D0203495

From Belasco to Brook

Recent Titles in
Contributions in Drama and Theatre Studies

FROM BELASCO TO BROOK

REPRESENTATIVE DIRECTORS OF THE ENGLISH-SPEAKING STAGE

Samuel L. Leiter

Contributions in Drama and Theatre Studies, Number 33

Greenwood Press
New York • Westport, Connecticut • London

Library of Congress Cataloging-in-Publication Data

Leiter, Samuel L.
   From Belasco to Brook : representative directors of the English-
speaking stage / Samuel L. Leiter.
      p. cm. — (Contributions in drama and theatre studies, ISSN
   0163–3821 ; no. 33)
   Includes bibliographical references and index.
   ISBN 0–313–27662–5 (alk. paper)
   1. Theatrical producers and directors—Great Britain—Biography.
   2. Theatrical producers and directors—United States—Biography.
   3. Theater—Production and direction.   4. Theater—20th century—
   History.   I. Title.   II. Series.
   PN2597.L45   1991
   792′.0233′0922—dc20
   [B]   90–45350

British Library Cataloguing in Publication Data is available.

Copyright © 1991 by Samuel L. Leiter

All rights reserved. No portion of this book may be
reproduced, by any process or technique, without the
express written consent of the publisher.

Library of Congress Catalog Card Number: 90–45350
ISBN: 0–313–27662–5
ISSN: 0163–3821

First published in 1991

Greenwood Press, 88 Post Road West, Westport, CT 06881
An imprint of Greenwood Publishing Group, Inc.

Printed in the United States of America

The paper used in this book complies with the
Permanent Paper Standard issued by the National
Information Standards Organization (Z39.48–1984).

10 9 8 7 6 5 4 3 2 1

To the memory of my mother and father

Contents

Preface

When this book was first written, it was a rather novel offering in a field of theatrical research that was just then coming into its own as a matter of serious concern. Apart from Toby Cole and Helen Krich Chinoy's important collection of documents, *Directors on Directing* (rev. ed. 1963), only one prior book in English (Norman Marshall's excellent *The Producer and the Play*, rev. ed. 1975) had been published purporting to survey, in some depth, the careers of the most important stage directors. And Marshall's otherwise comprehensive book had not even ventured to look at American practitioners.

Meanwhile, as the present work languished in the hands of a succession of publishers (three to be exact), each of whom ran into catastrophic financial problems and had to scuttle the project (which as early as 1981 had been printed in galley form and was being advertised), a series of useful writings on directors began to appear. These ranged from such surveys as Edward Braun's *The Director and the Stage* (1982) to David Bradby and David Williams' *Directors' Theatre* (1988), along with a series of carefully researched monographs on specific directors, a number of whom are also discussed in the following pages.

At long last, the project found in Greenwood a publisher who had long been interested in it (Greenwood having published a considerable number of my other books), and the decision was made to divide what had become a rather unwieldy tome into two complementary volumes, *From Belasco to Brook: Representative Directors of the English-Speaking Stage* and *From Stanislavsky to Barrault: Representative Directors of the European Stage*.

Both books were thoroughly revised and updated through the years to take account of newly published materials and of new activity by the three directors who remained active (Abbott, Barrault, and Brook). The text represents all such developments through 1989.

For assistance in my research I would like to thank the staffs of the Lincoln Center Library for the Performing Arts and of the Gideonse Library, Brooklyn

College, City University of New York. I would also like to thank Erika Kralik, head of documentation at the Théâtre Renaud-Barrault, Paris, and Clive Barker of *New Theatre Quarterly* for their helpful responses to my inquiries.

For keeping me sane during these trying years, for helping me with numerous editorial details, and for compiling the indexes, I must thank my wonderful wife, Marcia.

Introduction

Ever since Western theatre began in ancient Greece, there has been someone—an actor, playwright, producer, stage manager—to fulfill the basic functions of the stage director, although no particular term identified his role in the production process. In most cases, his responsibilities were primarily those of organization and traffic management; interpretation, albeit limited, must now and then have played a role as well. Still, for all its innate importance, it is generally agreed that stage direction was not accorded recognition as an independent theatrical art until the 1870s, when George II, the Duke of Saxe-Meiningen, formed his court troupe and, through a series of international tours, showed Europe what could be done when a play was completely realized in performance through the application of a single, unified directorial vision.

The revolution in theatrical production effected by the Meiningen company was not accomplished overnight. It was necessary for a number of other distinguished members of this new breed of artists—men like André Antoine, Otto Brahm, Aurelian Lugné Poë, and Augustin Daly—to make their mark before the need for directors became a theatrical commonplace. Even the terminology used to refer to directors and their art remained vague well into the present century. It is only in recent years, for instance, that the British have begun to lean toward the term ''director'' and away from ''producer,'' which, of course, has entirely different connotations in the American theatre. Nevertheless, by the end of the nineteenth century experienced theatregoers were, for the first time, talking about a growing number of individuals who were virtually transforming the nature of the theatre experience by the application of their personal touch to stage production, even when they were neither in the play nor credited with its writing. An age was dawning when audiences would increasingly attend the theatre not to see the work of some famous star or dramatist, but to confront the individualistic expressions of specific directors; this new period was to be called the ''age of the director.''

It is not difficult to identify who these directors are. What is problematic, however, is to select those who might be considered representative of this still young and continually evolving art. The choices made in *From Belasco to Brook* and its companion volume, *From Stanislavsky to Barrault,* will unquestionably differ from those others might have made. They have been selected to cover the broad spectrum of directorial art as it has developed during this century. It is not my intention to defend each of my selections. I would, however, like briefly to discuss all the directors in both books in aggregate and to identify some of the salient aspects of the director's art that they exemplify. These, I believe, are comprehensive enough to embrace a considerable range of available methodologies and, to a large extent, to be applied to those many outstanding directors not dealt with in these pages.

The first thing that identifies these directors is their diversity of taste and accomplishment. If we look, for example, at the matter of repertory we see those like David Belasco and George Abbott, whose entire output was of the strictly commercial, escapist, entertainment-for-entertainment's-sake variety; the former concentrated on contemporary and historical melodramas, the latter on contemporary melodramas, comedies, farces, and musicals. Contrasting with them are directors like Bertolt Brecht and Vsevolod Meyerhold, who devoted much of their careers to making the theatre intellectually provocative and politically viable from a Marxist point of view. Some of these directors, like Harley Granville-Barker, Tyrone Guthrie, Margaret Webster, and Peter Brook, can thank Shakespeare and other classics for the foundations of their reputations, while others, like Elia Kazan, David Belasco, George Abbott, and Bertolt Brecht rarely could be found within a stone's throw of a play older than themselves. Then again, Kazan could be cited as a director whose greatest successes come from the work of one or two specific modern playwrights (in his case, Tennessee Williams and Arthur Miller), while Konstantin Stanislavsky, for all his other accomplishments, is indelibly linked with the plays of Anton Chekhov. Several of the directors here were major playwrights; Brecht, for example, unquestionably the most outstanding German dramatist of the century, only staged someone else's plays on a handful of occasions, while Granville-Barker, Abbott, and Belasco directed plays both by themselves and others. Max Reinhardt, Jean-Louis Barrault, Jacques Copeau, and Joan Littlewood directed new plays and old, classics and avant-garde, and consequently had rather eclectic repertories, with no single playwright or type of dramaturgy occupying an undue share of their credits.

The directors in these books also represent a cross-section of the modern theatre's stylistic attitudes toward production. Thus we have Belasco's use of minutely detailed naturalism in the service of each and every play; Stanislavsky's "spiritual naturalism" marked by a preoccupation with investigating the means for creating psychological truth in acting; the objective theatricalism of Meyerhold's biomechanics and constructivism; Reinhardt's never-ending search through every variety of style and environment for the perfect *gesamtkunstwerk*; the flexible adaptability of a naked stage and the disciplined ensemble expres-

siveness of Copeau; the quiet naturalism and modern Elizabethanism (or Elizabethan modernism) of Granville-Barker; the rapid-fire, door-slamming comedic
techniques of Abbott; the estrangement devices of Brecht's anti-Aristotelian,
Marxist-oriented epic theatre; Guthrie's "wouldn't-it-be-fun-if" interpretations
of the classics; Webster's domestication and popularization of the Bard; Kazan's
hard-hitting psychological theatricalism; Barrault's employment of mime and
Artaudian "total theatre"; Littlewood's improvisational and anti-Establishment
left-wing antics; and Brook's multifaceted concept of the "empty space" and
his never-ending exploration of the essences and ritual structures of theatre.

Similarly varied is the approach of these directors to their work with actors;
their own backgrounds, however, do not reveal such dissimilarity. Ten of them
first established their careers as actors (Belasco, Stanislavsky, Meyerhold, Reinhardt, Granville-Barker, Abbott, Webster, Kazan, Barrault, and Littlewood);
most continued to act—for varying lengths of time—either in their own productions, in those of others, or both. Guthrie gave up acting very early on,
Copeau began acting only when he also began directing, Brecht occasionally
performed in cabarets but not on the legitimate stage, and Brook never acted at
all.

In their rehearsal methods a number of these directors (Meyerhold, Belasco,
Abbott, Reinhardt, and the early Stanislavsky, for example) were essentially
autocratic, even dictatorial, using any method, foul or fair, to get desired results.
Others (such as Brecht, Littlewood, and Brook, and the later Stanislavsky) gave
their companies great freedom, allowing the actors to discover their own movement and behavior through the employment of a wide assortment of creative
techniques, especially improvisation. Some brooked no interference from others
who might have suggestions to offer; others were openly collaborative, often
codirecting and even accepting critical comments from casual rehearsal visitors.

Some came to rehearsals with every move blocked out in advance, every vocal
nuance preplanned; this could be in an extensive promptbook or it could be
entirely in their heads. Others followed the tabula rasa approach, and used the
rehearsal process to discover what the play was about, what its theatrical possibilities were, and what the actors involved could bring to realizing it onstage.
Then again, there were those who would accept a script and respect it implicitly
(Granville-Barker, Copeau, and Webster are good examples), and there were
those who could not direct a play without making extensive revisions in the text
or having the playwright do so (see, especially, Meyerhold, Kazan, Abbott, and
Littlewood).

On other fronts there is a surprising homogeneity in the approaches of these
directors. An impressive statistic is the number who were devoted to working
within the concept of a repertory company, with a band of permanent players
who would appear in one play after another during one or more seasons. Even
if they often had to work within the restrictions of the typical one-shot commercial
milieu, they would return whenever possible to the less financially lucrative
company idea where they could explore challenging plays with a fixed group of

players under conditions which, more often than not, permitted relatively protracted rehearsal periods. Company directors, and some of the companies they headed, include Stanislavsky (Moscow Art Theatre), Meyerhold (Imperial Theatres, St. Petersburg; Meyerhold [State] Theatre, Moscow), Reinhardt (numerous theatres), Granville-Barker (the Court and Savoy theatres, London), Copeau (Théâtre du Vieux Colombier, Paris), Brecht (Berliner Ensemble, East Berlin), Guthrie (Old Vic, London; Festival Theatre, Stratford, Ontario; Guthrie Theatre, Minneapolis), Webster (American Repertory Theatre, New York; Marweb Shakespeare Company, touring), Barrault (Compagnie Madeleine Renaud—Jean-Louis Barrault, Paris), Littlewood (Theatre Workshop, London), and Brook (Royal Shakespeare Company, London; International Center for Theatre Research, Paris). Kazan, after a successful career as a commercial director, fulfilled a dream when he took over the new Lincoln Center Repertory Company, but left the theatre when bureaucratic circumstances frustrated him. And if one looks at the careers of the two other commercially oriented directors in this book, it is clear that even Belasco and Abbott kept a "company" idea in mind when casting for their shows.

Another thing that ties many of these great directors together is the multiplicity of their theatre talents. Most of them are *hommes* and *femmes de théâtre*. For example, putting aside their directing abilities, we can point to such representative individuals as Belasco, who wrote popular plays, acted (in his early career), and was a master lighting designer; Meyerhold, who designed sets and acted; Granville-Barker, who was an important playwright and actor; Copeau, a critic turned playwright, actor, and theoretician; Abbott, a hit playwright, producer, and leading man; Brecht, the outstanding German playwright and theoretician of the century; and Brook, who not only designed many of his productions, but composed the music for them as well.

We see, moreover, in the careers of many of these directors a continuing fascination with the shape and function of the performance space. The traditional proscenium with its fourth-wall realism may have been the *sine qua non* for directors like Belasco, Stanislavsky, and Abbott, but most of the others were seriously alienated from the picture-frame stage. Meyerhold continuously sought to break through the "fourth wall" with aprons built over the orchestra pit, and Granville-Barker did likewise; the latter also discovered a suitable tripartite method of arranging the stage for Shakespeare so that Elizabethan conventions could be combined with contemporary styles of decor. Copeau reinvented the architectural stage on his *tréteau nu,* while Guthrie was almost single-handedly responsible for the reintroduction into contemporary theatre architecture of the three-quarters round stage combined with a permanent, but variable, scenic arrangement. Max Reinhardt made the revolving stage essential to the best-equipped theatres, and also showed what could be done by staging plays in circus arenas, on church steps, in wooded glades, on Venetian canals, in eighteenth-century ballrooms, in immense U-shaped indoor amphitheaters, and in tiny chamber theatres. Peter Brook regularly put on plays in the orchestra area of a burned-out nineteenth-century theatre, and in such natural environments as the awesome hills of Persepolis and the open, dusty, unadorned squares of African villages, with nothing but a carpet for a stage.

The majority of these great directors wrote about their theatre ideas, some of them extensively. Many of these works form the foundation for Western theatre thought in our times. A glance at some of the highlights of such writings (with reference to only those foreign works that have been translated into English)[1] would focus attention on Stanislavsky's books, from *My Life in Art* through his three major tomes on acting; Meyerhold's miscellaneous articles and treatises as translated by Edward Braun in *Meyerhold on Theatre*; Brecht's numerous theoretical works, including *The Messingkauf Dialogues* and *The Little Organon*; Granville-Barker's multiple *Prefaces to Shakespeare* and many other books, including *The Exemplary Theatre* and *The Study of Drama*; Tyrone Guthrie's *In Various Directions, A New Theatre,* and others; Webster's two-volume autobiography and her *Shakespeare without Tears*; Barrault's *The Theatre of Jean-Louis Barrault* and *Memories for Tomorrow*; and Brook's *The Empty Space* and *The Shifting Point*. It may not be too far-fetched to say that not only have their productions had a profound effect on the shape of the modern theatre, but that their ideas as communicated through the written word may have made an even more powerful impact because they were thus able to reach a far vaster audience than could ever have attended their productions.

Finally, the men and women of these volumes are linked by their having contributed productions which may easily be seen as beacons charting the progress of the modern theatre. Hopefully, the capsule descriptions of many of these landmark works in the pages that follow will make apparent the changes that have marked the theatre of our times from Belasco's *The Young Mrs. Winthrop* to Brook's *The Mahabharata*.

A few words are in order about the approach taken to the subjects of these volumes. Each chapter is organized into numerous subsections, but the essential pattern is to first discuss the individual's career, then his or her overarching conception of theatre art and directing, and finally his or her actual working methods. Each chapter ends with a brief chronology that focuses on plays directed; apart from one or two exceptions, operas and films are not included, but, in some cases, musicals and operettas are. Because of the different natures of the directors' careers, the listings vary slightly in format from one director to the other.

Thus, almost every chapter has information on a director's repertory, major productions, theoretical concerns, techniques of working with actors, playwrights, designers, and composers, casting methods, production preparations, and rehearsal processes. There are as many approaches to directing as there are directors, and no one technique or ideology can be held up as an ideal. Each director must discover for himself or herself the best way of working; some of the greatest, such as Peter Brook, have gone from one method to another as experience taught them what was most appropriate to their own personalities and situations. One of the purposes in writing these volumes was to reveal this wide divergence of directorial styles and techniques and to thereby open the reader to the kaleidoscopic multiplicity of avenues open to exponents of the art. The treatment of the book's subjects, then, is not critical, but descriptive. It implies that for some the paternalistic authoritarianism of a Belasco or Meyerhold may actually be appropriate, while for others the collaborative, investigative, and experimental methods of a Brook may be the route to travel.

It is a given that, in his or her own time, each of the directors described here was—despite obvious pockets of criticism—widely considered a master of the art. Today, some of these artists have been subjected to the whims of revisionist thinking which scorns techniques no longer in fashion. Occasionally, comment on negative contemporary criticism of various directors has been included, but just as it was never my intention to write hagiography, it was also not my aim to denigrate individuals selected because I deemed them representative of certain schools of directing.

The theatre is no longer the monolithic structure it was in premodern times. Each new theatrical venture potentially expresses a new vision of the art; each new director has the option of following and expanding one of the many existing traditions or striking out on his own in search of some idiosyncratic notion of what the theatre's expressive potential might be. Every director discussed in these books has brought to the theatre a special viewpoint that has enriched its literary, architectural, decorative, and performance facets. These works are dedicated to all directors, conservatives and radicals, and every shade in between, for it is only through a healthy heterogeneity of styles and methods that the theatre of the future will survive and flourish.

NOTE

1. Much remains untranslated, both by those cited here and by Copeau, whose work has appeared in English only in scattered essays. A collection of his essays in translation is reported to be in preparation, Norman H. Paul (ed.), *Jacques Copeau: Texts on Theatre, an Anthology*.

From Belasco to Brook

David Belasco

(1853–1931)

During a sensational career which saw his active participation in 123 Broadway shows, David Belasco came to be called by a number of vivid nicknames—"the Wizard," "the Bishop of Broadway," "the Governor," "D.B.," "Mr. Dave." He might equally have been dubbed "Mr. Versatility," for he was a highly skilled actor, playwright, producer, designer, technician, and, of course, director. More than any of his contemporaries, he was in *total* control of his productions. Though he hated the ideas of Gordon Craig and the New Stagecraft, he came closer to Craig's ideal of the super-artist of the theatre than almost any other director of his time.

EARLY YEARS

He was born in San Francisco of Portuguese Jewish parents who had emigrated there from England at the height of the gold rush fever. The family soon moved to Victoria, British Columbia, where he was raised. He claimed to have made his stage debut in the latter city by being carried on as a tot, but his earliest documented appearance was in San Francisco when, at eleven, he played the Duke of York in Charles Kean's production of *Richard III* (Kean was then on a farewell world tour). Though only twenty-three years old when he moved from California to New York in 1876, Belasco had behind him an extremely varied theatrical background as actor, director, playwright, and stage manager for about three hundred productions. Prior to 1882 he made a brief New York appearance in James H. Herne's *Hearts of Oak,* which he coauthored and directed. In 1882 after his play *La Belle Russe,* staged by Lester Wallack, opened, he had a considerable success directing and acting in Bronson Howard's *The Young Mrs. Winthrop.*

In California Belasco had gained an enormous amount of experience working in every theatrical capacity. He was especially active as a special effects expert creating the illusions of fires, storms, explosions, and eruptions in spectacular melodramas. He also gained much knowledge of the new electric lighting techniques and made a number of technical advances in this field. He claimed to have eliminated footlights as early as 1879 and to have used as a spotlight a locomotive headlight hung from the front of the balcony.

His directing work soon was recognized by the actors with whom he worked in California stock companies, as evidenced by a letter written to him in 1878 from the young leading man James O'Neill (in his pre–Count of Monte Cristo days):

> Your quick apprehension and remarkable analytical ability in discovering and describing the mental intentions of an author—are so superior to anything we have heretofore experienced that we feel sure that the position of master dramatic director of the American stage must finally fall on you.[1]

BELASCO IN NEW YORK

Beginning with *The Young Mrs. Winthrop,* Belasco was employed by the sanctimonious Mallory brothers, who ran the Madison Square Theatre where they produced clean, wholesome plays completely lacking in "significant social or moral commentary and devoid of profanity."[2] Belasco directed six more plays at the Madison Square before leaving the Mallorys. Among his last productions for them was the successful *May Blossom* (1884), with which he began his custom of making a shy, embarrassed curtain speech in response to the audience's cries for the author.

Following his experiences with the Mallorys, Belasco signed up to direct at the Lyceum Theatre, where actor-director-playwright-inventor Steele MacKaye held sway. MacKaye soon left, however, and Daniel Frohman became Belasco's superior. At the Lyceum, Belasco staged such plays as *The Main Line, or Rawson's Y* (1886), *The Highest Bidder* (1887), *The Wife* (1887), *Lord Chumley* (1888), and *The Charity Ball* (1889).

Belasco's Lyceum productions were mainly of poorly written melodramas brought to life by his expert staging, especially of the thrilling climaxes which held his audiences spellbound.

BELASCO THE STARMAKER

Belasco's career took a new twist in the late 1880s when he agreed to undertake the stage training of the notorious ex-Chicago socialite, Mrs. Leslie Carter. Mrs. Carter had just gone through a painful divorce proceeding which had found her guilty of adultery. Deprived of financial support, she decided to capitalize on her beauty and personality by making acting a career; the up-and-coming "Mr. Dave," as she always referred to him, was the perfect choice to be her tutor. He apparently saw in her a magnificent opportunity to mold an exciting individual with striking personal attributes into a star of the first dimension, one over whom he could exercise complete control. During a two-year period Belasco spent a tremendous amount of time and energy developing the talents of this flame-tressed lady into those of a first-rate actress. He had her study ballet and jig dancing, boxing, wrestling, fencing, music, and thirty to forty standard roles. His training method was essentially an external one and not based on psychological principles. As he said, "I taught her how to weep. I would weep myself for hours until I looked like a wet rag. I would tear and scratch myself. I taught her to weep for the different emotions in a different way."[3] Mrs. Carter was the first in a series of performers Belasco transformed into leading stars. In her case, much of her original success was due to her position as a figure of scandal, but she soon convinced critics and audiences alike that she was possessed of a genuine acting talent and continued to play important roles for many years, even after she and Belasco parted company in 1906.

Belasco first starred Mrs. Carter in the ill-fated *The Ugly Duckling* (1890), but had better luck with *Miss Helyett* a year later. He had a considerable success with *The Girl I Left Behind Me* in 1893, failed with *The Younger Son* the same year, but bounced back strongly with Mrs. Carter in his own play, *The Heart of Maryland,* in 1895. In the climax of this stirring melodrama, Mrs. Carter displayed her considerable athletic prowess by swinging from the tongue of a huge alarm bell in order to still its sound so that her lover could escape. Other outstanding successes with Mrs. Carter followed, including *Zaza* (1899), *DuBarry* (1901), and *Adrea* (1905).

With Mrs. Carter established as a star, Belasco concentrated on two new performers, Blanche Bates and David Warfield. Blanche Bates was an independent soul who had quit the redoubtable producer-director Augustin Daly when she realized she would always be playing second fiddle to Daly's star Ada Rehan. In 1900 Belasco cast her in the leading role of a new play he had adapted from a short story by John Luther Long, *Madame Butterfly,* and the play and its star soon made history. A year later Blanche Bates rose to greater renown with her performance as Cigarette in the Belasco-directed *Under Two Flags,* in which—true to her master's predilection for spectacular flourishes—she had to ride a horse up a mountainside composed of interlocking risers. She played another Japanese role in Belasco's *The Darling of the Gods* in 1902, and starred in several other Belasco productions until 1910 when she retired from the stage.

David Warfield, who became the world's wealthiest actor, was a burlesque performer when Belasco decided to make him a legitimate theatre star. Warfield's first play for Belasco was *The Auctioneer* (1901), in which he played a Jewish-dialect part, a role at which he excelled. Warfield had a number of immense successes with Belasco, including *The Music Master* (1904), *A Grand Army Man* (1907), and *The Return of Peter Grimm* (1911). After a period of separation from Belasco, he returned to play Shylock in *The Merchant of Venice* (1922), the director's only attempt at a classical revival.

When Mrs. Carter left Belasco in 1906 to get married, Belasco turned his back on her and decided to build up another actress, Frances Starr, to replace her. This talented performer played leads for him in *The Rose of the Rancho* (1906), *The Easiest Way* (1909), *Marie-Odile* (1915), *Tiger! Tiger!* (1918), and *Shore Leave* (1922), among others.

Though many other major actors and actresses first gained a solid footing in the theatre through their work with Belasco, few were as closely associated with his career as these four and Lenore Ulric, who first worked for Belasco in *The Heart of Wetona* (1916). Greater acclaim came to her in *Tiger Rose* in 1917, followed by *The Son-Daughter* (1920), *Kiki* (1921), *Lulu Belle* (1926), and *Mima* (1928).

THE BELASCO THEATRE

In 1900 Belasco set himself up as an independent producer, and for the rest of his career was in complete control of all aspects of his productions. He leased Oscar Hammerstein's Republic Theatre in 1902 and, after remodeling it extensively, renamed it the Belasco. One of New York's best equipped theatres, it was resplendent with such features as multiple trap doors, an elevator-platform for shifting scenes, a counterweight flying system, and resistance dimmers. In 1906 he built his own theatre, the Stuyvesant. An ornate Georgian colonial-style playhouse, it, too, was outfitted with the finest in contemporary equipment and opened in 1907 with David Warfield in *A Grand Army Man*. In 1911 it became known as The Belasco; the first Belasco then reverted to its original name.

BELASCO NATURALISM

More than anything else, Belasco is remembered for his emphasizing detailed naturalistic visual effects and acting. Belasco settings were remarkable for the attention to detail with which they were composed. The average example was "a curiosity shop of a hundred and one exhibits, any few of which might have better served his purpose,"[4] according to critic and historian Montrose J. Moses. A Belasco production was the last word in fourth-wall pictorial illusionism. This attention to naturalistic convention was achieved regardless of the plays, from those set in contemporary times to those set in the past, including his one Shakespearean production. Every scenic element was carefully selected or approved by Belasco, who was responsible for the entire mise-en-scène, though he did not actually design the settings. So assiduously did he build up, piece by piece, the impression of exact pictorial illusion that he became the paragon of stage realism in the American theatre, gaining the admiration of most of his peers, including the Russian master of naturalistic staging, Konstantin Stanislavsky. Every element of Belasco's sets and properties had to be as real and authentic as possible, including real jewelry, real food, and real wallpaper. In a Belasco interior, wrote theatre theorist Sheldon Cheney, there is hardly a square foot of wall space that is not broken up by a vase, a projection, an ornament, or whatnot. A Belasco room looks as if the designer had wandered about . . . with a basket of "natural" objects and with an irresistible desire to stick them up on every bare spot.[5]

The wealth of objects thus dispersed about the scene may have created serious problems of focus, as a spectator's eyes were likely to be traveling about among the properties instead of settling on the actors and their behavior.

Production after production received rave reviews for the staging and decor, but the plays themselves invariably were found wanting. As a reviewer wrote after seeing *The Rose of the Rancho* (1906), theatregoers knew "that no matter how poor the fare may be, the dish is always so daintily served that it looks appetizing, even if the taste be a disappointment.''[6] Comments on the inadequacy of the plays Belasco staged normally took a back seat to the gushing descriptions of the scenery. A typical review contained descriptive passages like the following for *Adrea*:

The pomp and circumstance of a semi-barbaric court, the symbols and curious weapons of forgotten dynasties, the tramp of armed men in strange-fashioned garb and headpiece, the smiles of courtesans and the cringing of slaves—all this mingled in a splendid, glittering pageant of pleasing sound and color.[7]

The Belasco legend contains a number of striking examples of the extent to which the man would go in seeking out scenic authenticity. One famous example occurred when he purchased the fading wallpaper from a third-rate boardinghouse for a boardinghouse scene in *The Easiest Way*. Even more extravagant was his set for the third act of *The Governor's Lady* (1912). The scene took place in a Child's Restaurant at midnight in midwinter. Child's decor was as well known to most theatregoers as the interior of a McDonald's is to people today. Few would have been unfamiliar with its "geometrically arranged assortments of provender, its burnished coffee boilers, its neat, white-aproned 'Ham-an' waiters.''[8] For this play Belasco practically put a Child's Restaurant on the stage.

All of the fixtures—tables, chairs, hat and coat racks and stands, cash desk, cash register, cigar counter and food counters, coffee boilers, ovens, heaters, dishes, icebox and the griddle-cake cooker in the window—were obtained from the Child's Restaurant Equipment Company, and were installed by employees of the concern exactly as if a new restaurant were being opened! It is complete even to the signs: "Watch Your Hat and Overcoat," "Not Responsible for Personal Property Unless Checked by the Manager." . . . There is, also, the familiar white clock, keeping actual time, on the stage.[9]

The writer of the above continues in rapturous detail, itemizing all the other realistic elements of the setting. Only the walls, floor, and ceiling were made of normal scenic materials; the walls were built as light as possible to enable the show to travel efficiently. They were tiled, however, to simulate the actual walls of a Child's with "a hard rubber-like asbestos composition."[10] Actual Child's food, delivered fresh nightly, was set on the stage and used in preparing the meals eaten at each performance.

Not content with the naturalistic decor of the rooms shown onstage, Belasco, like Stanislavsky, even had offstage rooms built and decorated with extreme authenticity, visible through open doors. Similar attention was paid to exteriors seen through windows.

He was fond of shopping for most of the properties himself and loved to haunt antique and curio shops in search of the proper objects. When necessary he would import these from abroad, as when he sent to Japan for the furnishings required by *The Darling of the Gods*. His excessive literalism in the scenery and props often produced such heavy sets that the audience had to endure long waiting periods as scenes were changed. *Sweet Kitty Bellairs* (1903), for instance, had a running time of five hours and forty-three minutes; a normal production probably would have ended in less than three hours.

Despite the evidence in his work of excessive attention to details, Belasco and his supporters often claimed that his approach was far more selective and artistically suggestive than that for which he was given credit. This seems to have been especially true in the later period of his career when critic James Gibbons Huneker wrote that, despite what Belasco's critics may have said, the director's work had grown "more impressionistic. He suggests rather than states."[11] What Huneker implies is that Belasco did not merely plunk down, willy-nilly, the more obvious attributes of realism on his stage, but that he took considerable pains to dispose his effects in a totally integrated way through a careful arrangement of color, texture, and composition. In particular, his often brilliant lighting effects were responsible for achieving atmospheric results of which few other directors were capable. He stated clearly that, to him,

to surround the mimic life of the character in drama with natural aspects of life, to seek in light and color the same interpretive relation to spoken dialogue that music bears to the words of a song, is . . . the real art, the true art of the theatre.[12]

LIGHTING

Belasco was keenly aware of the power of light to create emotional and atmospheric effects: he spent long hours experimenting onstage and in a specially equipped lab with his electrical technicians to devise perfect lighting. For many years, Louis Hartmann served as his chief electrician and helped Belasco to achieve many breakthroughs in this young field. Belasco believed that a prime requisite for a director was a knowledge of color and the effects of light and shade. Although the symbolic, emotional values he ascribed to different types of lighting were somewhat simplistic (sunlight implied happiness, moonlight suggested romance, etc.), his taste for illusionistic effects is revealed when he suggests a director have adequate knowledge of geography so the lighting in a play might simulate the natural lighting of that geographical region in which the action occurs. The descriptions in his book, *The Theatre Through Its Stage Door,* are often exaggerated and even unfounded in some of their claims. But he did accurately describe the uniquely Japanese qualities achieved by his lighting for *The Darling of the Gods,* a description supported by contemporary accounts. Montrose J. Moses even heard him shout during a rehearsal of this play, "I don't want a moon, I want a Japanese moon,"[13] and this, apparently, is what he got. Even more outstanding in this production was the eerie quality Belasco achieved for the "River of Souls" scene, which took place in a sort of Japanese purgatory in which the bodies of the dead were seen drifting in limbo between heaven and hell. Unable to capture the precise effect he wanted by the use of various tricks, he accidentally came across the approach that was finally used. As the stagehands were striking the set he noted the effect of two calcium lights shining on a gauze curtain. A stagehand passing behind it cast a weird shadow and Belasco realized that he could duplicate this effect for the "River of Souls." Immediately, he began to rehearse the new effect, even though it was six in the morning. All who saw the play found the scene unforgettable.

Belasco's most famous demonstration of geographically correct lighting was that devised for *The Girl of the Golden West,* where a California sunrise in the Sierra Nevadas was captured after three months of experiment and the expenditure of five thousand dollars. Such lighting effects were frequently noted in discussions of his productions. Moses described how the atmospheric quality of California was conveyed in *The Rose of the Rancho:* "For six minutes the curtain was up before a word was spoken . . . it was a somnolent scene; those who saw it felt the drowsy vapor of the glow, the still air, and the enervating heat."[14] Or, as another journalist, watching a dress rehearsal of *Adrea,* enthused: "the atmospheric effect of pale yellow light, filtered through a grove before falling aslant of weather-aged stones, was so masterful in its conception, and so perfect in its harmonics as to suggest a dream of ancient Greece."[15]

To discover his effects, Belasco thought nothing of keeping his actors onstage for hours as he toyed around with the lights, checking the effects of various colors and intensities on the living presences before deciding which to use.

MUSIC AND SOUND

Music usually played an important role in Belasco's work, to conjure up the appropriate atmosphere. He was very insistent, however, that the music should be thoroughly integrated into the performance and never draw attention to itself. As in much modern cinema, the effective relation of the music's rhythmic values to the acting was a notable feature of a Belasco production.

Sound effects helped build the illusion of Belasco's stage worlds, and he took as much pain in creating them as he did with other aspects of the play. In one play, for instance, a crew of over thirty stagehands was used to simulate the effect of raging gale winds. However, so closely did some sounds match their real-life counterparts that they were likely to distract the audience by their *trompe l'oreille* efficacy. In a play called *The Woman* (1911), a highly suspenseful scene took place in an upstairs hotel room. As the audience waited breathlessly to see whether a certain character was about to enter the heroine's room, a sudden dramatic pause intervened, during which the authentic squeaking sound of an elevator could be heard. This effect was so like the sound of a real elevator that the audience momentarily lost interest in the action and began wondering how the effect had been achieved, thereby dissipating the dramatic mood.

Belasco could, however, be less literal and more suggestive in his employment of sound effects. In *Marie-Odile* the actors rehearsed against the sound of a drum, forcing them to speak loudly over the booming. When no drum was used in the performance, the way the actors shouted their lines gave the illusion that they heard offstage cannon fire.

STAGE BUSINESS

Even in this world of illusion, the acting had a vital role to play, and Belasco's performers strove diligently not to be outshone by the decor. Just as he was reluctant to leave too much to the audience's imagination in the sets and furnishings, Belasco sought to make sure his actors implied little but stated all. So thorough was he in his manipulation of his players that many were simply unable to work effectively under any other director. Step by step he led them through every moment of their roles—clarifying, justifying, and motivating everything for them. He attended to even the smallest details of the acting, letting nothing go by if it failed to satisfy his craving for authenticity. His distrust of the actor's creative imagination is clear from his belief that the actor could successfully achieve truth and believability onstage only when he was surrounded by a scenic world as close to reality as possible.

Belasco was a master at devising clever stage business, enriching the theatrical life of a play with physical activities not specifically called for by the script. He was able to build up a vivid sense of reality through his attention to pantomimic action and could hold an audience enthralled by the richness of detail in the playing. Often this ability was used for what would today be considered melodramatic techniques more likely to be found in the cinema than on the stage. For example, in *The Girl of the Golden West* the wounded outlaw-hero, Dick Johnson, is hiding in the rafters of a cabin when the sheriff comes to search for him. As the sheriff is on the point of leaving, a drop of blood falls from above on his hand, then on his handkerchief. The ability to create tension in the audience by such effects was one of Belasco's trademarks.

Belasco considered himself an innovator in the development of stage activity, despite accusations that he was old-fashioned. In an interview he once revealed some of the unusual advances with which he had experimented. These experiments are good examples of the lengths to which he would go to increase the illusion of reality on the stage. For instance, his production of Avery Hopwood's

Nobody's Widow (1910) consciously attempted to eliminate all audience laughter which might interfere with the flow of the play as the actors waited for the laughs to die. Instead of overt guffaws, Belasco sought a sense of warm but quiet humor, because he was certain the audience would receive more actual pleasure this way than when it burst into laughter "only to settle back into the cold, grey proceedings until the next outburst."[16] To achieve these ends all strong laugh lines were cut or revised so as to gloss over them and allow the play to proceed smoothly, and in a more "lifelike" manner.

When he produced *The Concert* (1910), Belasco aimed to strike out every piece of stage movement other than what might actually have been done if the play's action were real instead of theatrical. Feeling that most stage business was artificial and meaningless, he went counter to his own normal procedures for this "experiment." Concluding that stage action is more cerebral than physical, he allowed only movement which would be performed in life. "When two men sat down to talk things over, I had them sit there as they would have done if another wall had cut off the stage from the auditorium, and they didn't move until they would naturally have moved."[17]

A number of Belasco techniques remind one of the movies. Most notable of these is the "pandown" effect he used with great success at the opening of *The Girl of the Golden West*. It involved a clever use of lights, curtains, and drops as he first displayed the general area and atmosphere of a scene, then dimmed the lights and changed the scene drop, repeating the process several times until the actual room in which the scene took place was revealed. In *The Girl of the Golden West,* the transitions went from a vista of Cloudy Mountain to the Sierra Nevadas, showing a cabin on the mountain and a path leading to it. In dim light this was slowly rolled up to reveal another panorama of the cabin itself, actually a saloon. As the lights dimmed again, the inside of the saloon was seen with the people in it going about their business.

Another unique Belasco device reminiscent of the cinema was to end a powerful scene by dropping the curtain on a tableau, raising the curtain a few seconds later to display a tableau set several moments later in the action, and to repeat this one or two more times.

His imagination was ceaselessly at work transforming the prosaic scenes of the scripts he staged into theatre magic. He could make dull situations dramatic by the way in which he arranged a set, communicating at a glance the drama inherent in any situation. In *Accused* (1926), produced but not directed by Belasco, the audience was supposed to know that when the curtain rose on Act II the lawyer in the play had been up all night preparing to defend his loved one against a murder charge. Seeing that George Middleton, the play's adapter and director, was having trouble bringing life to the script, Belasco gave him an instant lesson in the stage director's art. With the help of the prop master,

authentic French law books began suddenly to appear. Large strips of paper were torn up dramatically and hectically placed between the pages to mark citations the lawyer had discovered. Cushions were thrown upon the floor and a myriad of crumpled paper scattered about, to reveal his mental confusion. A lamp was left lighted in the early sunlight, a curtain half opened, and the French window widened to catch the morning air. And, as a crowning touch, the head cushion on the couch was pushed in to indicate where his head had rested in his futile efforts to relax. "This is how the room should look. Anyone can see now what he had been through," Belasco said.[18]

The incident perfectly illustrates Belasco's remarks in a magazine article in which he declared that the director in rehearsal

must see that the story unfolds itself intelligently and simply; he must fit the action to the word, the word to the action, and make both move so briskly that the dramatic value of each situation may be made the most of. Above all, he must *think in pictures,* so that each scene of the play . . . may provide ceaseless occupation for the eye as well as the ear.[19]

THE MERCHANT OF VENICE

Although Belasco staged only this one classic play, a look at his approach to it as reconstructed by Lise-Lone Marker should serve as a convenient summation of his theatrical methodology in general. This production was seen by Stanislavsky during the Moscow Art Theatre's American visit in 1922–23. He wrote to his partner, Vladimir Nemirovich-Danchenko, of how amazed he had been by the quality of Belasco's lighting, staging, technical resources, and acting company, especially David Warfield. (When Stanislavsky wrote a mise-en-scène several years later for *Othello* [not produced], his ideas reveal that he saw Shakespeare in much the same way as did Belasco.) Belasco's Shakespeare was a spectacular, pictorially realistic production in the fashion of the old-time actor-managers. No expense was spared in making Venice a palpable reality within the picture-frame stage. As had Stanislavsky, Belasco and designer Ernst Gros undertook extensive historical and geographical research in preparing the designs. Choosing the early sixteenth century as the scenic period, because of its romantically picturesque possibilities, Belasco placed onstage heavy, three-dimensional scenery requiring numerous scene changes that kept the audience in their seats until quarter past midnight. This scenic method made it necessary, as it had in other directors' productions, to rearrange a number of the play's scenes. This included the placing of the casket scenes in tandem in Act II. Some scenes, such as the Prince of Arragon's casket scene, were cut. Surprisingly, Belasco's scenic solution, despite his research, was not the typical nineteenth-century stage Venice, with its familiar canals, bridges, and popular architectural attractions, but a more generalized Italian city, with drapes used as framing elements at the sides. In this we see something of the impressionism which Huneker described as representative of Belasco's later years.

The relatively "simplified" decor aside, Belasco peopled the stage with a myriad of realistic actions, often creating extensive scenes of pantomimic business, fashioning the believable illusion of a sixteenth-century city brimming with living characters. They moved off and on through the realistic streets, entered their homes, appeared at their windows, and helped to project a truly plausible environment; the set was thus as integral to the production as were the actors.

Lighting had its crucial role, of course, and the first scene between Antonio, Bassanio, and Shylock was especially noteworthy for its effect of showing the gradual transition from late afternoon's fading light to the glow of sunset, to darkness, with a single beam falling aslant the solitary figure of Shylock at the climax.

Some of the stage business was in the nature of interpolations borrowed from earlier productions, including the idea of bringing on reveling masquers during the scene of Jessica's elopement. This was followed by silence, and the picture of Shylock crossing to his now deserted house to knock on the door as the lights dimmed. Here, however, Belasco's directorial imagination conceived an effective interpolation of his own. According to Marker's reconstruction, the new scene took place in Shylock's home, immediately following the scene in which he was about to knock on the door.

As the curtain rose, Shylock was heard knocking on the door—seen from the outside in the previous scene but now shown from the inside—and calling: "Why, Jessica, I say!" The knock was repeated; then in an interesting foreshadowing of later cinematic technique, the door swung open and Shylock was revealed standing in the doorway, "amazed at finding his dwelling unguarded." He entered, calling again for his daughter. The sounds of revelry outside, heard faintly, increased. Shylock again went outside still calling for Jessica, re-entered—and stumbled first on a set of keys dropped in the doorway by his daughter and then on a jewelled ring. Snatching these things up and crying, "Jessica, my girl, Jessica!" he saw that a large, iron strong box had been left open. He uttered "a piercing cry" as he realized that he had been robbed. Turning, he discovered a letter and veil left by Jessica on a table. As he read, the masquers could be heard thronging past outside his house.[20]

Warfield was directed to play Shylock as an unpleasant, bitter character, filled with hatred and a desire for vengeance. Yet this was tempered by a note of pathos which was dramatically revealed in the trial scene. He lacked the Renaissance grandeur of the role and came off too undignified and petty, but managed nevertheless to evoke tears of pity for Shylock's wretched fate.

In summing up his perspicacious review of this production, critic Stark Young wrote, "scratch the Shakespeare hue and you will find Belasco, and that is really the best thing about the occasion. Good, bad or indifferent, it means at least a certain fullness and genuine theatricality."[21] Generalizing about Belasco's career, however, Young denies Belasco any "supreme gift," and attributes to him a taste "uncertain to the point of vulgarity," a lack of high artistic achievement among his actors and in his play selection, and an inability to take advantage of the newest ideas. Yet he finds it difficult to refute Belasco's strongest, positive feature, "theatrical sincerity."

WORKING WITH ACTORS

Although he contrived to give the impression of warm paternalism, David Belasco ruled his actors with a fist of steel. Some even say he "hypnotized" his players to get results; it would be closer to the truth to say he was psychologically adept, a person who knew how to use a wide range of techniques to elicit a desired response. Belasco himself contended that he did not have to bully his people because he was skillful at attaining his finest work by appealing to their imaginations; looks and gestures, he maintained, were more effective than scoldings. Despite his protests, however, Belasco was an autocratic bully who resorted to numerous stratagems in driving an actor toward a specific goal. The ethics of his methods were often questionable.

A magnetic man, whose powerful personality left few of his coworkers untouched, Belasco carefully created a legend about himself, painstakingly building up an environment and life-style which were calculated to give the impression that he was a wise and spiritually gifted guru. A notable achievement in this direction was the private "studio" in which he ensconced himself above the Belasco Theatre. George Jean Nathan, the caustic critic who often chided the "Wizard" for his overblown pretensions, described this sanctum sanctorum in words which suggest a tone of grudging respect for the director's audacity. Nathan saw here

a Ming dais, an altar candlestick, and a copy of the *Mona Lisa,* carpets ankle deep were laid upon the floor, the blinds were drawn, and Vantine's entire stock of joss sticks set to smell up the place with a passionate Oriental effluvium. In that corner a single wax taper, inserted artistically in a Limoges seidel, illumed the chamber with its ecclesiastic glow. . . . Upon the inlaid onyx commode that served as a desk rested carelessly a framed photograph of Dante, with the inscription "To my warm friend, Dave, in token of his services in the cause of art"—and duly autographed by the poet.[22]

Belasco would invite critics here, writes Nathan, to flimflam them into giving him favorable reviews. A large portion of Belasco's success, claims Nathan, was owed to this form of psychological manipulation. If the supposedly independent critics could be so bamboozled by the director's not so subtle charms, one can imagine how much more susceptible were Belasco's actors, who often thought of him as the next best thing to God.

Belasco's manner and stature were Napoleonic (he was five feet three inches tall); his intelligent, cherubic face was topped by thick, curly hair, silver in his later years, and set off by a dark suit and bib topped by a white priest's collar, giving him a decidedly clerical appearance. A reporter for *Theatre Magazine* wrote that when Belasco spoke at rehearsals, in his gentle, mellifluous voice, he created

an impression of perfect poise, which may be ascribed to supreme repression rather than expression of his mood. He strikes the stranger as an intense man, who controls himself because he will and must do so, but there are times when his great earnestness finds sudden vent and then his people listen to him as to an immortal.[23]

Belasco's method was to work with an actor first by talking to him about his role, reciting the story of the play as simply as he could, seeking to capture his interest while providing the needed information. He would arouse the actor's intellectual interest before involving him on an emotional level. When one actor would respond, he went on to the next. He would suggest what native qualities to play down but not what to exploit for fear of its being overused. Telling a woman how beautiful her smile was would lead to her smiling forever after. Though he preferred to be thought of as a director who never bullied actors, he was guilty of doing so—but only when the actors knew not to take him seriously. If he criticized an actor by saying, "You walk across the stage like a hog going to a snail's funeral," the actor realized that the walk was inadequate but did not feel any malice that would hinder his work. Such snide remarks would be totally out of place in dealing with "some sensitive, half-hysterical girl" who required a calm chat to avoid hurting her feelings.[24]

To judge by his remarks one would imagine that he rarely lost his own temper and never threatened his actors with harm. A director's job, he thought, is to lead, not to drive his players. Women especially require gentle handling, and the director must do all he can to gain their trust.

It is true that Belasco had reservoirs of patience, but it is also true that the reservoirs sometimes ran dry. An observer at a rehearsal for *Adrea* once witnessed him during an anxious moment, speaking to a group of minor actors:

"I thought . . . [yelled Belasco] that I was dealing with brains and heart, but at the eleventh hour . . . I see that I am dealing with idiots! Your souls! Where are they? If you have none, plunge a knife into your bosom in an effort to discover some."[25]

Yet, like the thespian-psychologist he was, he immediately turned kittenish, and his rage momentarily dissipated. It was not long before the fire erupted again, however, and a group of "wantons" heard him shriek, "Unless you can do better than that, I'll break up the show with an axe!"[26]

Belasco possessed a well-stocked arsenal of psychological weapons and knew precisely which to use for each occasion. One interesting tale comes from the famous actress Blanche Yurka, who recounts that Broadway's "bishop" was not above using one actress in a company to get results from another. Once, when he was having trouble getting a female star to reach an emotional climax, Belasco turned to another actress, a woman with excellent abilities but with looks that had held her back from being a star in her own right, and told her she had a chance for the starring role. This character actress immediately learned the role privately and put her all into achieving the results Belasco sought. One day Belasco stopped a rehearsal and told the star that she should take a break and watch a real actress play the part as it was meant to be played. When the subordinate player proceeded to act her heart out in the crucial scene, the humiliated star began to carry on hysterically. Interrupting, Belasco told her she was now producing precisely the effects he had been after all along.[27]

Perhaps the classic Belasco-actor's story is the one about how a lack of progress would so enrage him that he would smash a supposedly cherished watch to smithereens. Struck by the consequences of his tardiness in capturing what ''Mr. Dave'' was after, the guilt-smitten performer would push himself even harder to reach results. Needless to say, Belasco had a stock of cheap watches which he destroyed whenever the occasion demanded.

Hour after hour Belasco would pressure his actors in an attempt to wring from them his own goals. A twenty-hour rehearsal into the small hours of the morning was not uncommon in those preunion days. Belasco would have his actors repeat lines or business endlessly until they succeeded in pleasing him by producing exactly the intonation or subtlety of gesture he had in mind. Contemporary theatre people often shook their heads over stories of Belasco's practice of taking up a full day's rehearsal to work on a page-long soliloquy. He would drill a player to the extent of having him practice a single sentence for hours at a time. Nevertheless, instead of imposing a performance on a player, he preferred to work at getting qualities from them which he was sure were perfectly suited to their individual capabilities. What he wanted from one actor could never be gotten from another as each had his or her own peculiarities of temperament and physique.

In his attempts to attain psychological truth from his actors' portrayals he was not averse to having them make a thorough study of the environment from which their characters supposedly evolved. David Warfield, for example, made a close observation of life on the Lower East Side of New York for *The Auctioneer,* a technique strikingly similar to the new methods of the Moscow Art Theatre when its company visited a flophouse in preparing for *The Lower Depths.*

Many of Belasco's techniques are similar to those of Germany's Meiningen company of the late nineteenth century. Like the Duke of Saxe-Meiningen, Belasco was an expert in the handling of crowd scenes, individualizing each character in the mob by giving him a unique name and set of personal attributes.

Belasco is one of the few directors who has left specific advice on the handling of child actors. He was fond of children and knew how to get good performances from them. His theory was that children should be played with, even given toys during the rehearsal period. A director should spend a good deal of time with them even before rehearsals begin, to put the children in the proper, relaxed state of mind. Belasco would explain the whole play to them, not merely their scenes, making the narrative as interesting as he could. He went over their lines with them in detail and demonstrated not only how to speak them, but how to combine the words with movement. Though he acted out their roles for them, he advised the children not to mimic him. In a sense he seemed more apt to trust them to come up with the right way to do their scenes than he was with more mature actors.

CASTING

Actors for Belasco productions were found wherever there were performing artists at work. He scouted for talent constantly, even attending amateur productions, burlesque shows, second-rate stock companies, and musical reviews. The well-known Irish actor Whitford Kane, who worked for him, pointed out that Belasco had an incredible memory for actors he had seen.[28]

Belasco had the patience and drive to turn rough, untutored players into sensationally popular actors and, as we have seen, gained a great reputation as a "star maker." Though he "made" stars, he actually considered himself opposed to the star concept, favoring instead the smoothly oiled mechanism of a true ensemble. Rarely would he cast actors who were stars already, choosing to work with those who, by the sheer force of their talent and personality, became stars under his tutelage. He favored new actors because they were more pliable and could be more easily developed according to his own inclinations. Star actors who achieved their status before working with him came equipped with too many bad habits and were less easy for him to control.

He knew the minute he saw an actor if he could use him. This awareness was instinctual. He had an actor read only as a pro forma part of the tryout. He liked to appear as a mystic whose casting talents stemmed from psychic powers. When he came across a possible new actor, he had him come for an interview. He described his interview method thus:

I talk with him as to a new friend. I draw him out. I persuade him to talk of himself, of his life, and while he does so I am studying him—studying his face to see what it discloses, and what it hides, studying his hands, his feet, his body, to gauge their possibilities of expression. There are no rules of physiognomy I follow. I can tell; that is all.[29]

When auditioning and considering new actors, Belasco would listen to their voices, watch their expressions, and note how clever they were at grasping new ideas and conveying various suggested moods. A Belasco actor also had to be sincere—someone whom he could trust wholeheartedly. The five all-important factors in a Belasco actor's nature were ability, imagination (though we have seen how little he actually trusted this element), industry, patience, and loyalty.

Sometimes he took as much as a year to find precisely the right actors for an ensemble. The actor not only had to be the correct physical type, but he also had to have a spark that would bring the role to life. As Belasco pointed out, this often was no easy task. Seeking the perfect actor for a role could be like looking for a needle in a haystack, despite the availability in New York of many talented performers.[30] If he could not be found, Belasco would select a versatile player whom he knew could be bent into shape by the director's will. His concern with casting extended to the smallest roles, for he hated to have a company strong in its leads and inferior in the supporting parts, knowing that the smallest role could make or break a scene.

Typecasting was the norm, even to the extent of casting actors whose nationalities matched those of the roles they played. In assembling a company, a prime
essential was the vocal blend produced by their voices. The musical balance of
a leading actor's deep baritone would be carefully matched by the high-pitched
tones of his leading lady. Belasco found it easier to cast a play which had been
selected prior to considerations of its players than to have one or more actors in
mind for whom he would have to find a vehicle (which he normally wrote for
them himself). So closely did he work with his company on a show, and so
united with their characters were they in terms of his casting, that he could not
bring himself to cast a second company for any of his productions.

PREPARATIONS FOR PRODUCTION

Prior to the beginning of rehearsals, Belasco would make a thorough study
of the play and its physical requirements. He gave careful attention to the scenic
needs and to the nature of the atmosphere required. If the play was not one of
his own, he usually ignored the author's stage directions and conceived the visual
effects in terms of the stage values that he imagined would be most suitable.
The placement of windows, doors, and other scenic elements was thus dictated
by his own knowledge of stage requirements and not so much by what the
playwright believed was necessary.

His next step was to sketch a plan of the set he envisioned, carefully taking
the physical movement of the characters and placement of furniture and props
into account. The scenic artist, usually Ernst Gros, would then be summoned,
and together they would go onstage so that Belasco could act out the play in
rough form and demonstrate all the requirements of the setting. Over a period
of four or five evenings all groupings, entrances, and exits would be worked
out in this manner so that the set design would contain few or no flaws when
completed. Scene designs and models would then be created and needed changes
would be made.

Work on the lighting plans followed, with Belasco repeating the minute description of the play to his electrician until both were satisfied with the essential
choices.

Belasco did not contract out the building of his sets, but rather had them
constructed in his own scene shops. He disapproved of canvas stretched on
wooden frames, insisting instead on materials as close to the real ones as were
obtainable, including, when feasible, solid walls.

Costumes were the final consideration in his preparations for the visual side
of the production. Particularly in the case of modern-dress plays, costumes were
generally not considered until the show was in rehearsal at least a week so that
he could be sure of his actors. With plays demanding period clothing, he did
thorough research on cut, color, and fabric and then wrote up a full description
of each role's needs, including notes on beards, wigs, makeup, and so on. Only
then would he discuss the execution of the designs with a costumer. In modern-

dress plays he sought clothes identical to those worn by actual persons who resembled the characters. His selection of costumes was analogous to his work on scenery; often he would either purchase clothes from people he saw in the street or visit pawn-shops to find what he wanted.

THE REHEARSAL PROCESS

Belasco normally took six weeks to rehearse a play. He began the process by gathering the entire company and introducing them to each other, attempting to establish a cordial and intimate atmosphere by treating his actors more as "guests" than as subordinates. Following some general conversation, he would lead them to a reading room where they were shown scale models of the sets and given a pep talk about the need for unity, cooperation, and unselfishness. Whitford Kane says that the reading room had "no evident sign of ventilation, the only light is artificial, and the walls are hung with countless photographs and mementoes of all the past Belasco successes."[31] They were cautioned never to discuss the play outside the theatre. Belasco would then read the play to them without allowing any interruptions, following which the prompter distributed the actors' parts in the form of "sides." A lunch break ensued, succeeded by a read-through by the actors themselves. A general discussion of character psychology would also take place, and time was allotted for the correction of errors in the typescript. In cases where someone had to use a foreign language or accent, an expert in the given tongue would be present to help overcome any problems. In *Deburau,* for instance, a professor of French was hired to keep tabs on everyone's accents. Belasco gave the professor a role as a crowd member to insure the stability of all accents during the run of the play.

The company would adjourn after the reading and reconvene the next morning at ten-thirty. For a week the actors would sit and read their parts as Belasco studied their respective vocal attacks and the strengths and weaknesses they displayed. During this period he would attend to rewrites where necessary, cutting, making transpositions, revising, and retyping, for he believed that "plays . . . are built, not written."[32]

Blocking rehearsals would begin the second week, but strangely enough, Belasco placed the responsibility for them in the hands of his stage manager, who was roughly aware of what Belasco was after. This was the major opportunity for the actors to exercise their imaginations, for, when Belasco returned, the ruthless search for results allowed the actors little creative freedom. "I have always found it better," he commented, "to keep out of sight during the first experiments in the real acting, for when I am present the actors stand still and depend upon me for directions."[33] His stage manager was cautioned to let the actors have a loose rein during this early period.

Ultimately, Belasco resumed control and took the actors through their paces, spending about a week to ten days on each act. He left nothing to chance, having prepared every move and piece of business in a promptbook in advance. The results were all in his head before he even met with his actors; rehearsals were simply a way of arriving at his preconceived goals. He warned his players not to work at learning their lines until they had begun to firmly mold their characters. When the company had reached a stage of general smoothness, he would hold a rehearsal during which he tried to ignore the acting per se and instead watched the play itself, listening to the dialogue, weighing the values of the speeches, attending to the climaxes, and quietly dictating notes to a stenographer so as not to interrupt the run-through.

As the opening approached, the actors were given one day to attend to their costumes with the costume personnel. This culminated in a "dress parade" during which the actors appeared onstage in costume with the director seated in the house checking details and color balances. Then the curtain call would be practiced, and finally, a dress rehearsal would be performed. An extensive note-giving session was likely to follow, and it was not unlikely that Belasco would require several run-throughs before being satisfied. It was only at the final dress rehearsal that a small audience of a dozen or so was allowed to attend. Belasco would carefully study them to gauge their reaction to each speech or piece of business.

Belasco's final instructions to one of his casts before a New York opening have been preserved. Speaking onstage to a company of over one hundred actors, he said:

Remember, out there, in the darkened house, not ten feet away from you, will be sitting the best people from New York, from Paris, from London. I want to show them what the author of the play can do, what we can do. But my work is finished, the author's work is completed, all depends now on you.[34]

He then gave them explicit instructions on how they must remain quiet backstage, how the women with flimsy evening gowns must be careful not to catch drafts, how the children in the cast must care for their costumes, and how all should read the gilt motto on the callboard before leaving the theatre. It said, "A Sure Road to Success—Mind Your Own Business; A Sure Road to Happiness—Mind Your Own Business."

Belasco hated to open cold in New York and preferred two to four weeks of out-of-town tryouts before settling down to the metropolitan run. Constant revisions took place during these tours so that the play was as polished as could be when it opened officially. Many Belasco productions were forced to rehearse even after they had just given a performance to an out-of-town audience—often until the early hours of the morning. Belasco was indefatigable, able to outlast most people half his age.

When opening night finally came, usually on a Tuesday, Belasco would visit and encourage the performers before the curtain rose, but he did not watch the play from the auditorium. Rather, he would stand in the wings, continuing to inspire or correct the company, maintaining an air of positive energy, aiming only to instill confidence.

CONCLUSION

By 1930, the year Belasco staged his last production, *Tonight or Never,* he had become an American theatre legend, the "master dramatic director of the American stage," loved by thousands of theatregoers for whom he could do little wrong, and despised by many others who saw him as outdated, shallow, and the epitome of Broadway hokum.

During his long and colorful career, Belasco was constantly in the public eye, now fighting the Theatrical Syndicate, now battling in court against the many who accused him of plagiarism, now publishing articles on matters of domestic interest, now struggling against the new actors' union. He often produced and directed three or four shows a year, most of which he had a hand in writing, and continually amazed his audiences by his ability to display new facets of his gift for realistic staging.

Belasco was a great showman who gave Broadway audiences the finest presentations in the tradition of theatrical verisimilitude they had ever seen. Further, George Jean Nathan felt that, despite his many drawbacks, Belasco contributed to the American theatre "a standard of tidyness in production, and maturation of manuscript, a standard that has discouraged, to no little extent, that theatre's erstwhile not uncommon frowzy hustle and slipshod manner of presentation."[35]

Unfortunately, he produced plays of little lasting value (the most often revived plays of his repertory are Giacomo Puccini's opera versions of *Madame Butterfly* and *The Girl of the Golden West*). Few critics find any values more serious than melodrama and sentimentality in most of his output. He was essentially a man of the late nineteenth century; a Belasco production of the 1920s was already a theatrical anachronism in a world enthralled by the ideas of Gordon Craig, Adolphe Appia, Jacques Copeau, Max Reinhardt, and others of the New Stagecraft who were then revolutionizing the world theatre.

NOTES

1. Quoted in Craig Timberlake, *The Bishop of Broadway: The Life and Work of David Belasco* (New York: Library Publishers, 1954), pp. 62–63.

2. Ibid., p. 118.

3. Ibid., p. 170.

4. Montrose J. Moses, "David Belasco: The Astonishing Versatility of a Veteran Producer," *Theatre Guild Magazine* 7 (November 1929): 30.

5. Sheldon Cheney, *The New Movement in the Theatre* (New York: Benjamin Blom, 1971), p. 155.

6. Review of *The Rose of the Rancho, Theatre Magazine* 7 (January 1907): 4.

7. Review of *Adrea, Theatre Magazine* 5 (February 1905): 28.

8. Wendell Phillips Dodge, "Staging a Popular Restaurant," *Theatre Magazine* 16 (October 1912): 104.

9. Ibid.

10. Ibid., p. x.

11. James Gibbons Huneker, "American Producers III: David Belasco," *Theatre Arts Monthly* 5 (October 1921): 264.

12. David Belasco, *The Theatre Through Its Stage Door,* ed. Louis V. Defoe (New York and London: Harper Brothers, 1919), p. 167. The authorship of this book and of many of Belasco's articles is open to serious doubt, as it is known that press agents wrote much of what he passed off as his own. Instead of disputing the ideas of these publications as not being Belasco's, I have accepted them as representing what he wanted the public to believe were his theories, regardless of who actually penned the words.

13. Montrose J. Moses, "The Psychology of the Switchboard," *Theatre Magazine* 10 (August 1909): 65.

14. Ibid.

15. Aubrey Lanston, "A Rehearsal under Belasco," *Theatre Magazine* 5 (February 1905): 42.

16. Archie Bell, "David Belasco Attacks Stage Tradition," *Theatre Magazine* 13 (May 1911): 166.

17. Quoted in ibid.

18. George Middleton, "Adventures Among the French Playwrights," *New York Times*, 23 October 1938, sec. 9, p. 3.

19. David Belasco, "How I Stage My Plays," *Theatre Magazine* 2 (December 1902): 32. An excellent summation of Belasco's achievements in the art of pictorial illusionism as it related to nascent art of film realism is in Nicholas Vardac, *Stage to Screen: Theatrical Method from Garrick to Griffith* (New York: Benjamin Blom, 1968).

20. Lise-Lone Marker, *David Belasco: Naturalism in the American Theatre* (Princeton, N.J.: Princeton University Press, 1975), p. 196.

21. Stark Young, *Immortal Shadows* (New York: Hill and Wang, 1948), p. 41.

22. George Jean Nathan, *The Magic Mirror,* ed. Thomas Quinn Curtis (New York: Alfred A. Knopf, 1960), p. 57.

23. Lanston, "A Rehearsal Under Belasco," p. 43.

24. David Belasco, "David Belasco Reviews His Life Work," *Theatre Magazine* 6 (September 1906): 247–50, viii–ix.

25. Lanston, "A Rehearsal Under Belasco," p. 43.

26. Ibid.

27. Blanche Yurka, *Bohemian Girl: Blanche Yurka's Theatrical Life* (Athens: University of Ohio Press, 1970), pp. 54–55.

28. Whitford Kane, *Are We All Met?* (London: Elkin, Mathews and Marrot, 1931), p. 199.

29. Belasco, "Reviews His Life Work," p. 248.

30. Belasco, "How I Stage My Plays," p. 31.

31. Kane, *Are We All Met?*, p. 199.

32. Belasco, *The Theatre Through Its Stage Door,* p. 68.

33. Ibid.

34. Jane Dransfield, "Behind the Scenes With Belasco," *Theatre Magazine* 35 (April 1922): 228.

35. Nathan, *The Magic Mirror,* p. 62.

CHRONOLOGY

Only New York productions are given. Belasco revived many of his productions, sometimes more than once; those later receiving revivals are marked with an asterisk; most
such revivals are not listed, the focus being on new productions. See Craig Timberlake,
The Bishop of Broadway: The Life and Work of David Belasco (New York: Library
Publishers, 1954) for a fuller listing.

1853   born in San Francisco, California

1876   moves to New York

1880   Fifth Avenue Playhouse: *Hearts of Oak*

1882   Madison Square Theatre: *The Young Mrs. Winthrop*

1883   Madison Square: *A Russian Honeymoon; The Rajah, or Wyncot's Ward*; New
        Park Theatre: *The Stranglers of Paris*; Madison Square: *Delmar's Daughters*

1884   Madison Square: *Alpine Roses; May Blossom*; Fifth Avenue: *Called Back*

1886   Lyceum Theatre: *The Main Line, or Rawson's Y*

1887   Lyceum: *The Highest Bidder; The Great Pink Pearl* and *Editha's Burglar;
        Baron Rudolph; The Wife**

1888   Lyceum: *Lord Chumley**

1889   Lyceum: *The Marquise; The Charity Ball*; trains Mrs. Leslie Carter for an acting
        career

1890   Broadway Theatre: *The Prince and the Pauper*; Proctor's 23rd Street Theatre:
        Men and Women; Broadway: *The Ugly Duckling*

1891   Star Theatre: *Miss Helyett*

1893   Empire Theatre: *The Girl I Left Behind Me; The Younger Son*

1895   Herald Square Theatre: *The Heart of Maryland*

1897   Manhattan Theatre: *The First Born*

1899   Garrick Theatre: *Zaza**

1900   Herald Square: *Naughty Anthony; Madame Butterfly*

1901   Garden Theatre: *Under Two Flags*; Bijou Theatre: *The Auctioneer**; Criterion:
        *DuBarry**

1902   takes over the Republic Theatre and renames it the Belasco Theatre; Belasco:
        The Darling of the Gods

1903   Belasco: *Sweet Kitty Bellairs**

1904   Belasco: *The Music Master*

1905   Belasco: *Adrea*; The Girl of the Golden West**

1906   Belasco and Mrs. Carter end their professional relationship; Belasco: *The Rose
        of the Rancho*; builds the Stuyvesant Theatre

1907   Stuyvesant: *A Grand Army Man*; Belasco: *The Warrens of Virginia*

1908   Stuyvesant: *The Fighting Hope*

1909   Stuyvesant: *The Easiest Way**; Belasco: *Is Matrimony a Failure?*; Stuyvesant: *The Lily*

1910   Belasco: *Just a Wife*; Stuyvesant: *The Concert*; Hudson Theatre: *Nobody's Widow*

1911   the Stuyvesant is renamed the Belasco; the current Belasco resumes its old name of the Republic; Republic: *The Woman*; Belasco: *The Return of Peter Grimm**

1912   Republic: *The Governor's Lady*; Belasco: *The Case of Becky; Tainted Philanthropy; Years of Discretion*

1913   Republic: *A Good Little Devil*; Belasco: *The Temperamental Journey*; Criterion: *The Man Inside*; Belasco: *The Secret*

1914   Belasco: *The Phantom Rival*

1915   Belasco: *Marie-Odile*; Empire: *A Celebrated Case*; Belasco: *The Boomerang*

1916   Lyceum: *The Heart of Wetona*; George M. Cohan Theatre: *Seven Chances*; Belasco: *Little Lady in Blue*

1917   Belasco: *Polly with a Past*; Lyceum: *Tiger Rose*

1918   Belasco: *Daddies; Tiger! Tiger!*

1919   publishes *The Theatre Through Its Stage Door*; Belasco: *Dark Rosaleen*; Lyceum: *The Gold Diggers*

1920   Belasco: *The Son-Daughter*; Empire: *Call the Doctor*; Belasco: *One; Deburau*

1921   Knickerbocker Theatre: *The Wandering Jew*; Lyceum: *The Grand Duke*; Belasco: *Kiki*

1922   Lyceum: *Shore Leave; The Merchant of Venice*

1923   Lyceum: *The Comedian*; Belasco: *Mary, Mary Quite Contrary; Laugh Clown, Laugh!*; Morosco Theatre: *The Other Rose*

1924   Belasco: *Tiger Cats; The Harem*; Lyceum: *Ladies of the Evening*

1925   Empire: *The Dove*; Lyceum: *Canary Dutch*

1926   Belasco: *Lulu Belle*; Lyceum: *Fanny; Lily Sue*

1928   Belasco: *The Bachelor Father; Mima*

1929   Belasco: *It's a Wise Child*

1930   Belasco: *Dancing Partner; Tonight or Never*

1931   dies in New York

Harley Granville-Barker

(1877–1946)

During the first decade of this century, the English stage made its boldest attempt to smash the shackles of the actor-manager system, although the assault was to require many years before freedom was assured. Sirs Herbert Beerbohm Tree, Johnston Forbes-Robertson, John Martin-Harvey, and Frank Benson continued toiling valiantly in the well-plowed furrows of Henry Irving, who died in 1905. Yet, as elsewhere in Europe, the coming of the new century provided fertile seeds for exciting innovations in the English theatre; the ideas of William Poel and Gordon Craig were perhaps the most potent of those produced by the new breed of stage directors, although both men achieved far more through their influence than by their practical theatre work.[1] It was another man, Harley Granville-Barker, who emerged from this fruitful environment to electrify the theatre world as the first of the truly modern British directors. Like many others in this book, Barker[2] was an *homme de théâtre,* an all-around theatre man with a wide variety of skills, including playwriting, acting, directing, producing, and scholarship. Esteem for his diverse contributions has not diminished in the four decades since his death.

EARLY YEARS

Born in England, he was the son of an architect and a professional actress. He first began acting in his teens and soon developed into an actor of note. His early acting career included such outstanding experiences as playing the title role in Poel's production of *Richard II* in 1899, Christopher Marlowe's *Edward II* for Poel in 1903, and Marchbanks in the first production of George Bernard Shaw's *Candida*. Both Shaw and Poel had a profound influence on Barker's career. Despite his erudition, Barker never attended a university. A dedicated artist with lofty ideals, he disdained the commercial theatre and mainly took roles in dramas of serious pretensions such as those put on by London's Stage

Society at the turn of the century. The Stage Society had come into existence in 1899 to put on serious new dramas that were of little interest to commercial managements. They produced their offerings for a select audience on Sunday evenings and Monday afternoons, using well-known West End actors and performing in West End playhouses. It was largely through the efforts of the Stage Society that many of the most farseeing new plays of England and elsewhere, including the work of Shaw, Frank Wedekind, Maxim Gorky, and Luigi Pirandello, were first produced in London. Barker's directorial debut occurred under the Stage Society's auspices in 1900 when he staged three poetic one-acters for them; the plays were Maurice Maeterlinck's *Interior* and *The Death of Tintagiles* and Fiona MacLeod's [William Sharp] *The House of Usna*. During the next few years, while continuing to gain recognition for his acting, he directed half a dozen more pieces for the Stage Society, most of them for only a pair of performances; among them were Shaw's *The Man of Destiny* and *The Admirable Bashville,* as well as his own play, *The Marrying of Ann Leete.*

THE COURT THEATRE

The work being done by the Stage Society ultimately had to prove frustrating to Barker, who was growing more and more convinced that London required a subsidized, fully professional repertory company producing the world's finest plays, new and old. Such a company would be representative of the most advanced ideas in staging and decor and would boldly discard the worn-out clichés associated with nineteenth-century acting and design. The goal toward which Barker aspired was that of an endowed national theatre; before long he and famed critic and Henrik Ibsen translator William Archer would draft the first of several proposals for such an institution, which Barker would not, unfortunately, get to see realized during his lifetime. However, his published descriptions of such a theatre and the work he achieved in practical theatrical terms demonstrated with crystal clarity the possibilities of his dream.

Barker passionately longed to produce the best of the new socially relevant, uncommercial drama for a subscription audience that would pay low prices to see frequently changing bills with an expertly drilled nonstar ensemble of serious artists. In such a theatre there would be unwonted intellectual stimulation for actors as well as audiences bored with the trite conventionalities of most of what then passed as commercial drama.

Barker's dream began to turn into reality when, in April 1904, he was asked by a man named J. H. Leigh to direct *The Two Gentlemen of Verona.* Leigh had leased the intimate, 642-seat Court Theatre, situated in a relatively accessible but not West End location, in order to feature his actress wife in a series of Shakespeare plays. Barker agreed provided that he be permitted to stage several matinees of Shaw's not-yet regularly produced *Candida,* written in 1895 and given by the Stage Society in 1900. The Shakespeare and the Shaw were both successful (Barker played Speed in the former and repeated his outstanding Marchbanks in the latter). The warm critical and public reception led Barker to align himself with Leigh's business manager, J. E. Vedrenne, and to arrange to give a series of matinees at the Court in the autumn of 1904.

During the next three years they carried out one important production after another for limited runs, with the emphasis primarily on new plays. Their original policy was a six-matinee run during a period of two weeks, but this soon was altered to three-week runs of eight or nine matinees each. In their second season this too was revised so one play could run for six nights a week while the matinees were given over to another production. Some plays were allowed extended runs, 176 performances being the longest and two performances the shortest. However, two weeks constituted an average run. During the three years of operation the Court offered 988 performances, then popularly referred to as the Thousand Performances, of which 701 were of eleven plays by Shaw. Shaw was so closely bound up with this enterprise that he even had to go to his own tight pocket to rescue it from financial disaster. The Court productions of Shaw's plays, which Shaw either directed himself or codirected with Barker,[3] succeeded in making him the most prominent British playwright of his time (Shaw was actually Irish, of course). Henrik Ibsen, John Galsworthy, Arthur Schnitzler, St. John Hankin, John Masefield, Gerhart Hauptmann, and Barker himself were among the other distinguished authors whose works were staged at the Court. The chief play by Barker was the highly respected *The Voysey Inheritance* (1905). There was also *Prunella* (1904), a lesser work coauthored with poet Laurence Housman. Even more noteworthy were the productions of three Euripidean tragedies—*Hippolytus* (with which daring choice the venture bravely opened), *The Trojan Women,* and *Electra*—in translations prepared by Gilbert Murray. The only other play by Euripides ever professionally produced on the English stage before this was *Medea*. In later years, Barker would return to Euripides for some of the most outstanding productions of his career. The importance of the Euripides stagings to the Court has recently been underlined by Eric Salmon, who declares that the entire venture may have been owing more to the inspiration of Murray's version of *Hippolytus* than to the influence on Barker of Shaw's works: "*Candida* had been a way of getting an example of the 'new drama' into the Court, but *Hippolytus* inspired the idea of using the Court for a whole series of plays—standard works as well as new works—presented in repertory."[4] A series of plays such as these, directed with care and taste, came as a revolutionary step forward in the development of the modern English theatre.

Barker directed all the non-Shaw plays, acted in many of them, as well as in Shaw's works (he was Jack Tanner, for example, in *Man and Superman*), and oversaw all aspects of the theatre's artistic direction. It was not long, however, before he gave up acting so that he could devote himself to all his other theatrical interests.

Desmond MacCarthy, the respected critic, summed up the Court's achievement by providing an interesting set of parallels between the Court and one of its important predecessors in the Independent Theatre movement of the day, André Antoine's Théâtre Libre. These theatres resembled each other in

that both succeeded in getting the public to appreciate a more natural style of acting, that both were practical protests against the tyranny of the "well-constructed" play, that both produced their plays for short runs, and lastly, that both very quickly collected around them a new school of young playwrights.[5]

There were striking differences, of course, most notably the eclectic nature of Barker's repertory when contrasted with the emphasis on naturalism seen at the Théâtre Libre, but there is no question that each was determined to abandon the sham theatrics of the typical nineteenth-century theatre, and to return to an honest realism of movement, speech, and emotion.

Because of the Court's slightly out-of-the-way location, it depended for support mainly on the people in its vicinity. It also proved too cramped for some of the more expansive productions which Barker was considering. Moreover, the subscription idea was never carried out (although an attempt was made to do so) and the prices were not any cheaper than those of commercial managements. Thus, a move to the West End itself began to seem inevitable.

OTHER STAGES

After the Court was forced to close, Barker and Vedrenne (with whom Barker split up in 1911 as the result of various personal and financial pressures) became involved in ventures at a series of London theatres beginning with the Savoy, a West End house, in 1907. The increased expenses here—despite stringent cutting back wherever possible (the actors willingly accepted rather low salaries, for example), and despite the frequent loans of Shaw—made it an impossible undertaking. The system of producing a healthy sampling of plays in brief runs had continually to be sacrificed to commercial considerations whenever a play promised to bring in money through an open-ended run. Barker was further pained when his play *Waste* (1907) was banned by the official censor (Barker was to spend a considerable amount of time hereafter in battling the British censorship system). At the Savoy, Barker directed (or, as Kennedy asserts, co-directed in the case of Shaw's plays) six plays during the 1907–1908 season, two of the plays on the same bill. He did not direct here again, however, until 1912, when he staged *The Winter's Tale,* the first of his three famous Savoy productions of Shakespeare, the last being given in 1914.

Aside from several brief runs and special matinee performances at such London theatres as the Haymarket and the Royalty, Barker's directorial work was not much on display during the last three years of the 1900s; for one nineteen-month stretch between 1908 and 1910 he directed only Galsworthy's *Strife* (1909), seen at the Duke of York's (before it transferred elsewhere). Soon after *Strife*, Barker began what promised to be a significant enterprise with the American commercial theatre impresario, Charles Frohman, at the Duke of York's. Frohman was led to believe by playwright James M. Barrie that London was ready for a major repertory company and that Barker was the chap to run it. Still, Barker's authority was not complete and the project, which began in February 1910 and was formally dubbed ''The Repertory Theatre,'' ultimately foundered when theatregoers were not inclined to turn out in force for a rotating repertory season of challenging new British plays (the season began with such works as Galsworthy's *Justice,* Shaw's *Misalliance,* and Barker's *The Madras House*). Before long, ''safer'' works were being offered; seventeen weeks after it began, its coffers seriously depleted, ''The Repertory Theatre'' became an entry in history's pages. Among the fine actors involved were Lewis Casson, Sybil Thorndike, Frederick Lloyd, Dennis Eadie, and Mary Jerrold.

Barker was married to a lovely and highly respected actress, Lillah McCarthy, who performed leading roles in many of the plays he directed. He was one of many directors who made his marriage into a working partnership with a talented spouse.[6] Early in 1911 the couple teamed up to present a series of matinees at the Court, with Barker directing and McCarthy starring. Following a brief season in which two plays by Masefield (one of them an adaptation of a Swedish play) and Barker's own one-act farce *Rococo* were produced, the couple began a more regular managerial enterprise at the Little Theatre in Adelphi, opening with Schnitzler's *Anatol,* Barker himself playing the title role of the Viennese rake. Ibsen's *Master Builder* and Shaw's *Fanny's First Play* (directed by Shaw) were produced before the Barkers decided to move to the Kingsway Theatre, another intimate playhouse. Here, and at the St. James's Theatre and the Savoy, from February 1912 to the end of 1914, a substantial list of plays was produced, including, among others, Euripides' *Iphigenia in Tauris,* its staging under the obvious influence of Max Reinhardt's *Oedipus Rex,* Arnold Bennett's *The Great Adventure* (which had a substantial run), Shaw's *Androcles and the Lion* and *The Doctor's Dilemma,* Molière's *Le Mariage Forcé,* and a forward-looking version of Thomas Hardy's lengthy poetic drama, *The Dynasts.* Among his other directorial work of these years was a spectacular staging in 1914 of Masefield's *Philip the King* at Covent Garden. *Iphigenia* was also given three performances at an outdoor Greek theatre built in a chalk pit at Bradfield College. Barker's performance as Orestes marked his final work as an actor.

During these years Barker's reputation grew rapidly and he was recognized internationally as the leading British representative of the modern theatre movement. As a consequence, in 1908 he was invited to New York to consider the management of the New Theatre, then popularly referred to as the ''Millionaire's Theatre,'' a grandiose new enterprise being launched by a group of wealthy New Yorkers. He turned it down, though, when he saw how unwieldy the new playhouse was going to be. Winthrop Ames thereupon accepted the offer, but the project eventually proved a gigantic failure. Barker did work in New York, however, when, in 1915, he staged a repertory of *Androcles and the Lion,* Anatole

France's short play *The Man Who Married a Dumb Wife,* and *A Midsummer Night's Dream.* (*The Doctor's Dilemma* and *The Madras House* were scheduled but not given.) He also successfully staged two Euripidean tragedies, *Iphigenia in Tauris* and *The Trojan Women*, at a number of outdoor stadiums on college campuses, including the Yale Bowl, Harvard Stadium, and City College's brand new Lewisohn Stadium (*The Trojan Women* was its inaugural event and 20,000 attended). No one was more important than Barker to the establishment of English-language productions of Euripides.

Although he had headed several attempts at a repertory company, Barker never was able to arrange for the type of theatre he would have found ideal. This would have been a playhouse in which there were two stages, one for production and one for experimentation. The results of the work in the experimental theatre— experimental in terms of playwriting, acting, and all the arts of design—would have fed the work in the regular theatre. Also a part of this dream theatre would have been a gymnasium in which the company members could constantly work on gymnastics and dancing to improve their physical prowess and grace.

DIRECTING CAREER ENDS

Barker's marriage to Lillah McCarthy ended in divorce, and his second wife, Helen Huntington, a well-known American poet and novelist, was instrumental in forcing him to break with direct involvement in the theatre. He spent his remaining years as a writer and lecturer, returning to direct (or, more likely, to work on someone else's production) sporadically and often without taking credit. Usually, these productions were of plays he and his wife had translated, such as those by the Quintero brothers, or of revivals of his own works. The most significant of these occasions, because of the star and the record he has left of Barker's methods, was John Gielgud's *King Lear* (1940) at the Old Vic. The direction for this production was formally credited to Lewis Casson, but the program noted that it was based on Barker's preface to the play and also benefitted from his personal advice.

PRODUCTION STYLE

Barker's production style was always directed at making the events transpiring onstage as lifelike and believable as possible. He struggled valiantly to rid the stage of the clichés of nineteenth-century acting and scenic techniques by paying immense attention to the details of the mise-en-scène. He wanted life, or the effect of life, on the stage; he sought an aura of actuality which would compel the audience's belief. Broad, theatricalist effects were, for the most part, anathema to him; instead, he worked for quiescence, simplicity, understatement, and even austerity. Many of the plays he staged at the Court were in the naturalistic style then in fashion, to which his techniques were perfectly suited. Dennis Kennedy notes, though, that there were actually four types of plays at the Court;

in addition to the realistic plays there were the "translations of Euripides; the poetic, non-representational work of Maeterlinck, [Maurice] Hewlett, Masefield, and *Prunella;* and the 'ideational comedies' of Bernard Shaw."[7] Whatever the play, his close work in rehearsal with the actors led to an atmosphere in which the living qualities of the characters replaced the artificial, superficially observed behavioral attitudes of conventionally realistic productions. C. B. Purdom, a Barker biographer, however, found Barker's stress on lifelikeness to be an "inherent fault," as the resultant "understatement, under emphasis, a tendency even towards what seemed to be inarticulateness [caused] his rhythm to go underground."[8] A contrary opinion is that of director Hugh Hunt, who feels that Barker's "naturalistic tendencies were balanced by his sense of the rhythmical values of the text."[9]

Barker's naturalism had an inner rather than an external orientation. Although desirous of creating a truthful stage picture, he was far from convinced that the theatre's purpose was to provide a total reflection of reality. The surrender of the audience, he wrote, "to illusion, however allowable, is only the crudest form of enjoyment the theatre provides. And it is the cruder sort of acting that contributes to it, the impersonative, not the interpretive."[10] It is the latter which people hope to view at classic plays, he said, the former being appropriate only for "crudely realistic plays." Barker implies that an actor's attitude toward a role and the understanding of it that he displays are ultimately more important than the degree to which he can convince the spectator that he and the role are one. Barker wanted the audience to clearly distinguish the actor from his role and urged that "any identification of the player with the part implies a lowering, not a heightening, of artistic achievement."[11]

Barker felt that the actor was both a creative and interpretive artist, and that it was his duty to play his character and not himself. The actor was to avoid the temptation to exploit himself; he had to make a conscious effort to detach himself from his own personality and transform himself into the role, while simultaneously interpreting it. Although vague on methodology, he wanted the actor to find subconscious means for this achievement. Assiduous study of the text, he assumed, would allow the actor to surrender himself to his role; as he began to apprehend it, he would find growing in him a "mysterious second personality, which will not be himself and yet will be a part of himself. He will be wedded to his idea."[12] Barker's ideal actor identified himself *with* the character; he did not identify himself *in* the character. He acted what the character would do in the given circumstances, not what the actor would do if he were the character. Barker's ideas in this regard resemble those of Stanislavsky's disciple, Michael Chekhov, who differed from the master on just these grounds.

In Barker's opinion, physical activity on stage was overused in most productions. Stage movement is of very little importance, whereas the interior action of the characters is the crux of a performance. The director should employ unusual stage movement only for scenes of acrobatics, dancing, or fencing—all other stage movement should be limited to what derives from the well-trained actor's impulses within the scenic circumstances. It was in his Greek and Shakespearean productions that Barker had the fullest opportunity to exploit the possibilities of movement; his Greek productions inevitably employed considerable choreography for the choruses. When they were given in the huge American stadiums the choreography had to be as striking as possible because of the dimensions involved. Similarly, as can be discerned from the available photographs, the gestures of the principal players had to be extremely expansive and nonrealistic merely in order to communicate across the vast spaces.

Few English actors of his day measured up to Barker's standards, however, and in 1922 he declared that most native thespians were of inferior quality. In his eyes they lacked the vocal, facial, and physical talents needed for artistic work, although he was pleased to find them generally better educated than their forebears. He would have liked to see actors undergo a long and arduous process of training. According to his first wife, Lillah McCarthy, who said she shared his ideas, such training would have entailed three years of studying music, rhythm, elocution, and voice production followed by three years of playing in a provincial stock or repertory company. A weekly repertory requiring the acting of eight different roles was recommended for such an actor-in-training. This, McCarthy concluded, would prepare the player for work in the better theatres in the larger towns.[13]

Among Barker's various targets was the ubiquitous star system. Because he aimed for a total harmony and unity in production, he saw the system which stressed the work of one or two leading players as artistically bankrupt. Only through ensemble playing could the effects of naturalness, of reality, and of truly felt emotions be communicated. This approach was alien to a system in which the actor-manager reigned supreme and where superficial scenic and acting effects distracted the audience's attention from the weaker parts of a play. Barker's actors were never required to perform bizarre or foolish actions, but were given only that which could be acted believably and honestly, in as natural a fashion as possible.

To Barker, plays were written to be acted, not read; they were only alive when embodied by the actor's presence. "As well praise a yacht for being built to stay safely afloat as exalt a play because it is more fitted for the study than the stage,"[14] he wrote. Nevertheless, he held supreme respect for the text of the play, and attempted to avoid idiosyncratic effects which would point attention to the director. His aim was always to bring out the play's values and not his own. It is ironic that, despite Barker's own efforts to avoid clever directorial gimmicks, Peter Brook and Tyrone Guthrie, two of the most outstandingly "pyrotechnical" directors of the century, were both powerfully influenced by his work. Yet Barker ridiculed just those production techniques from which these two directors were to gain their reputations.

There is nothing . . . [he claimed in 1934] to justify the translating of the *Agamemnon* into modern slang, his entry riding on a tank flanked by machine guns; or a symbolic staging of *Hedda Gabler;* or the playing of Othello as a puppet jerked about by Iago; [or using *Hamlet* as a] mockery of the ridiculous morality of the bourgeoisie.[15]

He thought such "aberrations" should be punished by placing the director in the pillory and cutting off his ears. Even in his Shakespearean productions, the use of overt theatricality was meant to suggest the world of the play as he believed the author had imagined it, and not an externalized conception forced on the play against its spirit.

Because he saw in each play its own inherent style and possibilities, and not those of some generalized method of stage production, Barker was close to the sort of eclecticism associated with Max Reinhardt. As Lillah McCarthy observed of him,

One great truth about my husband is that there is not a Granville Barker school, or manner of treatment. He attacks each new play with all the freshness of view and openness to impression and desire for individual treatment as though he were a beginner. He has no set form of production, not even in the matter of lighting. Every new play is a new problem.[16]

MUSICAL VALUES

Like many directors Barker introduced musical values into his productions, working in great detail on the subtle rhythms beneath the apparently natural surface. He concentrated on the "repetition of the rise and fall of the action, variations in time, the relation of speech to movement—in fact, the action as a whole."[17] He was convinced that the evocation of a play's meaning could be largely achieved through rhythmic means. He would spend long hours at the pianola, developing a rhythmic basis for a production. All the dramatic action would be keyed to specific rhythmical and musical ideas so that the play corresponded to those elements one might find in musical composition.

Theodore Stier, musical director at the Court, recalled the extreme care taken by the director to guarantee that every phrase was musically orchestrated. He would tell an actor to play one line crescendo, ask for a firmata, and then demand a pianissimo. Or he would make analogies with musical instruments so that an actor would perform his proper role in the orchestral ensemble.[18]

CLASSICAL REVIVALS

In directing the classics, Barker's aim was to find as close an approximation of the play's original staging conditions as he could and then temper these to satisfy modern tastes. To ignore the old conditions is folly, especially in the case of Greek, medieval, and Elizabethan plays. The director must not fail to consider the modern audience's capacity for accepting various stage conventions of the past in choosing ways to make the work palatable, but the closer he can get to reproducing the essence of the original, the better. Barker was sure that the old plays became much clearer the greater the attention paid to their original methods. In staging a Greek tragedy, for example, the architectural relationships of a circular orchestra to a shallow stage area, and to the encircling audience, must be visible in the director's mind as he conceives his staging patterns. Only by a reimagining of these fundamental principles could a production successfully convey those architectural principles of composition, mass, and line.

THE THRUST STAGE

Having considered the various types of stages, Barker came to feel that the ideal arrangement was a thrust stage surrounded by a horseshoe auditorium, as opposed to a picture frame proscenium faced by straight rows of seats. Barker found that an audience surrounding the stage and able to see the other spectators created a friendly, united atmosphere. The spectator could be aware of both the play and the other theatregoers at the same time. To Barker the audience's response to the play was tied up with the way its members related to each other. A good performance was marked by a spirit of friendliness among the viewers. He disliked an arena arrangement, however, as in the circus, because he wanted the play to be the primary focus and the audience secondary. Reinhardt's London production of *The Miracle* was weakened by just such an approach.

Barker's ideas on the relationship of audience to actors were largely unfulfilled during his own career, although directors such as Tyrone Guthrie later made something of a fetish of similar notions. Compromise arrangements were all Barker ever achieved. He was hindered by being forced to work on Shakespeare and Euripides within a proscenium arch. Despite the horrible sight-line problems he encountered, he tried to bridge the aesthetic gap by such measures as an extended forestage and the clever employment of curtains. He remained convinced, however, that a new theatrical form was capable of being designed to accommodate both a proscenium stage (with a variable opening) and a thrust for use in Elizabethan productions. Removable seats would be provided for conversion of the front of the auditorium into a usable orchestra for Greek choruses. (The often criticized Vivian Beaumont Theatre at Lincoln Center in New York is a major example of such an arrangement.)

Barker's dreams of a flexible theatre did not extend to the inclusion of mechanical means for making scene changes. The more he experienced such devices as revolving stages, wagons, elevator traps, and other methods, the more a bare stage seemed the best solution to most scenic problems. He was especially antagonistic toward the revolve (a favorite device of his great contemporary, Max Reinhardt), which he deemed out of place in most classical productions, as well as in the majority of modern plays. He himself had made exciting use of the revolve in *Androcles and the Lion,* to show the shift from the gladiators' room to the arena and back again, but realized that this technique required too confining a scenic plan to be widely useful.

SHAKESPEAREAN STAGING

Although the conditions under which he worked were far from ideal—forcing him to make painful concessions to the demands of the proscenium stage—Barker nevertheless was so successful in his classic stagings that these are remembered far more vividly than any of his other work. His Greek and Shakespeare productions were, for their time, strikingly original versions in which he employed a forestage built out over the orchestra pit, in order to bring the action nearer to the audience. He had learned the value of the forestage when working with Poel, the great innovator in Shakespearean production whose idea it was to return the Bard and his contemporaries to an Elizabethan-type platform. Simplified sets requiring only a minimum of change so that the action could proceed swiftly from scene to scene replaced the pictorial splendor of archaeologically correct re-creations of Shakespeare's locales. However, for all Barker's awareness of the importance of allowing the audience to imagine, when necessary, the places of the action without recourse to scenic literalism, he was himself dependent on localized scenery, albeit of a far more theatrical and fanciful type than was currently the convention. Poel labored diligently to convince his contemporaries of the worth of simplicity in Shakespearean decor, but it took Barker to make the idea finally acceptable. Barker's Shakespeare settings were not Poel-like attempts to re-create the actual details of the Elizabethan stage, but sought instead to capture the essence of the stage's functional basis as seen through the prism of a modern use of color, line, and form. Norman Wilkinson and Albert Rutherston (formerly Rothenstein) designed the formalistic ''post-impressionist'' sets and costumes for these stagings which, in their startling *au courant* feeling and style, created a sensation.

Barker broke sharply with the pictorially illusionistic sets of the romantic-realist school, as represented by the work of actor-managers like Henry Irving and Herbert Beerbohm Tree. He aimed for a frankly theatrical and symbolic decor which would require swift but simple shifting to serve for all the scenes of the play. His appearance came at a time when West Enders were more concerned with the personalities of their favorite players and the trappings of the spectacle in which they appeared than in the words and events of Shakespeare's plays. The texts were cut to shreds, usually to allow time for scene changes. Barker's scenic concepts fell between the excessive bareness of Poel and the sumptuousness of Tree. Many of his ideas were suggested by contemporary experiments in the German theatre—Reinhardt's work, in particular—where stripped down, highly simplified, three-dimensional settings employed light, color, and the play of mass and line to do away with the old-fashioned two-dimensional flat and backdrop sets. Some of these were equipped with semi-Elizabethan arrangements that attempted to provide a fore, middle, and rear stage area such as Shakespeare's theatre was believed to possess. (German experiments in approximating the arrangement of Shakespeare's stage date back to the Dusseldorf activity of Karl Immermann in 1840.)

Similarly, Barker's Shakespeare sets were divided into three areas—fore, middle, and rear. A false proscenium was set into the arch and upstage of it was a rear stage formed of a four-stepped platform across which curtains were hung. Between the steps and proscenium arch was the middle stage, and, somewhat lower, was a curved forestage, twelve feet deep at the center and eleven feet at the sides, extending over the orchestra pit and several rows of the auditorium. Doors in the proscenium gave access to the middle and forestage. Footlights were absent, the principle illumination coming from powerful lamps mounted at the front of the rear balcony. Bright, decorative curtains and drapes were run across the rear and middle stages to allow for rapid alternation of scenes. The formal, "hieroglyphic" scenery prevented the scenery from seeming representational and thus allowed the actor to move out onto the forestage without seeming to be stepping out of a picture. Curtains on which scenic locales were painted were treated merely as decoration, no attempt being made to disguise their folds.

These Shakespeare settings were not quite as simple as they might appear. Barker's use of curtains, drops, and scenic units to represent each major scene was actually quite complex. For example, in *The Winter's Tale*, nine differently colored, suggestively painted curtains were used to denote locales and changes in the seasons. Their swift deployment allowed the action to move steadily forward without the need for time-wasting scene shifts. As a new scene began, its curtain would be brought in as the dialogue proceeded unimpeded. Walter Prichard Eaton's description of *A Midsummer Night's Dream*, quoted below, gives further details on Barker's creative use of curtains.

Regardless of his awareness of the Shakespearean convention of place as being either insignificant or suggested by the lines when sufficiently important to the dramatist, Barker's sets, as noted, attempted to conjure up images of specific locales, although by an aesthetic unfamiliar and therefore not easily assimilated by contemporary audiences. The attention given the sets in reviews of Barker's work gives the impression that these decorative solutions were more distracting than the director would have liked, especially in their striking coloration. Also distracting were the cloth hangings used to picture trees, columns, and other scenic elements as they waved or flapped loosely on the drafty stage.

Few directors have revealed as deep an understanding of Shakespeare as has Barker. His *Prefaces to Shakespeare* displays his "genius for directing Shakespeare on paper," says critic Laurence Kitchin.[19] The plays he analyzed but did not direct were later staged with deference to many of his ideas by such important artists as Harcourt Williams, John Gielgud, and Tyrone Guthrie. Barker saw the plays as acting vehicles for an ensemble of skilled players and comprehended their multileveled meanings specifically as these related to the crucible of stage production. Kitchin praises his abhorrence of "pedantic irrelevancies" and notes that "no other critic conveys the feeling of sitting next to the dramatist at rehearsal."[20]

Barker believed that Shakespeare's words should be spoken with ease and facility, "trippingly on the tongue," yet his actors were much criticized for the unfamiliar rapidity with which they flew through their lines. Edward Fales Cow-ard wrote, for example, of Barker's *A Midsummer Night's Dream* when it played in New York:

The tempo is *vivace, multo vivace*, so much so that though the speech is impeccably true in its delivery, the thought by its very haste of expression becomes blurred and confused. This is particularly true of the quartet of lovers which by their fluency of diction and movement lose the dominant notes that particularize the different characters in their changing moods as influenced by Oberon's potions.[21]

Barker reasoned that the audience was simply not used to listening to these words and was unable to adjust to a delivery which he thought was far more natural and real than the high-flown, drawn-out theatrics of conventional verse-speaking. Cultured Elizabethan speech was spoken quite quickly and with a much more energetic delivery than was currently the case with spoken English. Barker cut only the more archaic and bawdy sentences and words, and these excisions were kept at a minimum. Restoring the text to a basically uncut version was a sig-nificant innovation in an age when the average director freely applied the blue pencil to Shakespeare. Intermissions (which Barker would have liked to eliminate entirely) were included for the convenience of the audience, not the scene shifters, as the sets required little changing of any but their decorative elements, and these could be managed instantaneously.

The first of Barker's famous Shakespearean presentations was *The Winter's Tale*, produced in September 1912 with settings by Wilkinson and costumes by Rutherston. The almost uncut performance (only six lines were dropped) aston-ished audiences by its fiery pace and scenic innovations. Leontes's palace was represented by white side walls and a colonnade of pillars at the rear, backed by gold curtains. (The extensive use of curtains has been alluded to above.) A variety of palace interiors were created by the rearrangement of curtains and furnishings. The sheep-shearing scene used a fairly representational cut-out paint-ing of a rustic cottage shown in a simple, unadorned manner. (The Morris dancers in this scene were accompanied by an onstage quartet of musicians playing antique instruments.) Bright white light illuminated most of the play, although there were effective variations in its intensity according to the specific scenes; one scene, indeed, was lit by little more than a brazier burning onstage. So curious did the whole thing appear to the critics that they floundered desperately in trying to assess it, although many found the major weakness the racing dialogue.

Critical perceptions were more acute for *Twelfth Night*, which opened in November, two months afterwards. Wilkinson did both sets and costumes. Ac-cording to Edward G. Moore, the permanent set revealed Olivia's

formal garden with white staircases right and left leading down to a cupola in the centre supported by columns of pink and gold; smaller columns were used for porches at the top of the staircases. Four steps below the cupola were black and white benches with gold seats. . . . Two formal wooden yew trees—obviously wooden—painted a dark green flanked the centre cupola.[22]

This permanent set was varied by the use of curtains and various convention-alized elements (such as a prison grate) downstage of it, or by additions to it. The kitchen scene—done in an inset inspired by the Elizabethan "inner stage"—was realistic enough to be likened to the productions of Beerbohm Tree.

The production drew attention to Barker's novel interpretations of the familiar characters. He pointed out, for example, that Viola, when acting a boy, must be as straightforwardly masculine as she can, or else the balance of the love scenes, written for a boy actor, would be disturbed. The disguise should not be played as a joke (which was conventional at the time), but must be acted seriously with Viola doing all in her power to make the audience believe she is male. Otherwise she will knock, "for the sake of a little laughter, the whole of the play's romantic plot on the head."[23]

Sir Toby and Sir Andrew were no longer the typical stage sot and his cretin companion, but bore themselves like gentlemen. Fabian was seen not as a sec-ondary part for a young actor, but as an old-retainer role worthy of a senior player; Feste, played brilliantly by Hayden Coffin, a musical comedy star without Shakespearean experience, also was aged to suggest the pathetic quality of a fading entertainer. Malvolio, acted by Henry Ainley, was played against tradition as an unsympathetic figure. These revisions stressed Barker's view of the play as a passionate romantic comedy of character and not an excuse for a broad comic turn.

A Midsummer Night's Dream, February 1914, was Barker's last and most controversial Shakespeare staging. It was also the most popular and ran for ninety-nine performances. The old-fashioned, romantically extravagant sets and costumes were banished and replaced by an exotic decor which showed the influence of modernist, continental scene designers such as Leon Bakst. Here is how the stage appeared to an American observer, critic Walter Prichard Eaton, when the work was produced in New York:

When the audience gathers in the theatre, it sees the forestage (built out as far as Row C), bathed in white light, and hanging just inside the proscenium, framed by a second proscenium of plain gold, like a box, a curtain of whitish color, with a frail green and gold floral design upon it. Just in front is a black seat, on a slightly raised platform. As trumpets sound, four negro slaves enter, by the passage made by the elimination of the stage box, and they are followed by Theseus, Hippolyta, and the Court. The costumes are not the traditional Greek, but are full of barbaric color, which is perhaps more nearly authentic . . . for the next scene, all that is required is the raising of the curtain. Six inches behind it is another curtain, painted with a quaint, formal representation of a window or two and a glimpse of the city. It is a cloth curtain, hanging in folds. Before this Bottom and his fellows plan their play. Then this curtain also rises, and behind it (it will be seen that so far the real stage, behind the proscenium, has not been used at all) is a third curtain, painted plain Nile green on the bottom edge, and above that deep blue, spangled all over with silver stars and a huge moon.[24]

The full set was used in the next scene, at Titania's bower. In it a large, green, dome-shaped mound occupied most of the acting area. Suspended above it was a "quaint ring, or wheel, or purple grapes and leaves. Surrounding it on all three sides are long, upright strips of Nile green cloth, between which you see only an indefinite blueness. They are, presumably, the forest trees."[25] In and out among these strips the characters appeared and disappeared. In the last scene the full stage was used, with a wide expanse of jet black steps rising about six feet, and on top of which stood "a forest of round silver columns supporting white crossbeams through which you glimpse the night sky. Black and silver—that is all."[26]

The set for the *Dream*, it has been observed, was a visual metaphor for a forest, just as Shakespeare uses verbal metaphors to suggest the same thing.[27] Puck, dressed in bright red, was actively engaged throughout as "the presenter of the play's fond pageant" with Barker employing him frequently to perform bits of theatrical legerdermain suggesting his controlling powers. For instance, Puck gestured for the lights to be dimmed; then, with his line, "We may effect this business yet ere day," communicated that his magic was responsible for the raising of the curtain which effected the change.

Perhaps the most controversial ingredient was the fairies, thirty robotlike beings painted from head to toe in gold leaf that made them seem like living statues. Only four of the fairies were played by children; the remainder, like Puck, were acted by adults, each of whom was clearly individualized, being given such names as the Major, the Professor, the Twins, the Old Man Fairy, and the Doctor. The problems posed by the fairies were a major incentive in Barker's selecting this play for production. His fairies seemed to be unearthly creatures, and were hardly the charming winged sprites beloved of audiences at traditional revivals. Some believe them to have been aesthetically out of synch with the rest of the presentation, with whom they appeared to have little in common.

Barker's approach to the play had as dynamic an impact on the theatre world of his day as did Peter Brook's version in 1970. Indeed, Barker once admitted that the scenic arrangement grew from his conviction that the machinery and technical apparatus of the modern stage were "well enough," but when it came to the *Dream* "what is really needed is a great white box. That's what our theatre really is. We set our scenes in a shell."[28] The set's colors of blue and green were added later to tone down the harsh effects of the whiteness. Barker's original vision, of course, was captured unforgettably in Sally Jacobs's white box for the Brook revival.

Summing up the Barker approach to Shakespeare, we may point to the uncut text, the respect for the author's sequence of scenes, the rapid alternation of scenes with only one intermission break, the fore, middle, and rear stage ar-

rangement with curtains, the swiftness of the dialogue, the modernistic, nonillusionistic decorative scheme, the fresh approach to characterization, and the
general unity of conception.

EURIPIDEAN STAGING

His production of Euripidean tragedy likewise gained Barker great acclaim.
His analytic powers served well in his detailed direction of the difficult speeches
in these works. He looked for and found the contemporary value of Euripides'
ideas and taught his actors to project them, thereby communicating the time-
lessness of the old plays. His productions were remarkable for the naturalness
and believability of the main characters, although his handling of the choruses
was not consistently well received. At first the choruses were composed of eight
women; later Barker used twelve, divided into two equal groups. Few critics
found the vocalizing totally successful, though. As for movement, the limited
space at the Court greatly confined the director's imagination for the plays he
staged there. He sought a relatively natural, but not overly formalized, style of
movement that occasionally seems to have worked in harmony with the realistic
character portrayals. Also problematic was the nature of the music used to support
the choral chanting. Various approaches were tried, but success does not seem
to have been reached until the outdoor stagings in America.

Scenery was spare and suggestive. In *The Trojan Women,* for example, one
writer has noted that ''a great gateway in the ruined city was seen under the
varying lights, while in the background were the white towers of Troy standing
out vividly against a blue sky, and in the distance shone blue waters.''[29] Excellent
lighting effects helped the stage say more than mere sets could; few English
productions at the time revealed so masterful a use of the electric switchboard.

When Lillah McCarthy acted in the highly acclaimed 1910 Reinhardt production of *Oedipus Rex* in London, Barker was greatly impressed by the Austrian
regisseur's techniques and borrowed some of them for his own version of *Iphigenia in Tauris* at the Kingsway Theatre in 1912. For example, he built an apron
stage out over the first three rows of the auditorium with a runway, which was
used for entrances and exits, leading into the house. When appropriate, however,
he could produce brilliant theatrical effects on his own. Among these was his
conception of Pallas Athena in *Iphigenia in Tauris.* Wearing a mask, Athena
appeared as an immense, almost totemic figure, thrilling the audience with her
veritable incarnation of divine presence. Years later, Guthrie surprised audiences
with a similar effect in his staging of *The House of Atreus.*

The outdoor stagings of *Iphigenia in Tauris* and *The Trojan Women* in America—with McCarthy as Iphigenia and Hecuba—were of such interest to the public
that within thirty days over twenty-five thousand copies of the plays were sold.
These productions—produced in bright daylight at 4:30 P.M.—held their vast
audiences' attention with the aid of Norman Wilkinson's essentially accurate,
highly decorated (especially in *Iphigenia,* where they actually may have erred

on the side of gaudiness in an attempt to capture a feeling of barbarism), and vividly colored costumes. It was, indeed, something of a task to hold their attention, as something of a circus or sports event atmosphere surrounded the show, what with all the backstage preparations clearly visible to the throngs, with vendors at the Yale Bowl loudly hawking not only copies of the play as if they were scorecards but selling peanuts as well, and with the shouts from a nearby baseball game audible to spectators at Harvard Stadium. The costuming for the women in *The Trojan Women* included sandals with soles several inches thick, although the high-soled *cothurnus* was actually a Hellenistic innovation and was not employed in the classical Greek period.

Wilkinson's striking settings were built to be transported to the various stadiums at which the plays were shown. Audiences were seated at one end of the oval-shaped stadiums, their placement corresponding to the three-quarters wraparound configuration of a Greek *theatron*. Before them was placed a massive three-doored set conforming to a generalized conception of a *skene* house fronted by a circular orchestra one hundred feet in diameter; this latter was patterned in huge geometric designs that assisted in the choral choreography. The *skene* sat on a low stage reached by several steps that ran all along its edge; before the central door, which was slightly larger than those at either side, the stage had a thrust attached that brought that portion of it several feet closer to the orchestra. The main characters employed the central door, the lesser characters the side doors, and characters arriving from elsewhere came on from either side of the *skene,* mounting the steps on their entrance. The chief difference in the settings for the plays was the addition for *Iphigenia* of an altar in the center of the orchestra for the chorus to dance around. In these spatially expansive settings Barker was finally able to bring to the choral movements a sense of their original grandeur. *Iphigenia in Tauris* was notable primarily for its spectacle while *The Trojan Women* was marked more by verbal felicity; in both plays, however, problems of projection were serious, and critics were surprised that as much of the text as was communicated did come across. Extremely detailed ritualistic choral movements indicative of the play's every emotional transition were choreographed by Barker and expertly carried out.

PREPARATION FOR PRODUCTION

Harley Granville-Barker took great care in the preparations made for his productions. His concern was with the interior life of the play and the shaping of its thought processes. Although he admired Stanislavsky's idea that a play should not be presented before the public until it is ready—no matter how long a rehearsal process is required—circumstances forced him to put a production together in an average of three weeks, and sometimes less. Thus, despite his many pronouncements about how a play should be rehearsed, economic reality compelled him to compromise his ideals by working at a more intense pace in search of results.

WORKING WITH THE DESIGNER

After selecting the designer best suited to the play's style and giving him a general idea of the desired look, Barker would be shown a rough draft by the artist. After some discussion, Barker would allow the designer to finalize his concept. Regardless of his self-described casualness in regard to the development of a fitting scenic embodiment, the scenic elements he employed often drew more attention than any other feature of his period productions. We know, for instance, that when he and Albert Rutherston discussed the costumes for *The Winter's Tale,* they shared the notion that the look should be "Renaissance-classic, that is, classic dress as Shakespeare saw it," which was suggested to Barker by a reference in the play to Giulio Romano. He had the designer look Romano up "and there the costumes were much as we had forethought them."[30]

Among Barker's other outstanding contributions to the art of setting the stage was his choice of the young Robert Edmond Jones to design the curtain-raiser, *The Man Who Married a Dumb Wife,* produced in New York in 1915. This much-reproduced design is often pointed to as the first successful instance of the New Stagecraft to be seen in the work of an American designer. Jones' black and white setting was in the two-dimensional style of the "relief stage," a concept popular in avant-garde European theatre in the century's first decades. Moving against the friezelike background, were a progression of lovely red, yellow, and orange medieval costumes, also created by Jones.

CASTING

Casting for these productions was emphatically in favor of the versatile, highly skilled, and dependable actor as opposed to the major star. Although some stars did work for Barker, they were only those who favored ensemble playing. He chose to use players whose ability and methods he knew well. Such an approach guaranteed that little time and nervous energy would be wasted on them at rehearsals. Actors in his companies were paid rather low salaries compared to those received by players on the West End or Broadway. However, many serious performers sought employment with Barker, for he offered them fine roles which they might otherwise never have had the chance to act elsewhere. When he comanaged the Court on a limited repertory principle, talented players were likely to be used for leading roles in one production and supporting or even minor roles in another. Small roles, played by an actor such as Edmund Gwenn, took on a life unknown in the work of other directors where lesser rules were glossed over in favor of principals. Unity of effect could only be achieved by true ensemble playing. No star, no matter how outstanding, could create, by himself, the effect of harmonious excellence produced by a team of talented players working together in the spirit of serving the play, not themselves.

When casting, particularly for the more challenging plays, Barker sought the advice of those he respected, and his letters to such persons as Shaw reveal the difficulties he often confronted in finding the right actor for a difficult role.[31]

IN REHEARSAL

Barker typically began the rehearsal process by reading the play aloud to the cast. He aimed to give a sense of the play's totality and read with simplicity, conveying the outlines of the characters rather than fully acting each part vocally. He then moved on to a discussion of the play with the cast, but the three weeks normally at his disposal would put serious limits on the time thus spent. A profound believer in rehearsals ''at table,'' Barker would have liked to discuss the play at great length before blocking it, an approach he had learned under Poel.

He saw the director as the chairman of a committee, as did Guthrie in later years. Outlining the procedural rules for discussion, he wrote, ''The producer discusses every scene for he is interested in them all, an actor must only discuss those in which he is personally concerned. The chairman may closure a debate and no doubt he will have to closure many.''[32] Actors may not always be able to argue rationally, he claims, as instincts and emotions are such powerful forces with them. In fact, the director may have to rely on a good actor's instincts rather than argue endlessly on a point. Some plays require a minimum of discussion, others require much more. The proper amount of discussion should lead to the evolution of the play's ''natural form.'' Blocking out the action should not be attempted until this form is clear. In this ideal situation the actors should be given some movement work only when the discussion seems to need revitalizing through an external stimulus. Only a scene or two should be attempted, and not necessarily in sequence, in order to keep the actors' involvement fresh. The actors were instructed to do no more than mumble their words as they focused on their blocking.

This exercise should not last too long [he insisted], nor should the scenes that are tried follow too much in sequence, for above all things, the physical action of the play must not be defined while the thought and feeling that should prompt it are still unsure.[33]

Only after the three steps of textual understanding, physical activity, and memorization of dialogue were absorbed would Barker encourage the cast to play full out. Further corrections would then be concentrated on whichever of the three points was most greatly in need of them.

To insure that his actors were in tune with him throughout the rehearsal process, he thought they should have full copies of the script, not the ''sides'' in which only the actor's own lines and cues were printed. This allowed each performer to feel he was part of the totality.

Barker warned that all the actor's work on his role should be done at rehearsal, in concert with his fellows, and not on an individual basis at home. The latter approach led to individual performances and detracted from the ensemble. As he explained:

> To study the play, apart from studying your fellow-actors in the play, is to prefer dry bones to flesh and blood. There is much to be said for the method of the seventeenth-century music teacher, who locked up the instrument upon his departure for fear that his pupil might practice.[34]

In his writings, Barker often said that the externals of stage action were secondary to the internal action of conflict and character relationships. As suggested by his fondness for long discussions, he did not want actors to worry over their blocking since this was a trivial concern compared with the psychological and emotional action. Where a character sat or stood, or which arm he gestured with, was of lesser importance, he claimed.

When staging a work requiring the marshalling of a large number of bodies he could be as specific as the Duke of Saxe-Meiningen in his requirements. His Reinhardt-like production of *Philip the King* employed a vast number of extras for the crowds, and he had to insure the correctness of their blocking by giving each extra a booklet containing the requisite movements, with their moves denoted in a letter and number-based code.

Even when doing smaller productions, however, he thought it a good idea to assist his actors in understanding their stage positions to have the stage manager build a rough model of the set, one-inch in scale and filled with dollhouse furniture, and to keep it before the actors as they worked.

WORKING WITH ACTORS

Barker was convinced that acting was the foundation of all theatre art, its raison d'être. Accordingly, he worked very closely with his actors yet gave them, initially, a great deal of freedom in the development of their roles. A *New York Times* reporter, observing him at rehearsal, noted that he came off as "a director of gentle manner and infinite patience, superhuman almost in the calm displayed at times under exasperating circumstances."[35] Barker had a temper, but he frightened actors more by his general demeanor than by shouting. Hesketh Pearson noted:

> His curses are neither loud nor deep; they are atmospheric. It is what he doesn't say that paralyzes one. He looks; and having looked, he turns his back to the stage—and you can still see him looking through the back of his head. You feel that he is saying quite a lot of things to himself, saying them thoughtfully and witheringly—annihilating things. . . . Sometimes he will execute a little dance, a quiet, solitary waltz with ghastly possibilities. That is when you are unimaginably shaking in your efforts to get what he wants. . . . The best thing to do is to hide yourself from him completely until he calls you back. By that time he will have recovered, and will be quite charming. . . . Later, you will ask someone what happened after you had gone away. You will be told that nothing happened—nothing

whatever! That is the appalling thing about Barker. Nothing happens. But all sorts of things are *going* to happen. He is the supreme artist of suggestions.[36]

A fruitful discussion period, felt Barker, would provide the impetus for the actors to bring their capacities for interpretation and execution to bear on their roles. All the director should have to do is eliminate from the actor's work that which is ineffective. He would merely have to say, "No, that does not quite express it. Try again." He must guide the actors subtly, never dictating their performances. The director should function as an ideal audience. Once having brought his company to a mutuality of feeling and understanding of the play, he can safely allow them full participation in the evolution of the performance. Barker was a flexible director, always allowing his own ideas to be altered by those of the players, provided it was the play they were concerned with and not themselves. He said he would suggest to them "the general lines I want them to follow and leave the filling in to them. I am the architect and they build upon my plans. This is what I conceive to be directing as opposed to driving."[37]

Unlike many directors, Barker did not view his job as comparable to musical conducting. The actor's means are not as precise as the musician's, nor is the terminology he uses. One should leave room for the actor's humanity when it comes to setting his performance. An actor must display discipline and control, but there must be as well a necessary degree of freedom in his performance. An overly mechanical directing method aiming at the precision of ballet or singing can only produce deadness onstage, he believed. As we shall see, disagreement exists as to whether Barker actually achieved these antidictatorial ideals.

Irrespective of his claims of great freedom for the actors, Barker worked quite meticulously and intimately with them on their parts. In blocking a scene he often moved an actor physically to his position. Although his notes during run-throughs in the later stages of rehearsals were delivered before the entire company, he frequently took actors aside to talk privately to them during early rehearsals. He did not praise his actors freely, so a rare compliment from him meant a great deal. John Gielgud, who starred in the 1940 *King Lear,* which was Barker's final work in the theatre, remembers that his "praise was often rather implied than stated. 'You did some fine things today in that scene' he would say to me, 'I hope you know what they were!' and then proceed to read me a long list of my mistakes."[38]

Barker frequently demonstrated what he wanted when verbal explanation was unsuccessful. As an actor he was skilled at showing the appropriate movement or effect he desired, just as he might read aloud the lines as he wanted them spoken. Gielgud writes that at the times Barker chose to instruct by reading the lines himself, he displayed "extraordinary power and repose, though [he had] no great range of voice."[39] While staging *Androcles and the Lion* Barker was not averse to getting down on all fours and crawling about the stage for hours, roaring aloud for the benefit of the actor playing the lion. Still, Barker preferred to communicate through explanation rather than action. John Fernald, a noted director, remembers being directed by Barker in the Gielgud *Lear*. He found Barker capable of going

invariably . . . straight to the point, explaining with penetrating clarity what he wanted an actor to do and how he should do it. If he could not get what he wanted, however, he would persist in pressing on with his attempt, with a relentless and unflagging energy which left the actor utterly exhausted.[40]

Gielgud corroborates these remarks:

In dealing with the actors he was quite impersonal, calling everyone by the name of the part they were playing. He neither coaxed nor flattered, but at the same time, though he was intensely autocratic and severe, he was never personal or rude. The actors had immediate respect for his authority. They did not become paralysed or apathetic, as can so often happen when a strong director is not excessively sensitive. They were constantly dismayed, however, by the high standards he continually demanded of them, and by the intense hard work to which he subjected them without showing any appearance of fatigue himself. For, the moment they appeared to begin to satisfy him in one direction, Barker was urging them on to experiment in another.[41]

Gielgud would not agree with Fernald's judgment, however, that Barker's methods led to creative "suffocation" for the actor.

Fernald's dissent raises the question of how much actual freedom Barker's actors had. We have seen, for instance, that even Gielgud, who reveres Barker's memory, has called him "autocratic" and "severe." Shaw also criticized Barker's dictatorial powers. Had he been an ideal director, wrote Shaw, he would have been the actor's guide and helper but never a dictator.[42] Perhaps the bitterest enemy of Barker's methods was critic Huntley Carter. Carter castigated him as a tyrannical artist who left the actor "no scope for creation," his players being simply "mummers" who got pushed into predetermined forms by the despotic director. To directors like Barker, claimed Carter, "actors are automotons."[43] Barker must have been shocked to see himself described in such terms. Most records indicate he was not autocratic except in the final stages of rehearsal when the pressures of an opening forced him to demand particular results. Actress Cathleen Nesbitt, who worked with Barker on several occasions, from *The Winter's Tale* to the Gielgud *Lear,* was one of the most outspoken defenders of Barker as a director who gave actors breathing space.

He was not one of those directors who do a lot of homework with a set of puppets, and then say to the actors, "I have you standing stage left on that line and moving stage center on this." He worked *with* his actors and the only thing he ever bullied one about was *speech*: he wanted tremendous speed and clarity, a difficult combination.[44]

Barker wrote in a number of places that a director must never succumb to becoming a drill sergeant, no matter how urgent the matter, but should always exercise diplomacy. He should "hint and coax and flatter and cajole, do anything rather than give orders; let them [the actors] if possible still be persuaded that the initiative is theirs, not his."[45] He did admit this to be an ideal, stating that ultimately orders have to be given, but the less this was necessary the better. He wanted actors to create their roles organically and recognized that arbitrary direction could only stifle them. No matter how precise the technical requirements of a production might be, including the careful orchestration of voices and movement, the work must evolve in an organic, coherent way and never by external imposition. Aside from his occasional practice of demonstrating lines and movements, in theory, he stressed that no director should "sententiously" tell an actor, as Hamlet does the players, to "Speak the speech, I pray you, as *I* pronounced it to you." Actors are interpretive artists using their own personalities to create a performance. It is they, not the director, who bring a play to life, he insisted.[46]

When he worked on *King Lear,* he had only ten days in which to rehearse. Therefore, Gielgud's and Fernald's comments that he forced the actors strenuously may be understood in view of the pressure he was under. Gielgud does say, after all, that Barker "did not *at first* try to force his views upon the actors or attempt to discourage their ideas"[47] (my italics).

Barker wanted his actors to approach their roles by giving careful thought to the character's biography. He once tried to make this method clear to an actor by telling him that a close look at his role revealed "that his childhood had been unhappy, that his father had been an enthusiastic golfer, that part of his life had been spent in an unhealthy spot on the coast of South America, and that his favorite author was Balzac."[48] Barker's biographical method aimed to make the actor live the part with truth and sincerity. It was quite an unusual technique for his day and actors normally were confused by it, yet he managed nonetheless to seduce from his players performances they themselves did not know they were capable of.

During the final phase of rehearsals Barker would not interrupt his performers but allow them to run through scenes or acts while he sat in the house and took copious notes. While rehearsing in New York, he watched the run-throughs from a seat in the balcony, obviously because he wanted the actors to project. He sat with an aide who noted whatever was amiss among the supernumeraries and bit players while Barker took more than one hundred loosely scribbled pages of notes. When the scene was over Barker moved to the stage, where he gathered the cast around him in a large semicircle and read his notes chronologically. Occasionally, he rose and acted out a passage to clarify his meaning. For longer passages he would portray a few characters, one after the other.

Each actor, no matter how small his role, in *A Midsummer Night's Dream,* was treated as an individual worthy of attention and respect. As noted earlier, he gave all crowd members, all "fairies," names, so they could feel the individuality of their characters.

A sense of Barker's precision and attention to detail is conveyed by Gielgud's rehearsal copy of *Lear* in which the actor noted Barker's numerous directions. Here is an extract.

ACT I. SCENE I

(Lear enters ceremoniously from the side carrying a huge staff. . . . Reaching the centre of the stage, on his way to the throne . . . he suddenly stops, and striking the staff impatiently on the floor, raps out his first command to Gloucester—then he gives the staff to an attendant and mounts the throne. Pleased. Happy.)

Line

102   *Nothing will come of nothing.* First note of danger.
106   *How now, Cordelia, mend your speech a little.* Grind. Intimidation.
124   *By the sacred radiance of the sun.* Big without ponging (actor's slang for hamming).
131–2   *The barbarous Scythian.* Oath over, sulk over this. Descending passage.
139   *I loved her most.* Justify himself.
152   *With reservation of an hundred knights.* He thinks this disposes of the whole thing, lean back, happy as at opening.
178   *Kent, on thy life, no more.* Dead quiet. Turn. Stare at him.
. . . .
(After exit of Kent) Lear—complete change—smooth, courtly, charming, anger vanished. (To Burgundy) Irony, smooth, cruel about Cordelia, urbanity, very ironic, schoolmaster showing up dunce.[49]

Even when a show was opening, Barker's notes were always before his actors. J. C. Trewin states, for example, that when *The Winter's Tale* was produced, each actor had a card with notes placed on his dressing room mirror. The player of Autolycus had one reading, "BE SWIFT. BE ALERT. BE DEXTEROUS. PITCH THE SONGS HIGH. BE SWIFT. BE ALERT."[50]

CONCLUSION

Barker was without any question England's first great modern director. His presence was a crucial one in the evolution of the modern British theatre. It can still be felt today in his directing methods, his scholarship, and his plays, which are revived from time to time. Had he not been as active as he was in the drive for a national theatre, England might not have one today. He renovated Shakespearean production, helped make Shaw popular, and made productions of Euripides acceptable by modern audiences in both proscenium stagings and huge outdoor stadiums. He also demonstrated not only the value of an excellent repertory company but the basic importance of the repertory concept, taught several generations of leading players and directors their craft, and introduced vital new scenic and architectural techniques. He moved smoothly from the realistic mode to the symbolic to the Elizabethan to the Greek, making him an exemplar of the eclectic tradition best represented by Reinhardt, who, indeed, was a strong influence on his work. Moreover, as Hugh Hunt has suggested,

Barker's career evokes extraordinary parallels with that of his French contemporary, Jacques Copeau.[51] Both men represent the cornerstones of twentieth-century theatrical practice in their respective countries, and their influence has continued unabated to the present moment.

NOTES

1. Craig's total directorial output comes to barely more than a dozen productions, several of which involved amateurs. Though his stagings were artistically significant, they were not nearly so successful in revolutionizing theatrical ideas as were his published designs and writings. Poel practiced more frequently, but his work was largely with amateurs, too, and succeeded more in its historical impact and influence on the ideas of others than in any intrinsic artistic quality of its own.

2. His father's name was Albert James Barker and his mother's was Mary Elizabeth Bozzi-Granville, although he was christened Harley Granville. He was usually known as Granville Barker or Harley Granville Barker until he began to publish books in 1921 with his byline using the hyphenated Harley Granville-Barker. He will be referred to here as Barker.

3. Dennis Kennedy recently has argued that Barker was an important assistant to Shaw on these productions. See Kennedy's *Granville Barker and the Dream of Theatre* (Cambridge, Eng.: Cambridge University Press, 1985), pp. 68–72.

4. Eric Salmon, ed. and annot., *Granville Barker and His Correspondents* (Detroit: Wayne State University Press, 1986), p. 197.

5. Desmond MacCarthy, *The Court Theatre, 1904–1907: A Commentary and Criticism,* ed. Stanley Weintraub (Coral Gables, Fla.: University of Miami Press, 1966), p. 11.

6. Others in this book and its companion volume are Meyerhold, Stanislavsky, Barrault, Brook, Brecht, and Reinhardt. Also, Ewen MacColl often acted in plays staged by his wife, Joan Littlewood.

7. Kennedy, *Granville Barker,* p. 41.

8. C. B. Purdom, *Harley Granville-Barker: Man of the Theatre, Dramatist, and Scholar* (London: Barrie and Rockliff, 1955), p. 41.

9. Hugh Hunt, "Granville-Barker's Shakespearean Productions," *Theatre Research* 10 (1969): 46.

10. Harley Granville-Barker, *The Exemplary Theatre* (Boston: Little, Brown, 1922), p. 164.

11. Ibid. p. 166.

12. Ibid., p. 243.

13. Quoted by Ada Patterson, "Behind the Scenes with Mrs. Granville Barker," *Theatre Magazine* 21 (May 1915); 253.

14. Granville-Barker, *The Exemplary Theatre,* p. 7.

15. Harley Granville-Barker, *The Study of Drama* (Cambridge, Eng.: Cambridge University Press, 1934), pp. 22–23.

16. Quoted in Patterson, "Behind the Scenes," p. 253.

17. Purdom, *Harley Granville-Barker,* p. 164.

18. Cited by Kennedy, *Granville Barker,* p. 37.

19. Laurence Kitchin, *Drama in the Sixties: Form and Interpretation* (London: Faber and Faber, 1966), p. 124.

20. Ibid., p. 127.

21. Edward Fales Coward, "Barker's New Shakespearean Spectacles," *Theatre Magazine* 21 (April 1915): 198.

22. Edward G. Moore, preface to Harley Granville-Barker, *More Prefaces to Shakespeare*, ed. Edward G. Moore (Princeton, N.J.: Princeton University Press, 1974), p. 14.

23. Harley Granville-Barker, ibid., p. 29.

24. Walter Prichard Eaton, *Plays and Players: Leaves from a Critic's Notebook* (Cincinnati: Stewart and Kidd, 1916), pp. 236–37.

25. Ibid., p. 238.

26. Ibid., pp. 238–39.

27. Charles M. Barbour, "Up Against a Symbolic Painted Cloth: *A Midsummer Night's Dream* at the Savoy, 1914," *Educational Theatre Journal* 28 (December 1975): 522.

28. Quoted in Karl Schmidt, "How Barker Puts Plays On," *Harper's Weekly*, 30 January 1915, p. 115.

29. Noel K. Thomas, "Harley Granville-Barker and the Greek Drama," *Educational Theatre Journal* 7 (December 1955): 297.

30. Granville-Barker, *More Prefaces to Shakespeare*, p. 24.

31. See, for example, Eric Salmon, *Granville Barker and His Correspondents* (Detroit: Wayne State University Press, 1986).

32. [Harley] Granville Barker, "Rehearsing a Play," *Theatre Magazine* 30 (September 1919): 142.

33. Granville-Barker, *The Exemplary Theatre*, p. 23.

34. Ibid.

35. "A Glimpse of Mr. Barker from Behind the Scenes," *New York Times*, 21 February 1915.

36. Hesketh Pearson, *Modern Men and Mummers* (New York: Harcourt, Brace, 1922), p. 169.

37. "A Glimpse of Mr. Barker."

38. John Gielgud, *Stage Directions* (New York: Capricorn Books, 1963), p. 54.

39. Ibid.

40. John Fernald, *A Sense of Direction: The Director and His Actors* (London: Secker and Warburg, 1968), p. 165.

41. Gielgud, *Stage Directions*, p. 53.

42. George Bernard Shaw, "Barker's Wild Oats," *Harper's Weekly*, 19 January 1947, p. 53.

43. Huntley Carter, *The Theatre of Max Reinhardt* (New York: Benjamin Blom, 1964), p. 16.

44. Cathleen Nesbitt, *A Little Love and Good Company* (Owings Mills, Md.: Stemmer House, 1977), p. 51.

45. Granville-Barker, *The Study of Drama*, p. 58.

46. Granville-Barker, *On Dramatic Method* (New York: Hill and Wang, 1956), p. 29.

47. Gielgud, *Stage Directions*, p. 53. An excellent discussion of these issues, particularly of the relative autocracy of Barker's methods, is in Cary M. Mazer, "Actors or Gramophones: The Paradoxes of Granville Barker," *Theatre Journal* 36 (March 1984): 5–23.

48. Hesketh Pearson, "A Great Theatrical Management," *Theatre Arts Monthly* 31 (September 1955): 94.

49. Gielgud, *Stage Directions*, pp. 121–22.

50. J. C. Trewin, *Shakespeare on the English Stage, 1900–1964* (London: Barrie and Rockliff, 1964), p. 53.

51. Hunt, ''Granville-Barker's Shakespearean Productions,'' p. 44.

CHRONOLOGY

All productions London, unless noted. A number of works directed for the Stage Society were for single matinees only. Works with an asterisk were first given at matinees and later offered at evening performances. In some cases, the management team responsible for a production is given. For a more detailed chronology see Dennis Kennedy, *Granville Barker and the Dream of Theatre* (Cambridge, Eng.: Cambridge University Press, 1985). Plays that Kennedy suggests were codirected with George Bernard Shaw are so listed.

1877   born in London, England

1891   enters Sarah Thorne's acting school at Royal Theatre, Margate

1900   Globe Theatre (Stage Society): *Interior; The Death of Tintagiles; The House of Usna*

1901   Comedy Theatre: *The Revolted Daughter; The Man of Destiny* (single matinees)

1902   Royalty Theatre (Stage Society): *The Marrying of Ann Leete*

1903   Imperial Theatre (Stage Society): *The Waters of Bitterness; The Admirable Bashville*

1904   King's Hall (Stage Society): *The Philanthropists*; comanagement of Court Theatre with J. H. Vedrenne: *The Two Gentlemen of Verona; Candida* (codirected with G. B. Shaw); Lyric (later at Court): *Hippolytus**; Court (Stage Society): *Where There is Nothing*; Duke of York's Theatre: *The Pharisee's Wife*; Court: *John Bull's Other Island** (codirected with Shaw); *Aglavaine and Selysette; Prunella*

1905   Court: *The Pot of Broth; In the Hospital; How He Lied to Her Husband* (codirected with Shaw); *The Thieves' Comedy; The Trojan Women; You Never Can Tell** (codirected with Shaw); *Man and Superman** (codirected with Shaw); *The Return of the Prodigal**; *The Wild Duck; The Voysey Inheritance; Major Barbara** (codirected with Shaw)

1906   Court: *Electra; A Question of Age; The Convict on the Hearth; Pan and the Young Shepherd* and *The Youngest of the Angels; Captain Brassbound's Conversion* (codirected with Shaw); *The Silver Box; The Charity That Began at Home; The Doctor's Dilemma** (codirected with Shaw); marries Lillah McCarthy

1907   Court: *The Reformer; The Campden Wonder; The Philanderer* (codirected with Shaw); *Hedda Gabler; Votes for Women!; Don Juan in Hell* and *The Man of Destiny; Joy; The Devil's Disciple* (codirected with Shaw; transfers to Queen's Theatre); *Medea*; Imperial (Stage Society): *Waste*; Savoy Theatre: *Arms and the Man* (codirected with Shaw); publishes *A National Theatre: Scheme and Estimates* with William Archer

1908   Haymarket Theatre: *The Tragedy of Nan*; Royalty (transfers to Haymarket):
         Feed the Brute; Haymarket: *The Chinese Lantern*; rejects offer to run New
         Theatre in New York

1909   Duke of York's: *Strife*

1910   Duke of York's Theatre Repertory begins: *Justice; The Sentimentalists; The
         Madras House; Prunella; Helena's Path*; Royalty Theatre, Glasgow: *The Witch*

1911   Court: *The Witch*, for Lillah McCarthy's management; Palace Theatre: *Anatol*
         (three scenes, one each for three weeks); Court: *The Tragedy of Nan*; McCarthy-
         Barker management, Little Theatre: *Anatol; The Master Builder*; Queen's: *Bon-
         ita*; McCarthy-Barker, Little: *The Twelve Pound Look; Rococo; The Sentimen-
         talists*

1912   McCarthy-Barker, Kingsway: *The Secret Woman; Iphigenia in Tauris* (also at
         His Majesty's and Bradfield College; Barker's last acting work); McCarthy-
         Barker, Savoy: *The Winter's Tale; Twelfth Night*; McCarthy-Barker, Kingsway:
         The Eldest Son

1913   McCarthy-Barker, Kingsway: *The Great Adventure*; McCarthy-Barker, St.
         James's: *Androcles and the Lion; The Harlequinade; The Witch; The Wild
         Duck; Le Mariage Forcé; The Tragedy of Nan; The Doctor's Dilemma; The
         Silver Box; The Death of Tintagiles*

1914   McCarthy-Barker, Savoy: *A Midsummer Night's Dream*; Covent Garden: *Philip
         the King*; McCarthy-Barker, Kingsway: *The Dynasts*

1915   Wallack's Theatre, New York: *Androcles and the Lion; The Man Who Married
         a Dumb Wife; A Midsummer Night's Dream; The Doctor's Dilemma*; Yale Bowl
         and other stadiums: *Iphigenia in Tauris; The Trojan Women*

1917   second marriage, Helen Huntington

1920   Royalty: *The Romantic Young Lady*

1921   Gaiety Theatre: *The Betrothal*; Ambassador's Theatre: *Deburau*

1922   publishes *The Exemplary Theatre*

1923–27 publishes Prefaces to *The Players Shakespeare* (7 volumes)

1925   Ambassador's: *The Madras House*

1927   Strand: *The Kingdom of God*

1931   moves to Paris

1934   Sadler's Wells: *The Voysey Inheritance* (codirected with Harcourt Williams)

1936   Westminster Theatre: *Waste* (codirected with Michael MacOwan)

1940   Old Vic: *King Lear* (codirected with Lewis Casson)

1940–45 resides in New York

1946   dies in Paris

George Abbott

(1887–   )

In 1931, Brooks Atkinson, drama critic of the *New York Times,* observed that the art of Broadway stage direction had taken a great step forward five years before when a play called *Broadway* opened. A mediocre script (coauthored by Philip Dunning and George Abbott, with most of the credit due to Dunning) had been transformed by the colorful staging of the authors (with the bulk of the honors going to Abbott) into a thrilling, fast-paced melodrama that ran for 603 performances. Whereas the average play had about twenty or thirty entrances and exits, *Broadway* had 243, requiring masterly directorial skill. So expert was the play's handling, wrote Atkinson, that swift staging and colorful action soon became the hallmark of a slew of new directors.[1]

The title of that landmark production is fitting, for George Abbott's multitalented and prolific presence has typified the New York commercial theatre scene for well over sixty years. He has garnered fame as an actor, a director, a producer, a playwright, and a play doctor, normally exercising several of his talents on the same show. His record for longevity as an active worker in the theatre will probably never be surpassed. Abbott's one hundredth birthday was feted by Broadway at a gala revue in his honor held at the Palace Theatre. Many of the great stars who worked for the ageless theatre artist paraded across the stage. But he still was not ready to call it quits. In 1989, at the incredible age of 102, he wrote the book for and directed *Frankie,* a musical about the Frankenstein monster that moved from a closed reading at the Coconut Grove Playhouse in Miami to an Off-Broadway run at the York Theatre. Had it not met with universally negative reviews, the centenarian director would have tried to move it to the Great White Way.

EARLY YEARS

George Francis Abbott was born in 1887 in Forestville, New York, attended Rochester University, and later studied playwriting under George Pierce Baker at the latter's famous Harvard workshop. Abbott's first Broadway role was in *The Misleading Lady* (1913). His directing career began eleven years later with *The Fall Guy* (1924), which he wrote with James Gleason, the popular actor-playwright. Assigned codirecting chores with Gleason, Abbott took over full control when Gleason's time was taken up with his new hit show, *Is Zat So?* The actors, however, showed distrust for his untried ability. In the 1920s an experienced company, especially one with stars, was not ready to have a new-comer tell them how to enter and exit. Compromise on Abbott's part was the solution, though he "longed to go deeper into the action, to control the whole stage, to make everything fit like a jigsaw puzzle."[2]

Abbott showed considerable pluck in getting the play on, even refusing a demand by his producers, the Shuberts, to make a major cast change during the pre-Broadway tryout. With his coauthor's support, he held his ground, and the play opened in New York to excellent notices. Now that he had a hit, he was offered many shows and accepted every one he could. He admits that he was unable to reject any offer that came along.

In 1926 Abbott's directorial fame was launched with a new play that others had rejected. As he remembered in 1987,

Phil Dunning had sent *Broadway* [the title Abbott selected after dismissing Dunning's original, *Bright Lights*] to over 20 producers before I took it on and rewrote it . . . It had a great atmosphere—Phil knew the nightclub world—but a lot of poorly written characters and no story. I was able to give it some shape.[3]

Despite, or perhaps because of, Abbott's success, producer Jed Harris refused to pay the director royalties for the hit, and Abbott vowed never to work for the notoriously meanspirited Harris again, although Abbott did—at the request of Helen Hayes—hire him several years later to restage *Coquette*. The conflict with Harris was a powerful element in convincing Abbott to become a producer himself, although he admits producing is not something he likes. "I only became one so I wouldn't have to deal with producers,"[4] he declared.

PRODUCTION SURVEY

Like most of Abbott's early directorial work *Broadway* was a fast-moving melodrama, filled with dynamic activity. Though he continued to stage mel-odramas during the thirties and early forties, the former decade was marked by his comedy work and the latter, and afterwards, by musicals. Among the melo-dramas Abbott directed were *Chicago* (1926), *Four Walls* (1927), *Spread Eagle* (1927), *Lilly Turner* (1932), *Heat Lightning* (1933), *Small Miracle* (1934), *La-*

dies' Money (1934), *Angel Island* (1937), and *Goodbye in the Night* (1940). As one journalist noted in 1934, Abbott's work normally found him "enmeshed in murder, rapine, blackmail, larceny and the darker side of the sorceries and misdemeanors."[5]

Beginning with the hugh success of *Three Men on a Horse* (1935), which he coauthored, Abbott's work came to be largely identified with farce and comedy. The thirties saw Abbott's special flavor bring bubbling life to such comic hits as *Boy Meets Girl* (1935), *Jumbo* (1935), *Brother Rat* (1936), *Room Service* (1937), and *What a Life* (1938).

In the mid- and late-thirties he increasingly turned his attention to musical comedy, beginning with the spoof on ballet, *On Your Toes* (1936), and continuing with the pathbreaking use of Shakespeare's *The Comedy of Errors* for a musical comedy, entitled *The Boys from Syracuse* (1938). *Too Many Girls* (1939) and *Pal Joey* (1940) continued his string of musical successes, all of them by Richard Rodgers and Lorenz Hart. Long-run hits of the forties included *Best Foot Forward* (1941), *On the Town* (1944), *High Button Shoes* (1947), and *Where's Charley?* (1949). *Call Me Madam* (1950); *A Tree Grows in Brooklyn* (1951); *Wonderful Town* (1953); *Me and Juliet* (1953), which marked a return to the music of Richard Rodgers; *The Pajama Game* (1954); *Damn Yankees* (1955); *Once upon a Mattress* (1959); and *Fiorello!* (1959) were memorable hits of the 1950s. The sixties saw considerable activity but, aside from the comedy *Take Her, She's Mine* (1961), the musical *A Funny Thing Happened on the Way to the Forum* (1962), and another comedy, *Never Too Late* (1962), the veteran director faced one flop after another. In a career as prolific as his, he had often met with failure, but no previous decade had been as disastrous for him as this one. Though he continued directing in the 1970s, there was a considerable decrease in his output. In 1973 Abbott staged *Life with Father* at the Seattle Repertory Theatre, the first regional theatre production of his career. His last Broadway staging of an original work was the 1976 disappointment, *Music Is,* which he adapted from *Twelfth Night.* He could usually tell why a show was weak, but with this one he was surprised at the critical reaction and said that he was no longer happy with the theatre. He decided to write a novel; the result was *Try-Out,* published in 1979.

Abbott returned to New York in 1978 to direct a new comedy, Lee Kalcheim's *Winning Isn't Everything,* a cynical play about unscrupulous political campaign maneuvering, for the Off-Off-Broadway Hudson Guild Theatre. It was his first such noncommercial venture in New York. The energetic, six foot plus, blue-eyed, ramrod straight, unstoppable nonagenarian followed this with the spectacular feat of restaging *On Your Toes,* his 1936 Rodgers and Hart hit (for which he had written the book), in a highly effective 1983 Broadway revival that garnered him the Tony for musical direction. (Abbott, it might be added, despite the many musicals he has directed, cannot read music.) In 1986 he was still involved with *On Your Toes,* directing a Los Angeles revival with ballerina Natalia Makarova, the star of the 1983 production.

Meanwhile, in 1985 he worked on a new musical called *Tropicana,* for which he wrote the book; it was shown under workshop conditions at a small downtown theatre on Second Avenue by Musical Theatre Works, a group dedicated to the development of new musicals. In 1986 Abbott staged a revival of *Damn Yankees* at New Jersey's Paper Mill Playhouse; the *New York Times* reviewer thought it had "the sort of drive and momentum that define big-time Broadway at its professional best."[6] Around that time, when most people lucky enough to be alive at his age are withering into second childhood, Abbott also wrote *Irwin,* a new play based on the Dracula story, and revised *Broadway* as *Speakeasy,* a dialogueless rock musical in the vein of the Webber-Rice musical, *Evita. Speakeasy* never did get off the ground, but *Broadway* itself did when, in 1987, Cleveland's Great Lakes Theatre Festival asked Abbott to consult on their revival of it and another Abbott classic, *The Boys from Syracuse.* He wrote back to the festival's artistic director, Gerald Freedman, "I don't know what a consultant does in the theatre," adding, "I'm available." The hint was taken, and Abbott was hired to stage *Broadway* at the Ohio Theatre; to celebrate his participation the festival held a well-attended weekend conference in Abbott's honor, called "Classic Broadway." Many of the most famous Abbott protégés took part, including Harold Prince, who delivered the keynote address. The show was produced on Broadway itself in June 1987, but despite Abbott's "characteristic zippy pacing and clean delivery,"[7] the Cleveland cast was deemed to be of less than Broadway quality, and *Broadway* died after four performances.

In the twenties his work as an actor gradually wound down as his directing, producing, and writing picked up speed (he coauthored many of the plays he staged). After his poorly received portrayal of John Brown in *John Brown's Body* (1934), he did not reappear as an actor until 1955, when he played Mr. Antrobus in a revival of Thornton Wilder's *The Skin of Our Teeth,* directed by Alan Schneider, in a cast including Helen Hayes and Mary Martin. But he was so active with his other theatre work that it was rare for a Broadway season not to be represented by at least one, if not as many as seven, of his productions. For much of his career he directed hit after hit, concentrating almost exclusively on new works and adaptations. Thirteen of his shows ran for more than five hundred performances. The total number of Broadway or Broadway-bound shows in which he has been involved is over 120. He won only two directing Tonys (he already had garnered one as colibrettist of *Fiorello!*), the first for *A Funny Thing . . .* and the second for his *On Your Toes* revival, but was given the even greater honor in 1965 of having the Fifty-fourth Street Theatre named after him. (It has since been torn down.) He also received a number of special awards, such as the Handel medal—New York City's highest cultural honor—and the first of the annual Lawrence Langner Awards for his lifetime of service to the American theatre. In 1982 he was presented by President Ronald Reagan with a Kennedy Center Honors award for lifetime achievement. Abbott also was awarded two honorary doctorates.

THE ABBOTT TOUCH

George Abbott was renowned for the so-called Abbott touch, a slick, professional veneer he brought to all the plays he staged. Journalist Maurice Zolotow suggested that

the essence of the Abbott touch is speed. Curtains rise and fall quickly. Actors enter and exit on the run. Lines of dialogue are spit out feverishly. Characters cross in front of one another with dizzying rapidity. Doors are forever being jerked open and slammed shut.[8]

Abbott protégé Garson Kanin remembers that Abbott was a terrific ballroom dancer, and declares that he had an "instinctive feel for liveliness of sound and get-on-with-it movement." Kanin offers his own definition of the famous "touch" as "a heady blend of innocence and sophistication, formal structure and daring innovation—usually played in jazz rhythms."[9]

Thus, the Abbott touch can be viewed as a combination of driving energy, abundant movement and activity, and dynamic and rhythmic pacing; within this vivid framework, the key to success was always the high level of believability sustained by the actors.

An excellent example of the Abbott touch was seen in the comedy *Twentieth Century* (1932), about events aboard a speeding train. Critic Percy Hammond wrote that the director

keeps it in motion as smooth and swift as that of the great ambulance from which it gets its title. The conductor, the brakemen, and the porters are more real than those of the Pennsylvania System or the New York Central. . . . By a cunning manipulation of curtain and machinery Mr. Abbott enables you to believe that you yourself are a passenger. The whistles, the bells, and other mechanical instruments of railroad atmosphere are faithfully counterfeit, and cause you to feel that you are really on route from Chicago to New York with a cargo of sensational companions.[10]

In the melodrama *Ladies' Money*, Brooks Atkinson remarked how "The action scampers from one room to another with the nimbleness of a dancing routine. Characters run up and down the stairs, dodge the landlady, burst into each other's room; and the comedy and melodrama are neatly juggled."[11]

Abbott's 1978 production of *Winning Isn't Everything* was in much the same format. The set, a seedy hotel room (recalling such Abbott hits as *Three Men on a Horse* and *Room Service*), had three doors and four phones. Characters kept entering and exiting, going into the closet and to the bathroom as the phone rang incessantly, the movement to the doors and phones keeping the large cast within a small set constantly on the go in a comic ballet that sometimes bordered on pandemonium.

Abbott could take the simplest materials and build them into breathless moments of hilarious pantomime. A classic instance was the scene in *Room Service* where three characters, not having eaten for eighteen hours, attack a dining table laden with food and gorge themselves for a full five minutes without a word being spoken. Through the precision of selected gestures and moves the scene became the funniest in the play and one of the most memorable in modern comic staging. However, Abbott disciple Harold Prince points out that to think of the "Abbott touch" as nothing but fast-paced, constantly moving, door-slamming comedy is to oversimplify the matter. "At the heart of the matter," he says, "is a demand that things be honest, that responses be motivated, that performances be honest."[12]

CLEAR SPEECH AND TRUTHFUL COMIC ACTING

Douglas Gilbert may have written of Abbott in 1936 that he was "head man of the socko school of directing,"[13] but Abbott liked to think that his touch was most apparent in the clear speech heard in his productions and in their truthful acting. He maintained that getting the actors to say their final syllables was a major factor in his success. Kanin quotes Abbott on this matter:

What happens is that players learn their parts and when the time for delivery comes, they often begin a line, then knowing that they know it, let it fade as their attention goes to the *next* line. If I am remembered for anything as a director . . . it will be for my insistence on projecting the ends of lines.[14]

An enemy of the miked performance, he cast musicals by first making the actors prove they could project without artificial amplification. He held that good diction and correct pronunciation could make almost any actor audible. The actor is often unaware of his indistinctness and, in his search for an interesting performance quality, neglects to concentrate on his articulation. To Abbott, Method actors were guilty of this fault, as they overemphasized their emotional interpretation to the detriment of verbal communication. To guarantee good projection Abbott would sit in various parts of the house to test his actors, and would shout out that he couldn't hear them when they were inaudible.

As Prince observed, truthfulness to life is another distinguishing feature of the Abbott touch. The director avoids anything which draws attention to its artificiality and always seeks total conviction and believability in the acting. Abbott considered this believability the essence of his comic success. No matter how wild the comedy, he admonished actors not to overdo, to play for character, to act straight. Actor Hal Linden recalls that when he worked for Abbott, the director's favorite word was "actory." "If he catches you doing something he doesn't like, he says 'That's too actory.' What he really means is that he doesn't believe it."[15]

Abbott's work on reality begins at the first rehearsal. After the first company read-through of Act I in *Take Her, She's Mine,* he told the cast:

What I would try next time . . . is to read it a little rougher, with a kind of flatness, a lack of any sweetness, almost with cynicism, as it were, a little more worldly. . . . We sound so much better when we're believable. Let's not try to frost the cake. We don't think it's farce. We think it's real.[16]

He was at his best with plays in which the laughs grow from the situations rather than from gag lines delivered for their own sake. For instance, there is an exchange in *Boy Meets Girl* when the waitress, Susie, brings a tray of food for the producer and a pair of writers and then collapses.

C.F.: Do you get these epileptic fits often?

SUSIE: I didn't have an epileptic fit.

C.F.: Then what's wrong with you?

SUSIE: There's nothing wrong. It's only natural.

C.F.: Only natural for you to come into my office and collapse on the floor?

SUSIE: Oh, no sir. It's only natural for you to feel sick when you're going to have a baby.

In Abbott's production, the final line garnered an immense laugh, not because of its innate humor, which is barely revealed on the printed page, but because of the perfect timing of the actors and the contrast of the characters. C.F.'s rough and hard-hitting speech style contrasted with the slow and measured cadences of Susie, thereby heightening her expressiveness. A lot of telephone byplay and shifting group attitudes made the action so clear words were not needed to point out its meaning.

A knockabout farce directed by Abbott in which the seriousness of the characters was effectively employed as counterpoint to the mayhem of the action was *In Any Language* (1952), which starred Uta Hagen. Brooks Atkinson reported:

The pace is fast. The style is broad. The acting is noisy. The stage lighting is glaring. Although the characters are behaving like strong imbeciles, they are desperately serious. Every moment in the performance is a crisis for one or the other of them. No matter how boisterously the audience may be laughing, the characters never intimate that the rumpus in which they are involved is crackbrained and ludicrous and a travesty on the life the audience thinks it is living outside the theatre.[17]

One can understand from these remarks on Abbott's deadpan approach to comic style why he was terribly upset at the improvisational antics of Zero Mostel, who starred in *A Funny Thing* . . . , despite his respect for Mostel's comic genius. Anything deviating from the goal of stage illusion made Abbott uncomfortable. Mugging is for children, not for mature, professional actors. To him, the lowest form of humor was custard-pie comedy. (He also hated cruelty as a source of laughter, being opposed to everything that derives humor from the infliction of pain.)

In Abbott's eyes, America's favorite comedy style grew out of the period when the division between the comic and emotional parts of a play were sharply divided. Then directors like David Belasco and Winchell Smith (both powerful influences on Abbott) came along and began to work toward stage realism and illusion, their attention to detail creating well-rounded characters who behaved truthfully, rather than like pasteboard clowns. The resulting fusion of the serious and the comic led to what Abbott considered one of American acting's most accomplished styles. This is comedy acting that proceeds from a human basis. The laughter is closely tied up with the warmest emotions so that one laughs even as one is on the verge, or in the midst, of tears.

Abbott's ideas, however, do not precisely reflect his own practice; most observers agree that his shows were rarely emotional or sentimental. One associate was quoted as saying, "Too much emotion embarrasses Mr. Abbott . . . He doesn't want it in his personal contacts and he doesn't want it in his shows."[18]

Although he was considered a master of farce directing, he chose not to think of his shows as farces (despite his occasional use of the term). As he told Lucius Beebe:

Farce I conceive to be merely comic lines and situations spoken and mugged and overplayed, while fast comedy, which is how I like to describe my shows, is based on funny situations and sides spoken by actors whose characterizations are cleverly drawn.[19]

TASTE

A taciturn, laconic man of modesty and reserve, who normally wore a jacket and tie at rehearsals no matter what the weather, Abbott bore such an aura of dignity and aloofness that only a few intimates called him by his first name. He was "Mr. Abbott" to the legions of actors and technical personnel with whom he worked, even those who were with him for years. This distinguished elder statesman of the commercial theatre felt that his success was bound up with the "taste" he displayed as a director:

By taste I mean artistic judgement—the decision as to just how much to do or not to do, at what point to leave one scene and get into another, and for the actor, how much to express and how much to imply.[20]

Abbott's taste may also be suggested by the type of plays he staged. It was a popular taste, one shared by the average Broadway showgoer. It displayed an anti-intellectual bias in favor of solid production values. Simple situations, obvious but colorful characters, and straightforward dialogue were more in his line than what might be seen as self-consciously artistic or literary writing.

He never staged a classic,[21] although he was fond of Shakespeare, whom he defined as a writer of "shows," not literature. Convinced that current productions of the Bard completely missed his theatrical qualities, Abbott tested his ideas on Shakespeare's stageworthiness by doing some experimental work with his Broadway actors in the 1930s. At two or three afternoon rehearsals a week he staged his own abbreviated versions of plays such as *The Merchant of Venice, All's Well That Ends Well,* and *King John.* From these experiences he emerged satisfied that actors must do more than pay lip service to Hamlet's advice to the players about holding the mirror up to nature. The verse is secondary to the reality of the characters. He wanted actors to play the lines conversationally, and to avoid an old-fashioned bombastic approach.

Instead of seeking works of literary importance, Abbott opted for plays that had immediate audience appeal, with qualities of topicality and contemporary relevance, provided they contained little controversy. His business was to make money, not create artistic precedents. Still, an overview of his career shows that he often selected plays that, in their own way, were novel or trend-setting within the limitations of Broadway production. *The Boys from Syracuse* was the first American musical comedy based on a Shakespearean text. *Pal Joey* had an unsympathetic leading character and captured the cynicism of the John O'Hara short stories from which it had been adapted. *The Pajama Game* dealt with the touchy subject of labor problems and strikes. *New Girl in Town* (1957) used the sombre Eugene O'Neill drama *Anna Christie* as its source. *A Funny Thing . . .* was probably the finest transposition of Roman comedy the modern theatre has seen.

A list of Abbott's ten favorite plays published sometime in the 1930s reveals a taste for modern drama, especially of the more flamboyant Broadway type in which he specialized. Most of the plays are American, although there are several British examples. Seven are from the 1920s, two from the 1930s, and one from 1910. Not one classic or European play is listed.

1. *Journey's End*
2. *Rain*
3. *Broadway*
4. *They Knew What They Wanted*
5. *What Price Glory?*
6. *Yellow Jack*
7. *The First Year*
8. *She Loves Me Not*
9. *Justice*
10. *Desire under the Elms*[22]

Few of these plays are now taken very seriously, although most of them see occasional revivals and still have the power to grip an audience when well performed. Their value is theatrical, not literary; they represent the ideals of a man whose extremely long life in the theatre has never veered from an interest in the play as something to be acted, not read.

PREVENTING BOREDOM

Abbott has been deathly afraid of boring an audience and would take whatever measures possible to keep its attention riveted to the stage. Keeping its interest was more important than the director's reverence for the script. If cutting would help, then cut he would, no matter how painful the extraction. However, Abbott sometimes would cut not only boring material, but also scenes and dialogue that were working well. His aim was to provide a well-balanced production, and material that stood out too obviously, at the expense of the rest of the show, was likely to be removed. Thus, he eliminated a hilarious scene in *Boy Meets Girl* wherein various tests were conducted to select a baby for a new film. Some superb comic dialogue was thereby tossed out in the interests of the play as a whole. Similarly, in *Three Men on a Horse,* twenty-five to thirty laugh lines were cut to speed up the show.

Boredom often derives not from the script, but from the actors. Abbott would keep going back to his shows to look for actors who tried to make the most of their scenes by lengthening pauses, being slow on cue pickups, pumping for laughs, and seeking self-enhancement at the expense of the ensemble. He would remind them of their tendency to fall into these traps, even demonstrating how they had fallen off the pace because he knew that actors cannot truly hear themselves; extraneous pauses creep in and destroy the desired effect. "Take out those air spaces!" he was likely to demand.

Another technique to prevent ennui is to keep everything clear. Nothing artificial or pretentiously murky found a place on Abbott's stage. He opposed what he saw as an excessive tendency toward subtle and vague effects in modern staging; to him the results were simply confusing. Clarity of approach was always an Abbott signature. He demanded clear-headedness from everyone creating a show. A definite goal was established, and all moved in a straight line toward achieving it.

Abbott demonstrated that audience interest can often be aroused by music, in straight plays as well as in musicals. Music puts the audience into a unified frame of mind, a most essential factor in any production seeking success. He had the overture for *Three Men on a Horse* made up of various musical selections dealing with horses, thus getting the audience into the proper mood for a play about horse racing. For the Hollywood comedy, *Boy Meets Girl,* the orchestra played an arrangement of "California, Here I Come." Military numbers preceded *Brother Rat,* including the anthem of the military school at which the action is set. This usage was considered an advance over musical overtures that bore no relation to the play. Likewise, music accompanying the action was quite carefully considered before being chosen.

RAPID PACING

Probably no other boredom-dispersing element in Abbott's directorial style gained the notoriety of the rapid pace at which his productions frequently were staged. Abbott never simply told his actors to perform as quickly as they could, despite the impression of theatregoers that the performance was racing at break-neck speed. He told Morton Eustis that "the one thing a play should not have, is just simple uncontrolled speed. The director who thinks that pace is just hurry makes a tragic mistake and produces a noisy, violent hodgepodge devoid of any illusion."[23] In addition to stressing the all-important picking up of cues, Abbott achieved the illusion of rapidity through the subtle means of temporal variety and by an intelligent use of contrast in characters, staging effects, and vocal tone rather than by racing his actors at top speed through the words and action. For instance, there is a scene in *Three Men on a Horse* where a gambler keeps begging the character Irwin for a horse's name. The action is fairly repetitious and does not develop much, though variety in the playing keeps the audience's attention. In Abbott's production, when someone ran in with the name of a horse race winner, the moment was played at a much quicker pace, giving the audience the impression that the actors had hurtled headlong through the whole scene.

In scenes of rapid action Abbott was sometimes willing to lose some small laughs by having the actors run into each other's laughs. By suppressing the moderate laughter he got the audience to guffaw with full energy at the big joke, providing them with a chance to express their delight completely.

Eustis capably summed up Abbott's approach in 1936:

What the director actually does to establish the desired tempo is to emphasize contrast both in speech and movement; to make the audience, instead of the actors, supply movement, by turning their eyes from one portion of the stage to another; to build up the volume, the speed, the intensity of the tone of voice here, chop it there; accelerate the motion of the actor, both in movement and gesture; speed up the rhythm of the company as an ensemble, slow it down, then build again; in short, to approach *every problem* related to everything the audience sees, hears or thinks about with variety, inventiveness and *still more variety*.[24]

In addition, the frequent employment of music, both in overture and accompaniment, served a useful function in stimulating the actors to play at a specific tempo. But other auditory devices, such as the constant opening and slamming of doors and the ringing of phones, had a similar purpose.

CASTING

In view of Abbott's commercial orientation, which led him to get the greatest output from the most efficient means, it is not surprising that he believed type-casting the best casting method available. In his opinion, careful matching of actor to role leads to far more artistic results than any other method. As he observed, "People today say typecasting isn't any good. But an old man is more likely to play an old man well than a young man, and a pretty girl has a step up in a love story."[25] The repertory system's main value is as an actor-training school; its use of actors in roles for which they may not be well suited broadens the actor's range, but weakens the production. One can easily judge a director's competence, he averred, by noting closely the acting of the lesser roles. "If they are well acted, it usually means the director is in control. But if the butler is lousy, perhaps the director is lousy."[26]

How a show is cast can seriously affect what a director can do with it. For example, having selected dancer-actress Gwen Verdon for the lead in *New Girl in Town,* he wanted her to play a character who did a minimum of dancing; however, audience expectations forced him to revise his concept and have the choreographer create dance routines for her.

Abbott always employed casting directors to help in the search for new talent and to advise on those who were more familiar. A thorough filing card system was kept, with information on every actor interviewed and auditioned. Their appearance, experience, talent, height, weight, and complexion were duly noted. The casting directors attended as many stock, amateur, and other local theatricals as they could.

At auditions, Abbott would treat actors with great courtesy, regardless of their lack of talent. He could not, however, abide an actor whose audition went on too long, and would stop him in the middle and dismiss him. He advised auditioning actors to keep their material brief because any director of insight can tell almost immediately if he can use an actor for his show. He also preferred people to get cast on their ability and not on their connections.

Regardless of his various warnings, if an auditioning actor proved to be of unusual interest, Abbott would allow him to extend his tryout, even experimenting with him to see his range. Abbott claimed to have been the first on Broadway to institute auditions by reading from the script; before then, he states, directors merely interviewed prospective players.

One of Abbott's pet peeves concerns actors who approach their craft from an overly internal standpoint. He often was irritated by the audition behavior of Method actors who removed their shoes and went into a corner to prepare while everyone waited. These actors were considered phonies who had little grasp of acting technique. He considered a technically well-equipped actor to be one who has the ability—through knowledge, training, and experience—to grasp immediately the essentials of a character or a scene.

Although forced to use it, Abbott actually had little faith in the audition system; too frequently actors cannot audition well, even the best of them. He turned down Marlon Brando half a dozen times, but wondered, when he saw him in *A Streetcar Named Desire,* why he had never seen him before. Brando's audition technique was not up to the Abbott standards, and the actor was a mere nonentity until he showed what he could do in an actual performance.

Well known for his frugality, Abbott enjoyed casting actors who were willing to work for minimum salaries. He once told Maurice Zolotow, "You're better off if you can do without a star. . . . Besides saving money, I like to concentrate on the play, not the star. A play can't ask you to come back stage to her dressing room and complain about her troubles."[27] Nevertheless, he had no objection to big stars when working for producers who were willing to pay for them.

Because his eye for new talent was usually so perceptive (aside from rare exceptions like Brando), Abbott succeeded time and again in making his nonstar policy work. "I've had many shows panned for the writing, but never for the acting," he observed. "I never had any fear of using an unknown actor for a big part, if I thought he was right for it."[28] Among his discoveries and those whose careers were boosted by working for him were Gene Kelly, Nancy Walker, Shirley Booth, Ezra Stone, Carol Haney, Van Johnson, Eddie Bracken, Kirk Douglas, Everett Sloane, Tom Bosley, Desi Arnaz, Paul Muni, José Ferrer, Helen Hayes, Eddie Albert, Barry Sullivan, Garson Kanin, Teddy Hart, June Allyson, Royal Beal, Joyce Arling, Betty Field, Richard Widmark, Shirley MacLaine, Joan Caulfield, and Sam Levene. Abbott liked to hire new faces because he wanted to give them a chance, remembering how tough it was when he had to struggle to get an acting job in his youth.

This willingness to use new people was actually one of the outstanding features of his career. Many of these new people, of course, left for Hollywood stardom after gaining recognition in an Abbott show, but many more were loyal. His successes were so numerous that he built up a reservoir of over one hundred actors who came to be popularly known as the Abbott Acting Company. The same actors appeared in one Abbott show after another. If he had nothing for them in a new show, they were sure to be used in one of the replacement casts for a long-run production or to be sent out in one of the various road companies he always had working. He shifted them from show to show to keep them fresh and energetic, and to provide a chance for their talents to diversify.

Not only new acting talent had a benefactor in George Abbott. Untried lyricists, designers, choreographers, playwrights, and composers often found him willing to take a chance on their possibilities. A good example of a show in which most of the creative staff was new was *Best Foot Forward;* here only designer Jo Mielziner and Abbott himself were veterans. John Cecil Holm had never written the book for a musical, Gene Kelly had never choreographed a Broadway show, costume designer Miles White had designed only one other musical, and the score and lyrics were by total newcomers Hugh Martin and Ralph Blane. A long run of 326 performances paid Abbott back for his faith.

PREPARATION FOR PRODUCTION

During most of his career Abbott would test out his response to a script which interested him by having a group of his familiar actors read it to him. The reading often led to the casting of some of these actors in the show itself. If his interest was held at the reading, he knew an audience would likely be just as caught up by it. Once selected, the script received little preparatory work other than re-writes, to which Abbott normally attended.

Abbott's first task upon reading a new script was to visualize it in general terms for the stage. When he did *Small Miracle* he saw the necessity of using a staircase as a central component of the action. In *Boy Meets Girl* he visualized the importance of doors in the set and realized that only if they were properly separated from each other would the movement have an appropriate "sweep." Similarly, the placement of a piano across the stage from the doors was neces-sitated by his realization that it served as a destination requiring interesting crosses for those entering through the doors. For a time, he used accurate ground plans to work out the movement patterns in advance, though these were likely to be changed considerably in the course of rehearsals. It was enough for him to be clear on the fundamental relationships between scenic elements and char-acters.

Abbott liked to have all script problems ironed out before rehearsals, though this was not always possible and revisions sometimes had to be done while working with the actors.[29] The presence of the author was crucial at rehearsals, so that the director could discuss whatever cuts and changes were necessary. Abbott never changed a line arbitrarily, but made his revisions collaboratively with the playwright. While working on *The Education of H*Y*M*A*N K*A*P*L*A*N* (1968), Abbott wanted to add the word "something" or "noth-ing" to the line "I hope I didn't interrupt." The writer chose "nothing." The actress spoke the new line, Abbott and the writer looked at each other, and the writer then decided to remove the entire line. Abbott agreed and rehearsal pro-ceeded.

Abbott seldom had trouble working with the authors of plays he staged because his own enormous success as a playwright granted him a sort of immunity in their eyes. They trusted him to make any needed alterations. He was sure that the most essential problems that crop up in a production are script problems, not actor problems. His collaborators were usually in favor of making cast changes when trouble arose, but he thought that if the script was strong any decent group of actors could play it, even a stock company.

In those cases where he went into a show which was floundering in its tryout period, he had to adapt another attitude, that of the play doctor. This could be a terribly confusing arrangement, as he admitted upon taking over the reins of *How Now, Dow Jones* (1967) from Arthur Penn. He pointed out that "there have been a lot of experiments to try to make things go well, and the first thing is to try to straighten out the story line. Then you accent your assets and minimize your liabilities."[30] This philosophy led to more colorful effects in the main production number, to the replacement of two other numbers, and to revisions in the casting, choreography, dialogue, and sets. However, the time to write and stage a new musical number required about two weeks, during which the director had to be extremely patient while living with a number which did not work.

Ironically, Abbott himself had to call in a play doctor at least once, during the rehearsals of *A Funny Thing* . . . . Jerome Robbins, himself a product of the Abbott showshop (*On the Town, Billion Dollar Baby* [1945], *High Button Shoes, Look Ma, I'm Dancing* [1948], and *Wonderful Town*), was brought in during the out-of-town tryouts and provided some very valuable suggestions, such as those that led to the popular opening number, ''Comedy Tonight,'' as a replacement for the original opening. Robbins staged the number and redid several others as well as reblocking the big chase scene at the end. Here was a perfect instance of the master learning from his pupil.

The *Funny Thing* . . . incident also illustrates one of the most often remarked upon features of Abbott's personality, his apparently total lack of ego when it came to getting a show across. He was never unwilling to listen to others' ideas and to go with them if he felt they would help. As Richard Hummler noted in this regard,

In a field legendary for temperament and emotional impulsiveness, Abbott is a byword for calm, good sense, clear-eyed pragmatism and professional discipline. Whatever claims his ego may have made on his personality have always been deferred to the requirements of ''the show.''[31]

REHEARSAL PROCESS

Abbott's work as an actor under Guthrie McClintic taught him the value of beginning rehearsals with company readings of the play. He preferred to have the cast do this for several days, a procedure which gave him a chance to gauge what the actor could do in the role and how he could help the actor with his characterization and line readings.

Blocking followed the reading sessions. When Abbott first began directing plays, he prepared a promptbook with great diligence, preplanning all the actors' movements in detail. He came to find such careful preparation meaningless, however, when working with the living actors who are not puppets. His promptbook blocking had to be discarded and new moves worked out in rehearsal. He thereafter preferred going to rehearsals with a completely open attitude, one that allowed him to develop his ideas in the heat of the rehearsal process. Even the stage directions in plays he himself wrote were likely to be ignored when he rehearsed.

Abbott's rehearsal preparation was minimal, which often surprised his performers. Blocking per se was far less important to him than getting everything to look natural. The early blocking was rather tentative and open to change either at the director's or the actor's instigation. Abbott had no qualms about changing his mind when he realized he had made a mistake. One of Abbott's most distinguished protégés, Harold Prince, noted that, ''Abbott alone, in my experience, possesses the self-confidence to alter his opinion without getting involved with 'losing face.' ''[32]

Abbott's early blocking may have been sketchy, but he had an extraordinary knack for suggesting the appropriate moves to his actors. He would state what he wanted in very precise terms. Actress Maureen Stapleton remembers that in *Norman, Is That You?* (1970), ''He would tell you to walk behind the third pillow, wait two beats, and then say the line. Lou Jacobi and I used to look at each other and shake our heads—he was always exactly right.''[33]

Scenes were staged by Abbott with surprising swiftness. William Goldman attended a rehearsal in which a five-minute scene took only fifteen minutes for Abbott to block. At this rate it was not unusual for a show to be blocked in roughly one week's time. Because he wanted his actors letter perfect, he went easy on blocking details for about a week following the first week's rehearsals.

When he worked on a show Abbott would become obsessed with it. Anything that distracted him from it was resented. He therefore worked with total absorption at rehearsals, refusing to be distracted by anything but the business at hand. His attitude was quiet and intense, with few overt displays of emotion. Goldman observed him sitting

slumped in a wooden-backed chair. An actress doesn't know the new scene that they are to rehearse, and Abbott says quietly, ''We'll prompt you.'' The stage manager tells him that one of the actors is late. Abbott says quietly, ''We'll jump around.'' Nothing ruffles him.[34]

During the early rehearsal period when the actors were becoming used to their moves and learning their lines, the stage manager would correct any paraphrasing, no matter how minor, since actors have a tendency to alter lines to make them sound ''natural.'' The playwright in Abbott, believing the original lines to have a sharpness and vitality lacking in the actor's version, insisted upon such corrections, realizing that once the actor has ''set'' his paraphrasing, rectification can be disturbing and confusing.

Abbott dispensed directions with the sureness of an old general. An autocrat in the best sense, he ran his rehearsals with an air of civility and politeness toward his actors, whom he referred to by the names of their characters. He would laugh loudly to let them get a sense of audience reaction to funny lines and business. His comments were normally quite terse and workmanlike. During a rehearsal of *Winning Isn't Everything,* he made such remarks as these:

''Hold your line, please,'' . . . ''Let the phone ring before you say that.'' Or, ''Say the line first, *then* cross.'' . . . Or, ''Let's say the line standing up, then collapse after the line.'' . . . Or, ''Excuse me, we'll have an extra pad, so that's your motive for going over there.''[35]

The director functions as a father figure, Abbott believed, but this paternalistic role should be played with modesty. By no means should the director be a tyrant. Directors who get off smart cracks at the actors' expense were despised by this veteran stager. He compared them to schoolteachers who mock their slow-learning students. He did recognize, however, that on occasion it becomes necessary to get a company in line through less civil methods, and realized that if the director does not put his foot down and show the cast who is boss the production will soon be in big trouble. There are several stories of his handling of stars who created obstacles to a smooth rehearsal process. His usual method was to show the actor that he was not intimidated and that if the actor was not happy he could leave. After telling Paul Lukas, during preparations for *Call Me Madam*, "I'll be glad to see you relieved of your contract," the ornery actor settled down and went on to give a superlative performance.[36] Abbott's cool, impersonal tone at rehearsal helped to prevent petty emotional squabbles; he approached each work session as if it were a business meeting. All potential conflicts were squashed immediately. Once, when an egotistical star was creating a scene and blaming everyone but himself for his own inadequacy, Abbott walked out of the rehearsal as if the matter were too trivial to deal with. He constantly showed an attitude of strength and dauntlessness which contributed to the confidence and respect all his coworkers placed in him. If he did not dominate the situation precious minutes would have been lost. Dancer-actress Gwen Verdon reminisced about the lesson she learned from Abbott's directorial authority:

When you work with George Abbott, it's a one on one relationship, and he's the boss. I think that was a very important thing to learn, that the director is the boss. The director is responsible for your performance and you're responsible to him. Not to the people who invest the money. And not to the producer.[37]

Abbott's productions were so carefully controlled during most of his career that he had a reputation on Broadway as the director who more than any other brought his shows in on the dates specified in the advance billing.

Abbott was extremely punctual and insisted on the same from his actors. He got right to work when he arrived at rehearsal, says William Goldman, noting that Abbott showed up for an 11:00 A.M. rehearsal at 10:59 and had it underway at 11:04. When an actor came in late, Abbott quietly said to him, "You're the villain in the show; don't be one to us."[38] Actor Art Carney notes that "When Mr. Abbott called for rehearsal at nine in the morning . . . that didn't mean get to the theater at nine in the morning. That meant start talking at nine in the morning."[39] Wishing to avoid confrontations with stars who came late, he initiated the practice of having the understudy rehearse when the star was tardy. He explained his reasoning:

Now no star is afraid that the understudy will take her part away or show her up by being better; nevertheless, it is *her* part, she feels possessive about it, and it's not pleasant to come in and find some one-cylinder bit player saying your lines. It usually works, and it is a device which I recommend to all punctual directors.[40]

Among the performers this trick was tried on was Ethel Merman, who arrived late to the first two days of *Call Me Madam* rehearsals. After arriving late on day three and seeing her understudy doing her business, she never came late again.

Another cause of irritation to this efficiency-oriented director was the practice of lengthy thematic and analytical discussions of the play and its characters. Such intellectualizing he saw as an unnecessary delay of the proceedings. A good director should be obeyed and trusted implicitly. Actors with clear speech, proper volume, and appropriate energy levels were far more valuable to Abbott than those who worried so much about what they were feeling or thinking that they were unable to make their lines register with the audience. He also dismissed as phonies those directors who work from an in-depth psychological standpoint.

Abbott attended to every aspect of the production, from the minutest details of costuming to the excision of major scenes and numbers. In working on a musical, though, he tempered his autocratic tendencies to blend with the collaborative process he believed was essential. Each creative contributor would offer his ideas but kept an objective attitude, thinking of the whole and not just his part of it. In the ideal situation the team would be filled with delight at being part of the creative process and would work with unbridled spirit and a sense of communal affection. He gave each team member the feeling of full creative participation. For example, the choreographer was allowed to work unhindered during the early stages to avoid making him feel the pressure of the director looking over his shoulder and stifling him. When Jerome Robbins worked with Abbott, the choreographic rehearsals began a full two weeks before Abbott himself started to rehearse.

WORKING WITH ACTORS

Even though he strongly criticized Method actors, most performers who worked with him affirm that Abbott used basic Stanislavsky techniques, such as always requiring motivation for all stage activity. No one did anything for purely arbitrary reasons in an Abbott show. Dance numbers, songs, slamming doors, characters running about, and other ingredients were always required by the dramatic action and were never imposed merely for effect. Humorous lines were not read to stir laughter but to express a character's actual thoughts; an actor did not dash across the stage to look ridiculous but to reach his destination because of a pressing need.

As Abbott rehearsed, he would listen closely to make sure the actors were speaking with a sense of inner justification, and not merely mouthing their words as if listening to themselves. He wanted actors to avoid carefully mulled over readings and to speak naturally and simply without overstressing key words.

The actor was to remain fresh and alert in his role and provide the "illusion of the first time" rather than seeming to anticipate what he knew would soon happen or be said.

Abbott liked to work the same way with all his actors, but admitted that there were occasions when he profited from giving an exceptionally gifted player the freedom to work in his or her own way. He was frustrated during rehearsals of *The Drums Begin* (1933) when the young Judith Anderson refused to put her all into the early sessions. Instead, she would mumble so that her lines were inaudible. He let her work this way, though doubting the value of building up a role in so slow and private a way. He ultimately realized, however, that her personal approach did pay off in an excellent performance.

Abbott's rehearsals were held either in rented rehearsal halls or in the theatre itself. In the latter instance, the noise onstage, especially in a musical, was likely to require more than lung power to call the company to a halt for a correction. At such rehearsals Abbott was known to resort to mechanical means, such as the blowing of a whistle to stop rehearsal and an electric megaphone to shout out his orders. Actors who worked with him claimed to know by the volume of his whistle just how perturbed he was.

A sign of Abbott's talent was his ability to call on his own experience as an actor in talking to his cast. He preferred to direct by demonstrating rather than discussing; this method saved him a lot of valuable time. Abbott favored demonstration to discussion, even if this meant giving line readings. He let the actors go with their own interpretations at first, trusting them, and then later would add what he could where needed. He rarely gave a reading without telling the actor the reason for it. Such rationales were short and to the point. When an actress in *The Education of H*Y*M*A*N K*A*P*L*A*N* read "Our whole class is dressed up" in a monotone, he corrected her. " 'Our whole *class* is dressed up.' . . . You're proud."[41]

Harold Prince, who observed Abbott on many occasions, emphasizes Abbott's totally flexible approach to working with actors.

He'll try whatever he knows will work to get the result he wants—a line reading for this actor, a motive for that actor, a movement for another actor. Then he wants them to go home and work on it and know it the next day.[42]

Abbott was aware that some directors choose to give their notes to actors on an individual basis, privately, but he liked to do so in front of the whole company. This allowed him to deter the selfish actor, who might be trying to steal scenes, by saying, "Please don't make that move because it hurts so-and-so's effect."[43] The offending actor was thereby put under the scrutiny of everybody else, making him self-conscious and careful not to provoke anyone's ire. Abbott points out,

If you talk to him privately, he may want to weasel out of a situation with a lot of double talk; but if you simply say it's good for the show to do it in such and such a way, he has very little comeback.[44]

On the few occasions when Abbott directed himself, he made a point of
knowing his lines early and well. Once he had worked out a scene in an apparently
satisfactory manner, he would have an assistant go through the business, script
in hand, and he would watch the scene from the house. As others have admitted,
though, the job of directing and being onstage presents serious problems of
concentration. While he was watching the others from out front, Abbott's mind
would keep reverting to thoughts of his own performance.

OBSERVING THE AUDIENCE

Abbott thought a show should have considerable audience exposure before its
official opening. He valued several weeks of out-of-town tryouts (Baltimore was
his favorite tryout city) as a vital part of getting a show ready, especially when
it was a musical. During the brief ten days he had for *On the Town*, a complete
musical number, two songs, and an attractive set were cut while a new song
and a new scene were added. He watched the audience intently at these tryouts,
believing that its reaction is the best way to gauge how a show is going. The
director and his collaborators are simply too subjectively involved to see the
problems clearly. Coughing, looking at programs, and any other such restless
behavior is an immediate clue to spots in need of the blue pencil. He often spoke
to people after the performance to elicit their responses. To get a valid reaction
he would make a critical remark and see if they agreed or not. Shortly before
opening night, invited audiences would attend final dress rehearsals or run-
throughs. The audiences were made up of friends, associates, and others in the
business. If the rehearsal was a run-through on a bare stage, Abbott often appeared and told the audience about what they were going to see, describing the
set, the shifting, and any other problems. He or an associate might also have
reminded the audience that they were guests at a rehearsal and that it might be
stopped if something needed fixing.

LONG-RUN PROBLEMS

Having produced and directed so many long-run hits, Abbott was inevitably
concerned over the effects such runs had on his casts. The mechanical quality
which performances begin to take on after actors have played in a piece two
hundred or more times eventually affects audience reactions adversely. Dissatisfied audiences soon have an effect on a show's box-office income. Abbott
wanted his companies to remain in first-class shape no matter how long the run.
Once a show had hit the two hundred performance mark, the cast would be
either completely rerehearsed or replaced, provided the new company was selected and rehearsed with the same care given the first. In actuality, second and
third companies for Broadway shows were usually put together sloppily, the
director concerned only with matching the externals of the original and not its

inner life. Abbott, though, attempted to give his replacement and touring companies the same attention he gave the original cast.

Believing an actor needed a vacation from a long run, Abbott began an innovative practice in 1936. This involved planning month-long staggered summer vacations for the actors while bringing in others who would form the fall touring company to perform for those on vacation. When the entire original company returned in the fall their performances would be refreshed while at the same time the new actors would have had a month of rehearsals under the best conditions—acting with the original cast before a New York audience.

WORKING WITH THE DESIGNER

Abbott gave his designers a good deal of freedom and did not participate excessively in the decorative aspect of his productions. He designed lights for at least one production, *A Holy Terror,* but his basic attitude toward lighting is perhaps indicative of his feelings about the decor in general. It has to be clear, workable, and attractive. Three top designers who worked with him numerous times were John Root, Jean Eckart, and Jo Mielziner. Harold Prince has written that when Abbott directed a musical, his approach was simple: ''lights up for the scene, and lights down for the song, with George Abbott shouting from the orchestra, 'more light on those faces—this is a funny scene.' And when the laughs didn't come, still more light.''[45]

CONCLUSION

Abbott is a unique phenomenon in the history of Broadway. His consistently shrewd, businesslike, yet tasteful approach to the world of theatre has made him the longest-lived success on the Great White Way. Unabashedly commercial, he came equipped for the fray not only with savvy and know-how, but with discretion, honesty, artistry, and taste. Because he looked on the theatre with one eye firmly fixed on the box office, his opinions are not likely to be popular with those whose theatrical interests are primarily artistic. For instance, he opposed subsidization of the theatre, feeling that any worthwhile theatrical enterprise should be able to succeed within a commercial context. Adversity leads to creativity, and the cushion provided by subsidy will hamper, not foster, theatre excellence. Art thrives through competition and not through patronage.

George Abbott has given the world laughter and excitement for close to three-quarters of a century. He directed, produced, acted in, or wrote some of the most popular shows of the period, during a career remarkable both for its longevity and abundance. Actors who worked for him hold him in the highest regard for his wit, insight, talent, class, and know-how. As actress Elizabeth Ashley remarks, in a typical encomium:

With George Abbott there's no such thing as politics. There is professionalism. He is absolutely the best because he goes right to the bottom line. Mr. Abbott is the genuine article, a real hero. He stands for championship. I like to remember that I worked for George Abbott, who is far and away the best of our time.[46]

The words of another great commercial director, Bob Fosse, might be cited here as well: "In my opinion, George Abbott is the greatest all-around director in the American theater."[47]

If Abbott's work has not plumbed the depths of profundity, has not taught the world any grand new lesson, and has not revolutionized the art of the stage, it has provided countless thousands with sheer pleasure, devoid of guilt, with charm, glamor, good music, and many other fascinating and delightful elements of entertaining theatre.

NOTES

1. Brooks Atkinson, "Morales for Kings," *New York Times*, 27 September 1931.

2. George Abbott, *"Mr. Abbott"* (New York: Random House, 1963), p. 264.

3. Quoted in Richard Hummler, "Still Rolling Up Those Sleeves after 100 Years, Abbott Keeps Perpetuating 'Mr. Broadway' Tag," *Variety*, 24 June 1987, p. 103.

4. Ibid.

5. "All the Four Horsemen," *New York Herald Tribune*, 24 November 1934.

6. Alvin Klein, " 'Yankees,' Hit of Old, Is Revived in Milburn," *New York Times*, 28 September 1986, sec. 11, p. 23.

7. Richard Hummler, *"Broadway,"* *Variety*, 1 July 1987, p. 140.

8. Maurice Zolotow, "Broadway's Most Successful Penny-Pincher," *Saturday Evening Post*, 29 January 1955, p. 71.

9. Garson Kanin, "A Born Dancer's 'Abbott Touch,' " *Variety*, 24 June 1987, p. 103.

10. Percy Hammond, "The Theatre," *New York Sun*, 8 January 1932.

11. Brooks Atkinson, Review of *Ladies' Money*, *New York Times*, 2 November 1934.

12. Quoted in Alan Wallach, "He's Still Got the Abbott Touch," *Newsday*, 11 May 1986, Part 2, p. 3.

13. Douglas Gilbert, "Making Plays into Shows," *New York World Telegram*, 21 January 1936.

14. Quoted in Kanin, "A Born Dancer's 'Abbott Touch.' "

15. Quoted in Charles Kipps, "Remembrances of 'George,' " *Variety*, 24 June 1987, p. 104.

16. Stuart Little, "It's an Old Story for Abbott—The Rehearsal of a New Play," *New York Herald Tribune*, 3 October 1962.

17. Brooks Atkinson, "Slapstick Comedy," *New York Times*, 9 October 1952.

18. Quoted in Neil Hickey, "Mr. Abbott, Sir!" *American Weekly*, 15 May 1960, clipping, Lincoln Center Library for the Performing Arts, New York.

19. Quoted in Lucius Beebe, "Stage Asides," *New York Herald Tribune*, 30 May 1937.

20. Abbott, *"Mr. Abbott,"* p. 264.

21. Unless one considers his productions of such musical comedy adaptations as *The Boys from Syracuse* and *Music Is* as Shakespearean revivals. During the thirties, Abbott

considered doing Anton Chekhov's *The Seagull* and Shakespeare's *The Merchant of Venice* (with Sam Levene or Philip Loeb), but these plans did not materialize.

22. George Abbott, "My Ten Favorite Plays," *New York Sun* (n.d.), clipping, Lincoln Center Library for the Performing Arts, New York City.

23. Quoted in Morton Eustis, "The Director Takes Command," *Theatre Arts Monthly* 20 (February 1936): 122.

24. Ibid., pp. 120–21.

25. Quoted in Hummler, "Still Rolling Up Those Sleeves," p. 104.

26. Abbott, *"Mr. Abbott,"* p. 104.

27. Zolotow, "Broadway's Most Successful Penny-Pincher," p. 69.

28. Hummler, "Still Rolling Up Those Sleeves," p. 104.

29. A good picture of Abbott's problems with a script during rehearsals is provided by Craig Zadan in *Sondheim and Co.* (New York: Macmillan, 1974), in which the preparations for *A Funny Thing* . . . are described.

30. Quoted in Edwin Bolwell, "George Abbott Again Caring for a Broadway Bound Patient," *New York Times*, 10 November 1967.

31. Richard Hummler, "Still Rolling Up Those Sleeves," p. 103.

32. Quoted in Harold Prince, *Contradictions. Notes on Twenty-Six Years in the Theatre* (New York: Dodd, Mead, 1974), p. 92.

33. Quoted in Howard Kissel, "Going Through the Paces with George Abbott," *Women's Wear Daily*, 12 April 1976.

34. William Goldman, *The Season: A Candid Look at Broadway* (New York: Bantam Books, 1970), p. 363.

35. "The Talk of the Town: Rehearsal," *New Yorker*, 30 October 1978, p. 34.

36. Quoted in Gilbert Millstein, "Mr. Abbott: One Man Theatre," *New York Times Magazine*, 3 October 1954, p. 60.

37. Quoted in Kipps, "Remembrances of 'George,' " p. 104.

38. Goldman, *The Season*, p. 363.

39. "Working for Abbott No Leadpipe Cinch, Art Carney Recalls," *Variety*, 24 June 1987, p. 104.

40. Abbott, *"Mr. Abbott,"* pp. 170–71.

41. Quoted in Goldman, *The Season*, p. 363.

42. "Prince Recalls: 'Abbott Was First to Tell Me, You Are a Director,' " *Variety*, 24 June 1987, p. 104.

43. Abbott, *"Mr. Abbott,"* p. 256.

44. Ibid.

45. Prince, *Contradictions*, p. 37.

46. Quoted in Kipps, "Remembrances of 'George,' " p. 102.

47. Quoted in ibid.

CHRONOLOGY

All productions New York, unless otherwise noted; only shows directed are listed.

1887   born in Forestville, New York; raised in Salamanca, New York, then Cheyenne, Wyoming

1911   graduates from University of Rochester

1912   attends George Pierce Baker's playwriting course at Harvard

1913   Broadway acting debut, *The Misleading Lady*

1914   marries Ednah Levis

1924   assumes direction of *The Fall Guy* in mid-rehearsal

1926   Sam H. Harris Theatre: *Love 'Em and Leave 'Em*; Broadhurst Theatre: *Broadway*; Music Box Theatre: *Chicago*

1927   Martin Beck Theatre: *Spread Eagle*; Maxine Elliott's Theatre: *Coquette*; Henry Miller's Theatre: *Gentlemen of the Press*; John Golden Theatre: *Four Walls*

1928   Broadhurst: *Ringside*; Longacre Theatre: *Jarnegan*; Biltmore Theatre: *Poppa*

1930   John Golden Theatre: *Those We Love*

1931   Masque Theatre: *Louder Please*

1932   Morosco Theatre: *Lilly Turner*; Selwyn Theatre: *The Great Magoo*; Broadhurst: *Twentieth Century*

1933   Booth Theatre: *Heat Lightning*; Shubert Theatre: *The Drums Begin*

1934   Ethel Barrymore Theatre: *John Brown's Body*; Booth: *Kill That Story*; John Golden: *Small Miracle*; Ethel Barrymore: *Ladies' Money*; Mansfield Theatre: *Page Miss Glory*

1935   Playhouse: *Three Men on a Horse*; Hippodrome: *Jumbo*; Cort Theatre: *Boy Meets Girl*

1936   Imperial Theatre: *On Your Toes*; Fifty-first Street Theatre: *Sweet River*; Biltmore: *Brother Rat*

1937   Cort: *Room Service*; National Theatre: *Angel Island*; Biltmore: *Brown Sugar*

1938   Biltmore: *All That Glitters; What a Life*; Alvin Theatre: *The Boys from Syracuse*

1939   Biltmore: *The Primrose Path*; Lyceum: *Mrs. O'Brien Entertains*; Imperial Theatre: *Too Many Girls*; closed out of town: *The White-Haired Boy*

1940   Biltmore: *The Unconquered; Goodbye in the Night*; Ethel Barrymore: *Pal Joey*

1941   Ethel Barrymore: *Best Foot Forward*

1942   Forty-sixth Street Theatre: *Beat the Band*; Mansfield: *Sweet Charity*

1943   Biltmore: *Kiss and Tell*; Cort: *Get Away Old Man*

1944   Hudson Theatre: *Snafu*; Adelphi Theatre: *On the Town*

1945   closed out of town: *Mr. Cooper's Left Hand; One Shoe Off*; Alvin: *Billion Dollar Baby*

1946   second marriage, Mary Sinclair; Broadway Theatre: *Beggar's Holiday* (with John Houseman and Nicholas Ray)

1947   Biltmore: *It Takes Two*; Martin Beck Theatre: *Barefoot Boy with Cheek*; Century Theatre: *High Button Shoes*; closed out of town: *You Never Know*

1948   Adelphi: *Look Ma, I'm Dancing*; St. James Theatre: *Where's Charley?*

1949   Music Box: *Mrs. Gibbons' Boys*

1950   Imperial: *Call Me Madam*

1951   Alvin: *A Tree Grows in Brooklyn*; Biltmore: *The Number*

1952	Cort: *In Any Language*
1953	Winter Garden Theatre: *Wonderful Town*; Majestic Theatre: *Me and Juliet*
1954	St. James: *The Pajama Game*; wins first Tony as coauthor of book; Forty-sixth Street: *On Your Toes* (revival)
1955	Forty-sixth Street: *Damn Yankees*; first acting role since 1934, in revival of *The Skin of Our Teeth*
1957	Forty-sixth Street: *New Girl in Town*
1958	Fifty-fourth Street Theatre: *Drink to Me Only*
1959	Phoenix Theatre: *Once upon a Mattress*; Broadhurst: *Fiorello!*; wins Pulitzer as coauthor of book
1960	Forty-sixth Street: *Tenderloin*
1961	Broadhurst: *A Call on Kuprin*; Biltmore: *Take Her, She's Mine*
1962	Alvin: *A Funny Thing Happened on the Way to the Forum*; wins Tony for its direction; Playhouse: *Never Too Late*
1963	publishes autobiography, *"Mr. Abbott"*
1964	Mark Hellinger Theatre: *Fade Out—Fade In*
1965	Alvin: *Flora, the Red Menace*; Ziegfeld: *Anya*; Fifty-fourth Street Theatre renamed in his honor; receives Award of Merit from Society of Stage Directors and Choreographers
1966	Booth: *Help Stamp Out Marriage*; Henry Miller's: *Agatha Sue, I Love You*
1967	Lunt-Fontanne Theatre: *How Now, Dow Jones*
1968	Alvin: *The Education of H*Y*M*A*N K*A*P*L*A*N*
1969	Lyceum: *Three Men on a Horse* (revival); Broadhurst: *The Fig Leaves Are Falling*
1970	Lyceum: *Norman, Is That You?*; Brooks Atkinson Theatre: *Not Now, Darling*
1971	Parker Playhouse, Fort Lauderdale: *Twentieth Century* (revival)
1973	Lunt-Fontanne: *The Pajama Game* (revival); Seattle Repertory Theatre, Seattle: *Life with Father*
1976	St. James: *Music Is*; special Tony for Lifetime Achievement
1978	Hudson Guild Theatre: *Winning Isn't Everything*
1979	Publishes novel, *Try-Out*
1983	Virginia Theatre: *On Your Toes*; Tony award for direction of a musical; Kennedy Center Honors; third marriage, Joy Moana Valderrama
1985	Musical Theatre Works (showcase): *Tropicana*
1986	Paper Mill Playhouse, Milburn, N.J.: *Damn Yankees*
1987	Ohio Theatre, Cleveland, then Royale Theatre, New York: *Broadway* (revival); his 100th birthday celebrated by "Classic Broadway" conference in Cleveland
1989	York Theatre: *Frankie*

Sir Tyrone Guthrie

(1900–1971)

Few individuals have been so singularly responsible for the popular characterization of this century as "the age of the director" as has William Tyrone Guthrie.
Throughout a career ranging from 1924 to 1971, the year of his death, Guthrie's
work epitomized for the public the advent of the theatre's newest artist, the
directorial genius whose imaginative conceptions are often more responsible for
the attention given a production than are the presence of its players or, indeed,
the play itself.

Guthrie's contributions extended far beyond his significant interpretations of
the plays he staged; no other director has had so considerable an impact on the
very shape of the modern playhouse. Were it not for Guthrie the open or thrust
stage might still be a relative anomaly rather than, as it has become, an increasingly common alternative to the proscenium.

EARLY YEARS

It is fitting that this representative of the director's age should have been born
in 1900, at the start of the century during which the art of directing was to come
into its own. The event took place in Tunbridge Wells, England, where Guthrie's
well-to-do father and Irish mother then resided. After studying at private schools,
Guthrie entered Oxford, where he acted in the Oxford University Dramatic
Society (OUDS) theatricals and also received his earliest directing experience
by staging the ballet sequence in *Le Bourgeois Gentilhomme*. While Guthrie was
at Oxford the Irish playwright-director James B. Fagan founded the Oxford
Playhouse, which he ran for two years (1923–25), staging the works of Oscar
Wilde, George Bernard Shaw, Carlo Goldoni, William Congreve, and other
dramatists of stature. Fagan's casts included such fledgling thespians as John
Gielgud, Robert Morley, and Flora Robson. Fagan hired the gangling, towering
Guthrie, six-feet-five-inches tall, as an actor for his London company in 1924.

The twenty-four-year-old aspirant soon realized, however, that acting would not be his métier.

Shortly afterwards, he and a friend, Christopher Scaife, opened their own theatrical venture, the tiny Barn Theatre at Oxted, where Guthrie staged Scaife's *The Triumph of Death* as his first professional effort.

For the next two years, 1924–26, Guthrie served as a pioneer in the infant industry of radio broadcasting, working for the British Broadcasting Corporation (BBC) in Belfast, Ireland. He gained enough attention for his skillful direction of various radio plays during these years to be offered the job of directing the semiprofessional Scottish National Players, a touring company situated in Glasgow. In 1928 he returned to England to do some more radio work for the BBC, and, in 1929, took over the artistic direction of the Festival Theatre, Cambridge, where Anmer Hall was the producer. Terence Gray had recently gained notoriety at the Festival Theatre with his eccentric stagings of the classics, but Guthrie later dismissed Gray's work as that of a dilettante who directed plays in what he thought to be an avant-garde style. Actually, some of Guthrie's own far-fetched approaches to the classics reminded some critics of the very excesses of which he felt Gray to be guilty. In the theatre's eighteenth-century building, Guthrie toyed with antirealistic methods, fostered by men such as Gordon Craig and Jacques Copeau, then very much in vogue. Using a sophisticated lighting system, he created many lovely effects in the thirty-some plays he staged. Averaging one play a week, he opened with a play he was to direct on several later occasions, Luigi Pirandello's *Six Characters in Search of an Author*, and soon worked his way through such authors as Euripides, Richard Brinsley Sheridan, Ernst Toller, Henrik Ibsen, Shakespeare, Arthur Wing Pinero, Molière, and Anton Chekhov.

After a year of radio work in Canada, Guthrie joined up once more with Anmer Hall—this time at London's Westminster Theatre where he staged James Bridie's *The Anatomist* (1931). This play, the first of his London productions, was followed that season by others at the Westminster, including an unconventional and beautifully performed *Love's Labour's Lost*, which helped gain him local attention. Soon he was directing in the West End, his first venture there being J. B. Priestley's provocative mystery drama, *Dangerous Corner* (1932). In 1933 he counted among his productions a *Richard II*, done at the Memorial Theatre in Stratford-on-Avon; this was a prestigious step forward. More important yet was his being invited to direct at the Old Vic in 1933, an assignment which lasted through the war years. He headed the Old Vic again in 1951–52 and directed there in 1953, 1956, 1962, and 1967. His Old Vic activity in the 1930s was a major development both in his career and that of the Vic. Overall, Guthrie was involved at the Old Vic for thirteen seasons, during which he staged thirty-eight productions. When Lilian Baylis died in 1937, he succeeded her as administrator of both the Old Vic and Sadler's Wells theatres.

THE OLD VIC

Long a bastion of conservative Shakespearean production, the Vic allowed Guthrie to bring in his new ideas only after much debate. He had found the work there depressingly dull and frowzy, and sought to bring color, excitement, and glamour to its stage. He began by overturning the old nonstar policy and by hiring the young Charles Laughton, then experiencing sensational acclaim for his stage and film acting. Guthrie objected to the old-fashioned pictorial illusionism associated with the productions of actor-director Frank Benson, preferring instead the simplified Elizabethan approach to Shakespeare rediscovered by William Poel and developed by Harley Granville-Barker and Robert Atkin. To combat the drawbacks of the Vic's proscenium stage, he devised an architectural arrangement aimed at duplicating the conventions of the Elizabethan theatre, an idea that continued to obsess him throughout his career. The set incorporated an alcove, a bridgelike upper stage suspended between two heavy pillars, a pair of curving staircases, and an apron built out over the orchestra pit.

Hoping to create an arrangement which would allow the plays to move swiftly from scene to scene without unneeded breaks or heavy scenery, Guthrie found that a number of problems, both aesthetic and practical, arose from his attempt. The major difficulty was the set's obtrusiveness, its tendency, no matter how lit or painted, to draw attention away from the actors to its own glaringly inappropriate presence.

Guthrie's Old Vic productions of the classics during the 1933–34 season immediately established him as a maverick director, from whom a never-ending series of surprises could be expected. His season commenced with a delicately choreographed *Twelfth Night* in Carolingian decor, followed by a *Cherry Orchard* staged for all the laughter of a comedy of manners, a *Henry VIII* cut to the bone, and a *Measure for Measure* styled to suit the sophisticated tastes and ideas of 1933 London. After having his biggest success with this play, his *The Tempest*, set with modern music, failed to please. Other works were *The Importance of Being Earnest*, *Love for Love*, and a *Macbeth* without its witches. For this production, starring Laughton, Guthrie followed Granville-Barker's belief that Shakespeare did not write the opening scene on the heath and that it should be cut and the play begun with Macbeth's entrance. Guthrie felt that it weakened the characters of Macbeth and Lady Macbeth if their behavior were seen to be a result of the power exercised over them by the witches. He wanted to stress that the downfall of the Macbeths was because of their own natures and not because of some outside force. Everything that might have stressed the supernatural influences in the story was suppressed, and the drama became instead a study in abnormal psychology.

During his subsequent years at the Old Vic, Guthrie continued to shock and delight with his versions of such classics as *Hamlet, The Country Wife, Henry V, Richard III, A Midsummer Night's Dream, Othello, She Stoops to Conquer,*

The Taming of the Shrew, Timon of Athens, Tamburlaine, Troilus and Cressida, The Alchemist, and *Tartuffe*, among many others. He guided the early work of such then-and-future stars as Laurence Olivier, John Gielgud, Sybil Thorndike, Edith Evans, Judith Anderson, Ralph Richardson, Alec Guinness, Ruth Gordon, and Michael Redgrave. Guthrie displayed dazzling virtuosity when he staged the same play more than once. Instead of repeating his original production he would find a completely new approach. An example was his 1937 interpretation of *Hamlet*, with Laurence Olivier, as a romantic costume melodrama and his 1938 version with Alec Guinness, done in a restrained modern-dress style.

With one hand Guthrie sought to entertain and charm the public, molding the lighter plays into escapist fantasies, while with the other he would add to the plays a tone of contemporary irony, playing up their darker aspects. This was especially noticeable in the performances of characters like Feste the clown in *Twelfth Night*, whose black garb was designed to suggest an air of fatalistic gloom amid the otherwise happy goings-on. Also in the 1930s Guthrie, enthused by the ideas of Ernest Jones in *Hamlet and Oedipus*, infused Freudian ideas into Shakespeare, making Hamlet the victim of an Oedipal conflict and Iago the bearer of an unrequited homosexual passion for Othello. (In 1955 he staged a *The Merchant of Venice* which underscored the love of Antonio for Bassanio.)

Guthrie's work at the Old Vic in the thirties suffered from an extreme lack of sufficient rehearsal time. Often he had to sacrifice polish and perfection, especially in the speaking of the verse—for which he was often criticized—in order to get the play on in time. Adherence to a clearly established concept did help to tie many of the loose ends together. At the very least, the lack of smoothness in the ensemble was offset by the novelty of the directorial *jeux*.

DIRECTORIAL DIVERSITY

Concurrent with his Old Vic activities, Guthrie was fast becoming a popular commodity at West End theatres, where he was staging productions of modern comedies, most of them now forgotten. His first Broadway show, Dodie Smith's *Call It a Day*, was produced in 1936. Another of his London hits, *Sweet Aloes*, was also done in New York in 1936, but Guthrie did not return to this city until 1946 when he put on Leonid Andreyev's *He Who Gets Slapped*. The postwar years found him frequently in New York and London, as well as in places as far-flung as Tel-Aviv, Helsinki, Edinburgh, Dublin, Minneapolis, Glasgow, Sydney, and elsewhere. He directed plays from every period and in every style, revealing extreme eclecticism in his material. Often he staged the same play several times, doing five *Hamlet*s, five *Oedipus Rex*s, three *Six Characters*, three *Richard III*s, three *Cherry Orchard*s, three *Henry VIII*s, and three *Taming of the Shrew*s. Many other plays had at least two Guthrie productions. There were also operas, operettas, and dramas Guthrie had written himself.

He seriously believed that any director worth the name should direct in every dramatic genre, for there is something he can learn from them all. The lighter plays are excellent aids in doing the more sober types. A snobbish attitude toward the popular theatre is irresponsible, and a good director should be able to put on an acceptable production of any work, from an Elizabethan tragedy to a sexy striptease. Yet perusal of Guthrie's list of productions reveals that, despite the wide range of styles and eras represented—once his career was established in the late thirties—he rarely got involved with any but the most challenging plays, new or old. He claimed that many lightweight Broadway comedies needed no director, but that one is surely required by more serious works for making the text meaningful, developing the rhythmic aspects of the performance, choreographing the action, and unifying the disparate elements into a harmonious whole. Though the capable director can direct all types of plays, there is really no more accurate a gauge for measuring talent than the classics.

Guthrie directed as often in the commercial theatre as in the institutional theatre, bringing his gusto and creativity to New York's Phoenix Theatre, to the Edinburgh Festival, to the Habimah Theatre, the Metropolitan Opera House, the Memorial Theatre at England's Stratford, and, most notably, to the great theatres he founded at Stratford, Ontario, and Minneapolis, Minnesota. He had popular productions with Thornton Wilder's *The Matchmaker*, staged in 1954 with Ruth Gordon, and Paddy Chayefsky's *The Tenth Man*, which he did in 1959, but these are exceptions in a career notably lacking in long-run successes. Commercial success was of relatively little interest to Sir Tyrone (or, as he was popularly dubbed, "Sir Tony"), for he would rather have dealt with the theatre's artistic opportunities than exploit the medium for personal enrichment. Broadway was stimulating to him only when commercial and artistic goals happily coincided.

REPERTORY

Reference has been made to the founding by Guthrie of two noncommercial theatres, the Festival Theatre at Stratford, Ontario, and the Guthrie Theatre at Minneapolis. These theatres, built according to the director's ideas on the ideal shape for a stage suited to a classical repertory, are among the most successful realizations of the possibilities of the open, or thrust, stage. The Festival Theatre began in a huge tent the summer of 1953 when Guthrie directed Alec Guinness in *Richard III* and *All's Well That Ends Well*. The tent was replaced by a permanent building with a semi-Elizabethan stage designed by Tanya Moiseiwitsch, who also designed the stage for the Tyrone Guthrie Theatre, launched in Minneapolis in May 1963. Guthrie directed at Stratford in 1953, 1954, 1955, 1957, and 1960. In the latter year his productions were seen at the second of Stratford's legitimate playhouses, the Avon. Three years later he began the first of three consecutive years of work at the Guthrie, returning for guest productions in 1967 and 1969.

Guthrie obviously preferred working in repertory. Repertory offered a young actor security, excellent experience, and a chance to play a variety of roles without being typecast. From the ensemble situation of collective activity in repertory came ensemble playing. Despite the drawbacks of internecine rivalry and boredom, and less money and glamour, a repertory company organized according to a seasonal contract, renewable as long as desirable to both parties, was a workable compromise between good and bad features. A year prior to the opening of the Guthrie, he published the names of the "10 Best for a Repertory Theatre," three of which he staged at the Guthrie.[1] They were *Agamemnon* (directed as part of John Lewin's *House of Atreus* version of the *Oresteia*), *The Alchemist*, *Love for Love*, Friedrich Schiller's *Don Carlos*, *Peer Gynt*, *The Cherry Orchard* (staged at the Guthrie in 1965), *Mourning Becomes Electra, Death of a Salesman* or *The Little Foxes*, Wilder's *The Long Christmas Dinner* and Tennessee Williams' *Twenty-Seven Wagons Full of Cotton* on a double bill, and George Abbott and John Cecil Holm's *Three Men on a Horse*. However, aside from the two plays selected for the Guthrie, only three others on this list, *Love for Love*, *The Alchemist* and *Peer Gynt*, were ever staged by the director.

THEATRE IS LARGER THAN LIFE

Guthrie's tastes ran to the bold and extravagant. He wanted to make plays larger-than-life, as an alternative to what he considered the small-size acting of television and films. Theatre should be more vigorous and colorful than in the average realistic drama. Musicals and opera had the bigness he sought in straight plays, despite their intrinsic weaknesses. He devoted himself to classical works because these were to him the bigger-than-life dramas he could not find in the modern repertory. To stage these plays required a largeness in conception from actor and director such as the plays were rarely afforded. Guthrie disdained the puniness of modern realistic acting as represented by those American Method actors with whom he was familiar. In his opinion, Actors Studio performers fell down seriously when it came to meeting the demands of the great plays.

To demonstrate what he felt an actor should be capable of, he staged Christopher Marlowe's *Tamburlaine,* first in London in 1951 with Donald Wolfit and again in New York in 1956 with Anthony Quayle. The scope of these historic productions is suggested by a climactic scene near the end of the play. The dying Tamburlaine, like a great beast, staggered onto the near-empty stage with his followers retreating into the shadows at his approach. He ordered his men to bring on a map, and when they did it was so large it covered the floor of the stage and spilled over into the orchestra pit. Tamburlaine moved about on it as if it were the earth itself and he a colossus able to encompass it with only a few steps, pointing as he moved to all his international conquests.

VIEWS ON ACTING

Guthrie's ideal of a well-trained actor had a musical voice, clear diction, and superb breath control. He took issue with acting teacher Lee Strasberg's Method approach for its neglect of good speech training. An actor should, without difficulty, be able to recite seven lines of blank verse in one breath, at a normal pace, and with a range of at least two octaves. Though accepting the value of certain aspects of the Stanislavsky System (the basis for the Method), Guthrie felt it was outdated and no longer answered the situation for which it was created. To him it was silly for an actor in a modern farce such as *Up in Mabel's Room* to go to a farm to study the play's environment. In making such remarks Guthrie revealed an ignorance of actual Method practice; he harped on typical exaggerations of the Method's teachings. His own approach was almost dogmatically pragmatic. Anything smacking of the mystical, spiritual, or studiously psychological was immediately suspect. The best acting lessons came from watching professional players achieving their effects by the tried and true methods of the stage. Much could also be gained from watching the reactions of different audiences.

Guthrie—himself a good singer and enthusiastic piano player—invariably considered a play's language as a kind of music and attempted to elicit a musical response from his actors when they spoke it. Speaking dialogue was not much different to Guthrie from singing lyrics, as a similar process was being employed. Pauses, rhythm, pitch, volume, and color are all qualities shared by speech and song, and the director must conduct the choral effects. He would often say such things as "More brio, Chris! . . . in crescendo, crowd, please! . . . Pianissimo, Patricia!"[2] A play like *Tamburlaine* was "a sort of sadistic concerto. Tamburlaine is the solo instrument, backed by a discordant symphony of savage henchmen."[3] Robertson Davies observed,

He may tell his cast that the scene on which they are working is a Coda—a summing up of what has gone before, and in which it is therefore desirable to give a display of technical brilliance, rather than a sober statement of what is in the lines. Or he may tell them that what they are doing is to be played at "finale pace," which is clear to anyone who has become acquainted with classical opera.[4]

Guthrie once came to a rehearsal of *Gideon* and described ecstatically the performance of an actor he just had seen in Jean Genet's *The Blacks* because of the musical way he had delivered a speech. Guthrie thereupon began to direct a scene in *Gideon* seeking a similar effect by orchestrating the actors' voices and creating an a cappella interlude. It is not surprising, then, that Guthrie considered the training of the actor's voice of principal importance; he found that the actors in America lagged far behind those of Great Britain in this area. It was his firm conviction that a professional actor should have musical training and be able to sing pleasantly enough for stage purposes.

One of his favorite musical concepts was rhythm, and he used the term frequently in his rehearsals. The subtle rhythmic and counterrhythmic effects of his productions were a large part of his success, and could not be duplicated when one of his shows was copied by another director (such as when his Old Vic *The Country Wife* was restaged in New York). An actor overexerting himself to produce an effect would be told, ''It's rhythm that does it, not energy.'' Or an actress's confused delivery of a line might be met with a shout of ''The rhythm is *wrong*.''[5]

STRENGTHS IN STAGING

Guthrie was famed not only for the ingenuity of his unique conceptions, but for the enormous skill and imagination he displayed in such elements as groupings, crowd scenes, business, tempo, and, when time allowed, ensemble work. His pyrotechnical brilliance often obscured the emotional underpinnings of a play. Rather than rely on a play's inherent values to emerge through straightforward performances, Guthrie usually would invent dazzling displays of showmanship, which were not always as appropriate as those of a simpler approach. An example of inappropriate showmanship noted by various commentators was his Phoenix Theatre production of *Six Characters in Search of an Author*. In it, the director was so intent on making the audience laugh—through the creation of hilarious sight gags—that the play's anguish and pain completely failed to come across. Kenneth Tynan summed up the problem succinctly by describing Guthrie's

familiar, infuriating blend of insight and madness. On the one hand we have the great conductor, the master of visual orchestration, conceivably the most striking director alive when there are more than six people on stage; on the other hand we have his zany *Doppelgänger,* darting about with his pockets full of fireworks and giving the members of the orchestra hot-feet whenever . . . feeling threatens to impend.[6]

Guthrie's productions were notable for their full use of all the theatre's resources, including keeping every inch of stage space constantly alive with movement and surging life. Clever bits of business were invented to help shine light upon the text. To cite a small example, his Minneapolis production of *Hamlet* had the ghost whisper his message into Hamlet's ear as if poisoning him with ideas on revenge, just as the ghost, Hamlet's father, had been poisoned by Claudius. The same motif was exploited later in the production in a moment between Claudius and Rosencrantz. Guthrie's physical staging, too, was always fully expressive and exceptionally striking to the eye. Paddy Chayefsky recalled that the stage pictures devised for *The Tenth Man* and *Gideon* were so beautiful that each moment was worthy of being ''photographed and hung for a painting.''[7] Like a kaleidoscope, the pictures kept shifting into ever more fascinating and revealing arrangements of line and mass.

Closely associated with Guthrie's type of stage activity is choreography. This was especially true in the case of his work on the open stage where actors have always to be on the move while always remaining clearly visible to all parts of the semicircular auditorium. But as Davies noted, "His choreography is not movement for its own sake, but a subtle physical expression of each scene—indeed, a dance."[8]

Guthrie's preference for ensemble effects over emphasis on a star's performance led him to invent such detailed business for the lesser actors that the principals were put into a more subdued light. Guthrie enjoyed devising interesting characters for all minor roles so that even spear carriers might find themselves busy with sneezing, scratching, or falling over their weapons. The star might be saying the most famous passage in the play while a group of courtiers was busy at some realistic byplay created to give the scene more life. At times Guthrie would even tell an actor to "throw away" an important speech, thereby surprising the audience into listening to it from a new perspective.

Guthrie was also the type of director who could discern meanings in lines or uncover character relationships that others had overlooked. An example of the latter was his discovery in rehearsal that the role of Hortensio in *The Taming of the Shrew* could be viewed as Katharina's advisor; to convey this to the audience the director had the actor nod and gesture in such a way during his scenes with Katharina that no one could miss the connection.

Whole scenes were often interpolated on the basis of the merest textual hints. For instance, the 1959 modern-dress *All's Well That Ends Well* at Stratford, England, included a new segment lasting ten minutes—an army review by the Duke of Florence—suggested by a twelve-line section in the text.

Guthrie knew just how to realize all the technical tricks he liked to incorporate in his productions. Norris Houghton remembers the many effects used in *Six Characters* at the Phoenix and how Guthrie knew

how to make all six Characters appear out of nowhere; how to make Madame Pace dissolve in a puff of smoke; how to turn the Boy into a sawdust dummy; how to make the Step-Daughter disappear before our very eyes with a blood-curdling shriek.[9]

Theatricalism, vivid hues, and a tendency toward the spectacular and pageantlike were Guthrie hallmarks, though he occasionally was guilty of excess and unnecessary exaggeration. Nevertheless, as Robert Hatch pointed out, all directors must focus on the visualization of a play, and "Guthrie more than others seems to revel in the moments when the scene bursts out in flashing jewels and swirling capes, with trumpets sounding, armies passing, and fortune on the wing."[10]

Guthrie had little interest in turning the theatre into a lecture platform where social or political views were expressed. Although his fondest directorial experiences in the theatre were those which afforded him the chance to express his intellectual appreciation of great plays, he sought above all to entertain, to cause laughter to erupt and tears to flow. If he could only transport the audience to the world of the play, he felt far better than if he had succeeded in educating or uplifting them. If the theatre has an educational power, he explained, it is not because it is a short cut to examination answers nor because it is morally uplifting, but because it widens the imaginative horizon by presenting ideas in the most memorable way. [These ideas are] primarily emotional. They drive consciously at the sources of pleasure and pain; and by that means produce impressions, not only far more vivid but also far more lasting, than experiences which are more purely intellectual.[11]

At times, however, Guthrie did articulate a social or political point of view in connection with a drama he was directing. His *Tamburlaine,* for instance, emphasized the title character's demagoguery in the light of contemporary counterparts, such as Joseph Stalin or Mao Zedong, "when once again the idea of Absolute Power in the hands of a single Dynast or a group of Oligarchs, begins to be not only familiar but attractive."[12]

SHIFTING PERIODS IN SHAKESPEARE

Perhaps the most notorious feature of Guthrie's work was his tendency to shift the period of a Shakespeare play to one in which various thematic concerns could be made suddenly relevant to a contemporary audience. So startling were some of his period choices that he was nicknamed by theatre journalists as "Naughty Tony." The drama critic of the *New Statesman,* T. C. Worsley, who respected Guthrie's genius, labeled Guthrie "the leader of what we may call the "Wouldn't-it-be-fun (just for a change) School,"[13] a phrase that continued to reappear in other appraisals of the director's work.

Guthrie seems to have felt, for example, that it would be fun to stage *The Taming of the Shrew* (1954) as if it took place in turn-of-the-century North America as a Wild-West farce "in which Katherine and Petruchio were both people of highly nervous temperament, essentially shy, and both afraid."[14] The specific locale was indeterminate, although San Francisco seemed a good guess to some. The general look may have suggested the turn of the century; there were those who agreed with Robertson Davies that "it had no period; it had only an atmosphere." Because of a hint in a line of the Lord spoken in the induction, Petruchio was played by William Needles as a country bumpkin, "with his trousers tucked inside his boots, his collar visibly chafing him, a cow's-breakfast hat on his head and, above all, that air of being in town for the fair."[15] Moreover, the character wore glasses and resembled Harold Lloyd; instead of behaving with the usual braggadocio associated with the role, he had an air of temerity about him that allowed him to say his bravado lines as if they went against his more modest nature. He was matched by an equally uncertain Katharina, and the effect (not to everyone's liking) was that "Katharina and Petruchio were afraid of each other."[16]

The other roles were equally original in visual conception. They included, according to Davies,

The dandified Hortensio, with his pink shirt with white collar and cuffs; Bianca, in the garments of an Edwardian flapper; the maidservants in the wedding scene (is there anything naughtier than four inches of white thigh above long black stockings?); the elegant motoring coat and grey bowler of Old Vincentio; the travel-stained "duster" of the Pedant; Petruchio's Spanish hat and cloak at the end of the play, which turned him into an advertisement for a famous brand of port.[17]

Guthrie's *All's Well That Ends Well* (1959) took many textual liberties and had the soldiers dressed "in the khaki drill tropical kit and black berets of something very like an Eighth Army Tank regiment, his court in Edwardian Styles."[18] More controversial yet was Guthrie's 1956 *Troilus and Cressida*, set in

a Merry Widow world of 1913 fashions, a period just close enough to bring home sharply . . . the futile absurdities of military heel-clicking and splendid uniforms. . . . Cressida made her first appearance in a riding kit, and Alexander became her—rather presumptuous—groom. Pandarus was a fussy old fribble . . . with neatly trimmed moustache and grey toupé, carrying field glasses and obviously just returned from the Trojan equivalent of Ascot. The Trojan heroes were hard-drinking young cavalry officers and Priam an aged Franz Josef. The Greeks became a more serious group of Prussians . . . Helen became an over-bright actress . . . and Thersites a sour-mouthed young war reporter.[19]

In the 1938 modern-dress *Hamlet,* starring Alec Guinness,

actors perched informally on wire-backed chairs and sipped Duff Gordon. When the players came, they suggested a touring company of the Benson era, and the reaction of the court was the derisive condescension of the 1930s. Ophelia's funeral, perhaps the most effective scene of the play, was entirely modern. The mourners were shown as people anonymously hidden under dripping black umbrellas. The passing of Fortinbras' army was suggested by actors, in modern military gear complete with gas masks and carbines, marching along the rear of the stage while Fortinbras . . . consulted with a sergeant who shouted orders into a field telephone.[20]

Guthrie chose modern periods for Shakespeare because he saw such means as a way of clarifying the play for a modern audience. He chose to open the Minneapolis theatre he founded in 1963 with a new modern-dress *Hamlet,* starring George Grizzard. It was designed as if taking place at a contemporary European court, the men in formal dress and the women in evening gowns. Conventional period costume often fails to convey as much about a character as can modern clothes, especially concerning such things as the time, the weather, and the occupations of the characters. Since the time of day was a crucial factor in his view of *Hamlet,* and the action from the advice to the players through Act, IV, scene iv, where Hamlet meets Fortinbras' army, takes place in one night, the clothing worn helped show this factor by presenting the characters dressing for the gala event of the play scene, only to have their garments become realistically disarrayed during the ensuing events, as would happen in real life. When Claudius' "wisest friends" were awakened late at night, their sleeping garments revealed that they had just come from bed. Guthrie also chose modern clothes to make the American actors feel more at ease than if they had to wear conventional costumes with which they had less familiarity. Props too were unconventional, including flashlights and revolvers, though candles and rapiers were employed when required.

Actually, Guthrie's modern-dress productions were in no way a contradiction of his demands for theatrical activity on a scale larger than life. He may have desired believability and ease of carriage in his actors, but he never let them forget that they were on a stage, playing the grandest characters in drama. These characters are far bolder, more colorful, and more interesting than the people we encounter in everyday life. Modern-dress costumes in a Guthrie production were never commonplace but, instead, glamorous, beautifully cut, and often strikingly elegant.

DIRECTORIAL PREROGATIVES

Guthrie belonged to the school that gave the director total freedom when staging a classic, with no compunction to bow before its inherited traditions. A director was bound to bring a subjective interpretation to the script and the result could only be one that had been filtered through his imagination, even though it may have been at complete variance with what its author had envisioned. Once created, a play was not restricted to its author's understanding of it, but was simply a prism which could reflect a myriad of interpretations according to the visions of those who chose to stage it. Faced with a Shakespeare production, a director has two options: to stage his personal impression of what the author wanted, or to stage a copy of what someone else has done. Of course, Guthrie always elected the former. To be ''faithful'' to the author was to Guthrie a non sequitur, for no one could possibly be so objective as to avoid personal interpretation. Even if a play's author were living, Guthrie would never ask him for help in understanding his play. No important drama is created with the author even vaguely aware of its meaning, since so much of the creative process is subconscious.

Since Guthrie looked on a script basically as raw material to be shaped by the director's hand, he felt no compunction about deletions or even additions where necessary. He thought that there were times when even masterpieces could be improved. Always, the reason for cuts or additions should be to make the text clearer. Some plays, like *Hamlet,* no matter how long, deserve uncut or only slightly cut productions, whereas a work like *Henry VIII* may be the victim of ruthless surgery. Guthrie was prone not only to cut but to rearrange Shakespeare, as when, in order to contribute to the contemporary coronation celebrations for King George, he altered *Henry V* in 1936 to make the king's character heroically pure. In *Hamlet* he transposed the plotting scene between Claudius and Laertes (IV, ii) to the end of the graveyard scene. He sometimes mixed dialogue from other plays into a production, as when he used material from *The Beggar's Opera* in *The Country Wife*. Not only would he add several helpful lines to a play like *All's Well That Ends Well* to clear up an obscurity in the plot, but he might even write all the adlibs for characters in crowd scenes, in order to help the actors bring an air of excitement and reality to the stage. For the 1963 *Hamlet* he wrote out pages of blank verse adlibs for the actors in the court scenes. They were not meant to be heard by the audience, but were only a tool for creating a truthful-sounding buzz of conversation as the scene developed. The following is a sample of such dialogue. (Most character names were invented by Guthrie, whose humor is evident in the lines.)

BACKLIN: Give me a merry play with songs and dances.

SLINGSBY: Agreed. I hate your melancholy plays.

BACKLIN: And poetry—don't you *hate* it?

SLINGSBY: Yes, I do.

BACKLIN: Your Aeschylus, your Sophocles and stuff.
    Let them all burn, say I, they're garbage all.[21]

THE OPEN STAGE

Guthrie's most lasting contribution to modern theatre practice was his participation in the revival of the open, or thrust, stage as an alternative to the proscenium stage. His ideas on the open stage developed slowly, beginning with his work on the thrust stage at the Festival Theatre, Cambridge. A step forward came in 1933 when he attempted to re-create the basic conditions of an Elizabethan stage at the Old Vic. Although these first attempts were not wholly successful, he continued to search for a way of producing Shakespeare at the Vic through the use of unit sets which would allow a compromise between the pictorial impositions of the proscenium and the fluid, nonillusionistic requirements of the plays. Instead of using illusionistic painted scenery, he found that far more could be suggested through the deployment of drapes, banners, scenic units, props, and costumes with carefully chosen colors and fabrics. In *Henry V,* as Thomas Turgeon describes it, the many-hued banners carried by the pages and soldiers served a number of scenic functions:

With their staffs lowered so their points touched over the stage, they became alternatively the tents of the English and of the French. Held upright, they became the gates of Harfleur. Pulled aside they indicated a change of scene, revealing actors in the central pavilion; and moving about, they were the flags of the opposing armies.[22]

Work at the Vic, despite an attempt at a forestage, was still confined largely to proscenium staging. In 1937 Guthrie had his first opportunity to see the potential of a true open stage. His presentation of *Hamlet* with Olivier was scheduled for an outdoor performance at Denmark's Elsinore Castle when rain forced the company to move indoors. The three-quarters-round stage he improvised in the ballroom of the Marienlist Hotel convinced him that such an arrangement was indeed feasible.[23] A decade later he made his first deliberate attempt at open staging when he directed a classic Scottish allegory, David Lindsay's 1540 *Satire of the Three Estates,* in Edinburgh. The audience sat around three sides of the stage, which allowed each spectator to feel as if he were taking part in a ritual.

This famous production, which became an annual event, was produced in the Assembly Hall of the Church of Scotland, a neo-Gothic structure consisting of a vast auditorium surrounded on four sides by galleries. At the heart of the space was an oblong area for the performance. On it a stage was erected. The gallery behind the stage was converted into a second level by building two sets of stairs leading up to it. An "inner below" was created by hanging curtains beneath the gallery. The Assembly Hall setup became the prototype for the more well-known open stage achievements of the fifties and sixties.

In the Assembly Hall's vast spaces, Guthrie played with color and movement in an exceptionally stirring example of pageantry. Yet he never lost sight of the dialogue's importance as the essence of drama; he knew just how to make the visual spectacle serve the playwright's words. Noteworthy of this technique was the entrance of Correction, during a static moment in which six persons were onstage

in the untidily vulnerable attitudes of sensual exhaustion. [Correction] came in . . . down one of the aisles to a *fortissimo* from the orchestra, reinforced by the Assembly Hall's organ, held in reserve for this purpose, and a visual blaze of soldiers with lances and pennons. He was Tom Fleming, looking taller than his actual six feet one and wearing grey robes in contrast to the vivid colours everywhere. While two sergeants stood guard over the twin doors under the gallery, the men-at-arms rested their lances on the platform stage and their feet on the steps leading up to it. A deep, static silence pressed down. Then Correction, speaking the beautiful Middle English lines very quietly in a rich Scottish voice, began telling us who he was. Guthrie was demonstrating what can be done by the spoken word.[24]

By the early 1950s Guthrie was persuaded that the open stage was the only acceptable solution to staging Shakespeare and other plays written before 1640. With Tanya Moiseiwitsch he applied his ideas to the design of the stage for the Festival Theatre in Stratford, Ontario. The main acting area consists of a large tongue surrounded by a horseshoe-shaped auditorium. Access to and from the tongue, or thrust, is by three steps ringing its circumference. Vomitories beneath the auditorium spill actors onto the stage or swallow them as they exit. Upstage is a permanent architectural facade with doorways at either side and a platform at the center with an inner stage beneath it. The central platform also has a gallery above. It thrusts out from the facade so that actors beneath or above the gallery can be seen from both sides of the house as well as from the front. Ten years later a similar, though less symmetrical, arrangement was designed for the Tyrone Guthrie Theatre in Minneapolis.

With the open stage there was a far greater sense of intimacy created between actor and audience than on the proscenium stage. The more densely packed the auditorium, the greater the excitement generated. The open stage is also most appropriate for a Shakespeare play, as the author had such a space in mind when he wrote his plays. Combined with a permanent architectural background, the open stage allows Shakespeare's lines to set the scene without the use of superfluous scenic elements. Nor need there be a break in the flow of the play for changes of scenery. A prime purpose of theatre to Guthrie was to transport the spectator out of the drabness of the everyday world, but not to the extent that he mistook fiction for fact and believed the scene before him to be "reality." The spectator must be made to feel that he is part of a ritual in which a regular and meaningful sequence of actions is played out for him; this can be accomplished through his awareness that he is but one of many undergoing a similar experience. Seated so that his vision encompasses both the actors before him and the spectators seated across from him, he soon recognizes his being one with the "mass-personality" attending the performance.

Guthrie discovered that producing Shakespeare on a proscenium stage too frequently forces his plays into realistic modes, even though realism is not a fitting approach for the great writer's plays. Shakespeare's flashes of realism must be accepted as part of a grander conception such as could be realized on the open stage. Here the actors would be kept moving in complex but revealing choreographic patterns, even during soliloquies. To be seen, as he must, by everyone in the auditorium, the actor dare not stand long in one position. Though masking is a potential problem, it can be alleviated by frequently shifting the grouping and by allowing the actors to stand in natural-seeming circular groups around the person or object that is the focus of the scene. Actors should be capable of expression with every part of their anatomies, even their backs, as the audience practically surrounds them in open staging. And, ultimately, the focus in such staging is generally on the total expressiveness of the group rather than the individual.

Even when Guthrie did a play on Broadway, he tried to deal with the impositions of the proscenium arch. If the play needed it, he would build a forestage into the auditorium, as he did with *Gideon.* Yet he wisely acknowledged the inappropriateness of open staging for many plays, classic and modern. A play like *The School for Scandal,* for instance, works far better behind the proscenium than on the thrust. However, his production of *The Cherry Orchard* on the open stage survived the transplant rather well. The point was not that one stage was better than the other, but that certain plays worked better on one than on the other and it was the director's task to recognize the fact.

THEATRE AS RITUAL

Another reason for Guthrie's fondness for the open stage is that it allows more people to sit in relatively close proximity to the acting area than is the case in proscenium theatres. As noted earlier, theatre performance to this director was a kind of ritual. The more intimacy established between the performers and the audience, the greater the sense of communion between the actor-priest and the audience-congregation.

Through its insistence on a nonillusionistic approach to performance, theatre could more vividly present to each audience member an image of himself and, consequently, the image of God. Just as the participants in the rite of Holy Communion do not actually believe that the priest is truly Christ incarnate, but an impersonation, an audience at a nonillusionistic performance does not assume that the actors really are the characters they are playing, but that they are the embodiment of universal human forces.

The universal forces in honor of which drama is performed are themselves aspects of divinity. Theatre continues to bear a deep relationship with religion, as in its earliest days, and though the spectator may be totally unaware of the religious forces, these operate on him subconsciously, disguised in tragedy as ethical and emotional concerns such as "enlightenment, justice, pity, and awe," while in comedy they take shape as the forces of "mirth, sex, satire, vanity, and money-making."[25]

Guthrie laid particular stress on the ritual underpinnings of tragedy, which he saw as the symbolic commemoration of the sacrificial suffering of a tragic figure. The tragic hero, be he Oedipus, Macbeth, or Willy Loman, is the priest figure whose ritual sacrifice stands for the death of a crowned king. All great tragedies are about sacrificial victims, persons who must endure great suffering in the course of the action. The audience shares in the ritual reenactment of the sacrifice, and only by its participation can the ritual be made complete.

In his productions of the Greek tragedies *Oedipus Rex* and *The House of Atreus* (Lewin's 1967 adaptation of the *Oresteia*), he made every effort to convey the ritualistic foundations of the plays. For the 1954 *Oedipus* (W. B. Yeats' version, titled *King Oedipus,* was used) at Stratford, Ontario, which became one of his most renowned productions, he examined the play's considerable use of symbolism and endeavored to bring as much of it as possible to his staging. James Mason played Oedipus in the 1954 version, and was succeeded in the 1955 revival by Douglas Campbell. Oedipus was interpreted as a sacrificial victim sharing much in common with Christ, an idea that allowed Guthrie to underscore the relation between ritual and religion in the theatre. He eschewed any sense of illusionism in the decor and acting, and collaborated with Moiseiwitsch in developing an abstract scenic scheme suggesting no specific place or time. The costumes were reminiscent of the outlines and weight of early Greek statues. All traits of individualistic personality in the actors were removed by the use of masks, with oversized ones being worn by the principal actors, and smaller ones by the fifteen chorus members. Those of the latter were highly stylized suggestions of the sorrowing masses, with exaggerated, almost grotesque, features. Oedipus' appearance contrasted strikingly in its regal grandeur. Guthrie saw in

Oedipus the Immanence of the sun god, Apollo, which led to the character's mask being golden-hued with spiky sun-rays emanating from it; these also managed to hint at Christ's crown of thorns. The behavior of the chorus toward Oedipus sometimes seemed like that of suppliants before a deity. Jocasta was masked and costumed in colors suggestive of a silver moon goddess (a choice Guthrie later rejected because it made her seem too cold and metallic), while Creon's dominant color was dark bronze. All the main characters walked on six-inch soles, like the *cothornoi* of ancient Greek tragedy, which obviously helped to make them larger than life. Their hands were covered in long-fingered gloves, thereby further accentuating their icon-like presences.

Guthrie's chorus was congratulated for the brilliance in which the formality of their dancelike movements were expertly blended with musical speech patterns that verged on song. (He attributed his success with the chorus to the unpressured rehearsal schedule allowed by the Stratford repertory system.) The overall atmosphere was dreamlike—clouds of incense filled the stage at the beginning—and highly ritualistic, much of the effect being conveyed by the incantatory style in which the dialogue was spoken.

Guthrie was responsible for numerous memorable directorial decisions, such as having Tiresias played as a man who was so closely associated with the birds he employed in his soothsaying profession that he was himself very much like a bird; by allowing Oedipus' lengthy speech to Jocasta in which he recalls the killing of Laius to be spoken as though he were in a trance; and by avoiding the realistic impression of Oedipus' gouged-out eyes by having him enter wearing a large robe of purplish crimson suggestive of blood, with his head covered by a thick veil of black fishnet. In addition, Guthrie chose to pad the normally intermissionless ninety-minute production to more standard length by introducing a break for the audience, and did so in a typically Guthrie-esque fashion: when the scene of Jocasta's prayer was concluded, she and everyone else onstage were kneeling as the silence was suddenly broken by the cheerful shout of "News! Good News!" from the Man from Corinth standing unseen at the head of one of the aisles. All the characters turned toward the source of this cry and began to rise, but as they did so the lights dimmed; when they came up again the stage was empty and the intermission had begun. The second half began with the lights dimming again and the actors returning, not to the places they were in when the first half ended, but to where they were when Oedipus had completed his confession a bit earlier. The entire scene with Jocasta was repeated, Jocasta made her prayer, and once again the Man from Corinth made his joyous entrance, but this time he was not interrupted. "By this means," writes Guthrie, "the second part . . . got off to a flying start. Actors and audience were given the moment of recapitulation to re-establish contact, re-establish something of the impetus which the first part of the play had generated."[26]

In *The House of Atreus,* which was brought from Minneapolis to Broadway after a successful run, an all-male cast played in a hieratic style, surrounded by

imposing settings and encased in huge costumes and masks. Athena was represented by an enormous movable effigy which seemed to bring the deity's
awesome presence right into the theatre.

CASTING

Like many directors, Guthrie was distrustful of the typical audition process
and preferred to work either with actors whom he had directed before or those
whom he had seen perform. He found it impossible to determine an actor's
physical appropriateness without seeing him onstage in a performance. Nor did
he trust interviews: from them only an inadequate first impression can be gained.
When forced to use the interview method, however, he could be amazingly adept
at sizing up an actor's capabilities in two to three minutes of casual conversation.
Those who worked with him in Minneapolis were struck by the director's cour-
teous manner in interviewing dozens of performers, giving none more than three
minutes and declaring it unnecessary to have them read a single line. Nor did
he take notes, keeping each actor's name and qualifications entirely in his head.

He opposed typecasting because it restricted the creative contribution of the
actor. According to Paddy Chayefsky, Guthrie cast "with an image of the whole
stage in mind, rather than one part at a time—and he casts for voice. He will
say of one, 'good, he's a tenor,' and of another, 'he's a basso!' "[27]

Guthrie's casting choices greatly determined the direction he gave a play,
especially a classic. One could often tell from the actors chosen how the play
would be interpreted. He came out against the inequities of the star system, but
being a practical theatre man, he used stars frequently. Not only did he recognize
their box-office drawing power, but also their uniqueness and capability for the
roles in which he cast them. Guthrie normally found it more interesting to work
with talented but unknown people. Norris Houghton recalled that "he would
much prefer a talented youngster whom he can mould or an old, albeit obscure,
colleague to an established star."[28]

PREPARING A PRODUCTION

Preparations for a new production began with Guthrie's reading and rereading
the script many times to discover the drama's meaning. He would sometimes
read it aloud to himself, as new values could be discovered through vocalizing
the lines. Reading scholarly writings on a play occasionally could be helpful,
but more often than not these were, to Guthrie, ineffably dull and pointless in
practical theatre terms. He once wrote of how pained he was to discover from
his research on Marlowe's *Tamburlaine* how little scholars realized of the play's
theatrical essence. None, he pointed out, saw "it as a ritual dance or [heard it]
as a kind of savage oratorio."[29] One's best ideas come forth spontaneously, but
there is danger in excessive reliance on such methods. Inspiration is only as
good as the technique which supports it.

Preblocking was done on a play-by-play basis. In general he planned his productions quite loosely before rehearsals. He began rehearsals with a flexible production plan in his head, one that could be changed at a moment's notice. He liked to work out the blocking, furniture arrangement, and other such details in the course of rehearsals, as dictated by the needs of the moment. Alec Guinness, who acted in a number of Guthrie productions, writes that

There was a spontaneity in all he did, a sort of whirlwind of activity and invention. I don't think I ever saw him consult a script or caught him with notes in his hand, all was straight off the top of his head, blessed as he was with a phenomenal memory, both visual and aural.[30]

Davies, who observed him frequently at Stratford, Ontario, in the fifties, adds:

He sets the actors to work, and as they work he improvises ceaselessly; he urges the players on to show him what they can do, and he makes use of whatever talents they bring with them, or uncover as they work. He builds up his production on the stage. His own concentration is complete and at rehearsal he is working at the very top of his form.[31]

He would have preferred to have ample time for a play to grow collaboratively with the actors during the rehearsal; however, the typical rush to get the show on usually forced him to have many of the specifics committed to paper in advance. To save time in rehearsal he liked to have prerehearsal conferences with his leading players, designers, and business managers, working out the general concept and look of the play so that all were in agreement from the start. Once rehearsals were under way, Guthrie had little patience with long-winded analytical discussions and did his best to discourage them. To him, these were all too often time-wasting and boring to the actors. If necessary, they were to be held outside of rehearsals, not in their midst.

WORKING WITH DESIGNERS

An important part of prerehearsal preparations was Guthrie's collaboration with his designers. He worked closely with them but never dictated, choosing to guide rather than coerce. He gave his designers freedom but was careful to exercise control when the designs were impractical. His favorite designer, and the one with whom he worked most intimately, was Tanya Moiseiwitsch. He even developed a ''shorthand'' method of communication with her, described by the director in the following passage:

we refer back to other things that we've done and say, ''If it were a little like this only not so black,'' and ''If this were dark black,'' and drawings are made on the backs of envelopes and half-sheets of paper of a very rough nature, and we exchange these drawings, and then the drawings give place, before any finished drawings are done, to rough models . . . and the thing is set up. . . . And if that is agreed, then the rough . . . model gives place to a tidy one . . . and the dress sketches go through a similar thing.[32]

He was cautious, however, against being fooled by a designer's drawings prepared in great realistic detail, preferring rather to have simple sketches "without any frills at all [showing] how the thing is made, what it's going to be made of and why it's being made in that particular way."[33]

According to Moiseiwitsch, Guthrie was skilled at sketching, even more so than she, and would not only work out the floor plan himself but illustrate all his other ideas through pencil drawings. This talent enabled him to make perfectly clear to his designers the entire visual scheme he required for a production. Moiseiwitsch also says that Guthrie had a fondness for "dark lovely rich surroundings," a taste which led some to call him "Rembrandtesque." He consciously chose certain artists' styles for specific productions—among these were Holbein, Van Dyck, and Franz Hals.

LIGHTING

Pageantry may have appealed to Guthrie, but his tastes in lighting were surprisingly simple. Like Bertolt Brecht, he preferred ungelled lights, believing that the color should be in the scenic decor and the costumes, appropriately illuminated. White lighting was sufficient for most stage purposes. Contrary to most modern practice, Guthrie favored the use of footlights, convinced that they were a necessity for fully lighting the actor's faces. His lighting ideas are obviously in keeping with his wish to avoid the illusion of real life onstage. He did not deny the decorative delight of atmospheric (which he called "fancy") lighting, however, and would occasionally employ it, even on the open stage. Guthrie noted that such atmospheric clichés as dimming the lights to suggest mystery or melancholy could be appropriate, but he felt it was wrong to dim the lights to suggest evening, because that was too illusionary, especially on the open stage.

REHEARSAL PERIOD

Guthrie worked in various rehearsal situations where he had from one week to two months to stage a play. A week was never enough time, especially when, as was generally the case, the same actors were performing another play in the evenings. In such cases he would be sure to work closely with the leading actor before rehearsals began, carefully dealing with the lines, movement, and look of the character, and then letting the actor take over and do what he could with it. Each play had its own specific needs regarding a rehearsal period; who was directing and who was acting in it could also affect the time required. Some plays can be rehearsed *too* much, and Guthrie was sure that he could stage *Hamlet* in two weeks if he and the lead actor were united in their approach.

As Guthrie took a serious approach to the conduct of rehearsals he abhorred anything that constituted a waste of time at them. If an actor disagreed with him, he preferred for the actor to show him what he would like to do instead of letting the actor argue a point while everyone had to listen. He therefore organized his schedule very carefully and never kept actors in attendance when they were not needed.

Similarly, he refused to lecture his company, seeking instead the briefest, most effective means of communicating his intentions. Indeed, he was famous for his clipped telegraphic style of speech, in which he would convey the essence of an idea in the most concise yet most distinct manner. Actors were astonished at how simply he could make things work for them. As Stella Adler, famed actress and teacher, remarked, "He simply gave it to you and made some theatrical suggestions. He never criticized, he didn't bother. He said, 'Go there,' and when he said 'Go there,' a miracle happened."[34]

Guthrie noted that the director's functions are diverse and, among others, may entail the responsibilities of a factory foreman, chairman of a meeting, or orchestra conductor. "He is also the . . . abbott of a monastery, and the superintendent of an analytic laboratory . . . with the patience of a good nurse, together with the voice and vocabulary of an old time sergeant major."[35] The foreman's responsibilities are to provide a proper working atmosphere, to come on time to rehearsal and to require the same of everyone else, to keep to a tight schedule, to avoid conflicts, and to keep everything running smoothly. Efficiency is his byword.

As a good chairman, the director helps create a delightful working environment and presides with goodwill over participants of varying temperaments. Rehearsals were as enjoyable and interesting as Guthrie could make them, with everyone kept active and involved. Alec Guinness declares, "His rehearsals were always stimulating, usually great fun—often too much fun, perhaps—and always something to be looked forward to. They never became stodgy or finicky."[36] Guthrie took enormous pleasure in his rehearsals and infused his own vitality and good spirits into all around him.

Almost every actor who worked for Guthrie found his rehearsals among the most refreshing of their careers. Yet Guthrie was never able to overcome one major obstacle in rehearsing: dealing comfortably with romantic scenes. He may have written of the importance of a rehearsal atmosphere in which believable love scenes could be worked on, but in point of fact usually glossed over such scenes and had the actors involved work on them alone, giving them little help in the process. Such scenes seem to have embarrassed him, though he was a married man whose personal and professional relationship with his wife, Judith, was extemely close.

Actually, some have criticized Guthrie for spending too much time on only those scenes that most interested him and leaving the less interesting ones to more or less take care of themselves, thereby creating an unevenness in production.

Guthrie's analogy of the director and the orchestra conductor is a common one. In his eyes, however, a classical actor's task in interpreting a role exceeds in difficulty that of an orchestral performer because so much of the actor's score is incomplete. Such an actor requires a good director for reinforcement of his perceptions; he does not need someone to tell him what to do.

Yet the director, more than a conductor, must exercise disciplinary control over his charges, employing "finesse" rather than "ferocity," being capable of roaring "like any sucking-dove," but aware of "when gently to tickle his patients with the velvet glove and when—at rare but terrible moments—to hand out a good sock in the eye with a mailed fist."[37] Alec Guinness observes,

New recruits were always treated with the utmost kindness and encouragement, the very old or incontinent with sympathy, but anyone in between, particularly if they were well-known personalities, was likely at some point to be verbally humiliated or reduced to anger or hysterics.[38]

At one of these "rare but terrible moments" he used the "mailed fist" on the great British star Marie Tempest, who had been misbehaving at rehearsals of Robert Morley's *Short Story* (1935). Guthrie strode down the aisle and, on reaching the stage, yelled, "Miss Tempest! Why are you being such a bitch?,"[39] a remark that immediately brought the grand dame into line and got rehearsals smoothly on the track again. Dispirited during a Stratford, Ontario, rehearsal of *The Merchant of Venice* by the mushy acting of the actress playing Jessica (Charlotte Schrager), he rushed to the stage "and reaching the actress . . . gave her a near karate blow on the bare leg and spoke in fury: 'You're feeling it, you silly little bitch! Your business is to make them feel it! . . . Do it again!' "[40] Or, as Brian Friel reports, without identifying the situation though it would seem to be at a rehearsal for the 1963 *Hamlet,* Guthrie exploded at the leading actor:

All very nice and charming what-would-mummy-say intonation! But for _____ sake you have a sword in your hand and murder in your heart! You're not a _____ Boy-Scout on _____ troop outing! You're simply _____ ing the whole thing up![41]

Davies reports:

One of these storms may impend, break and resolve itself into a dew as rapidly as the storm in the Overture to *William Tell*, but while it rages everyone quivers. This is no mere stage thunder, worked up to impress, it is genuine wrath.[42]

It is difficult to assess the reaction of actors to outbursts such as these, taken as they are out of context, though on paper they appear to be excessive. Yet most actors would have agreed that despite their sharpness, Guthrie's insults achieved their ends while rarely doing any serious damage to their recipients. This must be attributed to the man's enormous good humor, and the feeling that what he said was never meant to be taken personally. As Davies puts it, "It is clear to the whole company that though he may, at times, loathe, execrate and despise them as actors, he is genuinely cordial toward them as human beings."[43]

Guthrie's eccentricity of appearance was another of his famous traits. Brian Friel captures the Guthrie look in this description:

He comes to rehearsal usually in shirt, baggy flannels and navy tennis shoes. Because his stomach is more than slightly wayward he is constantly tugging at his trousers to keep them hoisted. This struggle undoes the bottom button of his shirt so that by the time work is well underway the actors find themselves being peeped at by his navel. . . . His eyes are calm and alert. He has a little military moustache. His hair is graying, and at times he scratches it with both hands at the same time.[44]

Throughout rehearsal he moved about restlessly, from one part of the auditorium to the other, and from the auditorium to the stage, even conducting a scene intensely as if it were an orchestral performance, "almost hurling himself bodily over the orchestra pit at moments of climax."[45] This image is not so far-fetched, as Davies declares that one of his fondest memories is of Guthrie in his Old Vic days placing his foot on the railing in front of the first row in order to "reach the stage by a startling leap over [the] abyss of the orchestra pit."[46] The procedure was often a noisy one, with Guthrie capable of an enormous assortment of approving or disapproving vocalizations, handclaps, or finger clickings. Most familiar was the thunderous handclap signal, of which Davies points out,

we quickly realize that this handclap is not really to compel attention, for he has everybody's attention the instant he speaks. Nor is it simply a mannerism. It is a sound which in itself expresses the quality of these rehearsals, their intense concentration and alertness, their incisiveness and their high nervous pitch. These handclaps seem to mark the rhythm of the work.[47]

FIRST READINGS

During the mature part of his career Guthrie rarely had his cast read a play through at the first rehearsal. He either skipped the reading entirely or had the company read for ten or fifteen minutes before setting them on their feet for the actual staging. Reading the play was a waste of time, he said, and only served to give the small-part actors a chance to show off when it was finally their turn to read. In the early years, however, he seems to have found cast readings somewhat more important. In 1932, he informed readers of the *Scottish Stage* how to conduct such a rehearsal. He said the cast was to read without moving around and then to discuss the play in great detail with the director. He felt at the time that "it is interesting and useful to have the matter threshed out and to send the cast away with a clear-cut idea of what you want them to aim at."[48]

Not only did he eventually reject cast readings, but he also came to think little of extensive talks or discussions at the first rehearsal. Nevertheless, he did sometimes use the occasion to address his company on certain crucial matters. For example, he addressed the actors in *The Three Sisters* (1963), describing to them the problems of open staging, telling them how they should be realistic but still act with larger-than-life vocal and physical dimensions, asking them to prepare emotionally for the performance by listening to chamber music, especially Beethoven quartets, and to think of the characters as musical chords.

BLOCKING AND WORKING WITH ACTORS

Blocking began as soon as possible, with the director giving rather precise directions at first to save time, though informing the actors that these could be altered later if they were found to be uncomfortable or if a better idea was forthcoming. He preferred to have his actors retain the blocking in their heads and not in notations made in their scripts. When the young Alec Guinness was noted marking down his blocking at the first rehearsal of a play, Guthrie reprimanded him for so doing, saying, in his clipped way, "Waste of time. If I've given you a good move you'll remember it; if bad, you'll forget it and we'll think up another."[49] Guthrie realized the need not only to be flexible, but also to establish a firm foundation immediately. Actors used to more leisurely methods sometimes froze at being so rapidly immersed in the business of the play, with Guthrie requiring meaningful readings of the lines even the first time they were spoken. The actors were practically rushed into playing their roles at the first rehearsal, since Guthrie wanted to clearly establish his authority at the start. He knew that he could soon let up on the reins to give the actors greater freedom in exploring their parts.

Guthrie's aim was not to dictate a performance, but to "evoke" one; too rigid a method would only hamper, not encourage, actors. Because he seemed to know so clearly what he wanted, actors felt great confidence in his technique. When he staged *Six Characters* for the Phoenix in 1955, he had to begin a week late because of another engagement. Norris Houghton ran the first week of rehearsals, but when Guthrie arrived and saw a rehearsal, he began again from scratch, working at "whirlwind speed" to redirect everything, pouring out ideas in a continual stream. He so captivated the actors by his brilliance and self-assuredness that they not only worked for five straight hours, but refused their dinner break and had someone go out for sandwiches and coffee as they continued to rehearse until midnight. Despite later changes the foundations for the production were set at this first rehearsal.

Actor after actor has testified to the freedom with which Tony Guthrie handled them. He would be very sure of what he wanted an actor to try for, but would immediately change directions if he saw the actor do something even more interesting. He was reluctant to get inside a character in working with the actor, and would, except in rare cases, instruct him in terms of pace, mood, physical business, and other technical concepts. Actors usually responded well to his offhanded way of giving them their head, and felt they were truly collaborating rather than being artful puppets manipulated by the king of puppet-masters. Guthrie's hints to actors could be so telling that they could even influence an entire career. Laurence Olivier, for one, reveals that Guthrie's merely telling him that he must love his character, no matter how repulsive, was a major turning point in his acting method. He had been very unhappy playing Sergius in Shaw's *Arms and the Man* until Guthrie gave him the key to unlocking the character's heart.

Davies provides an example of the type of stimulating imagery that could provoke an actor to do things other methods might never have achieved. During *King Oedipus* rehearsals Guthrie wanted Donald Davis as Teiresias to collapse suddenly as in a cataleptic trance. He asked the actor if he had ever seen a parrot faint, to which the actor responded that he had not. He then told Davis that parrots become so frightened by the stare of a cat that they fall forward in a dead faint. This brief lecture immediately produced the desired effect (the "Parrot faint" was how the other actors referred to it). Writes Robertson Davies,

It is not an ordinary mind which sees the connection between a bit of the vapours in a bird and the descent of divine truth upon a prophet. Yet it is this ability to see similarities between wildly dissimilar things which contributes to the imaginative insight of Guthrie's work.[50]

Guthrie's laconic manner was based on the assumption that he was working with professionals; an actor need only be told what the director wants for him to be able to find a way of doing it. If he learned that an actor was incompetent at his job, he blamed himself for having made a casting error.

Guthrie liked to have the actors learn their lines at once. In his 1932 article in the *Scottish Stage* he demanded that they should be letter perfect by the third rehearsal, even if rehearsal had to be suspended for a brief period until this was accomplished. Given a company of actors who had all their lines memorized, all the director would have to do was to have the cast continually repeat the play while he criticized and helped polish the performances. Although he may have followed a program such as this in his early career, Guthrie's later work rarely allowed him to give the actors time off from rehearsals to learn their lines. The best he could do was to demand that lines be learned immediately and hope for the best.

As Alec Guinness has observed,[51] while blocking a show Guthrie rarely looked at a script or promptbook, being too intent on watching the actors and adjusting his ideas in terms of what they were doing. In his blocking he aimed to produce a choreography of movement which would convey the emotional relationships among the characters through a subtle employment of lights, physical placement, and bodily attitudes. He emphasized that blocking is an allusive art, and not simply one of placing people where they could most readily carry out their business.

Sometimes Guthrie chose to direct by getting in among a crowd of actors and handling them at close range. At one memorable rehearsal for the last scene in *Hamlet* he walked onto the stage

and moved about as if he were a court member, shouting various comments to the combatants and to other court members. While the bouts were being played, you could see him, for instance, say something to a court lady and then give her a firm push in the direction of a guard six feet away—and she'd run to the fellow and point at the action excitedly; or he might pound a nobleman on the back as a hit was made. His physical and vocal presence *among* the cast seemed to generate even more excitement in an inherently exciting scene.[52]

It was impossible for Guthrie to describe precisely how a good performance could be evoked from an actor's conscious and subconscious self; it was some-thing that could be done, however, if the director's intuitive abilities made him the appropriate choice for the job. His own way was bound up with his personal charm and conviviality, as his offhand air immediately put actors at their ease. Apart from his occasional outbursts, he seemed to take everything in its stride, as if the work of doing a play should not create emotional cataclysms for any concerned, that it was, after all, just a play and not worth committing suicide for. When a calamity seemed imminent, he would normally encourage his cast by telling them to "Rise above it!" Yet, at least in his later years, actors held him so in awe and found his direction so effective that, despite his requests that they feel free to disagree with him, they rarely did. This proved to be a minor drawback in working with him as it put actors off and prevented meaningful discovery and debate. Many actors followed his instructions blindly, and only later—after the play had opened—did they realize how completely their own inclinations had been subordinated to his.

Guthrie was aware of the danger of a director overwhelming his actors by dint of his personal force. In his view many shows are harmed by a company's slavish adherence to the same directorial manner, as if the director were playing all the parts. Yet Guthrie himself could not escape the charge of having too strong an influence on the creative work of his actors. Shortly before his death he attempted to define his mature view of the actor-director relationship.

Absolutely I do not want him [the actor] to concede that, by virtue of my office, I am always right. That would be absurd. But I do hope he will concede me the right sometimes to be wrong; that if my point of view of a play or even of the actor's own point differs from his, then, if after reasonable argument we can reach no agreement, he must either play the part as directed, or play it in his way in another production. But this once granted, I expect the actor to feel completely free to make suggestions, to try experiments, to discuss, to argue, provided all this does not . . . take up too much of everyone's time at rehearsal; also that his suggestions and experiments do not conflict with the interest of other actors.[53]

The popular idea that a director was an autocrat who commanded actors to imitate what he demonstrated amused Tyrone Guthrie. He insisted that only the poorest, least talented actors need line readings. He wrote, "Imagine my saying to Dame Edith Evans, 'Do it this way, dear, copy me.' "[54] Nevertheless, Alfred Rossi reports that Guthrie did not hesitate to give line readings to actors in *Hamlet,* even on the first day of rehearsals, "with particular emphasis on phrasing, pauses for breath, and cushioning the 'r' sound in the middle of a word following a vowel as in 'buried.' "[55] And these directions were for important players as well as minor ones. Others who worked with Guthrie also report seeing him demonstrate, although John Gielgud is an exception in stating that he cannot recall any such approach. Davies recalls Guthrie being "right on stage with [the actors], demonstrating what he wants with broad gestures and occasional pushes and shoves, not unlike the presiding adult at a children's party." He demonstrated on a grand scale commensurate with his own great size. "There is a magnification about his gestures which," adds Davies, "I have never seen any actor successfully reproduce; nor is he meant to do so; he is expected to cut down whatever Guthrie has done to his own size."[56] Guthrie did prefer, however, to ignore demonstration in favor of exhortation and encouragement, so that the actor could find the means within himself and not by external mimicry. "Guthrie's desire is to find out what all the actors can do, and then persuade them to do it in the best possible way,"[57] notes Davies.

Finally, there came a time toward the end of the rehearsal period when Guthrie decided that it was better for him to remain silent, allow the actors to work unimpeded, and to take careful notes for delivery afterwards. At this point his notes would dwell on minor things,

but he watches all that goes on with deep concentration and the actors are strongly conscious of him. Now, more than at any previous time, they are acting *for* him, and they know if they win his approval they have succeeded, and no audience will have equal terrors for them.[58]

CONCLUSION

In his typically unconventional way, Guthrie claimed that it was perfectly honorable for an artist to borrow ideas from others and not to put too great a premium on originality. "We all learn, borrow, steal, if you like, from one another. But if this is theft, then all are thieves who have the wit to profit from other people's experience."[59] An idea he borrowed from the Austrian director Max Reinhardt, for example, was that the director at rehearsal should be a perceptive and "highly concentrated sounding board for the performance, an audience of one."[60] He should be like that ideal audience which gives and takes consistently and keeps the actor at his best throughout the play. Sir Tyrone Guthrie was an audience of one for over four hundred productions staged during a career lasting close to half a century. Few failed to recognize his genius or his eminence in an arena where the expected and the tried and true are standard fare. It is hard to take issue with an assessment such as that made over a quarter of a century ago by Laurence Kitchin that Guthrie was "the greatest director yet to emerge from the English drama."[61] His closest competitor would be Peter Brook. Two decades after Guthrie's death, his physically and artistically gigantic figure still overtops the field.

Guthrie's influence on contemporary staging has been enormous. For many directors it has become essential that each staging of a classic be a novel conceptualization, spilling over with clever directorial gimmicks and drawing attention to the director's ingenuity in making something original out of familiar material. Just as the Russian theatre of the thirties was often attacked for the infestation of "Meyerholditis," it has been possible to see the past forty years as infected by "Guthrieitis." Nor has the disease quite left us, as can be witnessed in any number of current classic stagings. But more important yet has been Guthrie's role in the popularization of the open stage, a theatrical form that now has spread throughout the world and is the dominant form in most new theatre buildings erected to house a classical repertory.

NOTES

1. Tyrone Guthrie, "10 Best for a Repertory Theatre," *New York Times* 9 November 1958, pp. 18–19.

2. James Forsythe, *Tyrone Guthrie, A Biography* (London: Hamish Hamilton, 1976), p. 219.

3. Tyrone Guthrie, "*Tamburlaine* and What It Takes," *Theatre Arts* 40 (February 1956): 86.

4. Robertson Davies, "Rehearsal—A Study in Rhythm," in Tyrone Guthrie et al., *Twice Have the Trumpets Sounded* (Toronto: Clarke, Irwin, 1954), pp. 16–17.

5. Ibid., p. 10.

6. Kenneth Tynan, *Curtains* (New York: Atheneum, 1961), p. 237.

7. Paddy Chayefsky, "Tyrone Guthrie: A Playwright's View," *Drama Survey* 3 (Winter 1963): 83.

8. Davies, "Rehearsal," p. 12.

9. Norris Houghton, "Sir Tony at the Phoenix: A Personal Memoir," *Drama Survey* 3 (Winter 1963): 88.

10. Robert Hatch, "Tyrone Guthrie: The Artist as Man of the Theatre," *Horizon* 5 (November 1963): 36.

11. Tyrone Guthrie, *A Life in the Theatre* (New York: McGraw-Hill, 1959), p. 144.

12. Guthrie, "*Tamburlaine*," p. 23.

13. T. C. Worsley, *The Fugitive Art* (London: John Lehman, 1952), p. 88.

14. Robertson Davies, "The Genius of Dr. Guthrie," *Theatre Arts* 40 (March 1956): 30.

15. Davies, "*The Taming of the Shrew*," in Guthrie et al., *Twice Have the Trumpets Sounded*, p. 34.

16. Ibid., p. 38.

17. Ibid., p. 35.

18. Laurence Kitchin, *Mid-Century Drama* (London: Faber and Faber, 1960), p. 89.

19. Roger Wood and Mary Clarke, *Shakespeare at the Old Vic, 1955–56* (London: Hamish and Hamish, 1956), n.p.

20. Thomas S. Turgeon, "The Super Artist of the Classical Revival: A Study of the Productions of Orson Welles and Tyrone Guthrie, 1936–1939" (Ph.D. diss., Yale University, 1968), p. 159.

21. Alfred Rossi, *Minneapolis Rehearsals: Tyrone Guthrie Directs "Hamlet"* (Berkeley: University of California Press, 1970), p. 43.

22. Turgeon, "The Super Artist," p. 168.

23. The story of this performance has been told in various places; an excellent recent version, by one of the participants, may be found in Alec Guinness, *Blessings in Disguise* (New York: Alfred A. Knopf, 1986), pp. 74–76.

24. Kitchin, *Mid-Century Drama*, pp. 93–94.

25. Tyrone Guthrie, *In Various Directions: A View of the Theatre* (New York: Macmillan, 1965), pp. 9, 30.

26. Tyrone Guthrie, "The Production of *King Oedipus*," in Robertson Davies et al., *Thrice the Brinded Cat Hath Mew'd* (Toronto: Clarke, Irwin, 1955), p. 160.

27. Chayefsky, "Sir Tyrone Guthrie," p. 83.

28. Houghton, "Sir Tony at the Phoenix," p. 87.

29. Guthrie, "*Tamburlaine*," p. 86.

30. Guinness, *Blessings in Disguise*, pp. 72–73.

31. Davies, "Rehearsal," p. 17.

32. Tyrone Guthrie, "Directing a Play," in *The Director in a Changing Theatre*, ed. J. Robert Wills (Palo Alto, Calif.: Mayfield, 1976), pp. 99–100.

33. Ibid., p. 100.

34. Quoted in Alfred Rossi, ed., *Astonish Us in the Morning: Tyrone Guthrie Remembered* (Detroit: Wayne State University Press, 1980), p. 111.

35. Guthrie, *A Life in the Theatre*, p. 151.

36. Guinness, *Blessings in Disguise*, p. 72.

37. Tyrone Guthrie, "Some Notes on Direction," *Theatre Arts Monthly* 28 (November 1944): 651.

38. Guinness, *Blessings in Disguise*, p. 72.

39. John Casson, *Lewis and Sybil* (London: Collins, 1972), p. 143.

40. Forsythe, *Tyrone Guthrie*, p. 255.

41. Brian Friel, "The Giant of Monaghan," *Holiday* 35 (May 1964): 95.

42. Davies, "Rehearsal," p. 14.

43. Ibid.

44. Friel, "Giant of Monaghan," p. 90.

45. Norman Marshall, "Guthrie Here, There and Everywhere: A Portrait of a Man Who Won't Sit Still," *Drama Survey* 3 (Winter 1963): 98.

46. Davies, "Rehearsal," p. 9.

47. Ibid., p. 11.

48. Tyrone Guthrie, "Producing a Play," *Scottish Stage*, February 1932, p. 320.

49. Guinness, *Blessings in Disguise*, p. 77.

50. Davies, "Rehearsal," p. 13.

51. Guinness, *Blessings in Disguise*, pp. 72–73.

52. Rossi, *Minneapolis Rehearsals*, p. 53.

53. Tyrone Guthrie, *Tyrone Guthrie on Acting* (New York: Viking, 1971), pp. 72–73.

54. Tyrone Guthrie, "An Audience of One," in *Directors on Directing*: *A Source Book of the Modern Theatre*, ed. Toby Cole and Helen Krich Chinoy, rev. ed. (Indianapolis: Bobbs-Merrill, 1963), p. 249.

55. Rossi, *Minneapolis Rehearsals,* p. 61.

56. Davies, "Rehearsal," p. 9.

57. Ibid., p. 10.

58. Ibid., p. 18.

59. Guthrie, *A Life in the Theatre*, p. 82.

60. Guthrie, "An Audience of One," p. 255.

61. Kitchin, *Mid-Century Drama*, p. 92.

CHRONOLOGY

1900   born in Tunbridge Wells, Kent, England

1923   receives degree from Oxford University

1924   first play directed, *The Triumph of Death*, Barn Theatre, Oxted

1924–26 BBC radio in Belfast, Ireland

1926–28 Scottish National Players, Glasgow

1929–30 Festival Theatre, Cambridge: *Naked*; *All for Love*; *Six Characters in Search of an Author*; *Gentleman Dancing Master*; *The Rivals*; *The Machine Wreckers*; *Marriage*; *Warren Hastings*; *Volpone*; *The Cherry Orchard*; *A Doll's House*; *Rosmersholm*; *Measure for Measure*; *The Merry Wives of Windsor*; *Lady Audley's Secret*; *Tobias and the Angel*; *Iphigenia in Tauris*

1930   marries Judith Bretherton

1931   Westminster Theatre, London: *The Anatomist*

1932   Lyric Theatre, London: *Dangerous Corner*; Westminster: *Love's Labour's Lost*; *Follow Me*

1933   Shakespeare Memorial Theatre, Stratford-on-Avon: *Richard II*

1933–34 Old Vic, London: *Twelfth Night*; *The Cherry Orchard*; *Henry VIII*; *Measure for Measure*; *The Tempest*; *The Importance of Being Earnest*; *Love for Love*; *Macbeth*

1934   Wyndham's Theatre, London: *Sweet Aloes*; His Majesty's Theatre, London: *Mary Read*

1936   Morosco Theatre, New York: *Call It a Day*; Booth Theatre, New York: *Sweet Aloes*

1936–37 Old Vic: *Love's Labour's Lost*; *The Country Wife*; *Hamlet* (also at Elsinore, Denmark); *Twelfth Night*; *Henry V*

1937   Lyceum Theatre, London: *Paganini*; Queen's Theatre, London: *School for Scandal*

1937–38 Old Vic: *Pygmalion*; *Measure for Measure*; *Richard III*; *A Midsummer Night's Dream*; *Othello*

1938   Vaudeville Theatre, London: *Goodness, How Sad!*

1938–39 Old Vic: *Trelawney of the "Wells"*; *Hamlet; A Midsummer Night's Dream*;
She Stoops to Conquer (codirected with Frank Napier); *An Enemy of the People;
The Taming of the Shrew*

1941 Old Vic: *King John* (codirected with Lewis Casson); *The Cherry Orchard*

1943 Old Vic: *Abraham Lincoln; The Russians*

1944 Old Vic: *Guilty; Hamlet* (codirected with Michael Benthall); Liverpool Playhouse Repertory, Liverpool: *Uneasy Laughter* (*He Who Gets Slapped*)

1944 Savoy Theatre, London: *The Last of Mrs. Cheyney*

1945 Liverpool Playhouse Repertory: *The Alchemist*; Old Vic: *Peer Gynt*

1946 Old Vic: *Cyrano de Bergerac*; Booth: *He Who Gets Slapped*

1947 Duchess Theatre, London: *He Who Gets Slapped*; Habimah Theatre, Tel-Aviv:
Oedipus Rex

1948 Broadway Theatre, New York: *Oedipus Rex* (Habimah production) (also at
Helsingfors Theatre, Helsinki); Assembly Hall, Edinburgh: *The Satire of the
Three Estates*; Sadler's Wells, London: *The Beggar's Opera*

1949 Assembly Hall: *The Gentle Shepherd*; Helsingfors: *The Taming of the Shrew*;
Shakespeare Memorial: *Henry VIII*

1950 Shakespeare Memorial: *Henry VIII*; Gate Theatre, Dublin: *Hamlet*; Assembly
Hall: *The Atom Doctor*; *Queen's Comedy*; Old Vic: *The Miser*; St. James'
Theatre, London: *Top of the Ladder*

1951 Lyric, Hammersmith, London: *The Passing Day*

1951–52 Old Vic: *Tamburlaine the Great*; *A Midsummer Night's Dream*; *Timon of Athens*

1953 Old Vic: *Henry VIII*; inaugurates Festival Theatre, Stratford, Ontario: *Richard
III*; *All's Well That Ends Well*

1954 Assembly Hall: *The Matchmaker* (then Haymarket Theatre, London); Festival:
Taming of the Shrew; King Oedipus

1955 Festival: *The Merchant of Venice*; *King Oedipus*; Gaiety Theatre, Dublin: *The
Bishop's Bonfire*; Assembly Hall: *A Life in the Sun*; Assembly Hall; Royale
Theatre, New York: *The Matchmaker*; Phoenix Theatre, New York: *Six Char-
acters in Search of an Author*

1956 Old Vic: *Troilus and Cressida*; Winter Garden, New York: *Tamburlaine the
Great*; Martin Beck Theatre, New York: *Candide*; Winter Garden: *Troilus and
Cressida* (Old Vic company)

1957 Belasco Theatre, New York: *The First Gentleman*; Festival: *Twelfth Night*;
Phoenix: *Mary Stuart*; *The Makropolous Secret*

1958 Belfast: *The Bonfire*

1959 Shakespeare Memorial: *All's Well That Ends Well*; Booth: *The Tenth Man*

1960 Phoenix: *H.M.S. Pinafore*; Martin Beck: *Love and Libel*

1961 London: *A Time to Laugh*; Phoenix: *The Pirates of Penzance*; Plymouth Theatre,
New York: *Gideon*; knighted by Queen Elizabeth II

1962 Old Vic: *The Alchemist*

1963 inaugurates Tyrone Guthrie Theatre, Minneapolis: *Hamlet*; *The Three Sisters*

1964   Guthrie: *Henry V*, *Volpone*; University of Minnesota: *Six Characters in Search of an Author*

1965   Guthrie: *Richard III*; *The Cherry Orchard*

1966   Bristol Old Vic: *Measure for Measure*; Alvin Theatre, New York: *Dinner at Eight*

1967   Guthrie: *The House of Atreus; Harper's Ferry*; National Theatre, London: *Tartuffe; Measure for Measure*

1968   National: *Volpone*

1969   Guthrie: *Uncle Vanya*

1971   Phoenix Opera Group, Brighton: *The Barber of Seville*; dies in Ireland.

Margaret Webster

(1905–1971)

Since its inception, the directing profession has been male-dominated. A few outstanding female directors have made their mark, but they have done little to alter the traditional imbalance. Gender, however, was only one anomaly in Margaret Webster's career. Even more unusual was the nature of her repertory. She chose to work primarily in the commercial world of Broadway, but rarely with what one thinks of as commercial fare. Her greatest successes were not with modern comedies and musicals, nor were they with the work of serious new playwrights. Instead, Webster's fame accrued from a series of outstanding Shakespearean revivals that, more than in the career of any other director, made the Bard a potent box-office commodity.

EARLY YEARS

Of all the directors discussed in these volumes, only Margaret (''Peggy'') Webster came from theatrical stock. She was the daughter of two acclaimed British actors, Dame May Whitty and Ben Webster. Born in New York in 1905 while her parents were on an American engagement, she represented the fifth generation of theatre artists in the family line. Her education and upbringing took place in England where she attended Queen Anne's, a ''public school,'' in Caversham.

Acting came naturally to her, and she played several parts in amateur theatricals during her childhood years. From Edy Craig, daughter of the great actress Ellen Terry and sister of designer-director Gordon Craig, she learned the rudiments of theatre art, from stage direction to lighting, costumes, and stagecraft.

Deciding not to continue her formal education, Webster turned down an opportunity to attend Oxford in order to travel to Paris. In her memoirs, she emphasized that a successful theatrical career required nothing but talent, luck, and perseverance: a college degree in theatre was not a passport to success.[1] For a time she studied acting at London's Etlinger Dramatic School, which her mother managed from 1921. Here the sixteen-year-old Webster met a young amateur actor, Maurice Evans, whose group rented the school's small theatre with the proviso that Webster be cast in the title role of their production of *Major Barbara*. Later, Evans would play an enormous part in her career.

Webster's first professional acting job came in 1924, when she played a member of the chorus in *The Trojan Women,* starring Sybil Thorndike, whose husband, Lewis Casson, directed. An active career as an actress in repertory—including highly influential seasons with Ben Greet and at the Old Vic—and in West End commercial vehicles ensued. Webster turned to directing in 1933 during the long run of *Richard of Bordeaux,* in which she was appearing with John Gielgud. Her work at the time was primarily with amateurs; among her mountings was *The Merchant of Venice* at a girl's school as well as a number of modern plays for other groups. In addition, she gained valuable analytical experience while serving as a judge of numerous British Drama League Festival competitions.

In 1934, while she was acting in *Queen of Scots* in London, she received her first salary as a director for the staging of a major amateur outdoor pageant version of *Henry VIII* for the Women's Institutes of Kent, with a cast of eight hundred women employed in the final baptism scene. The show was a vast undertaking, especially given the insufficient time allowed for rehearsals. The experience of handling huge crowds proved of inestimable value years later when she put on operas at New York's Metropolitan Opera House. Unbelievable as it may sound, she attempted to give each participant in the pageant a sense of individuality as a character. She would tell a player, for example,

You are a silversmith, your son is apprenticed to a shoemaker, you are in very good circumstances, but the taxation started by Cardinal Wolsey and his policy in domestic affairs seem to you very hard. You are, consequently, against him as a chairman and a statesman.[2]

It became one of Webster's artistic credos to insist that everyone onstage, no matter how many there were or how tiny their role, take an active part in the performance. This belief eventually led her to write out all adlibs for background actors, much as Tyrone Guthrie and Max Reinhardt did. These adlibs were not to be heard by the audience, but were to blend with all the others, creating the impression of life on the stage.

During the 1935–36 period she staged nine different productions for small noncommercial groups devoted to revivals and tryouts of new plays; several of these were for Sunday societies, groups that—using professional actors and facilities—were devoted to putting on Sunday evening performances for their members. Famed actress Flora Robson acted in one such presentation of *The Lady from the Sea* under Webster's direction. It was while directing a South African play in this season that Webster mastered the fundamentals of stage lighting technique. Ultimately she became a skilled lighting designer and executed the lighting for many of her own productions.

Webster did not at first allow directing to prevent her from continuing to take acting roles, and she remained an active performer on the London stage in other directors' plays. Even after she began to gain a reputation as a director, she did not abandon acting, although she preferred to take supporting roles in plays for which she herself was responsible.

RICHARD II

Webster's first commercial directing assignment in London was Keith Winter's warmly approved period piece, *Old Music* (1937), designed by Rex Whistler, and with a cast including the as yet unknown Greer Garson. She was then invited by Maurice Evans, who had been making a name for himself as an exciting Broadway star, to come to New York and direct him in a revival of *King Richard II*. Evans had so impressed wealthy producer Joseph Verner Reed that the latter had magnanimously presented him with a check for $35,000 to do a revival of the play, in which Evans in 1935 had caused a stir at London's Old Vic. The choice of *Richard II,* which deals with a king's abdication, made especially good sense because the news had just broken of King Edward VIII's decision to abdicate in order to marry commoner Wallis Simpson. Webster also intended to play the duchess of York, which she had played under Harcourt Williams' direction at the Old Vic in the 1929–30 season, with John Gielgud as the king; she eventually cut the character's scenes, however, believing them to be later accretions; she did not appear in the production. Sets and costumes were in the hands of another Briton, David Ffolkes, who had done the costumes for Evans' Old Vic performance. Evans and Ffolkes already had planned the staging of the play (Evans claims the production was "ready-made" for Webster, including the cuts), but Webster changed a great deal according to her own ideas. She and Evans developed a close working relationship; the actor's participation in the production amounted to near collaboration. Evans kept his mouth shut during the rehearsals but met privately with Webster during their lunch break and every evening, going over all that had been accomplished that day. He declares as well that it was he who established what the following day's staging would entail.[3]

Richard II had not been seen in New York since Edwin Booth's 1878 production; its last notable American showing had been Booth's three performances in 1884 Chicago. The Webster-Evans version, staged at the St. James, was an immediate success and ran for 132 performances followed by another 38 after the summer break; the total of 171 established a long-run record for the play.

Ffolkes' set was an excellent solution for dealing with the play, Webster found, although she thought an audience in the 1970s would find it "cumbersome."[4] It employed a small apron built over the orchestra pit, and a permanent arrangement of pillars and arches. Entrances could be made in the dark from the pit onto the forestage. A traveler curtain was used as masking for scene changes while some scenes were played downstage of it. The stage gave itself admirably to the swift playing of Shakespeare, especially when compared to the more unwieldy methods then employed.

New York audiences were seeing their first example of what would become Webster's unique pictorial approach to Shakespeare. Sparse for their day, her productions stressed the values to be gained from suggestive, yet beautiful, sets, and costumes. She acknowledged that *Richard II* was a play greatly in need of the visual excitement that a proper medieval environment could provide, with banners waving and heraldry abundant, but a fairly low budget forced her to use costumes salvaged from the recent New York production of *Richard of Bordeaux*. Ffolkes took the Motley-designed garments and touched them up to match his and Webster's conceptions.

Webster noted that in doing this play, the director's major problem is to get through the first half in which Richard is seen more as a reflection of the behavior of the other characters than as a presence himself. When he emerges in full form "with the armory of weakness, the gentleness of defeat, and the pure gold of the poetry in which he speaks," he will be sure to carry the audience with him. Until then, the director must develop the impact of the other roles, to "use them in their just proportion, blend and balance their component contributions so that they carry Richard lightly upon their shoulders and never seem to be doing so." Once this has been solved, the actor of Richard will carry the burden and the director "will do no more than regulate the tempo of the orchestral accompaniment."[5]

This then unfamiliar play came upon New York audiences—and those of many other cities on its extensive national tour—as if it were a virtually new work. Alan Downer wrote vividly of how Webster's production gripped the spectator from the moment the curtain rose. Especially noteworthy were her crowd scenes.

On the scene swept Richard and his court, engulfing the stage in a tidal wave of color and movement. The rhythm of the whole was established at the start. Spear carriers and mute courtiers were not hired from street corners, thrust into unfitted costumes, and instructed at the last minute by the stage manager, driven on stage to stalk self-consciously to plug a gap in the stage picture. They were given characters, reactions, even carefully muffled lines, and they were rehearsed to move with that sweep-and-dive which displays the costume . . . maintaining the tempo and rhythm at times when the principal characters had nothing to do but make obscure comments on an obscure situation.[6]

Richard II introduced Webster to the frustrations directors often have to face and the compromises they must make when dealing with the Broadway stagehands' union. The high costs of extra union help forced her to make many alterations in her staging so that actors had to be employed as pages to move small stools in shifts, or else the stools would have to be omitted and the actors forced to sit on platform edges or stand. She felt that such restrictions, despite the stimulating challenge they represented, could ultimately ruin a production.

Evans and Webster had hoped to produce a classical repertory program on Broadway, but *Richard II*'s long run forced their plan to be scrapped. She would, however, return to the idea of repertory on Broadway and achieve some memorable, if short-lived, results in this vein.

Webster's career continued to develop in America. After her 1937 production of *Old Music*, eighteen years were to lapse before she worked again in England. Her next New York venture was a play called *Young Mr. Disraeli* (1937), which closed after only six performances. New plays were never to be her forte; she staged slightly more than a dozen after *Old Music,* but none were significant successes. One of the few which managed a decent run (111 performances) was *Family Portrait* (1939), a religious drama about Christ and his family. Judith Anderson played Mary to Webster's Mary Magdalene.

HAMLET

Between *Richard II* and *Family Portrait* came two more Shakespeare mountings, *Hamlet* (1938) and *Henry IV (I),* both of which were successful financially and artistically. Evans starred in each, playing the title role in the former and Falstaff in the latter. *Hamlet,* produced in its entirety, came to be known as the "uncut" *Hamlet*; it lasted three hours and thirty-eight minutes. The performance began at 6:30 P.M., ran until 9:10 P.M., when an hour's break was taken, and then concluded around 11:15 P.M. Despite its great length, most critics said the performance seemed to be over in half the time. This was not Evans' first uncut *Hamlet,* as he had starred in a similar production at the Old Vic in 1935.

Evans claims to have worked diligently on preparing the production for six months and to have been responsible for almost every artistic choice made for it, including the sets and incidental music.[7] Webster—who never mentions Evans' research nor suggests that she herself was anything but the boss—points to the enormous amount of effort *she* put into the preparations.[8] She read everything she could about the play, seeking answers as to its proper period, the degree of realism to be encouraged in the decor and acting, and the nature of the characters. She later came to feel that too conscientious a study of the many writings on the great tragedies (*Hamlet, Othello, King Lear,* and *Macbeth*) would only end in confusing a director, and that one's safest bet would be a study of the plays themselves. Supported by an inspired actor—a genius—one "whose spiritual power enables him to make of himself the medium for a greater power," the director will provide for his cast a production scheme which seeks from the play all the power, passion, pace, and poignancy of expression with which their author infused it. "If the production is planned and patterned to Shakespeare's measurements, it will hold in the theatre under a diversity of different psychological interpretations" because of the director's universality of treatment.[9]

The director must make the story come alive, for the story is what Shakespeare started with. The playwright and his audiences found nothing vague about *Hamlet*. The figure of the prince only began to emerge as problematic in the mid-eighteenth century. Seen in their totality, Hamlet's ambiguities fall away, and he and his behavior become much clearer than one might have thought. The uncut treatment also brings out the fullness of Rosencrantz and Guildenstern, and makes their relationship to the plot valid and interesting. The balance of the entire play is restored through the revelation of the just proportions with which Shakespeare so expertly crafted it. All the characters become three-dimensional and real.

Webster wanted to discover *Hamlet* organically and not merely copy the devices of other productions. But she also recognized the value of traditional business and was willing to use it when necessary. Novelty for novelty's sake held no special charms for her. Finding the written scholarship unsatisfying from a practical point of view, she became aware that the text itself had to hold the answers. She studied the first folio and second quarto editions closely and found herself immersed in the historical and academic conflict raging regarding these versions. Her ultimate decision was to make her choices on the basis of her experience as actress and director. Thus she came to favor the first folio with the inclusion of its omitted passages, although she later regretted not using the scene sequence of the first quarto (the "bad quarto") which, in her opinion, has a more logical placement of the "To be or not to be" speech.[10] Evans permitted her full control over textual decisions and was satisfied with her decision to take an intermission after the "To be or not to be" scene that ends with Claudius' remark, "Madness in great ones must not unwatched go" (Act III, scene i).

Webster wanted her production of *Hamlet* to reach audiences in simple human terms:

It was our intention to bring the play close to its hearers, even to lead them by inference to believe that in this palace of Elsinore people led everyday lives much like their own, ate and slept and dressed and listened to music . . . Behind this facade of familiar things moves the spiritual pulse and emotional conflict of the play.[11]

The decorative scheme for the production avoided the choices made in recent Broadway *Hamlet*s by John Gielgud and Leslie Howard, the former having chosen the James I period and the latter having opted for a Viking look. Instead, the play's lusty Elizabethan flavor was attempted through a Tudor approach to costumes and sets. The ground plan was arranged to approximate the principles of the Elizabethan stage, including a forestage that allowed for entrances from the house, and a raised gallery at the rear. The latter was especially effective in the scene where Gertrude, Claudius, and Polonius see Hamlet approaching while reading a book; instead of having them view him coming from somewhere in the wings, they were able to observe him as he entered from the "inner above." A minimum of props and furnishings allowed the action to proceed without delaying scene shifts, but Webster's prediliction for establishing locales clearly may have gone too far when she allowed a room at Polonius' house to be conveyed through a fireplace and a window with a geranium. She also seems to have erred by having Ophelia's funeral depicted with piled-up snow, despite the text's suggestion of warmer weather.

Hamlet was seen as an extroverted young man, vigorous, masculine, and prone to action. He was quite unlike the conventional, morbid, melancholic Dane of so many other productions. Also untraditional was Hamlet's scene with Ophelia. As John Mason Brown described it,

By postponing Hamlet's glimpse of the hidden king and Polonius until "Where's your father?" Mr. Evans and Miss Webster change the whole meaning and value of "Get thee to a nunnery." In their hands it ceases to be the usual bitter, almost hysterical cry of rage. It becomes a tender proclamation of love, for Mr. Evans speaks the speech in a voice heavy and sweet and with affection. His arms are around Ophelia, his head is buried in her bosom. His one pathetic hope seems to be to protect her from the world full of sinners he has been forced into knowing.[12]

Claudius (Henry Edwards) was not played as an outright villain, but rather benignly, with a feeling of honesty and uprightness; he was clearly attracted to Gertrude (Mady Christians). She in her turn was appealing and sensual, but innocent of her husband's deeds. Her vanity was nicely communicated when she tried on an assortment of scarves while waiting for the embassy from England. Ophelia (Katherine Locke) did not appear as the usual lunatic in makeup and nightgown, and gave no hint of her impending insanity.

A perennial problem for interpreters of *Hamlet* is why the king does not notice the accusation performed by the dumb show, but only reacts to the playlet when it is performed with dialogue. Webster devised an interesting solution to the problem, described here by Downer:

Miss Webster's curtain arose to a great pounding of hammers revealing the players hard at work erecting a small stage for their performance. Here Hamlet addressed them on their art, then, as Gertrude and Claudius entered for the performance, stepped behind the curtain for a quick run-through before the play began. To anyone familiar with actors it was the most natural thing in the world to see this nervous conning of lines and last-minute brushing up in the details of the action. Claudius spoke his lines at the same time, but the audience paid little attention to him. They were too busy observing the fascinating preparations on the little stage.[13]

So popular was *Hamlet* in its full-length production that—apart from a pair of matinees during the first week of the run—a shortened version planned to succeed it never materialized. The uncut play proved much easier on the leading actor than shorter treatments because of the author's careful placement of scenes, during which Hamlet could be offstage resting. The production ran for 96 performances and then enjoyed a return engagement in 1939 of 40 more showings in a somewhat revised version.

HENRY IV (I)

While *Richard II* had been touring Webster and Evans began preparing a
production of *King Henry IV (I),* and rehearsed it with the *Richard* company.
They managed to give it two matinee performances in Philadelphia before shelfing
it to await Broadway production after their mounting of *Hamlet.* Once the way
for its showing had been cleared—it opened nine days after *Hamlet* closed—the
interests of economy were served via the resuscitation of the *Richard II* costumes
and sets, reworked for the new production. Many of the *Hamlet* actors remained
with Webster and Evans for the new play.

Once again, the physical appearance of Ffolkes' sets and costumes was a
combination of Elizabethan principles and modern pictorialism. Webster acknowledged later that the scenery may have been too obvious, but pointed out
that a work like *Henry IV* profits from a sense of spectacle, as do Shakespeare's
other history plays. Too bare a stage proves tiresome to the eyes. For *Henry IV,*
a drama brimming with action, there is much justification for heraldry and
pageantry.

Webster took several textual liberties with the script; her most obvious revision
was the placement of a trimmed-down version of the first Justice Shallow scene
from *Henry IV (II)* where Shakespeare's Act IV, scene ii normally occurs—the
scene about Falstaff and his recruits. Few appear to have noticed the transposition.
In his autobiography, Evans takes credit for the idea.[14]

Henry IV represented another triumph for Webster's detailed realism. She
made Shakespeare popular by making his characters as familiar as if they were
people the spectators might actually know. So lifelike was the behavior she
created for them that critics accused her of domesticating the playwright. One
favorite technique was to cover up long-winded and potentially dull passages
with a plethora of realistic activity. The audience was kept alert by characters'
"drinking, nose-blowing, turning the pages of a book, knitting, or simply [by
the director's] juggling the non-speaking actors for a better stage picture when
the big punch comes."[15]

MINI-SHAKESPEARE

An unusual project now turned up on the director's horizon. She agreed to
stage four Shakespeare plays in stripped-down, forty-minute versions at the 1939
New York World's Fair at Flushing Meadows. The space built for the shows
was called the Old Globe Theatre; it was a small theatre modeled after Shakespeare's Globe. A similar idea had been successful at an earlier World's Fair,
and although Webster did so with trepidation, she adapted *The Taming of the
Shrew*, *A Midsummer Night's Dream*, and *As You Like It* for this undertaking.
Her production of *The Comedy of Errors* used an adaptation by Thomas Wood
Stevens. Lehman Engel provided the music and David Ffolkes the decor.

A fiasco developed when the money promised to produce the plays failed to materialize. No funds were available to pay for costumes, musicians, or even the theatre and pavilion. The theatre that was built was completely inadequate, and the plays were produced under extremely disorganized conditions. Regardless of these obstacles, however, Webster managed to put on all the plays with a modicum of artistic success.

SOME UNHAPPY EXPERIENCES

Webster's next Broadway outing would have been Sidney Howard's *Madam, Will You Walk?* (1939); however, the show was marked by bad luck. Howard was killed in an accident on his farm during the rehearsal period, and star George M. Cohan proved badly miscast in the lead. The play opened out of town and folded there as well.

At about this time Webster accepted a contract to go to Hollywood, where she was to learn the film business and eventually get to direct movies. The experience was abortive, though instructive, and she never did get to make a film. She left Hollywood when it became apparent that she would not have the freedom to be in New York whenever she chose. An interesting chance to direct a film came along in the 1950s, but by then she had been sufficiently smeared by the innuendos of the infamous House Un-American Activities Committee hearings under Senator Joseph McCarthy for the offer to be withdrawn. The movie, a biography of the great American Shakespearean star Edwin Booth, starring Richard Burton, was made by someone else.

Another unhappy experience was that of directing *Twelfth Night* with Helen Hayes and Maurice Evans for the Theatre Guild in 1940, shortly after Webster returned from Hollywood. Evans had absolutely no say in the direction, which was entirely Webster's responsibility. She saw the play's main directorial problem as how to combine effectively its robust plot and characters with an atmosphere of fragility and evanescence. She felt she failed to strike the proper balance and thereby damaged the production. Having little control over the selection of her collaborators may have been partly responsible. The production period was rife with difficulties, as the Guild's methods struck Webster as disorganized and destructive to her needs.

Twelfth Night revealed Webster's occasional tendency to crib ideas from other directors. She openly admitted, for example, to stealing Michael Chekhov's conception for his Habimah Theatre presentation in which the conspirators carried around little potted palms and plunked them down to hide behind when necessary. She pointed out that when enough of this stealing continued it became "tradition."[16] Although she would have liked her own promptbook staging protected by copyright, she considered it a compliment to find her ideas used in another director's work.

Twelfth Night, despite its hassles, succeeded in delighting audiences with its comic verve. It contained lots of songs, pratfalls, and other farcical behavior. Malvolio's speech was a genteel cockney, and a black child, dressed as a page and carrying a pink parasol, followed him about. The stage was continually alive with business, and the audience erupted into laughter frequently, although more often at Webster's staging than at Shakespeare's comedy.

The Theatre Guild also sponsored Webster's next production, Tennessee Williams' *Battle of Angels* (1940) with Miriam Hopkins; this play was later revised and is now known as *Orpheus Descending*. Webster's respect for the Guild's great success continued to be tempered by her distaste for their methods, especially their indecisiveness and poor taste in casting. Also highly annoying was the Guild's demand for immediate results from its actors. Webster hated rushing performers; they needed time to grow and had to be handled with patience. The Guild, however, would often fire an actor if results were not apparent at once.

Williams was an unknown playwright in 1940, but Webster saw in him a poetic talent worth nurturing. She prepared for the production by visiting the author's hometown with him in order to absorb the local atmosphere and meet his friends, who were reflected in the play. A language-oriented director, Webster encouraged Williams but failed to direct his play effectively. It closed after a disastrous Boston tryout. The drama's physical demands, including a conflagration which almost smoked the audience out of the theatre, and a structurally flawed drama smoldering with sexuality, were among the causes of the play's demise.

THE EXPERIMENTAL THEATRE

Webster was a powerful advocate for any type of training opportunity that would develop fully rounded actors. She fought union restrictions which opposed actors becoming involved in nonpaying, educational productions; these offered actors the chance to play roles which would rarely come their way under the normal course of events. A system of such productions performed by Sunday societies in England had long provided a workable outlet of this sort, and Webster saw no reason for it not to work in the United States. Actors were too often out of work and bored by inactivity; they needed not only something to occupy their time, but a situation that would encourage the enhancement of their talents. Webster's constant efforts to solve this dilemma led to her establishment in 1941 of the Experimental Theatre, backed by the actor's union, Equity. The theatre planned to do a mixture of new plays and classics, using personnel ranging from stars to beginners.

Euripides' *The Trojan Women,* in Gilbert Murray's translation, was the first production. Webster directed it and starred as Andromache; her mother played Hecuba. This casting led to sharp criticism, especially by Equity, which tried to invoke its rules against the use of aliens. Webster defended her choices on the grounds that British actors were more successful than Americans at the classics, because so few training opportunities for the latter existed. Had she followed the logic of her reasoning, she would have realized that just such training opportunities as she created with the Experimental Theatre were those needed by American actors. There was clearly a confusion of purposes in the project at the outset.

The production was staged at Broadway's Cort Theatre, in front of the set for *Charley's Aunt,* which was masked by black velour curtains. Webster used Euripides to comment on the contemporary situation in Europe by incorporating an unsubtle new prologue written by Robert Turney concerning the Nazi attack on Rotterdam. The modern-dress costumes, barren decor, and overly realistic acting style clashed with the classical rhetoric of the translation and led to mostly unfavorable responses from the press. The Experimental Theatre did two more plays before expiring. Its noble example served to illustrate the need for such institutions; it was largely owing to its spadework that the American National Theatre and Academy (ANTA) was developed, as well as the Equity Library Theatre. In fact, the Off- and Off-Off-Broadway movements in general owe a debt to Webster's pioneering work. From 1942 to 1952 Webster, as a member of Equity Council, fought to establish a noncommercial Off-Broadway theatre and to convince the other theatrical unions to cooperate in its creation.

MACBETH

In 1941 Webster's Shakespeare production was *Macbeth,* starring Judith Anderson and Maurice Evans, and designed by Samuel Leve (sets) and Lemuel Ayers (costumes). (During the interim she had staged a play called *Viceroy Sarah* as a summer stock production starring her famous mother.) In conceptualizing *Macbeth* (she had played Lady Macbeth at the Old Vic) she was determined to emphasize the play's qualities of evil and witchcraft, a view slightly at odds with Evans' own idea of the play as a melodrama for two stars with the witches being a mere plot device designed to start up the action. She, too, saw the play as a melodrama but could not so easily dismiss the evil hags. This play has no villain, she declared, but in it the force of evil is so prevalent that it becomes "a protagonist in its own right."[17] How to evoke this force is the director's principal difficulty. As the action marches on and the atmosphere of terror grows thicker, the director must create a harmony of effect, although the witches are the only concrete manifestations of the evil powers motivating the protagonists. To present the witches effectively is a very difficult directorial task. Modern audiences no longer believe, as did Shakespeare's public, in the existence of such creatures. Somehow the witches' evil presence must be evoked without excessively literal methods. The play as a whole must project this presence so that the witches become a part of the pattern and not an aberration from it. Ultimately the director's fundamental materials are the play's characters and their actions—the revelation of human beings in conflict.

A limited number of cuts were made in the text, including the Hecate scene and Macbeth's fight with young Siward; moreover, the business of Macduff's entering with Macbeth's head was likewise blue-pencilled and replaced by Macduff forcing Macbeth over the battlements.

The production Webster staged was less successful than her other Shake-spearean projects, and she candidly expressed her dissatisfaction with its heav-iness and lack of spirit and mystery. Her greatest displeasure came from the opening scene, in which there were

bagpipes and drums (real, live music!), Duncan's army filing across the front of the stage, behind them a translucent backdrop of stormy sky, the clouds reforming into the shadows of the three witches, their couplets of doom (over an echo mike) whispering through the martial music, fading out as King Duncan spoke the opening line and the blood-spattered soldier reeled onto the stage and died at his feet.[18]

In her memoirs Webster gives some insights into her working relationship with Judith Anderson. Both had played Lady Macbeth before, and Anderson had previously worked under Webster in *Family Portrait*. Nevertheless, Webster had to defer to Anderson in various matters of role interpretation. She did not always agree with the star, but usually gave in to her ideas. Webster did manage to talk Anderson out of the latter's desire to have at least one scene in which she was seen in bed with Macbeth. She had to wait for Anderson to ask for her specific opinion before she would offer it. Such a deferential attitude of director to actor is unique among the artists of this book. Webster was never the totally powerful autocrat; often she let her leading players interpret their roles with great creative leeway—even when she desperately wanted to see the role done oth-erwise. In *Macbeth* the staging of the sleepwalking scene was based on Webster's ideas, but the method of execution was Anderson's. Webster directed the scene as a repetition of the action of the murder scene, to point out that Lady Macbeth cannot shake the horrible events from her mind. As Anderson described it, Lady Macbeth

enters through the same door, brings her candle and sets it down in the same place. She goes through the motion of taking the daggers, recalls fragments of what she thought that night, and in the end she goes out the door by which she left after the murder.[19]

Before returning to Shakespeare, Webster staged two foreign war plays in 1942 and 1943, but both were failures. *Flare Path* was a Royal Air Force play by Terence Rattigan. Its major significance lies in its having introduced Alec Guinness to American audiences. Janet and Philip Stevenson's *Counterattack* had eighty-five performances, considerably more than *Flare Path*'s fourteen, but not enough to pay its expenses.

OTHELLO

Webster's next production more than satisfied its investors, however. In 1943 her staging of *Othello,* with sets by Robert Edmond Jones, ran for 295 perfor-mances, establishing a long-run record for Shakespeare that still stands today.

Webster saw Othello not as a "coffee-colored gentleman who has been spending the winter in Tunisia,"[20] nor one whose character is centered in the heart or mind, but as a gut-level individual, a man "close to the jungle and the burning, desert sands."[21] He is filled with passionate feelings which, to those who unleash them, are almost incomprehensible in their naked power. To capture these qualities Webster was convinced a black man had to play the part. She declared that the Elizabethans so had conceived the noble Moor, and cited evidence in the play to establish Othello's "blackness."[22] Inaccurate theatrical traditions had developed for the role, but she determined to correct these by casting famed black athlete-actor-singer Paul Robeson. Today, audiences are used to seeing black actors as Othello, but in 1943 Webster's decision was a radical one. No black actor had ever played the part in a major American revival (Robeson, however, had played it in England), and her casting caused a furor. Many white actresses were loath to play opposite Robeson for fear of being stigmatized. The fear of controversy, in fact, had been so strong among potential producers that Webster had to first stage the play in summer-stock situations (in 1942), at the Brattle Theatre in Cambridge, Massachusetts, and at Princeton University before enough interest was aroused to buy the show for Broadway, where it was presented by the Theatre Guild.

As it turned out, Webster was never especially enthused about Robeson's performance, thinking him a less than skilled actor, yet she felt he brought something which was perfect for the role and the historical moment. Robeson had trouble giving the director the sustained emotional intensity she sought, despite his innate powers. No matter how she tried to draw out his rage and frustration as a black man living in America (and he had plenty of anger, considering his various political activities and statements), he could not always communicate these qualities, and tended to sermonize rather than "live" his role. Aware of her inability to elicit the proper responses from her leading man, Webster noted at the time, "My job is to jockey him into some approximation of Othello, and then make a kind of frame around him which will hold the play together."[23] She used various tricks of directing to move his performance along, such as emphasizing a rapid pace and having him barely move while everyone else was active around him.

Iago's motives for hating Othello were seen by many as the play's central problem, but Webster discounted this view. She felt that Iago must be played in a straightforward manner and accepted just as the playwright drew him. His principal trait must be an extremely frank and honest nature, without the smirking qualities of villainy with which he is so frequently interpreted. Webster cast Puerto Rican actor José Ferrer in the part and, although he never gave her all the honesty she desired in the role, was—in his first Shakespearean role—an excellent ancient. Uta Hagen (then married to Ferrer) was Desdemona, and Webster herself played Emilia in the first months of the run.[24]

Webster may have been proud of *Othello*'s long-run record, but she was not especially fond of the long-run system for Shakespeare's plays. She preferred to see them produced in rotating repertory, especially because the demands on an actor in a leading role were too great to be repeated at eight weekly performances. Knowing how a long run can throw off a performance, she devised a "coughing chart" during *Othello* to check on the audience's reactions. The more coughing, the greater was the audience's boredom, and the greater the need for tightening the show.

THE CHERRY ORCHARD

The Cherry Orchard (1944) was Webster's next venture. She coadapted and codirected it with Eva Le Gallienne, who also played Mme. Ranevskaya. When the star became ill, Webster took over the part. This was the beginning of Webster's collaborative relationship with the famed actress-director: their partnership had considerable significance in the annals of American theatre history. Their premiere presentation was successful, and Anton Chekhov was soon a popular Broadway dramatist, his *Cherry Orchard* achieving (for him) a record-breaking run of ninety-six performances.

Webster saw *The Cherry Orchard* as a comedy, much as its author had, although the critics tended to disagree. They preferred the traditional interpretation of Russian gloom, which had come to be associated (not very accurately) with the Moscow Art Theatre's version, and rejected the charm and lightheartedness of the new approach. To Webster, Chekhov was "the most delightful, touching, and in some respects, satisfying of all the dramatists."[25]

While no great problems arose in the process, codirecting proved an unpleasant task and Webster never did it again. Le Gallienne conceived the production style and handled the early rehearsals; as the actress began to work more deeply on her role, Webster took over the directing, concentrating especially on Le Gallienne's role as well as attending to the play's special technical requirements of lighting and sound.

THE TEMPEST

Shakespeare reappeared on Webster's stage as *The Tempest* came into being in 1945. She and Le Gallienne had wanted to do it as part of a repertory company they were hoping to form. With Webster's aid, Le Gallienne created her own scenic model on a revolving stage. The English firm of Motley translated the model into actuality and also designed the costumes. An island was built on a revolve and the lights were kept on throughout the performance, no curtain being used except at intermission. Had technical problems not arisen, Ariel would have flown on wires.

The temper of the times was always a vital ingredient in Webster's approach to a Shakespeare play. She was aware of *The Tempest*'s many pertinent thematic strains, among them the use and abuse of power . . . the search for freedom . . . shadowed with the penetrating implication that freedom often turns out to be different from what we had imagined, involving responsibility and not merely license, and that each of us must find his own way to the resolution of the conflict within himself. . . . Finally, the play is filled with the longing for peace and reconciliation.[26]

Webster cast Arnold Moss as Prospero, Canada Lee as Caliban, and [Vera] Zorina as Ariel. The latter choices were unusual. Lee was a black actor whom Webster cast not because of color but because of his unique ability to get inside the role. The parallel of Caliban's slavery with the plight of the American black man was clear to the director, but she insisted that the symbolism implied by her casting was not a primary consideration. Zorina, too, was a unique selection, as the tall Norwegian ballerina had no Shakespearean training nor much acting background of any sort. Also novel was the use of the famed Czech comic team of George Voskovec and Jan Werich as Stephano and Trinculo. Webster astutely opined that only great clowns could play such roles, not straight actors trying to be funny. Stuck with an actor who has nothing naturally comic about him, the director's only solution is to load on artificially conceived bits of farcical business; the more of these there are, the worse are the results.

Webster made some major cuts and alterations in the text. Among these was the cutting of the masque scene. She pleaded financial reasons for the deletion, but also considered the scene a later addition and not the work of Shakespeare. More noteworthy was her transposition of Prospero's "Our revels now are ended" speech from its usual place in the final scene to the play's closing lines, using it as an epilogue to suggest Shakespeare's farewell to the stage. As the lines were spoken the lights faded slowly and the actors behind him melted into the shadows. At last the lights on Prospero also went out, leaving only darkness. Despite the audacity of this change, critics tended to applaud it, even when they cavilled at other elements of the production.

Excessive use of stage trickery was not to be found in this *Tempest*. Downer noted that Webster's few gimmicks were restricted to

flash boxes for the entrances of Ariel, the magic table carried off in the dark, and the storm on board ship framed conveniently within the confines of a transparent sail with the actors busily rocking about on their legs to create the illusion.[27]

THE AMERICAN REPERTORY THEATRE

After failing with *Thérèse* (1945), an adaptation of Emile Zola's naturalistic *Thérèse Raquin* featuring Webster's mother, and a review called *Three to Make Ready* (1946), notable mainly for Ray Bolger's presence, Webster rejoined Le Gallienne to form the American Repertory Theatre (ART), a company which gave its premiere performance in Princeton, New Jersey, in September 1946, opened in New York in November, and closed in June 1947 with heavy losses.

Producer Cheryl Crawford handled the managerial duties of the troupe. Le Gallienne had run her own repertory enterprise years earlier, the Civic Repertory
Theatre, but despite its considerable acclaim, it failed to make ends meet, especially following the onset of the Great Depression. Similarly, the ART and
other subsequent American repertory troupes were to learn that repertory on a
major scale is an impossibility in this country without sizable subsidies to support
it.

The ART leaders would have liked to create a three-city repertory plan, each
city having its own company. The productions would be rotated with those of
the other cities, thereby providing a wide variety of plays for each. They hoped
such a plan could be effected on a purely regional basis, without including New
York, but lack of support forced them to reconsider, and it was in New York
at the International Theatre, a 1,100-seat house on out-of-the-way Columbus
Circle, that they eventually settled.

From the start the project ran into innumerable obstacles, financial and artistic.
A major hurdle was finding enough good actors willing to play at reduced salaries
for the joy of performing great plays in repertory. An all-American company
was sought, irrespective of the general lack of classical training then prevailing
in the United States. Among the best-known players they attracted were Walter
Hampden, Ernest Truex, Victor Jory, and Richard Waring. Newcomers to the
theatre included Eli Wallach, Anne Jackson, Julie Harris, Efrem Zimbalist, Jr.,
and William Windom. An unknown named Marlon Brando almost landed in
their net as well.

Webster's productions for the ART were *Henry VIII*, James M. Barrie's *What
Every Woman Knows*, George Bernard Shaw's *Androcles and the Lion* (all 1946),
and Henrik Ibsen's *Ghosts* and *Hedda Gabler* (both 1947). New plays the ART
considered but then turned down included Bertolt Brecht's *Mother Courage* and
Arthur Miller's *All My Sons*. These rejections were more exciting than the plays
selected, and might better have captured the public's attention. A solid but not
exceptional company, expensive tickets, and negative reviews—both for the
repertory concept and the individual shows—seriously undermined the company
and forced it to go out of business before it had time to learn from its various
setbacks.

Henry VIII was Webster's eighth Shakespeare revival in New York, and was
by far the most opulent. She had prepared a version several years earlier to be
produced by Billy Rose, but the project failed to come off. In the present
production, which she considered her most effective job of "obvious" direction,
a lot of money was spent to create a spectacular pageant designed by David
Ffolkes. Many liberties were taken with the text on the assumption that Shakespeare did not write all of it. The Cranmer subplot was removed and two Narrators
added. They spoke the lines given in the play to the two "Gentlemen," plus
some lines from Holinshed. The point was to clarify the political history behind
the play. Webster used a device in staging *Henry VIII* that she said later was
taken up by television. As the Narrators' text described Queen Anne's coronation,

the scene was enacted in mime upstage behind a scrim, in a dissolve effect. The same technique was used in the succeeding scene where the visions of the dying Queen Katherine were enacted as a divine analogue to the coronation taking place on earth.

THE MARWEB COMPANY

Webster's pioneering spirit, still eager for new adventures despite the debacle of the ART, found an outlet in the 1948–50 period when she organized a bus-and-truck touring company of twenty-two actors designed to bring streamlined Shakespeare stagings to audiences throughout the nation. The Marweb Shakespeare Company, as it was called, eventually ended in bankruptcy, but during its brief life provided America with an outstanding theatrical contribution. The company played mainly one- and two-night stands under every conceivable condition, from fully equipped theatres to meeting halls and gymnasiums. Audiences were made up primarily of school and college students.

Wolfgang Roth designed a flexible plan of small platforms to be arranged in various patterns with a simple backing of curtains hung from rods. Projections were made but never used in performance because of the technical difficulties in hanging and setting the screens in order to shoot at the correct angle and with the proper focus. Webster herself was the principal lighting designer. *Hamlet* and *Macbeth* were in the first season's repertory, *Julius Caesar* and *The Taming of the Shrew* in the second.

Economy was served by using the costumes from the Maurice Evans *Macbeth*; *Hamlet*'s costumes blended modern dress with touches of period glamour. *Julius Caesar* used paramilitary modern dress, while the *Shrew* was designed to suggest a troupe of strolling Victorian actors. Webster toured with the company during its first season, leaving it for only a brief period when she had to go to London; she was with the troupe only sporadically in the second year.

The Marweb Company brought living theatre to areas where none had been seen in years, if ever. People traveled hundreds of miles to visit the productions. They saw full-length shows, only slightly cut, and played in the simplified scenic surroundings of Roth and designer Ben Edwards. During the twenty-nine-week first season thirty-three states were visited in addition to three Canadian provinces. The longest stay in one locale was for eight performances. Webster's company failed to make money, but the touring idea attracted other groups who were able to operate at lower costs. The regional theatres which blossomed throughout America in the 1950s and 1960s owe a great debt to the bus-and-truckers of the Marweb Shakespeare Company for inspiring love for classical plays.

THE EARLY 1950s

In 1950 Webster's career began a new chapter when she was invited by manager Rudolph Bing to open his first season at the Metropolitan Opera House

with her staging of *Don Carlos*. She was the first woman director to work at
the Met, even though she had never done an opera before. She went on to do
several others in the coming years, both for the Met and the New York City
Opera Company.

The same year Webster teamed up with her old partner, Maurice Evans, from
whom she had been separated professionally for seven years, directing him as
Dick Dudgeon in Shaw's *The Devil's Disciple* at New York's City Center. So
popular was the show that its limited run was lengthened and it moved to a
regular Broadway house. A few months later Evans appeared at the City Center
in Webster's revival of their old *Richard II* success.

Webster's important contribution of 1951 was a revival of Shaw's *St. Joan*
starring Uta Hagen and produced by the Theatre Guild. The play had a decent
run of 142 performances, but did not gain universal approval. As a young actress
Webster had appeared in the original version starring Sybil Thorndike and directed by Shaw himself. She therefore felt that her production would have met
with the great writer's approval.

At this time Webster was called as a witness by the House Un-American
Activities Committee because of her various theatrical union activities and liberal
views. Although the committee's suspicions of her possible communist sympathies proved groundless, the wave of antileftist feeling in the country was
strong enough to hurt her career seriously, merely on the grounds that she had
been required to testify.

The year she was summoned by McCarthy's committee, 1953, was her last
of theatrical importance in New York. She directed a Le Gallienne adaptation
from the French, *The Strong Are Lonely,* which ran for only a week, and then
a limited-run production of *Richard III,* starring José Ferrer, Vincent Price,
Maureen Stapleton, and Staats Cotsworth. This, too, was panned. Only two
weeks were given for rehearsing the misconceived project. A very simplified
platform set was combined with rear projections and atmospheric lighting effects.
Webster had never done as poorly with Shakespeare as with this mounting.

From 1954 on she was mainly involved with directing outside of New York.
Though the McCarthy hearings surely had their effect, she also recognized that
serious theatre such as she stood for was becoming less and less possible in the
commercial mainstream. However, American theatre did not yet offer directors
like herself viable alternatives. She had no burning interest in making the transition to television and films, but admitted the necessity of working in these
media if one was to earn a decent living. A number of television productions
benefitted from her talents.

THE MERCHANT OF VENICE

During the remaining years of her life, Webster staged an average of one play
a season. She also kept active with lecture tours and one-woman shows. The
Shakespeare Memorial Theatre at England's Stratford-on-Avon employed her

services in 1956 for a production of *The Merchant of Venice*. In undertaking the assignment she hoped to stage what she considered her then unconventional though logically justified interpretation of the trial scene. She believed that Portia's delay in mentioning that Shylock's bond did not allow him to take a "drop of blood" is unnecessarily sadistic. Rather than have her know all along the course she would take, Webster wanted Portia to light on her solution only at the last moment when she seemed about to lose the battle. Margaret Johnston originally agreed to play the scene this way (which has since been done by various actresses), but later changed her mind, threatening the whole production. Webster was unable to change the actress' mind and had to let her do it in her own way. Here again Webster can be seen to have taken a back seat to a domineering star in order to preserve the integrity of a production. If she had to force the actress to play the part according to the director's view, the result would be an untruthful performance. The actors are out there when the curtain rises; no one sees the director.

For her revival Webster reviewed the many classical approaches to the character of Shylock, from that of the comic fool to the dirty villain to the poor, downtrodden Jew. In her eyes Shylock is an unsympathetic character despite his moments of pathos—these actually depict him falsely. He is a greedy man who loves his every possession, animate and inanimate. His wife and daughter are but objects to him, things he cherishes for owning them. He is gripped by the madness of avarice, and his tragedy is more terrible than pitiable.

Having returned to England with *The Merchant of Venice,* Webster was asked to stage *Measure for Measure* at the Old Vic in 1957. John Neville was cast as Angelo and Barbara Jefford as Isabella. She came to see this ambiguous drama as having a "Heaven-Earth-Hell pattern, probably derived from the medieval mystery and morality plays which must have been familiar to Shakespeare." She viewed the characters as tripartite, each with three basic facets, "the man he would like to appear, his public image; the man he himself likes to think he is; and the man he *really* is."[28] The scenes were slightly rearranged, moving the second Isabella-Angelo scene to a later place so that Angelo would not drop out of sight for too long as he does in the original version.

The tripartite theme was carried through scenically with a three-level series of platforms, including a Hell of dungeons in the orchestra pit connected by steps to the main stage. In costuming, too, the theme was emphasized: "Angelo . . . first appeared dressed soberly in a scholar's black gown; was invested with the robes of office; and in the last scene, stripped of them, leaving the unadorned man."[29]

FINAL YEARS

New York beckoned once more in 1958, and Webster directed Arnold Moss in a shortened version of Shaw's *Back to Methuselah* for both Broadway and a national tour. Also in the cast were Tyrone Power, Faye Emerson, and Arthur Treacher. Critical reaction, though, was sharply negative.

Webster returned to England to do *The School for Scandal* in 1960 at the Birmingham Repertory Theatre and then did Noel Coward's *Waiting in the Wings* on London's West End. These experiences thus saw her touch all bases of the English theatrical scene from the two seminational theatres to provincial repertory to the London commercial stage. Starring in *Waiting in the Wings* was the couple under whom her professional acting career began, Dame Sybil Thorndike and Sir Lewis Casson.

In 1961, back in favor with official circles, Webster was sent by the U.S. Department of State to South Africa, where she staged Eugene O'Neill's *A Touch of the Poet,* an experience detailed in delightful fashion in her autobiography. She returned at a later date under a commercial management to do *Ask Me No More* and *A Man for All Seasons* (1962).

In the 1960s Webster's work was enriched by her several experiences directing college productions as a visiting artist. Her professional credits included Michael Redgrave's adaptation of Henry James' *The Aspern Papers* (1962) on Broadway with Wendy Hiller and Maurice Evans. *Carving a Statue* was staged by her Off-Broadway in 1968. London saw her fine production of *Twelve Angry Men* in 1964, and Guildford her staging of *Mrs. Warren's Profession* in 1970. She also did versions of *The Madwoman of Chaillot* and *The Trojan Women* (1966) for a new American touring company dedicated to the classics, the National Repertory Theatre; its star was Le Gallienne. Both productions were praised highly for their harmony of concept and ensemble. Unhappily, the company closed a short time after Webster left it.

Colleges which benefitted from her talent were the University of California at Berkeley (*Antony and Cleopatra,* 1963); Boston University (*Measure for Measure,* 1964); and the University of Wisconsin (*The Three Sisters,* 1969). *Antony and Cleopatra* was done in the school's huge outdoor Greek Theatre with a cast of amateurs and semiprofessionals. Webster reduced the stage size by placing pillars at either side; she overcame the problems of long and distant entrances by having actors appear from the darkness into the light, each entry being timed carefully. The production was on an epic scale owing to the large cast and great spaces involved.

APPROACH TO SHAKESPEARE

Margaret Webster became one of America's leading classical directors more by accident than by design. She had grown up in a theatrical environment where Shakespearean performances were constantly in front of her, but she had not intended to make a career of directing his plays. "In one sense I was born to Shakespeare, but in another I had him thrust upon me,"[30] she quipped. Influenced by her great British predecessors, notably Harley Granville-Barker, Ben Greet, and Harcourt Williams, Webster became not only a famous director but a respected scholar as well. Her popular book, *Shakespeare Without Tears,* has rarely been out of print. Webster's outstanding commercial success with the Bard had, in its turn, a strong influence on those who came after her. She staged fifteen of his plays, including the four abbreviated works at the World's Fair, and nine of these productions were produced on Broadway (including City Center) with respected American players. Apart from Shakespearean stars such as Walter Hampden who headed their own companies, no other modern director has achieved a comparable record in the American commercial theatre.

Much of Webster's success with Shakespeare was because of her general avoidance of attention-drawing "gimmicks." This is not to deny her occasional use of unusual textual interpretations or other unfamiliar theatrical devices, including controversial casting choices; essentially, however, she viewed the play as the prime element of theatre and felt that, ideally, her directorial presence should be invisible, although she realized that this is less easy for the staging of a classic than for a modern play. As the preceding has shown, her visibility was more apparent, perhaps, than she would have desired, but by and large, she tried never to impose herself between the audience and the text. She aimed for straightforward, universal qualities, not narrow and specifically relevant ones. The director and actors were merely channels for communicating the playwright's work; theatre exists to make his words live, for only the playwright's contributions will continue to survive when his interpreters are gone.

A brilliant director has the right to interpret a classic radically, she thought, including the use of anachronistic settings and a greatly rearranged text, but only if such concepts "heighten in its purest essence the fundamental intention of the playwright—whether that be the delineation of character, the unfolding of action, or the eternal conflict between man and circumstance which is both these things."[31] A Meyerhold can carry off such interpretations, wrote Webster, but for most others (including herself), unusual directorial impositions are intrusive and of little value.

Webster regarded the more sensational of contemporary Shakespeare stagings, such as Orson Welles' modern-dress *Julius Caesar* (1937), which used the play to make a statement about modern-day fascism, as "adaptations"; they were not the plays the author had written. She stressed the importance of textual authenticity as crucial to a faithful rendering, but was sometimes guilty herself of mauling a script. Her cuts were often justified in terms of modern audience needs, but she went too far at times as with her forty-five-minute stagings for the World's Fair. She had some qualms about preparing the script for *Henry VIII*, yet felt she was merely removing material which the playwright himself had never written.

Aware of her reputation for cutting texts heavily, Webster outlined her cutting practices in "On Cutting Shakespeare—And Other Matters," an article for the *Theatre Annual,* demonstrating how the majority of her cuts were of the archaic and of topical references which would be of little interest to contemporary spectators. At times she was forced to cut scenes which would have required heavy expenses to produce. For *Othello,* her cuts were made to guarantee an early enough curtain to allow spectators to catch their homebound trains. (Overtime union expenses for the stagehands were also a serious consideration.) And even then, it was one of the most complete productions of the text ever staged in America.

SHAKESPEARE WITHOUT TEARS

To Webster, the way a director approached a play by Shakespeare was basically the same as he approached any other. One searched not for a clue by which to make the material politically, morally, or socially pertinent, but looked instead to the reality of the characters, helping the actors bring the characters to life with vividness and truth. Webster saw nothing highbrow or abstract about Shakespeare's characters and sought to make them as lifelike and familiar as they must have been to an Elizabethan audience. Each role must be examined for its fundamental motivations, its psychological foundations; the director must then contrive stage business appropriate to the revelation of these interior forces so that the audience can follow the shifting patterns of the play through the expressive behavior of the performers. Webster's mastery of this technique accounted to a large degree for her enormous success in making Shakespeare not only comprehensible but entertaining. Shakespeare was no god, and audiences must learn that they can enjoy themselves at his plays as much as at those by anyone else.

At times Webster went overboard in her attempts to prove how accessible Shakespeare really was and burdened her shows with business and byplay which was excessively obvious and obtrusive. As the title of her book reveals, she viewed ''Shakespeare without tears.'' She may, in so doing, have removed much of his mystery and magic. Agreeing that she may have overoccupied herself with creating visual activity to make the action understandable, Webster nevertheless was sure that such business was crucial to bring the characters and situations to life since Shakespeare gave few staging hints in his own directions. Especially in the comedies, if the correct business can be invented, many lines no longer funny can once again command laughter.

Webster did warn, however, of the dangers of being too clever when staging Shakespeare, and noted that anything that interfered with the ''speed, cohesion and clarity'' of the plays should be eliminated. ''If people do not trust Shakespeare, I do not see why they bother to produce him at all.''[32]

TEXT SELECTION

We have seen the care Webster took in selecting a text for *Hamlet.* She was equally fastidious in her choices of all her other Shakespeare productions. Experience led her to believe that where quarto editions existed, these were worthy of serious attention by directors. Even the so-called bad quartos were deserving of some consideration, if not so much as the good ones; their stage directions, she believed, were sometimes illuminating. Further, their cuts and deletions were often very helpful to a modern director seeking to reduce a play to manageable proportions. Webster chose the best text she could find after examining all alternatives. Usually, these were folio texts because they were more familiar to audiences. Readings from the quarto would be added when the folio presented problems, although some scholars dispute such practices. The main reason, however, for constantly using the folio texts was that their words when spoken provided the clearest versions.

PICTORIAL SHAKESPEARE

The Shakespeare productions of Margaret Webster were physically beautiful, using lovely scenic and costume designs based on the historical periods associated with the plays. Although sometimes overburdened with pictorial values, the average Webster staging was an integrated whole, with a well-balanced blend of color, texture, and style. There were no jagged edges and everything flowed smoothly, with rapid scene shifts, usually effected by actors deployed in choreographic patterns.

Webster was not especially fond of using a stage that resembled the one for which Shakespeare wrote; her own experiments with a miniature version of the Globe, employed for the World's Fair, led her to find the Elizabethan stage "most inflexible, difficult and dull."[33] She was unable to arrive at effective group tableaus on this stage, and felt hampered by the awkward spatial solutions at which she was forced to arrive. The proscenium theatre was far more compatible with her style as it allowed for the pictorial arrangements she liked to contrive. Variations in levels through platforms and steps afforded a much greater range of effects than possible with the sparser dispositions of the Elizabethan stage. With a proscenium stage everyone in the audience could enjoy basically the same picture, whereas a platform stage surrounded on three sides by the audience presented extremely difficult problems of picturization; in the latter, each group of spectators sees something different from what the others are seeing from their different vantage points. Webster was certain that had Shakespeare lived in this century, he would have availed himself of all the modern theatre's resources, including the proscenium stage. However, the use of an apron connected to the proscenium stage was recommended because it provided a touch of welcome intimacy between the actor and the audience, and this could be especially valuable in certain scenes. At the same time time she noted that a superb actor like Alfred Lunt or Helen Hayes could establish rapport with the audience even without a thrust.

For Webster, one of the great advantages of the proscenium stage was its curtain, which could descend on a final tableau; Shakespeare's stage had to find some less effective means to clear the area of the bodies which so frequently lie scattered about at the end of the tragedies. Yet, a positive factor in favor of a thrust, or apron, stage was the freedom of time and place which allowed the action to move swiftly without time wasted in scene shifts.

Directors often have tried to realize the spare simplicity of Shakespeare's stage, especially in the tragedies, by arranging platforms and steps in dark gray tones, lit by bold shafts of light. These efforts were, to Webster, misguided. The characters were "dressed in the early Bathrobe period and sometimes ended by looking as if they had got themselves unintentionally beknighted on the steps of the Lincoln Memorial."[34] The stage allows for swift scenic movement, but the architectural features of the design hinder rather than aid the audience's imagination.

Shakespeare should be granted a far more lavish use of color and pictorial beauty than these gloomy, ascetic productions, wrote Webster.[35] That the highly simplified yet richly imaginative ideas of pathbreaking designers Gordon Craig and Adolphe Appia could be brought to Shakespeare's plays as transmuted through the vivid work of such later designers as Robert Edmond Jones. With an intelligent use of lighting, the audience can be made to focus on the actor; the background can be toned down by the lighting to prevent the scenery from drawing undue attention.

Although she was occasionally guilty of it, Webster cautioned against literalism in Shakespearean scene design. Instead of duplicating Shakespeare's verbal imagery with scenic devices, designers should let the audience use its imagination. Similarly, overzealous attempts at realistic sound effects, such as the thunder in *King Lear,* were more often distracting than effective, and the mood created by such devices should come more from the actor than from the stage technician.

Everything onstage must bear significance to the mind of the spectator, cautioned Webster—the colors, composition, groupings, poses, gestures, decor. These are what the audience remembers long after all else has faded. Among the fine designers who worked on Webster's shows were Jones, Cleon Throckmorton, Rolf Gerard, Donald Oenslager, Ben Edwards, David Ffolkes, Motley, and Stewart Chaney. She believed that the relationship between designer and director was as close as that between playwright and director, the pair seeking to discover and interpret via visual means the play's spiritual essence. She thus avoided dictating the visual approach, although she insisted on all designs for her shows being based on her own carefully prepared ground plans. Only the director could truly appreciate the various staging problems represented by a play, and the one time that she had to deal with a design not based on her own ground plans (for *Old Music*) created insuperable problems. In her preliminary considerations of decor, she considered not only the designer's ideas but those of her stars and producers. At times she suggested the visual concept, at others she helped develop someone else's ideas.

Whatever the final decision as to the design, the principal thing to be realized was that the sets in no way draw undue attention to themselves. She wrote, ''It does not matter whether the settings are realistically magnificent, suggestive and symbolical, authentic in the Elizabethan manner or quite simply non-existent, so long as they do not obtrude themselves in front of the play."[36]

SPEAKING SHAKESPEARE'S LINES

Despite her constant stress on the visual beauty of sets and costumes, Webster stressed that such concerns were secondary to the truth brought by a great actor to his role. Any such player can be put down in a Shakespeare set of any period and be trusted to bring life to his role at once. Every word must be spoken with conviction and sincerity and not for its mere aural beauty. If actors were properly trained to meet the demands of Shakespeare's dialogue—to solve the technical problems along with presenting a reality of interpretation—many of the director's most pressing burdens would be lifted.

Webster's greatest obstacle in directing Shakespeare with Americans was the actors' lack of classical speech training. American actors, she discovered, fall far behind their British brethren in verse speaking, despite their often greater sense of inner truth: "They find it hard to see imagery in visible form or to use the potency of sound and rhythm without loss of truth."[37] She explained that "the director has to pay the most careful attention to the *phrasing and punctuation* of a line or series of lines, *so that the key words are clear and the parenthetical groups of words fall into their proper and subordinate place.*"[38]

Breathing exercises were recommended by Webster for a Shakespearean company to enable them to speak six to eight lines of verse in one breath. The unique verse style of each play should be examined to extract its full values in performance. The director should then seek to orchestrate the actors' voices since Shakespeare's greatest scenes, in both tragedies and comedies, are symphonic in structure. A rapid tempo is also helpful, allowing the slower parts to increase in value by contrast.

Actors were cautioned by Webster not to become enamored of the colorful words that modify the main thoughts, but to keep their attention pegged to the basic ideas and to forget about being poetically musical at the expense of the sense. Breath control and vocal color must be backed by deep thought, especially in the longer, more convoluted passages. For instance, only the most forceful and direct thought processes can bring a scene like that of Claudius' prayer in *Hamlet* vividly to life. Yet, on the other hand, the more lyrical passages must not become prosaically earthbound, but must soar, as in song. Rather than adhere to a dry and academic generalized theory of proper verse speaking, a path which can lead only to a dead end because of the variables presented by each case, Webster stated,

The actor must read the lines with his eyes and his ears, his heart and his mind, till they have come to be a part of him, till he can express their meaning in no other possible way. He must . . . clear from his . . . consciousness all the cluttering egotisms either of arrogance or fear. He must not take pride in his own fine-sounding chest notes nor reduce the more poetic flights to a trivial level of common sense. Only then can Shakespeare fill his heart and speak the immortal music through his lips.[39]

Webster's attention to the verse did not prevent her from thinking seriously about the need for the actor's physical training. Actors should practice acrobatics and athletics as part of their stage education, for stage movement often requires more than normal grace, fluidity, and ease. Training programs should include movement classes as much as those for voice and improvisations. The latter she found suitable for advanced actors but not for the beginner, who should first work on more fundamental acting problems.

MUSIC

Concerned as she was with the music of the verse, Webster also had a deep interest in the use of orchestral music to accompany her productions. She collaborated with many outstanding composers to provide engaging background music, and was angered when the demands of the musicians' union became so exorbitant that they all but disallowed the use of live music to accompany straight theatrical presentations. Among those who provided original compositions for Webster's shows were Lehman Engel (perhaps her most frequent musical collaborator), David Diamond, Paul Bowles, Marc Blitzstein, Alex North, and Colin McPhee.

AN AMERICAN NATIONAL THEATRE

Had Peggy Webster been born a few years later, it is likely that her career would have been spent less on Broadway than in the regional (or resident, as many prefer to be called) theatres which now dot the nation. Then again, the thirst for theatre represented by these institutions might never have been awakened had she not fought as diligently as she did for their establishment. Quite early in her directorial career Webster was advocating the need for an American national theatre which would make theatre as important as music in the lives of Americans.

In her eyes, the American community theatre was neglecting the potentially immense audience outside New York. Why not have one hundred different theatres, each appealing to different tastes and interests, scattered throughout the country? She longed particularly for companies performing in alternating repertory, for only this type of institution could provide American actors with the training necessary to fully develop their abilities. It was the responsibility of the American government to subsidize such theatres; not to do so would be a disservice to the millions who would attend productions of fine quality. The appearance of successful theatres in regional centers around the nation during the fifties and sixties clearly has vindicated the pleas she made in the early forties, although most of these still struggle to survive with various forms of subsidy that are vastly insufficient to their needs. Webster's own efforts with the ART, the NRT, and the Marweb Shakespeare Company were of inestimable value in creating the climate for such theatres. Taken together with the impetus she gave to the development of Off-Broadway, Webster's contribution to American theatre marks her as one of the century's most noteworthy theatrical artists.

PREPARATION FOR PRODUCTION

Throughout her impressive career Webster followed certain basic precepts as a director. She always prepared thoroughly for each production, doing whatever academic or social research fit the task, from examining all the texts and scholarship for a Shakespeare play to visiting a playwright's home-town to soak up its atmosphere. She declared that this prerehearsal work was the director's most difficult. "He must make up his mind what he is setting out to do, what characterization he wants, what tempo, what climaxes, what amount of movement, and how he is going to handle the mechanics of it. But he should remain flexible."[40]

Once she knew the general outline of her approach, its major moods, tempos, characterizations, themes, and climaxes, she set about predetermining its movement patterns. These were worked out on a floor plan of the set with two-inch figures; the patterns were then written into her promptbook in a sketchy fashion. She always used a promptbook at rehearsals, but she never stuck rigidly to her preblocking ideas. As her just-quoted words suggest, flexibility was essential to her, and the blueprint was not considered holy writ. Because of the many variables represented by each actor, rehearsals were a time for adjustments and new ideas; however, not having something clear from which to start working would have led to time-consuming trial-and-error solutions. Light, sound, and music cues were also outlined in the promptbook. In actual practice, she learned, the use of prearranged blocking was more essential for English actors, who tend to work on their physical activities before doing their inner character work.

Because of the skeletal format of her jottings, Webster did not think that study of her promptbooks would be a valid guide to her direction, as most of the values of a production were brought forth during the rehearsals. Ronald Worsley investigated forty-six of her promptbooks and found the early ones to be vague and not well organized, with the basic movement, sound, and light cues listed in pencil scribblings. Webster's technique became more sophisticated as she gained experience, and she began adding cues in different colored writing. She rarely used ground plans to indicate blocking and showed desired movements by drawing a line from the dialogue to the margin and writing in the blocking or business there. Such notes are put in the simplest terms—who crosses where or sits or stands, etc. Elsewhere in the promptbooks, however, are extensive supporting materials, including ground plans, light plots with cues, scenery sketches, actors' stage positions during the use of the revolving stage, costume lists, prop lists, sound cues, curtain call plans, cast information with phone

numbers and addresses, and an itemized budget. In the cover pockets are musical
scores, illustrations, programs, blueprints, clippings, and congratulatory letters.[41]

CASTING

Casting was, of course, a vital concern. Webster's choices were often sharply
criticized, although just as often she was said to have cast her plays with great
skill. In many cases she made unusual decisions which surprised the theatregoing
public, but established important precedents. As a Broadway director her casting
was frequently decided on before she even joined a production. However, she
never undertook an assignment where the producer's casting seriously upset her.

She looked for actors wherever theatre was performed, but also held conventional auditions and interviews for each production. When she came to the United
States in 1938 to direct *Richard II,* however, the strange American casting
methods surprised her. About twenty-five actors would be summoned to each
audition by the producer's secretary, although word of mouth led to an attendance
by many more. The typical procedure was to have the actors read with a generally
unfeeling stage manager on a stage illuminated only by a glaring work light.
Meanwhile, their fate was being decided by some invisible presences gathered
in the impenetrable gloom of the auditorium. (Broadway actors still encounter
such methods.)

One hundred and twenty actors were seen during the first two days of *Richard
II* auditions (four times the number would probably confront Webster now).
Horrified by the conventional system, Webster and Evans saw each actor privately. Their polite procedures amazed the cynical New York players. They
asked each actor about his past experience and apologized for not being familiar
with it. A potential choice was given a script, some information about the role,
and requested to return for another audition. Such a policy was fairly unusual
in the late thirties, but is more common now.

Webster remained convinced that a good audition was an orderly and fair one,
and did her best to make hers a standard for emulation. When necessary she
helped her actors out by easing potential difficulties for them. Therefore, when
auditioning elderly actors for *Waiting in the Wings*, she read with them herself
to help them along.

She found it impossible to cast on impulse at a first audition. As each actor
read she attempted to give him her undivided attention, which she found to be
greatly dulling to the senses and memory. She would find herself hoping the
next actor to be so bad that she could immediately write him off. To help her
memory she would scribble hasty notes to herself. ''Blond—blue sweater—long
straggly hair—good voice—possible—not for this part.''[42] Codes like ''NDT''
(''no discernible talent'') helped her, too.

Actors were advised to read something they liked, not something chosen to
please their listeners. She suggested that they wear the same clothes to callbacks
or else dress in character, to help the director remember them more clearly.

Perhaps Webster's most controversial casting idea was her use of black actors in classical roles conventionally played by whites. Paul Robeson as Othello and Canada Lee as Caliban were the most conspicuous examples. Equally significant was her casting of two lesser-known blacks, Edmund Cambridge and Austin Briggs Hall, to join her bus-and-truck company. Such racial casting fully blossomed a few years later in the fifties in the work of producer-director Joseph Papp. Webster faced surprisingly few situations of outright bigotry aimed at her troupe, although the few she did encounter were extremely unpleasant. Unlike Papp, Webster refused to use black actors in roles for which Shakespeare's intentions might be thought to have been violated. She would, for example, never have cast a black man to play Claudius to a white man's Hamlet.

Her sensitivity to Shakespeare caused her to direct only actors of star caliber in the leading roles. She believed that lesser actors would never equal the demands made on them by the playwright. Often interpretation of the principal roles had to defer to the particular strengths of her performers, for the director, she noted, must take advantage of the talent at his disposal and not seek to distort it for a directorial whim.

EARLY REHEARSALS

As the first rehearsals for a new play approached, Webster experienced waves of fear and nervousness; afraid to let her insecurities show, she resolved to become well acquainted with her actors' abilities and personalities. Knowing whom she had to deal with greatly eased her trepidation. Doing this with a large Shakespearean company could be a terribly difficult chore, but she invariably succeeded at it.

Unlike most Broadway directors, Webster read the script to her cast at the first rehearsal, rather than having them read it themselves. Her reading made the work as clear as possible so as to save time in explaining all the lines. She recommended this practice if the director was an able reader, but admitted that for some experienced actors the procedure was really not very helpful. Through the director's reading the actors would not only be able to see something of the director's conception of the play, but the actors' minds would be taken off their own individual roles, allowing them to see the play as a whole. Another benefit was the method's ability to distract actors from their doubts about others in the cast who were not able to read effectively at such rehearsals.

Once the reading stage was over, blocking commenced. Webster displayed a model of the set to the cast, and then had a taped outline of the floor plan laid out on the floor. The actors were instructed according to her prearranged blocking, thus giving them a feeling of security from which to begin building their roles. Knowing where he is going helps the actor learn his lines quickly. Watching the actors rehearse according to a well-prepared plan not only allows the director to see where the performances can be further enhanced, but will allow enough time to alter poorly blocked moments and refine the actors' interpretations.

Webster blocked with great rapidity, doing about an act a day for three days, repeating each act or scene twice at each rehearsal. Judith Anderson described the Webster working manner:

Margaret Webster has a mind that cuts through non-essentials; she knows what she is aiming at. And yet she seems to be conducting rehearsals as though they were only play. She jokes with you. There isn't the least tension. All the time, though, she is driving ahead.[43]

Working in this relentless, though good-humored way, Webster managed to stage all of *Richard II* in four days. Yet, despite her speed in staging, she never rushed her actors into premature performances.

WORKING WITH ACTORS

Composer Lehman Engel offers this picture of Webster at rehearsals:

Physically, she was a "thing" to behold. Generally, she wore slacks. Her short hair fell in strips across her face. A cigarette always hung precariously out of the corner of her mouth, the smoke menacing her eyes and provoking violent fits of coughing. She was everywhere in the theatre at once and never accepted any nonsense from anyone. She was the first to laugh raucously at a joke, but her work was concentrated, and it proceeded without interruption from the first day of rehearsal to the last.[44]

Webster was what may be called an actor's director. She never claimed to be the focus of her productions. As we have seen, she normally gave her stars the freedom to play their roles much as they pleased. She saw directing as a process of give-and-take, the director and actor working in collaboration and constantly modifying their effects in light of the other's insights. Actors greatly enjoyed working with her, for she inspired them with confidence in their abilities and let them find their own way to the heart of a role. She was capable of excellently elucidating the text from her knowledge and perceptions, and, although allowing individual freedom, could usually blend one performance with another into a unified whole. Each actor had her personal attention, for she respected and loved performers, being one herself. She felt that an acting background was an absolute prerequisite for a director because of the insights it afforded into the player's creative processes.

Directorial autocracy was not a Webster trait. She did not like to give actors line readings or to demonstrate for them, although she often found herself forced to do so—especially when rehearsing period plays, since the special manners required of the characters were usually beyond the ken of any but the most experienced players. American actors lacked the proper training in period movement and the wearing of period costume; they had to be shown how to deal with these elements.

Lengthy discussions at rehearsal were distasteful to Webster, as was the occasional need to lecture an actor. She hated to parade her obvious erudition and would rather have seen an actor approach a problem through instinct and intuition than through analytical cross-examination. The result of such psychologizing was far too often colorless and uninteresting. All discussions had to be brief and to the point. She tended, therefore, to demonstrate her intentions rather than talk about them, but hoped the actors would not directly imitate her so much as capture the essentials of her aims.

Webster acknowledged the techniques and talents of Method-trained actors, but she was reluctant to condone what she thought an overly egocentric attitude on their part. The great stress on personal feelings rather than on the response generated in the audience created a style too limited in its means and effects. Only the naturalistic drama could benefit from such acting; the big plays, notably those of Shakespeare, required considerably more of the performer.

She helped her actors get the feel of their characters' reality by suggesting parallels to which they could relate. She told them to think of their roles in contemporary terms, as if the characters were alive and not figures from a history book. In directing *Othello,* for instance, she said, "Try not to forget . . . that when you arrive at Cyprus you are Europeans in a semi-tropical garrison town. Although the heat is getting on your nerves and the natives are not too friendly, you have to be pukkha sahibs."[45]

Since most of Shakespeare was very clear to her, she would occasionally grow impatient with an actor who failed to get the meaning of a speech. She might then turn to the puzzled player and say, "Well, just look at what Shakespeare *says. . . .* If you'd only bother to listen to him!"[46] When she herself was puzzled, she would pace back and forth, a cigarette hanging from her lips, pondering the meaning of a line, "until finally, with a jerk of her head, she whirls on the waiting cast and breaks the all but unbearable suspense."[47]

Most accounts of Webster describe her as a mild and even-tempered woman who rarely yelled or grew violent at rehearsals. She learned that directors who constantly scream soon find no one listening to them. A good scream should be used very sparingly; when it is, it will have a far more telling effect. However, Cheryl Crawford, the producer who ran the ART with Webster and Le Gallienne, and who also produced *Family Portrait,* tells a story strikingly at variance with most other reports:

Peggy Webster was a woman whose temper flared easily. At one rehearsal when the authors [of *Family Portrait,* Lenore Coffee and William Cowen] interrupted, Peggy blazed with fury, flung her new fur coat on the stage floor and stamped up and down before leaving the theatre to cool off.[48]

Lehman Engel, who worked with her on eleven productions, agrees that "she could outscream anyone when provoked." However, he recalls one outstanding incident during rehearsals of Fritz Hochwalder's *The Strong Are Lonely* when he saw her quell her anger with an approach that worked wonders.

As we sat together during a run-through (no one else was in the theater), Dennis King, the star . . . , surrounded by a large cast, stepped downstage in the middle of a scene and delivered a noisy diatribe against the other actors . . . , against the play, and against Peggy. His screams seemed to go on for hours. Peggy did not move. The cast was frozen. As Dennis had no antagonist, he had to continue. Finally, little by little and even a bit pathetically, he "ran down" like a mechanical toy. Then silence. He stopped talking and froze like everyone else. After an interminable pause Peggy spoke up strongly and pleasantly: "Dennis, if that's all, we'll take the scene again from the top!"

Dennis had lost his battle. At the end of the scene, Peggy called a five-minute break, and Dennis hopped off the stage to embrace her and apologize.[49]

One thing that was sure to upset the director was an actor's lateness. Herself always punctual, tardiness from an actor seriously disturbed her. According to one anecdote, she once stood up to Maurice Evans (who was both producer and star) when he came in ten minutes late to a *Hamlet* rehearsal. Loud enough for all to hear, she sneered at him, "A star . . . has risen!"[50] The story relates that the star did not rise late thereafter.

DIRECTING HERSELF

Although Webster often directed plays in which she also acted, she did not recommend the practice to others, especially when the play was a profound one. Provided she had a good standby and a competent crew, her directing was as good as when she wasn't acting. But her own performance suffered badly in these cases. She always found it a struggle when onstage to concentrate on her part while ignoring those things that the director gets paid to oversee.

Having acted under the autocratic actor-director Sir John Martin-Harvey, Webster remembered how he would disconcert his company when he made his entrance by fixing a sharp eye on them to make sure all were where he had placed them and in correct postures. She resolved never to copy Harvey's method, but this was not always possible. When she asked a friend to observe her production of *Othello* so she could get some objective feedback, she received the following reply concerning her acting of Emelia: "Well . . . do you mean to play Emelia as an efficiency expert?"[51]

OPENING NIGHT JITTERS

Her cigarette smoking grew furious as opening night of a new production approached. When it finally came, she suffered indescribable tortures. What would the actors do before a live audience? They were never the same as they had been at rehearsal; some were better, some were worse. The unpunctual audience, the actors' nerves, and coughing in the house could drive a director insane, she said.

You nurse the actors through every speech, thrust every point home by muscular force, grin like a skull just ahead of every laugh. The members of the audience are thick-witted idiots with influenza. . . . The pace is intolerably slow, snail-like; what on earth do they think they're doing?[52]

Once her shows were open and running, Webster did not abandon them but came back often to make sure they weren't slipping. Without telling the cast, she would show up to watch, make notes on weak spots, and then discuss it with them afterwards. Special rehearsals were set up when necessary to get the show back in shape. The danger of sloppy work was prevalent especially in long runs, but Webster was unwilling to have any audience see a production of hers under less than optimum conditions.

CONCLUSION

Webster was not a particularly innovative or unusual director, either in the work she staged or her techniques of rehearsal. Yet she combined a powerful sense of what would appeal to a large audience with an inordinate love for Shakespeare's plays, and managed to convey these works in so appealing a way that they even made money for their producers. Stark Young succinctly summed up her strengths and weaknesses when he wrote, "Her theatre virtues are solid and respectable; what she lacks is the aesthetic sense to any notable degree." In a theatre where Shakespearean production was so rare, her presence was a fortunate one, although as Young pointed out, "in the realm of the blind, the one-eyed is king." His judgment seems overly harsh, but does contain at least a grain of truth. Webster's productions may not have been as technically brilliant as those of a Meyerhold or Brook, but, as Young admits, they had "a good breeding, a good sense, a certain kind of literalness and a sincerity that carry them a long way as both entertainment and box office."[53]

No other woman director in America has ever rivaled the accomplishments of Margaret Webster. Not only did she build a successful career in a field traditionally associated with men, but she did so with plays not even the most powerful male directors could continually make widely popular. Off-Broadway and the regional theatre movement owe her an undying debt, as do thousands of playgoers for whom she made the plays of Shakespeare and others come to colorful and imaginative life.

NOTES

1. Margaret Webster, *The Same Only Different* (New York: Alfred A. Knopf, 1969), p. 283.

2. Quoted in Ronald Craig Worsley, "Margaret Webster: A Study of Her Contributions to the American Theatre" (Ph.D. diss., Wayne State University, 1972), p. 257.

3. Maurice Evans, *All This . . . and Evans Too!* (Columbia: University of South Carolina, 1986), p. 110. Evans' account of the collaboration differs somewhat from Webster's

as outlined, for example, in her autobiography. As suggested in this chapter, each claims to have had the greater share of actual directorial responsibility for the production, although neither shows any awareness of the other's claim to priority.

4. Webster, *The Same Only Different,* p. 283.

5. Margaret Webster, *Shakespeare Without Tears,* rev. ed. (Cleveland and New York: World, 1955), pp. 169–172.

6. Alan S. Downer, "The Dark Lady of Shubert Alley," *Sewanee Review* 54 (January 1946): 123.

7. Evans, *All This . . . ,* p. 129.

8. Margaret Webster, *Don't Put Your Daughter on the Stage* (New York: Alfred A. Knopf, 1972), pp. 25–26.

9. Webster, *Shakespeare Without Tears,* pp. 210–11.

10. Webster, *Don't Put Your Daughter,* p. 26.

11. Webster, *Shakespeare Without Tears,* p. 213.

12. John Mason Brown, *Dramatis Personae: A Retrospective Show* (New York: Viking, 1965), pp. 222–223.

13. Downer, "Dark Lady," p. 127.

14. Evans, *All This . . . ,* p. 125.

15. Ibid., p. 130.

16. Webster, *Don't Put Your Daughter,* p. 98.

17. Webster, *Shakespeare Without Tears,* p. 223.

18. Webster, *Don't Put Your Daughter,* p. 25.

19. Quoted by Helen Ormsbee, "An Accessory to Murder, She Likes It," *New York Herald Tribune,* 23 November 1941.

20. Webster, *Don't Put Your Daughter,* p. 112.

21. Webster, *Shakespeare Without Tears,* p. 235.

22. Webster, *Don't Put Your Daughter,* p. 112.

23. Ibid., p. 110.

24. A fascinating glimpse of the various problems Webster had with her stars during the preparation of *Othello* can be found in Susan Spector, "Margaret Webster's *Othello*: The Principal Players Versus the Director," *Theatre History Studies* 6 (1986): 93–108. According to this account, Webster left the cast in a rage when Robeson would not back down on his demands that José Ferrer and Uta Hagen receive star billing on the national tour; this would have left Webster to take what she considered the embarrassing position of acting in "support" of the young Hagen.

25. Webster, *Don't Put Your Daughter,* p. 134.

26. Webster, *Shakespeare Without Tears,* p. 283.

27. Downer, "Dark Lady," p. 133.

28. Webster, *Don't Put Your Daughter,* p. 303.

29. Ibid., p. 304.

30. Ibid., p. 86.

31. Margaret Webster, "Credo of a Director," *Theatre Arts Monthly* 22 (May 1938): 344.

32. Ibid.

33. Margaret Webster, "On Directing Shakespeare," in *Producing the Play,* ed. John Gassner, rev. ed. (San Francisco: Rinehart, 1953), p. 438.

34. Webster, *Shakespeare Without Tears,* p. 75.

35. Ibid.

36. Webster, "Credo," p. 344.

37. Webster, *Don't Put Your Daughter*, p. 90.

38. Webster, "On Directing Shakespeare," p. 446.

39. Webster, *Shakespeare Without Tears*, p. 92.

40. Webster, "Credo," pp. 347–348.

41. Worsley, "Margaret Webster," pp. 126–28.

42. Webster, *Don't Put Your Daughter*, p. 345.

43. Quoted in "Miss Anderson Returns to Stage in Study of the Life of Christ," unidentified clipping, Research Collection, Lincoln Center Library of the Performing Arts, New York.

44. Lehman Engel, *This Bright Day: An Autobiography* (New York: Macmillan, 1974), p. 90.

45. Quoted by Barbara Heggie, "Profiles: We," *New Yorker*, 20 May 1944, p. 31.

46. Ibid., p. 30.

47. Ibid.

48. Cheryl Crawford, *One Naked Individual* (New York: Bobbs-Merrill, 1977), p. 107.

49. Engel, *This Bright Day*, p. 91.

50. Quoted in George Ross, "Broadway," unidentified clipping, Research Collection, Lincoln Center Library for the Performing Arts, New York.

51. Webster, *The Same Only Different*, p. 380.

52. Ibid., p. 385.

53. Stark Young, *Immortal Shadows* (New York: Charles Scribner's, 1948), p. 212.

CHRONOLOGY

All productions from *Richard II* (1937), New York City, unless otherwise noted. Return engagements are not noted.

1905   born in New York City

1918–23   attends Queen Anne's School, Caversham, England

1923   enters Eltinger's Dramatic School, London

1924   professional acting debut (as chorus member), New Theatre, London: *The Trojan Women*

1924–37   active as actress in London and in touring companies

1934   directs amateur pageant production of *Henry VIII* for Women's Institutes, Kent

1935   series of tryout productions, mostly for single performances; Whitehall Theatre, London: *Snow in Summer*; Phoenix Theatre, London: *Love of Women*; Gate Theatre, London: *No Longer Mourn*; Garrick Theatre, London: *The Lady from the Sea*

1936   Embassy Theatre, London: *Return to Yesterday*; *Heads I Win*; "Q" Theatre, London: *The Four Partners*; *A Ship Comes Home*; Aldwych Theatre, London: *Family Hold Back*

1937   Embassy: *Lovers' Meeting*; *Three Set Out*; first commercial production, St. James's Theatre, London: *Old Music*; St. James Theatre, New York: *Richard II*; Fulton Theatre: *Young Mr. Disraeli*

1938   St James: *Hamlet*

1939   St. James: *Henry IV (I)*; Morosco Theatre: *Family Portrait*; abbreviated versions
         of four Shakespeare plays at World's Fair, Old Globe Theatre, Flushing Mead-
         ows: *As You Like It*; *The Taming of the Shrew*; *A Midsummer Night's Dream*;
         The Comedy of Errors

1940   St. James: *Twelfth Night*; *Battle of Angels*, closes in Boston

1941   founds Experimental Theatre; Cort Theatre: *The Trojan Women*; National The-
         atre: *Macbeth*

1942   publishes *Shakespeare Without Tears*; Henry Miller's Theatre: *Flare Path*

1943   Windsor Theatre: *Counterattack*; Shubert Theatre: *Othello*

1944   National: *The Cherry Orchard*

1945   Alvin Theatre: *The Tempest*; Biltmore Theatre: *Thérèse*

1946   Adelphi Theatre: *Three to Make Ready*; cofounds American Repertory Theatre;
         International Theatre: *Henry VIII*, *What Every Woman Knows*; *Androcles and
         the Lion*

1948   Cort: *Ghosts*; founds bus and truck Marweb Shakespeare Company—opens at
         Erlanger Theatre, Buffalo: *Hamlet*; *Macbeth*

1949   Marweb opens at Woodstock, N.Y.: *Julius Caesar*; *The Taming of the Shrew*

1950   summer season with Marweb at Woodstock doing modern plays; City Center:
         The Devil's Disciple

1951   City Center: *The Taming of the Shrew*; Cort: *Saint Joan*

1952   tour opens in Parsons Theatre, Hartford, Conn.: *An Evening with Will Shake-
         speare* (one-woman show starring Webster)

1953   Broadhurst Theatre: *The Strong Are Lonely*; City Center: *Richard III*

1955   Picadilly Theatre, London: *The Strong Are Lonely*

1956   Shakespeare Memorial Theatre, Stratford-on-Avon: *The Merchant of Venice*

1957   Old Vic, London: *Measure for Measure*

1958   tour and Ambassador Theatre: *Back to Methuselah*

1960   Birmingham Repertory Theatre, Birmingham: *The School for Scandal*; Duke
         of York's Theatre, London: *Waiting in the Wings*

1961   Alexander Theatre, Johannesburg, South Africa, and tour: *A Touch of the Poet*

1962   Playhouse Theatre: *The Aspern Papers*; South Africa: *Ask Me No More; A Man
         for All Seasons*

1963   Greek Theatre, University of California, Berkeley: *Antony and Cleopatra*; tour-
         ing one-woman show, opens at Theatre de Lys: *The Brontës*

1964   New Arts Theatre, London: *The Brontës*; Boston University: *Measure for Mea-
         sure*; Queen's Theatre, London: *Twelve Angry Men*

1965–66 touring National Repertory Company, opens at University of North Carolina,
         Greensboro: *The Madwoman of Chaillot; The Trojan Women*

1968   Gramercy Arts Theatre: *Carving a Statue*

1969   University of Wisconsin, Madison: *The Three Sisters*; publishes first part of autobiography, *The Same Only Different*

1970   Yvonne Arnaud Theatre, Guildford: *Mrs. Warren's Profession*

1972   publishes second part of autobiography, *Don't Put Your Daughter on the Stage*; dies in London

Elia Kazan

(1909–)

During the 1940s and the 1950s Elia Kazan stood forth conspicuously as the representative American director of important contemporary native dramas. No other director was so closely associated with the postwar flowering of serious American playwriting, especially the work of Tennessee Williams and Arthur Miller. When British critic Kenneth Tynan castigated the English theatre in 1954 for its lack of directorial influence on acting, he pointed to two foreign directors who, though polar opposites in method, represented such forces as he wished were present in England. One was Bertolt Brecht and the other Kazan.[1] By the time Kazan stopped directing in the theatre, a decade later, he had garnered four Tony Awards, five New York Drama Critics' Circle Awards, and had staged five plays chosen for the Pulitzer Prize.

EARLY YEARS

Kazan, the eldest of eight siblings, was born to an Anatolian Greek family named Kazanjioglou in a small Turkish town near Istanbul on 9 September 1909. He grew up fluent in both Greek and Turkish. After living briefly in Berlin, Germany, his family moved in 1912 to New York; several years later they moved again to New Rochelle, New York, where his father set up a rug business. Although his family was Greek Orthodox, he was sent—despite his dislike—to a Roman Catholic school.

At Williams College, from which he was graduated in 1930, Kazan was encouraged to go to the Yale Drama School, where he studied playwriting with George Pierce Baker and directing with Alexander Dean, who later wrote a widely used text on the subject. Although he found Dean's method excessively technical, he appreciated his emphasis on the director's need to tell a story through stage pictures and his de-emphasis of the actor's importance: "I learned from him what the directors of the Group Theatre [with which Kazan was later closely involved] never learned: that directing a play should not be thought of simply as directing actors. Directing a play is an overall task, directing actors only a part of it."[2] His principal fascination at Yale—where he disliked the emotional sterility of the mannered, British-influenced production program—was with technical theatre, from lights to costumes to sets, and he was so adept that he even considered a career as a theatre technician. The experience stood him in good stead as a director, he claims: "No technician could tell me something couldn't be done; I'd very likely done it."[3] His extreme usefulness in all situations made even more appropriate the nickname he had picked up at Williams: "Gadget," generally shortened to "Gadg(e)," and descriptive of his small size but large reserves of nervous energy, which made him seem always to be in motion.

It was at Yale that Kazan met his first wife, Molly Day Thacher, whose taste in scripts and theatrical insights were of enormous assistance throughout his career; Kazan refers to her as an artistic partner as well as a spouse.

In the summer of 1931 Kazan landed his first directing job, S. N. Behrman's *The Second Man,* at Atlantic City's Toy Theatre, which did a new play every week. (Interestingly, the next to last play of his directing career to date was also by Behrman.) Aiming to be an actor, he joined the Group Theatre the following summer. The legendary Group was near the beginning of its climb to a position as America's foremost ensemble company, acting new plays of social significance in a style based on the ideas of Stanislavsky. While in the Group Kazan wrote several leftist plays; two were about strikes and another, *Dimitroff* (1934), co-written with Art Smith, was a short piece about the defense put up by the man accused of the Reichstag fire. This was the first play Kazan staged in New York and was originally on the same program as Clifford Odets' fiery *Waiting for Lefty.* Kazan acted in both. His next directing assignments were shared with Alfred Saxe under the auspices of the Communist theatre group, Theatre of Action; these were two politically radical plays, *The Young Go First* (1935) and *The Crime* (1936). When Kazan began work on *The Young Go First,* the third act had not yet been written. To supply it, the young director worked improvisationally, using a stenographer to write down all the actors' contributions, which were based on a scenario he devised. The edited results constituted the third act. Kazan's theatre ideas at this time were under the influence of the Russian masters, Vsevolod Meyerhold, Yevgeny Vakhtangov, and Konstantin Stanislavsky. Much of this influence came via the instruction of Group coleader Lee Strasberg. Kazan recalls one provocative idea in particular of Meyerhold's that came to him through Strasberg: "The actor no longer occupies the leading place upon the stage. The director will determine all life there."[4]

Kazan's social sentiments at the time also were expressed through an eighteen-month stint as a Communist party member. He left the party, disillusioned with its methods, but his membership came back to haunt him in the early fifties when he was called by the House Un-American Activities Committee to testify and name others whom he knew to have been members. His decision to face his responsibilities by naming names was a major cause of his rift with playwright Arthur Miller. Miller, who indirectly condemned Senator Joseph McCarthy's methods in such plays as *The Crucible* and *A View from the Bridge*, which view informers with disdain, and who, himself, refused to follow Kazan's example, was not reconciled with Kazan in the theatre until the production of *After the Fall* (1964). It should be noted that though Kazan renounced communism, he was offended primarily by Stalinism; he never abandoned his fundamentally left-wing political beliefs.

While waiting to be accepted as a full-fledged Group member, Kazan earned a living doing various assistant stage management jobs; it was on one of these, Theresa Helburn's bungled production of *Chrysalis* in 1932, that he first realized how much better he could be at directing than were the so-called important professionals. He was sure that if given the chance he could combine an actor's technical proficiency in voice and movement with subconsciously founded, emotionally intense and honest human behavior. He longed to fuse Dean's lessons about revealing behavior through visual ideas with the Group's Stanislavsky-oriented emphasis on character internalization.

The Group gave him his first shot at a major directing spot with Robert Ardrey's *Casey Jones* (1938); Kazan attributes part of the reason for the play's failure to his having allowed himself to be bullied by the star, Charles Bickford, and permitting actress Stella Adler to be brought in as a coach for an actress Kazan was convinced would have done better on her own (and who was eventually replaced). Kazan followed this work up with Ardrey's *Thunder Rock* (1939), an interesting play which flopped; Irwin Shaw's *Quiet City* (1939), which was shown only at six Sunday evening performances; and Clifford Odets' *Night Music* (1940), another defeat. Thus ended his directing career with the Group, which itself folded in 1941.

After several good roles on stage and in films Kazan left acting in 1941 and devoted himself to directing. In 1941 he directed Arthur Arent's *It's Up to You* for the Department of Agriculture, a documentary work about rationing influenced by the Living Newspaper style of the 1930s; it employed mixed media and even had the live actors talking to their images in a film.

His first hit (a modest one) came in 1942 with Hy Kraft's comedy about the Yiddish theatre, *Café Crown*. He learned various valuable lessons working on this unpretentious piece, including the notion that a director must not try to make more of a show than is there by pumping it up to a level it cannot sustain, and that it is harmful to impose a theme on a themeless play. *Café Crown* was succeeded by Irish dramatist Paul Vincent Carroll's drama about Scotland's bombardment by the Germans, *The Strings, My Lord, Are False* (1942), and then came Kazan's first megahit, Thornton Wilder's philosophical comic-strip allegory, *The Skin of Our Teeth* (1942), starring Fredric March, Florence Eldridge, and, memorably, for Kazan as well as audiences, Tallulah Bankhead as Sabrina. Nevertheless, he still had not found his groove, though his next three choices were not only interesting but were also successful. Helen Hayes starred for him in *Harriet* (1943), Mary Martin headed the cast of the musical comedy *One Touch of Venus* (1943), and Oscar Karlweiss and Louis Calhern starred in Franz Werfel's topical satire *Jacobowsky and the Colonel* (1944). Kazan was known to have been very helpful in staging Walter Kerr's cavalcade of American folk and popular music, *Sing Out, Sweet Land* (1944), but the direction was officially credited to Kerr and Leon Leonidoff. Less successful were the following pair: Barbara Bel Geddes acted in Arnaud D'Usseau and James Gow's controversial drama about religious prejudice, *Deep Are the Roots* (1945); and Richard Widmark, Dennis King, and Luther Adler were important figures in Behrman's *Dunnigan's Daughter* (1945).

By the time *Dunnigan's Daughter* was over, Kazan had concluded that he could not stand working for other producers, who had a propensity for pressing the panic button and pressuring him to do things he hated. Henceforth, all plays staged by Kazan were also produced by him either solely or in tandem with someone else. The first such project was his coproduction with Harold Clurman, one of the Group's leaders, of Maxwell Anderson's *Truckline Cafe* (1946), which Clurman directed, and in which an unknown actor named Marlon Brando proved electric during his five minutes onstage.

By now Hollywood had beckoned; although he had worked on several independent film projects in the thirties, Kazan's distinguished film-directing career began with the 1944 *A Tree Grows in Brooklyn*.

In 1947 Kazan staged his first play by Arthur Miller, *All My Sons*; he also coproduced it. His direction helped establish Miller as one of America's finest playwrights. Two years later Kazan was responsible for the premiere of Miller's most important play, *Death of a Salesman,* with Lee J. Cobb and Mildred Dunnock. Kazan has stated that his pre-Miller directing work was technically proficient but, on an emotional level, was just marking time; it was not until he was confronted by Miller's play that he felt he had found material which allowed him to put his own life's experiences into his work. A hiatus of sixteen years intervened, however, before Kazan did another Miller play. Kazan's enormous success with *Death of a Salesman* was remarkable, coming as it did right after his stunning victory fourteen months earlier with his first Williams play, *A Streetcar Named Desire* (1947), acted by Brando, Jessica Tandy, Kim Hunter, and Karl Malden. With Williams Kazan discovered the playwright with whom, even more than Miller, he was to have the closest emotional and artistic attachment. He found in Williams' writing a naked and vulnerable quality that made him feel protective of the playwright, despite his awareness of Williams' actual strength of character. Many consider *Salesman* and *Streetcar* to be two of the finest plays ever written in America; Kazan's having contributed as he did to their significance through his staging elevated him at once to a position as the nation's foremost director.

ACTORS STUDIO

His restless creative energies found a meaningful new outlet in October 1947 when he cofounded the Actors Studio in New York with Cheryl Crawford and

Robert Lewis. The Studio was designed as a place for professional actors to work on acting problems, using the principles of Stanislavsky. Kazan taught acting here for several seasons. Two years after Lee Strasberg joined in 1949, Strasberg became artistic director and the man most closely associated by the public with the Studio's work. The Studio was the "Temple of the Method," and Method actors soon provided playgoers with material for some of the most lively discussions of acting techniques the theatre has known. Method actors such as Brando, James Dean, Pat Hingle, Mildred Dunnock, Karl Malden, Eli Wallach, Geraldine Page, Lee J. Cobb, Ben Gazarra, and many others brought a new realism to the American stage. Critics often complained they were so true-to-life in their performances that audiences had trouble hearing their lines. Such excesses aside, the deep psychological probing typical of much Method acting breathed fresh life into many plays, finding suitable outlets in the multilayered realistic dramas of writers like Williams, Miller, Robert Anderson, and William Inge. Actors studying at the Studio were often used in Kazan's work.

At the Studio many ideas Kazan had picked up in his Group Theatre days were put into practice, especially the use of improvisations, through which actors could gain relaxation and believability in their work. These methods were also much used in Kazan's directing. Later he found the work of the Studio to have made an impressive mark on the American theatre and to have accomplished much good. Frequent grumblings about Method actors who lacked good speech and had slovenly habits were considerably distorted. Even if actors like Marlon Brando and James Dean gave rise to an unfortunate picture of certain Method mannerisms, they were far outnumbered by the many fine actors who were nothing like the stereotype.

The Studio gave actors a chance to act roles for which most producers and directors would never consider them. In fact, Kazan sometimes cast people after seeing them do atypical work at the Studio; such performances showed him aspects of their talent he might otherwise have missed. Geraldine Page, for example, was cast in *Sweet Bird of Youth* after Kazan saw her do an unusual part in a Studio class. Kazan maintained his association with the Studio until 1961, when he resigned from the board of directors to avoid a possible conflict of interest with his new position as artistic director of the Lincoln Center Repertory Theatre. Strasberg reportedly was perturbed that the whole Actors Studio operation had not been moved intact into Lincoln Center.

FINAL YEARS AS STAGE DIRECTOR

Though Kazan took the time to stage a successful musical, Alan Jay Lerner and Kurt Weill's *Love Life* (1948), he worked predominantly in the nonmusical field. A few failures littered the way, however; these were *Sundown Beach* (1948), with Julie Harris; George Tabori's *Flight into Egypt* (1952); and most painful of all, Williams' poetic fantasy, *Camino Real* (1953). Still, Kazan's success ratio was unusually high, with such works as Robert Anderson's *Tea and Sympathy* (1953), Williams' *Cat on a Hot Tin Roof* (1955), Inge's *Dark at the Top of the Stairs* (1957), Archibald MacLeish's *J.B.* (1958), and Williams' *Sweet Bird of Youth* (1959).

Sweet Bird was Kazan's last Broadway production. He had grown tired of the commercial pressures of Broadway work and longed for a situation where he could rehearse for more than four weeks and have the chance to do noncommercial plays. In 1961, he announced his retirement from the Broadway scene. As he observes in his candid autobiography,

I no longer wanted to handle the phalanx of backers and agents protecting each new play, deal with their anxieties and their hysteria, find the right actors, scenery, and costumes, and, while keeping everyone reassured, push the whole through to commercial success.[5]

He also notes that he had grown fed up with being the playwright's servant, and that he "no longer gave a damn about the themes of other men,"[6] which is one of the reasons he determined—to the great chagrin of the dramatist—not to do Williams' *Period of Adjustment* when it was offered to him at that time.

Several years later he became artistic director of the Lincoln Center Repertory Company, which he headed with Robert Whitehead. Here—apart from some work at the Actors Studio—he directed the last three works of his New York stage career.

PRODUCTION STYLE

By the late 1940s Kazan's personal style began to emerge; his direction had exciting physical activity, hard-hitting emotional climaxes, and a quality of deep psychological penetration in the acting. A gut-level realism in the performances was countered by a considerable theatricalization of sets and lighting. Similarly, Kazan's staging blended the ultrareal with the strikingly theatricalist. Terms like "selective realism," "poetic realism," "imaginative realism," and "stylized realism" were employed to define his unique approach. Yet, the overall impression one gets from the critics is that Kazan's work was predominantly realistic. This is largely because of his adherence to the Stanislavsky acting system, which requires close identification of the actor with his character. Kazan's effects almost always were inclined to foster illusionism, to convince the audience that they were witnessing real events, and to identify with the situations and the characters. He observed that "experience on the stage must be actual, not suggested by external imitation; the actor must be going through what the character he's playing is going through; the emotion must be real, not pretended; it must be happening, not indicated."[7]

He wanted the theatre to provide a searing emotional experience for dramatic action, not words. "The theatre . . . is not word, it is action. A play has to get you and do this to you,"[8] he once said while gesturing as if twisting a knife in someone's belly. And, for the most part, he succeeded. Kazan sought performances of psychological depth no matter what play he was directing. Even the overtly stylized *J.B.* elicited a reviewer's comment that "Elia Kazan has attacked [the play] with an energetic realism."[9]

Symbolic and expressionistic means were consistently injected into his productions through staging and decor. Kazan himself thought his work to be nonrealistic or "presentational theatre." In a 1964 interview with the *Tulane Drama Review* he said that theatre is by nature nonrealistic, since to operate effectively it depends on many accepted conventions.

I'm not interested in what is called realism. I don't believe I've worked "realistically" or "naturalistically" either. What our stage does is put a strong light on a person, on the inner life, the feelings of a person. These become monumental things. . . . They're out there living right in your midst.[10]

With the ability of films and television to present images of striking reality, theatre must rediscover its theatrical bases, which require the active use of the audience's imagination. Thus, in Kazan's mind, the most creative theatre work today is in the realm of musicals and dance.

Simple realism is a debilitating style to Kazan, one in which the actor can only experience anew what is already familiar to him. By the time he was appointed to Lincoln Center, Kazan had grown somewhat skeptical of a too slavish adherence to the Method. He criticized Studio actors who were better at theorizing than performing and yearned for actors who could provide not the theatrically modest quality of mere everyday truth but magnified acting combined with emotional immediacy. At Lincoln Center he wanted to forget about atypical Method actors and hire "a gang of wandering players, who could dance and sing, and who were, above all else, entertainers."[11] That he did not succeed in these aims is one reason for his ultimate debacle.

SCENIC STYLE

Kazan's illusionism was of the romantic, symbolic type, with ties much closer to Gordon Craig and Adolphe Appia than to the directing style of Stanislavsky. His was an inner realism projected through a wide variety of consciously theatricalist techniques. Kazan's designers, especially Jo Mielziner, who did eight plays with him, created simplified, impressionistic scenic milieus painted with chiaroscuro lighting effects. In *Cat on a Hot Tin Roof,* for example, Williams is extraordinarily detailed in his description of the scenery. He calls for a "bed-sitting room of a plantation home in the Mississippi Delta." Doors, balustrades, and walls are described. However, he is careful to emphasize the scenic atmosphere even more minutely than the set and props, and adds, "The set should be far less realistic than I have so far implied."[12] Mielziner transformed these instructions into a set that fairly did away with any resemblance to conventional realism, rejecting doors and walls for a set, in Eric Bentley's words, consisting of a square and sloping platform with one of its corners, not one of its sides, jutting out towards the audience. A corner of the ceiling is above, pointing upstage. On the platform are minimum furnishings for a bed-sitting room, and the room, steps and space suggest out-of-doors. The whole stage is swathed in ever-changing light and shade; at the outset ribbed light and shade projected on the front curtain suggest sunlight filtered through Venetian blinds.[13]

Similar sets, Bentley noted, with their simultaneous depiction of interior and exterior (a Mielziner specialty), were also used in *A Streetcar Named Desire* and *Death of a Salesman*. (A later example was the Lincoln Center production of *After the Fall*, although this was in an even more abstract dimension.) Such sets, wrote Bentley, ''present a view of man's exterior that is also a view of his interior, the habitat of his body and the country of his memories and dreams.''[14]

Probably the sparest set Kazan ever used was that for *After the Fall*. It was an open-stage arrangement devised for the thrust at the temporary theatre in Washington Square used prior to the opening of Lincoln Center's Vivian Beaumont Theatre. The scenery consisted merely of a variety of platforms and levels which could be used to represent any locale called for by the text; no actualistic props or furniture were used. Five blue velour-covered boxes served as all the required furniture and were moved whenever necessary. Nonliteral sets like this were an attempt to create a metaphorical embodiment of the play's essence. *After the Fall*'s set, for instance, captured the free-ranging quality of a man's mind as it followed the memory patterns of the drama's central figure.

The ultimate atmospheric effects of the sets in Kazan's productions owed a great debt to their lighting. Complex lighting plots (150 cues for *Death of a Salesman*) were typical, with a heavy use of mood-inducing colors, contrasts, and projections. Mielziner, in particular, created a complete integration of lighting and scenery by being responsible for both. Some critics, however, noted that Kazan overused atmospheric lighting to the extent that thematic values were obscured by the emotional effects induced. Among Kazan's singular uses of lighting were the transparency effects in *A Streetcar Named Desire*, the various projections of clouds and fireworks as well as the venetian blinds on the cyclorama of *Cat on a Hot Tin Roof*, the keeping on of the house lights for *J.B.* (until the action was well under way so the audience could be drawn into the play before the lights slowly faded), and the avoidance of blackouts in favor of gradual cross fades in *After the Fall* to illustrate the psychological movement of Quentin's mind.

PRESENTATIONAL STAGING

Kazan's staging harmonized with the essentially unrealistic decor. Moments of near naturalism often merged with formalistic ones, as in *Cat on a Hot Tin Roof*. Bentley described how attention is constantly called to the tableau, to what, in movies, is called the individual "frame." You feel that Burl Ives [as Big Daddy] had been *placed* center stage, not merely that he *is* there; in the absence of most of the furniture, a man's body is furnishing the room. When the man lifts his crippled son off the floor, the position is held a long moment as for a time exposure.[15]

Another critic, John Gassner, tells us that

Kazan's actors, standing on the quasi-Elizabethan platform, looked intently into space as though gazing into a mirror hanging on the fourth wall and addressed their thoughts, *treated as both soliloquy and colloquy* at the same time, to characters standing behind them.[16]

Thus, as the actors spoke to each other they also managed to speak directly to the audience.

An excellent description by director-critic Harold Clurman captures a moment of Kazan's staging genius in *A Streetcar Named Desire*. He concentrates on

the moment when Kowalski, having beaten his wife, calls for her to return from a neighbor's apartment where she has taken momentary refuge. He whines like a hurt animal, shouts like a savage, and finally his wife descends the staircase to return to his loving arms. Brando has been directed to fall on his knees before his wife and thrust his head against her body in a gesture that connotes humility and passion. His wife with maternal and amorous touch caresses his head. He lifts her off her feet and takes her to bed.[17]

Despite the powerful emotional effect of the direction, Kazan was apt to make choices which some believed upset the thematic balance of the play. In the example just quoted one can see how much sympathy must have been given to Kowalski from the staging. Various critics, including Clurman and Bentley, emphasize that by treating Kowalski in this fashion the character of Blanche is weakened and made less sympathetic than she is when Kowalski is played more brutishly. Kazan takes issue with such criticism, claiming that his direction of *Streetcar* was partly inspired by a note from Williams emphasizing that none of the characters is all hero or all villain, and that both sides of each character must be communicated. He notes also that when Clurman himself directed the road version of the play with Anthony Quinn and Uta Hagen, he emphasized Stanley's villainous nature, thereby, in Kazan's view, lowering the work to the level of a morality play about the destruction of a sensitive soul by the forces of evil in the world.

Kazan's staging went far beyond the narrow realm of psychological realism; it brought to the theatre a choreography of anguished souls. He had a talent for making the innately dancelike totally real. "Phantasmagoria," as Bentley says, were introduced even into the most fundamentally realistic plays. "Blanche Dubois' background was diaphanous walls and voices disembodied as Saint

Joan's. Willie Loman's life was shrouded in shadow and woodwinds and ghosts from Alaska.''[18]

Kazan's input was so expressive of the actions he uncovered in the drama's subtext that, as critic Gordon Rogoff declared, he was surely ''a kind of co-author to a theatrical event, the expert reader between the lines, the man who literally put flesh on [the] dreams''[19] of Williams and Miller.

Kazan's work often leaned strongly toward the melodramatic. His plays were usually fast-paced and constantly on the move. Bentley noted that ''things move fast in a Kazan show. So fast you can't see them. If anything is wrong, you don't notice. If a false note is struck, its sound is at once covered by others. One has no time to think.''[20] Rogoff echoes this:

There was never very much time for thinking. Drifters may drift, but the pace around them had to be frantic. If the spirit wouldn't work, there was always the body, something to plunder, something to kill. . . . On Kazan's stage, life came to a halt only after the body had been throttled into submission.[21]

Kazan's stress on the physical frequently tended to go too far. He was candid enough to admit this fault, realizing that his major problem as a director was a tendency to overdo things, exaggerating, pushing for effects, and not placing sufficient trust in the script. The critics agreed. Virginia Stevens observed in 1947: ''His faults are the excesses of his virtues: his energy, his boldness of invention, his desire to find new directions have resulted at times in a lapse of taste, an over-emphasis, a want of simplicity.''[22] It was critic George Jean Nathan who attacked Kazan for excessive reliance on melodramatic direction in the otherwise acclaimed *Death of a Salesman*. Nathan pointed out that Kazan's admirable handling of the physical action was marred by the poor quality of the vocal work.

Lines that should be read quietly are so shouted and yelled it seems he is determined to make the play a melodrama in spite of itself. There are moments, indeed, when the melodramatic screaming becomes so loud that it is next to impossible to make out what the father or his sons are talking about.[23]

SOUND AND MUSIC

Kazan was a genius at enriching the text through the creation of onstage action, often using background sounds to establish the environment of his characters. In *A Streetcar Named Desire* he established a major scene by devising a background ''ballet'' of a prostitute rolling a drunk, seen through a scrim at the rear. The noise of the background scene played a part in the main stage action as it interfered with Blanche's desire to escape. At the end of the background scene an orchestrated chorus of shouts, whistles, and sirens, only barely suggested by the script, was heard. *A Streetcar Named Desire* also effectively used New Orleans jazz and the occasional offstage cry of a woman's voice saying *"Flores para los muertos"* to immeasurably enhance the dramatic mood. In *Flight into Egypt* (1952) there was an offstage Egyptian heard every now and then uttering Egyptian cries; also audible was the chatter of street vendors, and the piercing cries of the muezzin. Kazan closed *Cat on a Hot Tin Roof* with a wonderfully expressive pantomime accompanied by the music of black folk singers Sonny Terry and Brownie McGhee.

Background music frequently was used to underscore the emotional values of a scene. Kazan was very specific about the music he required; the jazz music and blues piano used in *A Streetcar Named Desire,* the live four-piece band accompanying *Death of a Salesman,* and the circus music employed in *J.B.* were outstanding examples of a technique effectively incorporated into most of his plays and films.

LINCOLN CENTER: THE PRODUCTIONS

Like most controversial directors Kazan met with his share of criticism. However, never in his career did he encounter such vitriolic attacks as when he attempted to establish a repertory company at Lincoln Center. Not only was his directing of the three plays he staged there generally condemned, but his very raison d'être as a theatre artist was seriously called into question.

Kazan's selection to run, with producer Robert Whitehead, the theatre operation at Lincoln Center's much publicized multimillion-dollar performing arts complex was not a quirk. Aside from his eminence as America's foremost stage director, Kazan had been voicing concern for the establishment of a subsidized American repertory company for many years. In 1949 he grumbled publicly about the disgraceful fact that the world's richest nation was unable to provide a subsidized theatre such as those of which many European nations boasted. He was an outspoken critic of the Broadway commercial syndrome and a man who seemed to burn with an idea for a company such as the one the Lincoln Center board of directors felt was suited to their new establishment.

Kazan's idea was to create a company of forty actors whose main task would be to perform the best plays of the American past. His commitment always had been to the native dramatist, and he was not about to change. In 1958 he described his choice of plays for an ideal repertory company. All were twentieth-century American works which he considered of classic status: *Desire Under the Elms*; *Abe Lincoln in Illinois*; *The Skin of Our Teeth*; *Come Back, Little Sheba*; *Death of a Salesman*; *Awake and Sing!*; *Our Town*; *The Glass Menagerie*; *A Streetcar Named Desire*; and *Long Day's Journey into Night.*[24] These are plays of serious intent, the only comedy being the thematically weighty *The Skin of Our Teeth.* Of the ten, three are by Williams, two by O'Neill. Kazan himself staged the original productions of three of the plays. Obviously realizing the limitations of his selections, he also suggested that there be a second repertory for musicals and a third for great foreign classics, to be staged by American directors. During his brief tenure at Lincoln Center, however, none of these plays was produced. Kazan's first two Lincoln Center productions were no different from what he might have directed for the Broadway stage. His failure to go beyond the path he had already cut out for himself brought upon him the wrath of the critics.

Of the three plays he staged for the company, two were new dramas, *After the Fall* by Miller and *But for Whom, Charlie?* by Behrman. The third was a neglected Elizabethan play, *The Changeling,* deserving of a revival but castigated for its inept presentation. As critic Julius Novick commented, "It proved easier to take Kazan and Whitehead out of Broadway, than to take Broadway out of Kazan and Whitehead."[25]

Aside from the nature of the selections, the quality of the plays and productions was seriously called into question. *After the Fall* was the most impressive of the works, though it had a good share of negative reactions. Howard Taubman of the *New York Times,* for example, found few flaws in it and commended Kazan for a production "unfaltering in its perception and orchestration,"[26] but other critics leaped so readily to the attack that a lesser man than Kazan might have washed his hands of the business then and there. Richard Gilman began his remarks, for instance, by calling the company "a nightmare" and "a corpse." Gilman found Kazan's direction "atrocious"; after viewing *But For Whom, Charlie?* he thought that Kazan "either has no more ideas or he has suffered such a depletion of spirit that he is allowing his performers to handle their jobs the best way they can."[27]

Kazan's most interesting choice, Thomas Middleton and William Rowley's *The Changeling*, was conceived in terms which many thought augured well for the company. It exemplified Kazan's criteria for the selection of foreign classics since it had what he considered great relevance for the modern world. Kazan had said that he would only do such old plays if they were performed not as museum pieces but in productions through which the dramatic spirit could be made to live via the director's imagination. These works had to have something pertinent to say to a contemporary audience.

Kazan's own direction of *The Changeling* did not succeed in accomplishing these goals, irrespective of his vivid interpretation of the play as "modern in spirit, ruthless, amoral and existentialist. It could easily belong to the contemporary Theatre of Cruelty."[28] *The Changeling* was the first classic Kazan ever had staged, and the critics felt unanimously that he was not up to the task, though he rejoined that they had completely failed to see what he was trying to express. A rather dispassionate view of the production was taken by Julius Novick, who reported that it

was no worse than some of the shows that Joseph Papp puts on at his . . . Shakespeare Festival in Central Park. Kazan . . . was reasonably faithful to the script, and did not play games with it as American directors so often do when let loose on a Classic. Yet it is undeniable that *The Changeling* was badly done. Kazan's famous gift for abnormal psychology had deserted him. There was plenty of kissing and clipping and jumping into an onstage bed, and plenty of mayhem and mutilation . . . , but the emotions and desires, the tangle of loves and hates, the discoveries and internal transitions, that give meaning to the bed-bouncing and blood-letting, all this was less clear.[29]

Kazan and Whitehead hired a promising group of actors plus a sizable number of actors-in-training, and an acting program had been set up under Robert Lewis to help the latter develop their performance skills. The top actors in the senior company included David Wayne, Jason Robards, Jr., Barbara Loden, Salome Jens, Zohra Lampert, Ralph Meeker, and Joseph Wiseman. Although the actors were to be paid a decent salary, it was not designed to be competitive with what they could command on Broadway. Production choices were to include not only the outstanding new plays, major American plays of the century, and relevant foreign classics, but also daring and outspoken noncommercial plays that Kazan wanted to stage to let the voices of their authors, as he expressed it, be heard. So open an atmosphere did he want to create that he hoped the place would come to be called "Free Theatre."

LINCOLN CENTER: THE THEATRE

Kazan had helped to plan an innovative stage and theatre design for the Vivian Beaumont in keeping with contemporary developments in Europe and America. Jo Mielziner and architect Eero Saarinen collaborated on the design. Their planning led to the erection of two theatres, one full-sized (1,070–1,100 seats) and one smaller (299 seats), both with steeply raked auditoriums allowing for excellent sight lines. Both had thrust stages, so the audience could gather, as Kazan said, "around the stage as people might bunch around a fire on a cold night."[30] Mechanical advances such as revolves and wagons were likewise included.

The choice of a thrust stage was not made precipitously. Kazan and his designers had listened to many arguments pro and con for such a stage. Realizing that some plays worked better in a proscenium theatre while others were better suited to the open stage, they avoided an "either/or decision" and opted for a compromise. This required a permanent stage with a thrust extension that could be removed to add several additional rows of seats for proscenium staging. In other words, the theatre could be used for both proscenium and open-stage productions by rearranging the size and shape of the forestage area.

The theatre ultimately proved something of a white elephant, because of the huge proportions of its stage, sightline difficulties when the depth of the proscenium was employed, and other architectural problems, including the excessive plush of the decor.

LINCOLN CENTER: KAZAN RESIGNS

Kazan did not wait for his dream theatre to open before beginning to work with his company. He did not even wait for the complete script of *After the Fall* to be in his hands before commencing rehearsals. Seeing that the Beaumont would have to be a year behind its originally scheduled date of completion, he decided to have a temporary theatre built in Washington Square; when the Lincoln Center board refused to back him, Kazan got funding from the American National Theatre and Academy (ANTA). *After the Fall* opened there in January 1964. Kazan appreciated the unpretentiousness of this prefabricated building and would have preferred to continue in a theatre just like it rather than in the more ostentatious and otherwise problematical Vivian Beaumont.

Things went badly from the start.[31] As we have seen, audiences and critics balked at the play choices, and many found Kazan's directing inferior to that of his earlier work. The major successes were all of plays staged by outside directors. Impervious to the notion that a repertory company takes years of patient nurturing before it can find its niche, the board grew alarmed at the negative public reactions and, even more, at the large debts being incurred by Kazan and Whitehead. It was not long before a series of behind-the-scenes maneuverings led to Whitehead's resignation, followed by Kazan's, although Kazan actually had resigned privately several months before the brouhaha became public.

By the time the project was underway Kazan already had second thoughts about his position in it, and he did not relish the opportunity to hold an administrative job as artistic director of an acting company; he actually had to talk himself into the job despite his misgivings about his being an appropriate choice. Not only had he come to find distasteful the idea of being a long-range *pater familias* to a band of egotistical actors, he also cringed at the possibility of having to confront the classics, with which he had no production experience, and for which—with his background so heavily tinted by works of psychological realism—he had little talent or appreciation. A similar problem plagued the acting company, most of whom were chosen to fill the roles in Miller's play, and not to handle the demands of a classical repertory. Furthermore, he was a terrible administrator. Without the kind of burning commitment absolutely required to head a project like this, it was doomed to failure. Kazan also confesses that the company had no philosophy or specific goals. "We had no face. We hadn't made up our minds who we were going to be, rather tried to be everything for everybody."[32] When he quit the Lincoln Center post he also quit the theatre, and thereafter devoted himself to writing novels and making films, mostly from his own screenplays. Several times in the late seventies and early eighties he was on the brink of returning to the theatre; at one point he directed his own adaptation of the *The Oresteia* in a workshop production at the Actors Studio; at another he was planning to direct Richard Burton in *King Lear,* but the project was abandoned.

CHOICE OF PLAYS

As this survey of his career has shown, Kazan's direction was primarily of new American plays. Almost always these were works with strong social and psychological resonances. His film career, however, offers more examples of works that accord with his leftist sympathies. Aside from the two musical comedies of the forties, and a pair of light-spirited dramas with social messages (*The Skin of Our Teeth* and *Jacobowsky and the Colonel*), he staged serious works designed to stimulate the deep emotional involvement of the audience. Commercial considerations were less important than the impact a play made on him; if it were both emotionally exciting and intellectually meaningful it stood a good chance of capturing his interest. In addition, its potential was usually clearer to him than to its author. Tennessee Williams always was surprised at the way scripts he had conceived in the spirit of realism were transformed by Kazan into works of vivid theatrical romanticism.

WORKING WITH PLAYWRIGHTS

Kazan saw each play as representative of a specific social milieu and the characters as representatives of particular types within that milieu. In studying a play for production he attempted to determine how the characters in that milieu behaved. He frequently would travel to the area where the play was set to absorb the atmosphere; this was particularly important to him in the many plays he directed that were located in the South. It was important to him that he learn as much from the playwright as he could during his search. As a result he fostered intense working relationships with his authors, probing their psyches, digging deep to uncover the sources from which a play had sprung. Robert Anderson, whose *Tea and Sympathy* received a noteworthy Kazan treatment, wrote that the director would take long walks with him, trying to learn as much about him as he could. "It is not enough that he know the play [he noted]. He wants to know the person who wrote the play, wants to know the quality in him which made him write this kind of play."[33]

Kazan had great respect for the playwright, considering him the prime creative force in the theatre. He saw his own function as that of serving the writer and not himself, of using his own creative and interpretive powers to bring out what the playwright intended. Anderson remarked that so great was Kazan's respect for the writer that he was the epitome of "a playwright's director." He went on to note that "Gadge forms a union with a playwright in which they exchange mutual vows of honor and respect."[34] Tennessee Williams, too, said he felt this way, despite the major revisions Kazan often called for in a Williams script. With *Cat on a Hot Tin Roof* Kazan went so far as to require a total rewriting of the third act, yet, in the published version, Williams pointed out, "Elia Kazan and I have enjoyed the advantages and avoided the dangers of this highly explosive relationship [between the playwright and a director with a strong personal genius for interpretation] because of the deeply mutual respect for each other's creative function."[35]

In 1960 when Kazan and Williams had a dispute over Kazan's rejection of the playwright's new play, *Period of Adjustment,* the writer defended the director, saying that regardless of the critical reaction to many of Kazan's script revisions, "Kazan simply tried to interpret, honestly, what I have to say. He has helped me reach my audience, which is my aim in life."[36] Yet one must take comments like this with a healthy dash of skepticism. Williams was possibly acting coy by making such remarks, perhaps hoping he and Kazan could someday be reconciled. As will be seen shortly, Williams waited until many years later before publicly expressing his true feelings concerning Kazan's work on his plays.

A playwright's work may have captivated Kazan's profoundest admiration, but he normally felt that it required extensive revision before being worthy of a Broadway production. He did not seek extensive revisions in every play he staged, though. The most notorious of his reworkings was *Cat on a Hot Tin Roof*; Williams' earlier play, *A Streetcar Named Desire*, received only minimal changes (as did such plays as *Death of a Salesman* and *Tea and Sympathy*). Williams attributed this to the fact that Kazan received *Streetcar* when it was a completed script but *Cat* was given to him while still in draft form.

Kazan himself never rewrote a play, but merely made detailed suggestions for revisions. These were normally expressed in the form of letters to the author, followed by personal discussions. He placed his reservations in writing before agreeing to direct a play so there could be no misunderstanding later in rehearsals. He wanted everything out in the open at once so there would be no surprises during the course of rehearsals. If the author would not agree to Kazan's revisions, Kazan would refuse to direct the play.

Kazan's response to those who criticized him for interfering excessively in the work of playwrights is frank and to the point:

I've never regretted it. Too many people's hopes hang on the outcome of a play's production to allow above-it-all behavior. When I've felt strongly I've urged strongly. "You don't like it?," I've warned playwrights. "Then don't work with me."[37]

The crucial alterations Kazan called for in *Cat on a Hot Tin Roof* were made in the events and outcome of the third act. Williams went so far as to publish both the original version and that dictated by the director. In his own description of the revisions he says that Kazan demanded (1) that Big Daddy be on in Act III whereas he did not appear there in the original; (2) that Brick's talk in Act II with Big Daddy be shown to have made Brick change his attitude; and (3) that Maggie be made more sympathetic. In the note appended to his published version, Williams acknowledged that Kazan's alterations had been helpful, though he had strong reservations about them. He asserted that his acceptance of the adjustments stemmed from the popular and critical reception accorded the play. We have observed above how Williams continued openly to defend Kazan's work on his plays, even after the pair had split over *Period of Adjustment*. However, in 1975 he revealed his much deeper dissatisfaction, especially regarding the character of Maggie, whom he had conceived in a much harsher light than that in which Kazan wanted her to be viewed. Despite *Cat on a Hot Tin Roof*'s being Williams' "biggest . . . longest running play," he inwardly thought it "a failure, a distortion of what I had intended." After *Cat on a Hot Tin Roof*, Williams admits having gone into an artistic stupor leading to his dependence on artificial stimulants to get his "creative juices to flow."[38]

Another well-documented instance of Kazan's approach was with Archibald MacLeish's *J.B.* This play had had a very successful production at Yale under Curtis Canfield's direction when Kazan agreed to stage it for Broadway. It was Kazan's first attempt at a play in verse; he felt it needed extensive reworking and, as usual, communicated with the author through detailed letters. Though his first such missive claimed he was not calling for a major overhaul, he included five pages of detailed notes. The author responded eagerly and set to work on the script at once. As the work progressed, Kazan would inform MacLeish about new revisions he desired, the author would do his best to incorporate them, and Kazan would respond as to why he was or was not satisfied. After the New York version opened, the *Saturday Review* described the major revisions, including

(1) the elimination of some of the discursive dialogue . . . ; (2) the increasing of audience suspense, by the removal of lines which only remind it that there is no suspense; (3) the cutting of [redundant] speeches . . . ; (4) the changing of the idea that animals do not suffer as humans do by substituting inanimate objects like the moon and the sea for hawks and goats; (5) the manicuring of some of the speeches to remove some of the pretentious writing . . . ; (6) and a rewriting of the last scene.[39]

J.B. required extensive reworking not only before its rehearsals but also during them. Major problems with the second act continued to plague the show during out-of-town tryouts until Kazan finally recognized where the problem was and had MacLeish go immediately to work on it. This was the realization that the play required a recognition scene wherein J.B., "having accepted his insignificance and impotence in the face of the scale and the majesty of the universe, passes from dependence and humbleness to independence and dignity and pride in his own manliness."[40]

After the Fall seems to have been the only play Kazan began rehearsing without a completed script. Fortunately the ten-week rehearsal period with the Lincoln Center company allowed him to turn this drawback into an advantage. The second act was delivered after the first week of rehearsals and was rehearsed for ten days. Because of a weak scene at the act's end, it was returned to Miller, who was told by Kazan to take the second act to his country home and not to return until it was rewritten. Ten days later Miller returned with his new version and disaster was averted.

KAZAN'S NOTEBOOKS

In addition to his written notes to authors while preparing a production, Kazan always made it a practice to make written notes to himself. Following the practice of Harold Clurman, whose method he observed during the Group Theatre years, Kazan would prepare a notebook, sometimes in green ink, sometimes in blue, and keep a running, rambling commentary of his thoughts and feelings as he read and reread a play. These thoughts were tools for his private use and not to be communicated as such to the company during rehearsals. He could go back to them during the production process and refresh his perceptions by reading what he had placed there during his earlier cogitations. The notes were not written for any reader but himself, though various samplings from them have been published. They are not presented in discursive fashion but jump from thought to thought, feeling to feeling, subject to subject. The style is erratic and often vague. No specific method was used, though Leroy W. Clark, Jr. found that

Kazan generally analyzed the theme or ruling idea, the type of play, the basic directorial approach and style, the major characters, and the actions. In some instances when he thought it was important to the play he also recorded his ideas concerning stage business, props, and music.[41]

Thematic concerns were usually of ascendant importance. He would state and restate what a play was about. Thematic concerns always led him to organically consider all production concepts, so that his notes on set and costume design, for example, were couched in thematic terms. The relation of character to theme was likewise essential. *J.B.*'s title figure was seen as a tragic hero suffering from hubris, "pride combined with *no thinking*. This, of course, is America today."[42]

In pompous capitals matching what some felt to be the play's dramatic weakness, Kazan described the theme of *After the Fall*:

THIS IS THE STORY OF A

MAN

WHOSE MORALITY HAS

BETRAYED HIM.

HE HAD FOUND IT FALSE

AND HE IS

SEARCHING

FOR A NEW ONE.

THIS PLAY DRAMATIZES HIS

BEWILDERMENT,

HIS SEARCH,

AND WHAT HE DOES DISCOVER[43]

Despite the stress laid on theme in his notebooks, Kazan in his autobiography observes that from the time of *Tea and Sympathy,* he gradually moved away from his tendency—acquired in his Group days—to pin a play down thematically, at least in performance. He came to recognize that a play is weakened when its theme is spelled out and taught to an audience. It was more important, he discovered, to retain the ambiguities of a story, and not to resolve all loose ends, so that the audience had something to ponder when they departed. Theatre should be like life, this view insists, in which easy summaries are not ready to hand. "The theme," he writes, "should not be insisted on, in fact should be constantly and repeatedly contradicted. The viewer should not be bullied into agreeing with what a character says about the theme."[44] Thus, although he may have continued to make notes for himself about a theme, and even to have used such ideas to stimulate directorial choices, thematic underlining was given short shrift in the actual production process.

He often discussed plays in terms of the "spine," or what Stanislavsky called the "superobjective." His psychological orientation led him to think of the spine as "that lowest common denominator of personality that justifies even the most inconsistent details of behavior."[45] Each character was comprehended by the director in terms of his or her spine. For *A Streetcar Named Desire* Blanche's spine was "find Protection: the tradition of the old South says it must be through another person."[46] Maggie in *After the Fall* had the spine "to make herself a thing of the past."[47] Characters' spines were normally phrased in terms of an active verb leading to an objective. Kazan's ideas on a directorial approach often were couched in passages like the following for *Death of a Salesman*:

This play has to be directed with COMPASSION, which means with a quick and intense realization of the PAIN of each of the characters . . . and the real meaning of the "spine," which means the living and emotional meaning of the "spine."[48]

Characters are described by their actions, their personal qualities, and their physical attributes. For *After the Fall* there was this note on the hero: "Quentin discovers that one has to find his strength NOT through a person or cause, but IN ONE'S OWN BEING."[49]

Characters were also physicalized through constant reference to behavior patterns. Willy in *Death of a Salesman* was seen "defending himself," "justifying himself," "excusing himself," being "overwhelmed by . . . helplessness and seeking refuge," "asserting himself," and so forth.

Under the subheading "Direction and Style," he wrote for *Death of a Salesman* that

this play is essentially about Willy. Biff's importance is only as the love-object which "failed." But the play describes the *Process*—dramatizes the *Process in Willy's Mind*. In doing all this the elements of theatre magic are necessary. Tricks—music—disappearances.[50]

For *After the Fall* he specifically called for the use of a "freeze" technique by the actors, to suggest the idea of "doing something over and over. The one

most characteristic, most feeling, most eloquent attitude, glimpse, activity."[51]
He rejected the thought of blackouts for *After the Fall* by writing: "*Black Outs.
NO!* Try not to rely on them. They are stereotyped and 'empty.' "[52]

He noted the play's genre, comedy, tragedy, drama, or subtype, calling *A
Streetcar Named Desire,* for example, both a poetic tragedy and a romantic
tragedy.

Design matters usually were clearly represented in the notes, often by striking
images. He described what he wanted for *After the Fall* in metaphoric terms,
hoping to stimulate Mielziner's visualization. "It should be where murder was
discovered by the murderer," he wrote. "It should be cavernous, deep and dark.
It should be made up of the corners of [Quentin's] memory into which his mind
has never penetrated before, because it never dared to."[53] Kazan's scenic concept
for *J.B.* differed strikingly from that designed for the original Yale production
by Donald Oenslager. He tried to convey to his designer, Boris Aronson, ideas
such as these in his notebook:

(1) The set is not a circus. It looks like a circus . . . It is a plastic rendition of essences.
Example: "the family circle." The platform is where man naively imagines God to dwell
. . . This platform also exists in the circus. So that here, too, the set at first glance looks
like a circus. . . . (2) The tent represents the ecclesiastical claptrap, the churches pagan
and Oriental, the "props" of religions from the cavemen to the present.[54]

Kazan's desire to be as specific as possible for his set designers extended to
his preparation of ground plans for each production, often with precise measurements and ideas on the scale of the sets, before the design was prepared.
The plan was intended to inspire the designer, who needs as much help as the
director can give him. "You have to do more than hire a talented designer to
do the visual side,"[55] he declares.

Similarly, other production elements—like costumes, lights, and music—were
described, if not in his own notes, in letters to those responsible. For example,
his *J.B.* costume desires were contained in notes he submitted to Lucinda Ballard,
the designer. He emphasized his view of the characters as "types" and his belief
that the essence of each type should be conveyed by the costumes. He hit on
Wendell Wilkie as the type for J.B.—a representative of "liberal Capitalism."
Using highly expressive words, he described the leading characters and added:
"These aren't brilliant, but you get the idea. If you have designed *those,* you
would have stylized costumes . . . and costumes that fit the set."[56]

PROMPTBOOKS

Kazan's proclivity for written documentation of his thoughts extended to the
preparation of minutely analytical promptbook annotations. The notes were
placed on a page facing the text and included numerous useful jottings on
motivation and situation. According to Kenneth Thorpe Rowe, they were ar-

ranged in three columns, "the first for general situation, the second for more particular and internal analysis, the third for stage business."[57] Asterisks denoted the place in the script to which a note applied. Helpful Method terminology was used, with actions described in forceful verbs. Thus, in the scene between Bernard and Willy in *Death of a Salesman,* Bernard's notes are "find facts," "help," "avoid," "cutting right through," "wishes he were out of it," "trying to get out of it," and so on. Blocking is not as clearly defined in these annotations as is the physical activity expressive of the character's state of mind. By noting that Willy puts Bernard's tennis rackets down "guiltily," the director is prepared to offer a specific suggestion which can be of great help to the performer. In the Willy-Bernard scene, representative notes include (with their respective line number designations):

12. WILLY: Figure out what happened!!!???
Bernard is to Willy a mystery, an affront, an insult, a living humiliation.
   BERNARD: Put him at his ease, help him in a nice simple way. Bernard is proud to be known as the modest fellow. . . .
19. BERNARD: find facts. Bernard knows Willy is lying. . . .
20. *They are not talking to each other. They are examining each other.* . . .
36. WILLY: PLEAD.[58]

   These extracts from Kazan's notes display an incisive ability to cut through the surface patterns of human behavior, to expose the motive forces underlying them. As Arthur Miller expresses it:

When Kazan directs . . . he wants to dramatize the metaphor in every human action. There is always the overt action and something under the surface. You kill a man, but in what attitude? In anger? Or as though you were praying to him? A good deal of the time, Kazan finds the inner metaphor and that is why his best work has tremendous depth. . . . If he finds nothing below the surface, his work tends to get clouded or seems overloaded. He is always on the quest for metaphors. That is his art.[59]

CASTING

   The productions of Elia Kazan often were considered masterpieces of casting. He was able to see in actors qualities of which others were unaware. Among the actors to whose careers he gave enormous impetus by placing them in roles which earned them critical recognition were Marlon Brando, Pat Hingle, Karl Malden, Paul Newman, Kim Hunter, and Barbara Loden. He hated to cast through auditions, finding them extremely deceptive. Auditions were valuable for minor roles where the director wants a certain quality or look, but not for major parts. He would manipulate the audition process, however, when he wanted to convince the producer and author that he had found someone for a role better than the performer already cast. After spotting actress Evans Evans in a summer theatre production, he decided to use her in *Dark at the Top of the Stairs* and to release a previously contracted player to make room for her. Explaining the situation to Miss Evans, he told her that she had to give a brilliant audition to sway Arnold Saint-Subber, the producer, and William Inge, the playwright, to pay off the other actress and accept the new actress in her stead. He had his costume designer Lucinda Ballard dress her in a costume put together for the tryout. These preparations paid off when Miss Evans landed the part. A similar ruse was used to get Arthur Miller to accept Barbara Loden as Maggie, the Marilyn Monroe–like character in *After the Fall*. Kazan did what he could to disguise the actress's pregnancy, and dressed her in a blond wig for the audition, which helped her land this important role.

Because he wanted to see beyond the false facade that most actors throw up at an audition, he would sometimes provoke the actor to see if he or she displayed any ''temperament.'' He wanted to discover if some part of their personality was being hidden, for only then could he determine whether the actor was right for the play. He once told William Goldman:

As far as casting's concerned, begin with this: an actor can't be good in a lousy part. And unless the part is somewhere in the actor, you're never going to be able to fake 'em through it. That's why you've got to know what people really are, not their artificial egos.[60]

Therefore, Kazan found it pleasanter to cast people he knew, those whose qualities he had had time to perceive. He observed to Goldman, ''Most actors have that false front. That's why I have drinks with them, talk, anything. None of this intuition crap. And I cast people I know.''[61]

Typecasting, as generally understood, was not his method. He sought people with internal correspondences for the role more than those who looked the part. He recounted once how an actress he had cast in *All My Sons*

could not actually act the part for some time. She was too young and too nice. But out of these qualities I got a dual thing which was much more interesting than if I'd picked her for the obvious disagreeable qualities the character possessed.[62]

An ideal way of becoming familiar with the personalities of many actors was to work with them over a period of time in the confines of a company situation. Kazan found this approach helpful during the Group Theatre days and sought to recapture it at Lincoln Center. Also, his involvement at the Actors Studio over the years gave him wide knowledge of many actors practicing there. When he cast an actor with whom he had not worked before, he made strenuous efforts to learn what he could about him. For example, Kazan took Deborah Kerr for a long walk in an effort to find out things that might be useful in directing her in *Tea and Sympathy*. After an hour's stroll, they wound up in the Central Park zoo discussing Kerr's character and watching the seals.

Kazan rarely cast big stars in his plays, opting instead for young, talented unknowns. He has long claimed that stars become too much like merchandise once they are successful, and that they keep playing the same personality notes over and over while failing to develop. The director's task is made more difficult by his having to extract something deeper than the actor's salable exterior. American actors too often sell themselves to Hollywood and leave their acting potential behind. The unknown actor still bears with him the scent of freshness and promise, Kazan feels. "Marlon Brando has never been as good again as he was in *Streetcar*. It isn't the bloom that comes off the well-known star—it's the humanity."[63]

An aversion to stars may have begun to develop after Kazan had to deal with Tallulah Bankhead, who played Sabrina in *The Skin of Our Teeth*. Unhappy that she could not get Orson Welles to stage the play, instead of the fledgling Kazan, she "proceeded to make life hell" for him. According to a report by Lee Israel:

> She stormed out of rehearsal frequently, refused to take direction, requisitioned lines for herself which had been originally written for other characters to say. She fought about dressing rooms, tore at her costumes, ripped at the set, vilified, cried shrugged, shouted, and divided the company into allies and enemies. . . . One story tells how Kazan came to Tallulah's hotel, literally tied and gagged her, and proceeded to catalogue . . . what she was doing to herself, to the rest of the company, and to the play.[64]

Kazan makes no mention of physically binding the star, but he does talk at length about the experience in his autobiography, revealing some deliciously scandalous anecdotes about the famous star. In brief, he would combat her excessive behavior by calmly using her understudy when she failed to show up at rehearsal, and keep his seething emotions under cover, where she could not detect them. Her frequent tirades met only with his utter patience and seeming respect. However, one night at 3:00 A.M., after a catastrophic dress rehearsal, he finally blew his top at her outrageous behavior and could not be restrained, for which the entire cast and crew applauded him, a sign to him that he at last had become a real director. From then on, except for minor disruptions, the show sailed smoothly. However, Kazan determined never to have such a problem again by being much more careful in his casting.

In selecting an actor, Kazan looked for aspects of temperament and intelligence. He valued intelligence, because with it the actor could better comprehend his role and learn his lines. Actors with their own sharp interpretive faculties interested him because they could work without being totally dependent on him.

Another thing he looked for was the place at which the actor had trained. If he or she had not worked at the Studio, then a school with a similar orientation and reputation for success counted strongly in their favor. For instance, actors from the Neighborhood Playhouse stood a good chance of gaining his approval, as did graduates of Yale Drama School.

He always cast the principal roles first and then found actors to balance these in the secondary parts. The casting of one actor was matched by the casting of another; the actors had to look and sound right together, no matter how great their individual talent.

Kazan recognized that certain actors were better for certain playwrights than were others. For Williams, he knew that actors like Karl Malden, Eli Wallach, and Mildred Dunnock were appropriate since they have

the talent for tragicomedy . . . the ability to capture inner contradictions . . . an appreciation that nobility and foolishness can come on top of the other and that this coincidence and juxtaposition may be close to the essence of human character.[65]

Remembering his unsuccessful staging of Robert Ardrey's *Thunder Rock* for the Group, with a cast including many actors of Jewish background, he declared that the play might have succeeded had he cast it with actors who shared Ardrey's middle-American background, or even with English actors; such actors' "emotion is understated and generally accompanied by a wry humor,"[66] he noted. (Ideally, even the director should be of a background similar to the playwright's, he says.)

EARLY REHEARSALS

Rehearsals for a Kazan production began, as a rule, with the director reading the script to the cast, followed by the actors reading it aloud from their "sides." Kazan was one of the few mid-century American directors to read the script to his actors. He either read the entire play or parts of it at the first rehearsals. With *Jacobowsky and the Colonel,* for example, he read only the first three scenes. His reading communicated the ideas yet avoided suggesting how the actors should read their lines. In the case of *J.B.* he broke with the precedent and had the author himself read the play. As the play is in verse, he wanted the cast to realize how unburdensome the play's verse would be and how effective an asset it would be to their performances. He felt that through MacLeish's reading the actors might be able to grasp MacLeish's experience in creating the poetic dialogue. Kazan expected that during the reading the actors would be continually surprised as they realized how easy the speaking of the verse could be, how straightforward, clear, and pleasurable. If the actors could reach that point where it became as necessary for them to say the lines as it was for MacLeish to write them, they would have succeeded in achieving what Kazan hoped of them. Kazan actually disliked MacLeish's poetry, which he did not find "poetic." To make the play work, he downplayed the verbal elements, focused on the visual side, and kept the actors on the move, not allowing any speech of longer than three sentences to be spoken in stillness.

Kazan's general policy was to take his time before blocking a play. Several days, sometimes the entire first week, of rehearsals were devoted to reading and analyzing the piece. He clarified with the actors all their interpretations and set a solid intellectual foundation upon which his blocking could later build. He would then be able to concentrate primarily on movement and action at the proper time. During this time he would outline his ideas on the play and its characters and discuss what he hoped to achieve with the production. This procedure gave everyone a clear picture of their goals.

Before the actors themselves began to read he would make some basic remarks on how they should attack the play. For *Jacobowsky* he told them to "read with good normal speaking energy. Take it very easy—don't try to give a performance. But talk to each other, find out whom you're talking to and, especially, listen to what they're saying to you."[67] He then gave them advice on the flavor of the speech he wanted from them as European characters. Though he gave them only these general instructions, he cautioned them to give him what he asked for.

No sooner would an actor's reading get under way than Kazan was likely to interrupt. He would comment on interpretation, circumstances, intonation, style, and so on. To an actor reading with a British accent: "Remember you are Gallic, not English—your speech must be light and witty; you are not delivering yourself of wise remarks." To an actress reading her lines with too much obvious charm: "Cosette is not shy, modest, inhibited: remember she is a Frenchwoman, direct, a realist. She is an extrovert, and you must play her for that to contrast with the Colonel who is all introvert."[68]

REHEARSAL PRACTICES

Rehearsals for a Kazan production were extremely well organized so that the best use could be made of the brief time allotted. One reason he gave up Broadway was that he had only nineteen or twenty days in which to work with the actors before opening. He hoped for a six-month rehearsal period at Lincoln Center, but ten weeks was all he actually used when there. During the regular four-week Broadway period he came to rehearsals thoroughly prepared so that not a moment was wasted. At Lincoln Center, the ten weeks allowed him much greater freedom to experiment, even to send an author away for a lengthy period while he reworked his second act. One thing he never did, no matter how much time he had, was to keep actors at rehearsal when they were not needed.

Normally, the author was not permitted to attend rehearsals, except at designated intervals, though Kazan agreed to alter this practice when the occasion demanded it. MacLeish's presence at the *J.B.* rehearsals was one exception, though Tennessee Williams also attended rehearsals, where he sat right next to the director. Williams would show up late in the rehearsals, react audibly to what he saw and heard, and then leave. Kazan often found his comments helpful. Once, though, when Williams spoke to an actress about her work, he enraged Kazan, who told him never to come to another rehearsal or speak to the actors. Williams thenceforth obeyed the latter injunction.

Kazan dominated blocking rehearsals, mixing in freely with the actors as he manipulated them about the stage. The blocking had been preplanned to save time though it was done sketchily to allow for changes during rehearsal. He continued to expand and enrich his first suggestions as rehearsals progressed. If he had to demonstrate a piece of business, he did it broadly so as not to invite imitation, allowing the actor to fill in the details. The more the business is merely hinted at, the more the actor will be convinced that he can do it better and thus respond alertly to the stimulus.

As Kazan moved restlessly along with the actors while blocking them, seemingly playing each role, "his body [noted Maurice Zolotow] unconsciously moves like a pool player giving a caroming ball twinges of body English."[69] Zolotow watched him direct Gusti Huber and Paul Lukas in *Flight into Egypt,* observing that Kazan watched the rehearsal from the first row. In one scene the two Viennese refugees played by these actors were supposed to be waiting in their hotel room for their visas to the United States. Huber's character had to pack away her son's clothing in an old suitcase. Watching her, Kazan

restlessly stood up and leaned on a piano in the pit. Finally, he sprang up, leaped the flight of steps to the stage, and took the pajamas away from Miss Huber. He showed her how he wanted her to take the pajama tops and crumple them and then crumple herself against her husband's lap. As she repeated his movements, Kazan stood on the top step, both hands stuck behind him in his belt.[70]

Blocking was worked out by Kazan during his homework on a play and in rehearsal with the actors. He ignored the author's stage directions, believing their creation was his responsibility. Once, while rehearsing a scene, and stuck for a staging solution, he stopped the actors and proceeded to pace nervously for fifteen minutes while everyone present looked on anxiously. When someone finally interrupted his train of thought to ask what was wrong, he said he was trying to solve a staging problem; it was pointed out to him that the script already contained an answer in the author's directions. He flared up: "That chicken shit? I never read that. What do you think my business is in being here? I'm the director; I have to think of the business. I never read that kind of thing."[71]

Actors were expected to have their lines down soon after they were blocked, and Kazan was very strict about the lines being learned exactly rather than paraphrased. No matter how truthful the actor's emotional involvement, he had to give full value to the lines, especially in poetic and intellectual plays. A blending of inner and outer techniques was essential.

Nonstop run-throughs came during the third week of rehearsals, but he sometimes stopped dress rehearsals to work on the details of problem scenes. Once the show was set, he brooked no changes, aside from the most minute ones that enter a performance from one night to the other. But all basics such as business, moves, and blocking positions were not to be tampered with unless he approved the changes. After a show opened, the job of surveillance became the stage manager's. Kazan never came back to a show to run a refresher rehearsal. He was finished with the work once it opened in New York and did not stage the same play twice, nor did he do its road-show version or the London production.

The atmosphere at a Kazan rehearsal was exciting and inspiriting because of what the director brought to it. Anderson remembered that

Gadge creates a sort of friendship in all his work. He works happily. He is happiest when he is working. He is exuberant, full of joy and fun and contagious enthusiasm. With the delight of a child, he guides each person to realize the precious quality of self, the best that is in him.[72]

This attitude is owing to the influence of Harold Clurman, from whom Kazan says he learned "the general spirit of how to approach a play and how to deal with actors, what the rehearsal of a play can and should be—a joyous process."[73] The company was made to feel as if it were a family with Kazan the father figure whom the actors would obey implicitly.

Thomas Morgan saw Kazan in 1962 as

A short, congenial, ambiguous man with unruly-to-wild black hair [now white], eyes too close, nose too much, and a taste in wearing apparel that ranges from wrinkled tweeds to sweat shirts. He complains that strangers often mistake him for a taxi driver.[74]

Kazan is extremely informal in attire and attitude, unconventional, and dynamic in his public persona, Morgan said: "He wolfs food, smokes big cigars, calls males as well as females *baby,* and swears just about all the time, using all the words in any company."[75]

WORKING WITH ACTORS

This unusual firebrand of a man evoked some of the most sensational performances of the century from his actors. Few were those who lacked confidence in Kazan's approach, for he made each player feel as if he were special, as though no other actor could possibly have been better for the role. But he rejected the idea of instilling an actor with false confidence. He wanted the actors to realize that he was human and fallible. A director who gives an actor false confidence, acting as if nothing were wrong when clearly something is, is "full of it," he said. If a director says instead,

"I don't know—let's try it this way," and then he tries it that way with full conviction and full feeling, and then he says, "Let's try it another way," and he tries that way as fully as before—well the actors respond because they feel he's honestly searching.[76]

Actress Geraldine Page recalls, however, that sometimes Kazan's creative fickleness seriously annoyed his actors. She states that he would give the actors an idea and have them perform it.

Then he'd have another idea and a different way. After a while, we'd do it one way and it'd work and we'd all say, "Aha! We got this." The next day we'd do it again, and

because we were repeating what we did the other time, it wouldn't quite go, so he'd
think up something else. Finally, one day, I said to him, "All your ideas are marvelous.
We can't wait to act them, but can't you settle on one and let us get to try it? You've
got to let us mess them up a couple of times before we get hold of anything." He glared
at me, chewed on his cigar, and came up with another idea.[77]

In spite of his distaste for instilling an actor with false confidence, Kazan—ever
concerned about damaging the actor's ego—worried about how to tell an actor
that he had reservations about his performance. The director should try to be as
encouraging as possible, and not reveal his doubts: "He's supposed to be a
center of calm in a whirlwind of uncertainty. So why discourage actors?"[78] If
absolutely necessary, the director can resort to various subtle measures to suggest
dissatisfaction, such as leaving rehearsal without saying anything, thus planting
a seed of doubt, or by praising one actor and not the other in a scene. The
director must often be a dissembler to get the best results with the least psychological pain.

Fundamental to Kazan's approach is the Stanislavsky system as he learned it
with the Group. He did not adhere religiously to one interpretation of the Method
and recognized the existence of several variations. Nevertheless, regardless of
their differences, one essential factor was common to all: "The importance of
asking what the person on stage wants, what the circumstances are which he is
working in to get what he wants, and why he wants it—*and* how to make all
these important to the actor."[79]

For Kazan, a good actor demands to know the basics of a situation, to comprehend all the pertinent factors of the given circumstances. The character enters
having come from a specific somewhere which colors the way he comes on. He
wants something during his scene, but he has to overcome various obstacles to
achieve his goal. It is the director's job to establish the circumstances that will
allow the actor to achieve his *want*.

Characters always have objectives, and these must be the guiding light for all
their scenes. To achieve an objective a character will behave in a specific way,
will choose specific actions that help him overcome his obstacles. The actions
chosen by the actor to meet his objectives are of enormous importance in helping
him to develop the character's physical behavior. If the correct actions are chosen,
the actor will execute them with ease and appropriateness and will be likely to
feel something akin to the emotions supposedly undergone by the character. The
director's task then, according to Kazan, is to convert psychology into behavior.
Rather than emphasizing the Stanislavsky concept of the "magic if" (i.e., "What
would I do if I were this character in this situation?"), Kazan adheres to what
the Russian actor-director called the "method of physical actions," a method
which allows for work on the object or action itself and not a substitute or
parallel. Kazan believes that Stanislavsky "was saying, 'If you really invest the
moment itself—what's actually happening there—you'll get all the emotion you
need.' And that's what I believe, too."[80]

Another Stanislavsky term which often arises in Kazan's vocabulary is the "subtext," that underlying meaning found beneath the surface of every play. What a character says is rarely what he means; the actor's and director's job is to get behind that which is said to that which is thought. Arthur Miller, as we have seen, called this Kazan's search for the metaphor in every speech and action. One example is Stanley Kowalski's phone conversation about bowling in *A Streetcar Named Desire*. Kazan had Brando as Stanley play the scene so that it revealed the character's feelings, not about the subject of bowling, but about Blanche and Stella regarding an argument he had just been having. The behavior of Stanley on the phone had to be expressive of his emotional state in the situation with the two women.

Depending on the style he employed, Kazan either used very realistic props or had most props acted out in mime. When using props he chose those most indicative of the character. Stanley's cigar and beer bottle, for instance, expressed the character's oral fixation. Use of the actual props in rehearsal was crucial, and he usually managed to sneak them in despite objections from the stagehands' union, which prohibits anything but substitute props without the presence of a paid property person or crew. However, when Kazan used mime, as in *Cat on a Hot Tin Roof* and *After the Fall,* the actors had to rely on the Stanislavsky technique of sense memory, remembering what the actual prop or scenery would have looked and felt like if it were present. In *Cat* all doors had to be opened and closed believably, despite their being imaginary. When doing *After the Fall*, rather than using the "magic if" to help the actors conjure up the real scenery, Kazan had them use specific sense memories to capture the truthful attitude. To aid Paul Mann in feeling as if he were on a hospital porch, Kazan told him not only the type of porch he was on but that he should let the sun warm his face. This let the actor find the proper behavior to suggest that he was at peace prior to his receiving bad news.

Kazan felt that, when properly used, the technique of "emotional memory" or "emotional recall" was valid; to be so it had to be made specific and relevant to the scene. According to the Method, this technique refers to the actor's recalling an emotional moment in his own life analogous to that of the character in the scene. Most actors misuse this technique, being more in touch with their own feelings than those of the role, and consequently are outside the play while acting in it.

Actors who worked for instant results were cautioned by Kazan to take their time and allow for as much growth and discovery as possible. Yet the limits of rehearsal time forced him to push his players as soon as he could toward their goals. He tried every way he could to get the actors to become involved in the play's reality. Sometimes intellectual or psychological suggestions failed to get the desired response. At these times he might have resorted to physical means, provoking the actors by jabbing at them with a prop or throwing things and pestering them with commands. On the other hand, some actors were likely to find themselves being taken aside and spoken to in secretive, whispered tones.

Each actor demands a new and sometimes devious approach. Geraldine Page recounts how, for *Sweet Bird of Youth,* Kazan "sloshed" her with affection and, to make her comfortable in the part, left old movie magazines around hoping to inspire her with their photos of gorgeous screen stars. For Paul Newman, frightened of his impending performance on Broadway in the same play, he kept telling the actor over and over not to be nervous, and succeeded in making him so scared that he began to depend increasingly on Kazan and ended up playing the role with just the touch of nervousness that the director wanted all along.

Sometimes Kazan let his actors work out a problem on their own, using any method they found helpful. An especially delicate scene—such as the final one in *Tea and Sympathy,* in which an attractive older woman prepares to make love to a young man, thus assuring him of his masculinity—might be placed largely in the actors' hands provided they were secure enough in their characters to find the right approach.

Rather than apply a dogmatic method, Kazan was considerably liberal in his handling of actors. When he directed Mary Martin in *One Touch of Venus,* he gave her a great deal of freedom. At his first meeting with this star, prior to the start of rehearsals, she told him that her approach to a role was external. If she could determine the character's walk, the major problem of embodying the part would be overcome. Kazan found this a perfectly acceptable idea. He also told her that to play Venus, all she would have to do would be to imagine how she would feel if she were a statue coming to life after a thousand years. Venus sees the madly rushing life of the modern world and thinks that everyone must be crazy. This would be suggested by her playing in a totally different tempo, contrasting her legato to everyone else's staccato. This physical approach made her feel comfortable and helped her to succeed in the show.

The major technique Kazan and Stanislavsky had in common was their reliance on improvisation. Kazan used improvisations, however, only when he felt the actors were receptive to them, which he usually found to be the case with the younger players rather than the older. Improvisations were established with clear objectives, the characters *wanting* something and using the improvisation to discover how the want could be satisfied. Blocking and business often grew organically from these exercises. Improvisations were based on a variety of possibilities, such as what had happened prior to the play's actions. Each character was given his own objective, but those of the others in the scene were not known to him, as in life. In rehearsing *After the Fall,* Kazan set up an improvisation designed to help the character of the father, played by Paul Mann, feel that his wife has acted against his interests in her relationship with their son, Quentin. Since the father entered and spoke only a few lines, Kazan created an improvisation to deepen the moment and make it fuller. According to the improvisation, the father comes home, eagerly hoping to set the son up in business; in the course of the scene he discovers not only that the son is going to college instead, but that the mother is responsible for the son's decision. The devastating effect produced on the character in the improvisation was then used in the actual production.

Such imaginative devices were used in various ways. Believing that no actor should make an entrance unless fully prepared psychologically for the scene he is to encounter, Kazan would help his actors get into the proper frame of mind for their appearance by suggesting what might have happened to their character before the scene began. He chose this technique over group warmups, since it allowed him to deal individually with each actor's problems. He would also vary his suggestions on the present occurrences.

I say, "This happened right before you came in," or, "Yesterday this happened," or, "You haven't seen this person for so long." Then I start changing the circumstances under which the scene is played. I say, "You have to catch a train in ten minutes," or, "You have to do this so that no one hears you." I set the circumstances under which the scene is played.[81]

Kazan never insisted on a specific acting technique but allowed his players to find their own means for performing a scene. He would merely set the problem and tell them what it was he wanted them to achieve. They were trusted to discover their own way of solving a problem by making it real to themselves in a personal way. Only his great patience allowed him to place so much trust in the actors. He does state, however, that "patience is a good virtue for a director to have if the threat of violence is waiting underneath." His experience with Bankhead taught him that the director must be determined to get what he wants by hook or crook, "preferably by patient kindness or gentle, subtle manipulation, but if not by these means, by any that the situation calls for—an intimidating voice or the force of rage, simulated or genuine."[82]

Though he found little compassion for professional critics, Kazan listened to critical advice during rehearsals when offered by those he respected. He was not put off by well-argued contradictions from actors and felt that good ideas could come from anybody. He welcomed actors' rehearsal queries, having once been an actor himself, and being fully aware of their problems and insecurities. As a result, few who worked with him ever had anything but the highest praise for his methods and respect for him as a man.

CONCLUSION

In his autobiography Kazan provides a brutally candid assessment of his strengths and weaknesses.[83] Among the faults he finds are his inability to handle plays that do not directly relate to his own experiences; his noncatholic taste and limited artistic range; his nonintellectualism; his incapacity in the face of classics and poetic drama; his weakness at creating comic business; and his dependency on ideas stolen from others. On the plus side he lists such things as his daring, his ability to work with actors, and to inspire them, especially through his ability to break down their inhibitions by sharing his own innermost feelings and experiences. Although the emphasis seems here to be on the debit side, given the nature of a career spent almost entirely in the commercial arena, Kazan's accomplishments—circumscribed as they may be when compared to those of such men as Tyrone Guthrie and Max Reinhardt—nevertheless are great enough to place him high on the scale of American directors.

Kazan's presence is still felt through his films and novels. The lack of American directors of stature is as obvious today as ever. In the early seventies he told Michael Ciment that he could no longer even bear to read modern plays, because they seemed so out of sync with the real world. He feels his temperament is more suited to the cinema. "I have dreams, when I'm asleep, of working in the theatre again...but when I actually get up in the morning and I face life, I think of novels and films,"[84] he declared. In May 1986, when he appeared at a Museum of Modern Art salute to his movies, the seventy-seven-year-old director's principal concern was with a new film project he was developing. It seems highly unlikely, despite periodic news reports to the contrary, that Elia Kazan will ever again bring the incandescence of his touch to light up the American stage.

NOTES

1. Kenneth Tynan, *Curtains* (New York: Atheneum, 1961), p. 87.

2. Elia Kazan, *Elia Kazan, a Life* (New York: Alfred A. Knopf, 1988), pp. 49–50.

3. Ibid., p. 51.

4. Quoted in Kazan, *Elia Kazan,* p. 66.

5. Ibid., p. 596.

6. Ibid.

7. Ibid., p. 143.

8. Maurice Zolotow, "Viewing the Kinetic Mr. Kazan," *New York Times,* 9 March 1952.

9. Henry Hewes, "A Minority Report on *J.B.*," *Saturday Review,* 3 January 1959, p. 22.

10. Quoted in an interview with Richard Schechner and Theodore Hoffman, "Look, There's the American Theatre," *Tulane Drama Review* 8 (Winter 1964): 79.

11. Elia Kazan, "Theatre: New Stages, New Plays, New Actors," *New York Times Magazine,* 23 September 1962, p. 28.

12. Tennessee Williams, "Notes for the Designer," in *Cat on a Hot Tin Roof* (New York: New American Library, 1958), p. xiv.

13. Eric Bentley, *What Is Theatre? A Query in Chronicle Form* (Boston: Beacon Press, 1956), p. 55.

14. Ibid.

15. Ibid., p. 56.

16. John Gassner, *Directions in Modern Drama and Theatre* (New York: Holt, Rinehart and Winston, 1967), p. 125.

17. Harold Clurman, *Lies Like Truth* (New York: Grove Press, 1958), p. 79.

18. Eric Bentley, *The Dramatic Event* (Boston: Beacon Press, 1956), p. 109.

19. Gordon Rogoff, "A Streetcar Named Kazan," *Reporter,* 17 December 1964, p. 38.

20. Eric Bentley, *In Search of Theatre* (New York: Vintage Books, 1957), p. 83.

21. Rogoff, "A Streetcar Named Kazan," p. 38.

22. Virginia Stevens, "Elia Kazan, Actor and Director of Stage and Screen," *Theatre Arts* 31 (December 1947): 19.

23. George Jean Nathan, *The Magic Mirror,* ed. Thomas Quinn Curtiss (New York: Alfred A. Knopf, 1960), p. 244.

24. Elia Kazan, "Ten Best for a Repertory Theatre," *New York Times Magazine,* 9 November 1958, p. 74.

25. Julius Novick, "The Old Regime at Lincoln Center," *Educational Theatre Journal* 18 (May 1964): 131.

26. Howard Taubman, "Arthur Miller's Play Opens Repertory," *New York Times,* 24 January 1964.

27. Richard Gilman, *Common and Uncommon Masks: Writings on the Theatre, 1961–1970* (New York: Vintage Books, 1972), p. 261.

28. Quoted by George Oppenheimer, "On Stage: Kazan Answers the Critics," *Newsday,* 14 November 1964.

29. Novick, "The Old Regime," p. 132.

30. Kazan, "Theatre: New Stages," p. 18.

31. To make matters worse, Kazan's wife, Molly Day Thacher, died a month before the opening.

32. Kazan, *Elia Kazan,* p. 609.

33. Robert Anderson, "Walk a Ways with Me," *Theatre Arts* 38 (January 1954): 31.

34. Ibid.

35. Tennessee Williams, "A Note of Explanation," *Theatre Arts* 41 (June 1957): 62.

36. Quoted by Arthur Gelb, "Williams and Kazan and the Big Walk-Out," *New York Times,* 1 May 1960.

37. Kazan, *Elia Kazan,* p. 301.

38. Tennessee Williams, *Memoirs* (New York: Bantam Books, 1976), p. 213.

39. Hewes, "A Minority Report," p. 22.

40. Elia Kazan and Archibald MacLeish, "The Staging of a Play," *Esquire* 59 (May 1959): 144.

41. Leroy W. Clark, Jr., "The Directing Principles and Practices of Elia Kazan" (Ph.D. diss., Kent State University, 1976), p. 275. A thorough analysis of Kazan's notebooks for *A Streetcar Named Desire* is in David Richard Jones, *Great Directors at Work: Stanislavsky, Brecht, Kazan, Brook* (Berkeley: University of California Press, 1986).

42. Kazan and MacLeish, "The Staging of a Play," p. 144.

43. Nancy Meyer and Richard Meyer, "*After the Fall*: A View from the Director's Notebook," in *Theatre: The Annual of the Repertory Theatre of Lincoln Center, 1965,* ed. Barry Hyams (New York: Hill and Wang, 1965), p. 50.

44. Kazan, *Elia Kazan,* p. 505.

45. Meyer and Meyer, "*After the Fall,*" p. 47.

46. Elia Kazan, "Notebook for *A Streetcar Named Desire,*" in *Directors on Directing: A Source Book of the Modern Theatre,* ed. Toby Cole and Helen Krich Chinoy (Indianapolis: Bobbs-Merrill, 1963), p. 365.

47. Meyer and Meyer, "*After the Fall,*" p. 63.

48. Elia Kazan, "Notebook Made in Preparation for Directing *Death of a Salesman,*" in Kenneth Thorpe Rowe, *A Theatre in Your Head* (New York: Funk and Wagnalls, 1960), p. 50.

49. Meyer and Meyer, "*After the Fall,*" p. 67.

50. Kazan, "Notebook for *Salesman,*" p. 261.

51. Meyer and Meyer, "*After the Fall,*" p. 72.

52. Ibid.

53. Ibid.

54. Kazan and MacLeish, "Staging a Play," p. 144.

55. Kazan, *Elia Kazan,* p. 181.

56. Kazan and MacLeish, "Staging a Play," p. 144.

57. Rowe, *A Theatre in Your Head,* p. 51.

58. Kazan, "Notebook for *Salesman,*" pp. 52–56.

59. Quoted in Thomas B. Morgan, "Elia Kazan's Great Expectations," *Harper's Magazine* 225 (September 1962): 68.

60. Quoted in William Goldman, *The Season: A Candid Look at Broadway* (New York: Bantam Books, 1970), p. 208.

61. Ibid., p. 209.

62. Quoted in Stevens, "Elia Kazan," pp. 20–21.

63. Quoted in Morgan, "Elia Kazan's Great Expectations," p. 71.

64. Lee Israel, *Miss Tallulah Bankhead* (New York: Putnam, 1972), p. 215.

65. "A Quiz for Kazan," *Theatre Arts Monthly* 40 (November 1956): 32.

66. Kazan, *Elia Kazan,* p. 182.

67. Hermine Rich Isaacs, "First Rehearsals: Elia Kazan Directs a Modern Legend," *Theatre Arts Monthly* 28 (March 1944): 147.

68. Ibid., p. 148.

69. Zolotow, "Viewing the Kinetic Mr. Kazan."

70. Ibid.

71. Quoted in Cheryl Crawford, *One Naked Individual* (Indianapolis: Bobbs-Merrill, 1977), p. 129.

72. Anderson, "Walk a Ways with Me," p. 31.

73. Kazan, *Elia Kazan,* p. 123.

74. Morgan, "Elia Kazan's Great Expectations," p. 67.

75. Ibid.

76. Schechner and Hoffman, "Look, There's the American Theatre," p. 65.

77. Quoted by Richard Schechner, "The Bottomless Cup: An Interview with Geraldine Page," ed. Charles L. Mee, Jr., in *Stanislavski in America,* ed. Erika Munk (Greenwich, Conn.: Fawcett, 1967), p. 239.

78. Kazan, *Elia Kazan,* p. 73.

79. Schechner and Hoffman, "Look, There's the American Theatre," p. 71.

80. Ibid., p. 75.

81. Ibid., p. 73.

82. Kazan, *Elia Kazan,* p. 201.

83. Kazan, *Elia Kazan,* pp. 363–64.

84. Quoted in Michael Ciment, *Kazan on Kazan* (New York: Viking Press, 1974), p. 176.

CHRONOLOGY

All productions New York City, unless noted.

1909   born near Istanbul, Turkey

1913   family moves to New York, then to New Rochelle

1926–30 attends Williams College

1931   Toy Theatre, Atlantic City: *The Second Man*

1932   attends Yale Drama School; marries Molly Day Thacher

1933   joins Group Theatre as actor

1934   Group Theatre: *Dimitroff*

1935   Park Theatre (Theatre of Action): *The Young Go First*

1936   Civic Repertory Theatre (Theatre of Action): *The Crime*

1938   Fulton Theatre (Group Theatre): *Casey Jones*

1939   Belasco Theatre (Group Theatre): *Quiet City* (series of Sunday night perfor-
           mances); Mansfield Theatre (Group Theatre): *Thunder Rock*

1941   Department of Agriculture: *It's Up to You*

1942   Cort Theatre: *Café Crown*; Royale Theatre: *The Strings, My Lord, Are False*;
           Plymouth Theatre: *The Skin of Our Teeth*

1943   Henry Miller's Theatre: *Harriet*; Martin Beck Theatre: *One Touch of Venus*

1944   Martin Beck: *Jacobowsky and the Colonel*; International Theatre: *Sing Out,
           Sweet Land*; Hollywood film directing career begins

1945   Fulton: *Deep Are the Roots*; John Golden Theatre: *Dunnigan's Daughter*

1946   Belasco: *Truckline Café*

1947   cofounds Actors Studio; Coronet Theatre: *All My Sons;* Ethel Barrymore The-
           atre: *A Streetcar Named Desire*

1948   Belasco: *Sundown Beach*; Forty-sixth Street Theatre: *Love Life*

1949   Morosco Theatre: *Death of a Salesman*

1952   Music Box Theatre: *Flight into Egypt*

1953   National Theatre: *Camino Real*; Ethel Barrymore: *Tea and Sympathy*

1955   Morosco: *Cat on a Hot Tin Roof*

1957   Music Box: *The Dark at the Top of the Stairs*

1958   ANTA Theatre: *J.B.*

1959   Martin Beck: *Sweet Bird of Youth*

1962   publishes first novel, *America America*

1964   appointed codirector of new Lincoln Center Repertory Company; ANTA Wash-
           ington Square Theatre, Lincoln Center Repertory Company: *After the Fall; But
           for Whom, Charlie?; The Changeling*; resigns from artistic directorship of
           company

1967   second marriage, actress Barbara Loden

1983   third marriage, Frances Rudge; works on his new play, *Cutting the Chain,* at
        Actors Studio; optioned for Broadway, but no production to date; Kennedy
        Center Honors

Joan Littlewood

(1915–   )

To the world at large, the British theatre of the century's first fifty years was represented by a succession of polished actors, many with the title of "Sir" or "Dame" preceding their names, appearing in highly literate modern comedies and dramas or in well-spoken, pictorially tasteful revivals of the great classics, especially Shakespeare, and playing to a cultured audience of West End theatregoers. There was, of course, a more popular tradition, best represented by the music halls, and it was here that the English workingman found perpetual delight. Some mingling of the classes took place in both traditions, but until the advent of Joan Littlewood, working-class audiences did not form the raison d'être of any major non-musical hall theatre artist. Miss Littlewood undertook to inject the rumbustious spirit of the music hall tradition into the theatre of the spoken word, hoping to create a style which would appeal to those citizens for whom the West End was much more than a trip across town in the underground.

EARLY YEARS

A child of poverty, Joan Maud Littlewood was born in the slums of Stockwell, South London, in a year not clearly known but thought to be 1914 or 1915. Her mother, unwed at the time, later married a man who worked as an asphalter. Working-class life was in Joan Littlewood's blood; she never turned her back on her origins.

Though not a Catholic she attended a convent school because of its proximity to her home. At seventeen she won a scholarship to the Royal Academy of Dramatic Art (RADA). She had been interested in plays since early childhood and had even "starred" in her own presentation of *Hamlet* at age eleven. Early theatre experiences, especially those as an Old Vic gallery spectator, turned her off to conventional productions of the classics; she hoped that one day she could make these great works excite people of her own social background for whom

most contemporary productions were extremely dull. RADA, for which she
turned down scholarships to several prestigious universities, disappointed her.
She was appalled by its constraining approach to the teaching of acting. This
attitude helped her formulate an acting style in later years that became a keynote
of her art.

Leaving RADA before completing her course, Littlewood moved to Paris and
lived there as a painter until she was eighteen. Hard times were her lot in the
early thirties, as she lived a hand-to-mouth existence, her main source of sustenance being a BBC (British Broadcasting Corporation) job as a writer of doc-
umentaries with a left-wing slant. From 1933 to 1935 she had an active life in
radio, operating mainly in the industrial city of Manchester. It was here that her
theatrical career was founded.

In 1934, after a brief stint as an actress with the Manchester Repertory Company, Littlewood joined forces with Ewan MacColl (known then as Jimmy
Miller), a politically active writer and performer—he later gained fame as a
folksinger—who wrote agit-prop dramas for Manchester area performances. This
was a period of economic depression, considerable labor ferment, surging international fascism, and explosive energy among left-wing activists. Littlewood
shared MacColl's leftist beliefs; in 1934 they were instrumental in creating a
new touring repertory company, Theatre of Action. For a time, Littlewood earned
her sustenance by playing supporting roles with Manchester's Rusholme Repertory Company where, in 1935, she acted under German playwright Ernst
Toller's direction in his play *Draw the Fires*.

She and MacColl decided to learn what they could of the new European acting
and staging methods being developed by people like Vsevolod Meyerhold, Erwin
Piscator, and Rudolf Laban. These men were seeking a freer use of the body as
opposed to the static style current in the British theatre and which Littlewood
so hated at RADA. Littlewood and MacColl tried to create a style based on
political themes, using expressive techniques of movement, with lighting in the
Appian method. They rejected the trained and polished actors of the repertory
theatres as being too mannered and artificial and looked instead for untrained,
natural, and even slovenly spoken performers, hoping to build their method from
the ground up, through trial and error. Their audience was to be the poorer
classes, those who never went to the theatre under ordinary circumstances. As
Littlewood and MacColl viewed it, the great theatres of the past were almost
always popular theatres, using stories familiar to the people at large, but transformed by the power of great writers into works of universal art.

Working in makeshift surroundings wherever a space large enough for audience and performance could be found, and with whatever equipment they could
get to operate, the group put on one piece after another, often revising the scripts
writers gave them until they were unrecognizable. One forty-page play, staged
in constructivist style, was entirely rewritten, all the dialogue and characters
dropped, and the playing time cut to twelve minutes.

Their manifesto declared that it would provide a platform for the expression of working-class interests:

This theatre will perform, mainly in the working-class districts, plays which express the life and struggles of the workers. Politics, in the fullest sense, means the affairs of the people. In this sense the plays done will be political.[1]

The promise of these words was fulfilled by a repertory that stressed left-wing political material in innovative dramatic formats, much of it in proto–Living Newspaper fashion. (Theatre of Action's artistic iconoclasm was by no means welcome to those many other left-wing theatre groups which believed that the most effective way to handle communist themes was through the party-line aesthetic of socialist realism.)

Among the works done by Theatre of Action was the famous American agit-prop piece, *Newsboy,* Clifford Odets' strike drama, *Waiting for Lefty,* which had its first non-American production by this company, and a recent antiwar play called *Hammer,* which they thoroughly revised from a naturalistic script and made into a highly stylized, constructivist production in the Meyerhold style; they retitled it *John Bullion—A Ballet with Words.*

Plays were often rehearsed for two months, with frequent shifts in the casts as actors left to take paying jobs or had their work hours switched. Under such conditions, it was difficult for acting ideals to flower. All the current continental ideas of staging, such as constructivism and epic theatre, were employed. MacColl himself wrote many of their plays, and the direction was shared by MacColl and Littlewood, who became husband and wife. MacColl dealt mainly with the choral speech and movement of the group scenes, while Littlewood concentrated on the regular acting of the intimate scenes.

THEATRE UNION

Littlewood and MacColl, who had been expelled from the Communist Party because of their "formalist" artistic tendencies, both received scholarships to study theatre in Russia, and moved to London to await their visas; however, possibly because of their recent conflict with the party, the visas were not forthcoming, and, in 1936, when they ran out of funds—they had sustained themselves by giving theatre classes—they had to return to Manchester. There they began a new troupe, Theatre Union, and costaged Hans Chlumberg's antiwar *Miracle at Verdun.* Political aims continued to inform the team. Theatre Union's manifesto proclaimed a desire to provide Manchester with a communal theatre group to present "to the widest possible public, and particularly to that section of the public which has been starved theatrically, plays of social significance."[2] They existed primarily as a touring company, doing one-night stands in every conceivable circumstance.

Many applicants came to Theatre Union hoping to join the group, *The Good Soldier Schweik* auditions alone bringing out 160 actors. A huge warehouse was used as a work space, and here the company experimented with the ideas of Stanislavsky (whose *An Actor Prepares* had just been published), as well as with the concepts of Laban, Meyerhold, and Vakhtangov. A new source of inspiration came when they encountered the work of Nelson Illingworth, a teacher whose work on voice was seen as complementary to Laban's ideas on movement. ''You could work out a pattern, a scale of 'efforts' of voice as you could with movement,''[3] writes MacColl.

The company rehearsed six evenings a week and all day Sunday, while working at regular daytime jobs. Various warm-up and relaxation exercises began each session, followed by discussion of new theatre ideas, practice of Laban dance-exercises, and rehearsal of the current play.

Lope de Vega's seventeenth-century *The Sheepwell*, about a small town's rebellion against a cruel overlord, was chosen in 1936 as a Theatre Union comment on the Spanish Civil War and as a means of raising money for the Republican cause. Costumes and sets were the work of a group of sculptors and painters—the sheep and well were solidly sculpted in three dimensions. There followed the Czech antiwar comedy, *The Good Soldier Schweik* (1938); Irvin Kocherga's Soviet drama, *The Masters of Time* (1939); MacColl's Living News-paper–style *Last Edition* (1940); Aristophanes' classic antiwar comedy, *Lysistrata* (1941); Molière's *The Flying Doctor* (1941), a little-known piece based directly on a commedia scenario and which later also would be in Littlewood's postwar repertory; and the final Theatre Union presentation, *Classic Soil* (1941), which covered such concerns as the nineteenth-century exploitation of Lancashire loom workers and also offered a poetic disquisition about the insanity of war. In addition, the group also was responsible for presenting sketches, readings, and concerts.

MacColl—despite his inability to write or read music—composed the score for *The Sheepwell*, and music thenceforth became a trademark of all Theatre Union shows. This emphasis led to the requirement that the actors be capable of singing and moving well, and new actors were examined for these talents.

Living Newspaper techniques formed the basis for MacColl's *Last Edition*, a documentary which changed weekly to keep its ideas current. All of the material presented was researched by the cast itself, who selected major national and international events of the 1934 to 1940 period for theatrical examination. The ultimate goal was to excoriate capitalism as the world's most pervasive evil. Day-by-day topicality later became one of Littlewood's most marked production features, as did various other methods employed in this period. However, as might be expected in a theatre then still under the threat of censorship from a Lord Chamberlain, much of *Last Edition* was deemed too controversial for general consumption, and the diversionary tactic of producing the work under the auspices of a private club arrangement was attempted. Nevertheless, legal action was taken and the play was officially banned.

The unusual scenic arrangements for the Living Newspaper were adopted from whatever stage platform belonged to the hall they were in. Two long, stepped platforms were set up along the hall's side walls and these, with the stage, became an acting area surrounding the audience on three sides. A combination of staging methods was used, sometimes with all acting areas used simultaneously, sometimes with the action moving from one stage to another, sometimes with the action on the side stages used as a counterpoint to the action on the regular stage.

The company broke up in 1942 when many actors were drafted. During the war a nucleus of the company members prepared for the group's rebirth at the war's end by each becoming an expert in one area of theatre. One became a Greek theatre specialist (he died in the war); another (also killed) became a design expert; MacColl himself studied Elizabethan, Jacobean, and Chinese theatre; another examined the *commedia dell'arte*; another the Roman theatre; and so on. They shared their learning, no matter where the war took them, through writing they circulated among themselves. This historical and theoretical know-how gave them a firm intellectual foundation for their future activities. "By the end of the war," writes MacColl, "we had a group of people who, as a collective, probably knew more about the history of the theatre than any other group of players in the country."[4]

THEATRE WORKSHOP

In 1945, what was left of Littlewood's group re-formed in Kendal, near Manchester, and soon became a professional company known as Theatre Workshop. They rehearsed on a near-zero budget in a Manchester warehouse with MacColl continuing to supply scripts, but the business management was taken over by Gerry Raffles, who, in addition to his managerial responsibilities, became one of the most vitally creative ingredients in the Theatre Workshop amalgam. Technical aspects of the work improved with the addition of several specialists to the company.

Littlewood's aims had not changed; they had merely intensified. She still longed for a true "British People's Theatre" which would provide the common man with a pulsing, living artistic experience that spoke to his needs and tastes through an aesthetic program employing the most innovative contemporary theatre ideas. Her new manifesto included these words:

Theatre Workshop is an organization of artists, technicians and actors who are experimenting in stagecraft. Its purpose is to create a flexible theatre-art, as swift moving and plastic as the cinema, by applying the recent technical advances in light and sound, and introducing music and the "dance theatre" style of production.[5]

Her spirit was dead set against the commercial prostitution of the theatre as practiced on the West End and Broadway. She wanted her stage occupied not by mannequins, but by earthy, full-blooded people. The collaborative company effort was to be rewarded by a system of profit sharing. Like her earlier companies, Theatre Workshop had been established as an alternative to the "posh" theatre, a place to develop a whole new type of audience, a poor theatre playing wherever space and willing spectators could be found. A bohemian, arty bunch of vagabonds to many, they strove valiantly to break down the barriers to art appreciation which often frightened off the less cultivated of British citizens.

Born partly from dissatisfaction with social conditions outside the theatre, Theatre Workshop also was created out of internal theatrical frustrations. Its creation allowed Littlewood an effective alternative to the debilitating pressures of the long-run, short-rehearsal syndrome of the commercial theatre. Here she could work at peace with her "cell-like group of theatrical handymen dedicated to her proposition," as Anthony Bailey puts it, "that the finest theatre involves song, dance, movement, and plenty of lowlife idiom."[6]

For eight years, Theatre Workshop struggled to stay alive—mainly by touring—and did not come to rest in a permanent theatre until 1953. Tours were to England's industrial north, with some trips to the south, to Wales, and to the Continent. The ten-member company lived out of an old truck and often acted on the tailgate. New people joined up along the way, and some dropped out because wages were extremely low; hunger was a frequent companion. Their initial repertory was made up of two plays, *The Flying Doctor* by Molière and *Johnny Noble* by MacColl, with which they gave their first public performances in August 1945 at Girls' High School, Kendal. Both plays remained in the repertory for years, being revived frequently. The Molière gave Littlewood a chance to light up the stage with her exuberant love for *commedia dell'arte* techniques. *Johnny Noble,* a ballad opera, told of the drafting for war of a young fisherman, and was done in epic theatre style with an episodic structure and a considerable use of songs. Expressive physicalizations suggested such ideas as the firing of anti-aircraft guns. Simple sets were combined with a full use of lighting and sound to create an imaginative sequence of visual and auditory images.

Subsequent productions included Federico Garciá Lorca's *The Love of Don Perlimplín for Belissa in His Garden* (1945), Chekhov's *The Proposal* (1947), and MacColl's *Uranium 235* (1946), a play about the destructive uses of atomic energy. It was especially topical, being produced only months after the dropping of the atom bomb on Japan; MacColl took a three-month course in nuclear physics to prepare for it. The piece was a theatricalist endeavor allowing for a wide range of experimental techniques. Accepting the audience as a participant in the evening's experimentation, the actors would play the same scene several times, each repetition being in a different style. At later performances, improvisation became a regular feature of the show.

In November 1946 Theatre Workshop finally came to London, but only briefly.

This was at the Park Theatre, Hanwell, and St. Pancras Town Hall. Their official London debut, however, is usually cited as their appearance in 1947 at Rudolf Steiner Hall, where, with two other plays, they acted *Operation Olive Branch*, MacColl's new version of *Lysistrata*. Friedrich Wolf's 1933 German play, *Professor Mamlock,* about Nazi anti-Semitism, was the final offering of 1947, but it did not outlive its premiere in Brighton. In 1948 a new MacColl work, *The Other Animals,* was given a berth with the troupe; it was a challenging memory play with philosophical overtones which evoked the mental images of a political prisoner in solitary. There had been a brief trip to West Germany in 1947, and in 1948 the troupe went to Czechoslovakia and Sweden. Manchester was their home base, but they toured from it to Lancashire and Yorkshire for additional audiences, although they rarely played to full houses. Neither were their audiences as working class as they would have liked. Theatre Workshop's repertory was essentially middle class and did not draw the kind of spectators for which Littlewood always was on the lookout. New works joining the repertory briefly in 1949 were a "school version" of *Twelfth Night,* and an unsuccessful satire by MacColl called *Rogues' Gallery.* School tours, an important source of income at the time, soon offered trimmed-down versions of *As You Like It* (1949) and *A Midsummer Night's Dream* (1950). The failure in 1950 of *Alice in Wonderland* was of little help in maintaining morale and a living wage. Among other additions to the company's repertory were Irwin Shaw's *The Gentle People* (1950) and MacColl's *Landscape with Chimneys* (1951), a sort of British *Street Scene* about a year in the life of the residents of a representative street. A tour of Welsh mining towns came in 1951 with *The Long Shift,* a mining drama by Raffles and Littlewood. This play was staged with extreme realism, the costumes and makeup being so convincing that the actors were once taken for the real thing by the miners themselves and not permitted to enter the auditorium unless they first went home and washed up. A new Shakespeare production joined the repertory in 1951, *Henry IV, Part I,* and toured Welsh mining towns where it was played on an arrangement of three trestle tables.

Theatre Workshop began to participate in Edinburgh's annual theatre festival in 1949, when they produced *The Other Animals* there along with *Johnny Noble, Don Perlimplín, The Proposal,* and *The Flying Doctor*; they were very warmly received. They returned in 1951 with *Uranium 235,* presented MacColl's *The Travellers* there in 1952, mounted *The Imaginary Invalid* and *Uncle Vanya* for the festival in 1953, but did not return to Edinburgh until 1964, when they showed their new production of *Henry IV.* The most interesting of the earlier works was *The Travellers,* first produced in Oddfellows Hall and employing a set suggesting the interior of a train running down the center aisle of the auditorium, the seats on either side facing the aisle directly. Lighting and sound effects produced the sensation of a train—symbolic of Europe's nations rushing inexorably toward war—moving through the space, and the spectators felt that they were on it traveling with the actors.

Meanwhile, the company was making incursions onto the London scene,

beginning with a 1950 showing of *Alice in Wonderland* at Theatre Royal, Stratford (then called the Theatre Royal and Palace of Varieties), where in three years
they would find a permanent home; presentations of several of their standard
works at the Adelphi Theatre the same year; a successful two-week offering of
Uranium 235 at the Embassy Theatre, Swiss Cottage, in 1952, under the spon-
sorship of Michael Redgrave and Sam Wanamaker; and a single showing of the
same work at the West End's Comedy Theatre a few months later.

THE THEATRE ROYAL

In 1953, after a brief sojourn in Glasgow, the company took a six-week lease
on a terribly rundown 512-seat Victorian theatre erected in 1884 and located in
London's East End. In this theatre, a good thirty minutes by underground from
the Shaftesbury Avenue theatre district, surrounded by just such a working-class
neighborhood as she had come from and for whom she desired to provide
theatricals, Joan Littlewood and Theatre Workshop dug in for an extended stay.
All was not too happy, however, as Ewan MacColl opposed the permanence of
a London base for fear it would corrupt the company's ideals; when his pleas
did not prevail, he resigned. As it was, his prophecies eventually came true.

Not that hardship ignored them. Littlewood's twenty-year residence at the
Theatre Royal, Stratford-atte-Bowe (often referred to as Stratford East), marked
by many traumatic experiences, mingled with a number of highs that are among
the proudest of this century's theatrical achievements. At Theatre Royal, Littlewood at last had a permanent home for establishing her dream of a true repertory
company. The community of actors was to have no stars, and all roles, big and
small, would go to whoever could play them best. Plays would be produced for
brief runs, rather than in rotating repertory, with the more popular works being
revived from time to time to keep them alive for the interested public. Prices
were low enough to attract the local citizenry. Since the available money was
not enough to pay even a small company more than a subsistence wage, the
permanent troupe was supplemented with outsiders who were jobbed-in when
required. As it was, some actors were forced to make the theatre their home as
they could not afford flats. Even after several considerable successes in the
following years, the theatre could barely meet expenses. When Brendan Behan
was brought from Ireland to attend rehearsals of *The Hostage* in 1959, the only
room the theatre could afford to rent for him was unheated and had neither hot
water nor electricity. The success of *The Hostage* and several subsequent shows,
however, put a new face on things for a time.

A new production of *Twelfth Night* opened Theatre Workshop's tenure at
Stratford in February 1953. It was followed by mountings of plays by Molière,
MacColl, Sean O'Casey, George Bernard Shaw, Eugene O'Neill, and others.
Littlewood's directorial contributions at Stratford during the 1953–54 season
included her stagings of her own adaptation of Charles Dickens' *A Christmas
Carol* and Robert Louis Stevenson's *Treasure Island,* George Bellack's *The*

Troublemakers, Anthony Nicholson's *Van Call* (set in the vicinity of the theatre and written by a local reporter), *Richard II* (in which she also played the Duchess of Gloucester), John Marston's Jacobean drama, *The Dutch Courtesan,* Charles Fenn's propaganda piece about the war in Indochina, *The Fire Eaters,* and Henrik Ibsen's *An Enemy of the People*; there were also reprises of such earlier works as *The Travellers, Johnny Noble,* and *The Flying Doctor* (the latter two usually paired on the same program). During the 1954–55 season, Stratford audiences saw her adaptations of Honoré de Balzac's *Cruel Daughters* (based on *Père Goriot*), of Dickens' *The Chimes,* and of Mark Twain's *The Prince and the Pauper,* a new—and highly praised—MacColl version of *The Good Soldier Schweik,* Julius Hays' *The Midwife,* and a production of Ben Jonson's *Volpone*—which Littlewood viewed as scathingly anticapitalist—set in contemporary Italy and designed, according to Theatre Workshop veteran Howard Goorney, ''as a satire on spivs and hangers-on. Mosca rode a bicycle laden with pineapples and champagne, Corbaccio wheeled himself around in an invalid chair and Sir Politic Would-Be, the Englishman abroad, wore swimming trunks and carried a snorkel.''[7] In May 1955, *Volpone* and the rarely produced anonymous Elizabethan play *Arden of Faversham* represented Theatre Workshop at the Paris International Theatre Festival, where the company was a sensation, despite its shameful lack of financial support from its home government; reports of its acclaim filtered back to Britain where people soon were asking who this upstart bunch of radicals were that they should be so capable of raising an artistic fuss in France while being practically ignored at home.

Soon after the company returned to England, Littlewood's production of Brecht's *Mother Courage* and of *Volpone* were shown at the Devon Festival, Barnstaple. Littlewood herself played the title role in the former, and the pressures this created may have led to the production's failure. She had wanted to substitute another actress, but when Brecht heard of this, he threatened to withdraw his permission to do the play. She also suffered from a restrictive budget that forced her to cut all the songs.

Her new staging of *The Sheepwell* opened the 1955–56 season at Stratford, and her mounting of Eugène Labiche's nineteenth-century farce *An Italian Straw Hat,* was given soon after. Meanwhile, *Schweik,* which had had considerable popularity at Stratford, was revived and moved to the Duke of York's Theatre, the first of the company's West End transfers; it failed, however, to bring in the desperately needed manna. In July 1956 it represented the company at the Paris festival. The other Littlewood offerings of the season were her acclaimed productions of Christopher Marlowe's *Edward II* and of Brendan Behan's *The Quare Fellow,* a hit that transferred to the West End in July. What with the Paris success of 1955 and the productions of the 1955–56 season, the company was finally beginning to make waves which threatened to splash upon the British theatre establishment. However, with the arrival of the national critics at Theatre Workshop openings, and the growing trend of moving successful works to commercial auspices—which finally allowed the actors involved to be paid a living wage—

the company began to suffer serious internal problems stemming from such problems as the growing need to satisfy the critics and the difficulty of holding on to actors who were being lured away by the promise of more lucrative careers. The pressures of working at poverty-level wages (anywhere from two to four pounds a week) in a repertory system that was producing a new show every two or three weeks during much of this period also must have taken its toll; from February 1953 to April 1955 the troupe mounted thirty-six new programs.

Shakespeare's *Richard II* and Marlowe's *Edward II* were landmark productions in Littlewood's career, demonstrating her iconoclastic approach to the classics. She had first staged the former in January 1954, when it received little critical attention. Hearing that the Old Vic, the *sine qua non* of establishment classical theatre in the fifties, was going to do the play under Michael Benthall's direction, with John Neville in the lead, Littlewood revived her own staging as a rival version; it brought Theatre Workshop excellent publicity when the major critics arrived to compare it to the Old Vic's version. With a cast of fourteen (there were forty-five in the Old Vic production), Littlewood began an intense period of rehearsal that culminated in an exciting work in which the action sped rapidly along with no time for pauses. In place of the processional pomp and splendor of the Old Vic approach, the Theatre Workshop stressed ongoing and vivid dramatic action on a spare set that relied mainly on lighting for its effects. The Old Vic style was spectacular and poetic, that of Theatre Workshop gutsy and realistic. Contrasted with the regal and beautifully spoken Richard of Neville was Harry Corbett's interpretation in which the king was played, says Goorney, as "a less noble figure, slightly unbalanced, and with an effeminate streak. . . . He may have lacked some of the poetry of John Neville, but the lines were alive and their meaning unmistakable."[8] Though various drawbacks were noted, critical reaction was quite laudatory for the innovative interpretation, and Corbett was considered outstanding. According to Norman Marshall, *Richard II* was Littlewood's finest Shakespearean production. It took a Marxist point of view and made Bolingbroke the leading role as "the typical Marxist hero, the revolutionary who overthrows a regime."[9]

Edward II was likewise provocative. The stage floor was a raked platform on which a map of the southern counties was displayed. Upstage stood a single property, potent in its symbolism, a throne which was so designed that lighting changes could turn it from a stained glass window in a cathedral to a tombstone. During these years John Bury was the resident designer and built a highly successful career on the basis of his collaboration with Littlewood.

Littlewood's other 1955–56 production of note, Brendan Behan's *The Quare Fellow,* was a striking comedy-drama about the reaction of men in prison to the forthcoming execution of one of their number. The presentation made the author internationally famous. Behan was an Irish working-class author with a gift for theatrical vibrancy and relevance such as the director had been seeking all her career. Each was well suited to the other; the success with which this production was met was soon to be followed by one far greater. Littlewood's work on the script sharply deprived the character of Warder Regan of the prominence he has in the original, staged earlier in Ireland. She also made cuts designed to make the play suitable to an English audience. Specifically Irish and Catholic comments were excised to give the play a broader appeal. Bury's scenery consisted of an essentially bare stage, the brick theatre walls with their exposed pipes being visible and strongly suggesting the barren prison interior.

Soon Theatre Workshop was besieged with new plays by writers startled at the company's accomplishment with Behan's work. Most of them willingly submitted to her unusual approach in producing new plays; she used the text as a basis for creative collaboration with her entire company—this often led to a result quite different from the original.

The company's production schedule slowed considerably during the 1956–57 season, and designer John Bury directed those plays that were presented. Littlewood was back in harness in July 1957 with a production of *Macbeth* premiered in Zurich and then taken to the International Youth Festival in Moscow before opening at Stratford in September; set in the period between the outbreak of World War I and the end of World War II, it made various textual revisions to present a totalitarian Macbeth, whose life flashes before his eyes as he is about to be executed by a firing squad. Her other productions of the 1957–58 season were Henry Chapman's *You Won't Always Be on Top*; Edgard da Rocha Miranda's *And the Wind Blew*; an adaptation of Fernando de Rojas' classic Renaissance novel, *Celestina*; a double bill of two one-acters, Jean-Paul Sartre's *The Respectable Prostitute* and Paul Green's *Unto Such Glory*; and then, a work that would make a major contribution, *A Taste of Honey*.

With Chapman's play, the company made an excursion into the kind of naturalism later to be associated with certain David Storey plays; to tell the story of a day on the site of a construction project the actors—including Richard Harris—were required to construct a brick wall at each performance. But even more significant was the conflict that developed with the Lord Chamberlain when the actors' nightly improvisations in the roles of the construction workers led to charges that the play being performed was not the one that had been officially approved. One of the vulgar additions cited was Harris' imitation of what Winston Churchill might have said on the occasion of the opening of a public lavatory. Although those accused were ultimately fined for their transgressions, the public debate that was aroused surely contributed to the atmosphere that finally led in 1968 to the ending of official censorship of the British stage. Littlewood's frequent emphasis on the value of improvisation both as a rehearsal procedure and a performance technique would lead to trouble with the censor in later productions as well.

Stratford's local audiences continued largely to neglect the theatre, and Littlewood could only survive through a vigorous campaign of grantsmanship. It took many years, though, before Stratford was granted anything like a suitable public subsidy; by 1958 the company had received a total of only £2,350. Moreover, for the theatre to survive the entire company had to pitch in and keep the place clean and in a decent state of repair. To save fuel in winter, the heating system was not switched on until a half-hour before curtain time, and theatre regulars soon knew to come equipped with blankets and hot-water bottles. She regretted that her company played mainly to those who would otherwise have been attending West End theatres, but nothing she did seemed to supply the answer. She refused to leave the East End for a West End playhouse, holding tenaciously to her ideal of a people's theatre despite all pressures. To her, the ultimate irony was when commercial managements began requesting support grants in the 1960s.

A TASTE OF HONEY

With *A Taste of Honey,* the first play by Shelagh Delaney, a nineteen-year-old high school dropout, the theatre's financial burdens became somewhat less pressing. Although there was a considerable amount of improvisation during the rehearsals, Littlewood did surprisingly little tailoring of the script and surprised London with a seriocomic work about Cockney characters, a slatternly mother (Avis Bunnage), her one-eyed lover, her teenage daughter (Frances Cuka), a black sailor who fathers an illegitimate child, and a homosexual man (Murray Melvin) who sets up house with the girl. Backed by an onstage jazz trio, the characters acted with electric urgency, the mother often turning suddenly to address her comments to the audience. Such physical trivia as the drinking of tea and the eating of biscuits was mimed without props. As John Russell Taylor describes it, the "production . . . was in Joan Littlewood's characteristic manner, a sort of magnified realism in which everything is lifelike but somehow larger than life."[10] "Driving the play along at break-neck speed," wrote Lindsay Anderson, "stuffing it with wry and humorous invention, she [Littlewood] made sentimentalism impossible. The abandoning of the fourth wall, the sudden patches of pure music hall, panto-style, were daring"[11] but successful. The play went on to the West End and eventually, like *The Quare Fellow,* became a highlight of the modern repertory.

Littlewood later declared, "*Taste of Honey* I adapted and built up from dialogue sent to me by Shelagh Delaney, the love scenes alone being her original work untouched."[12] However, Taylor has shown conclusively that—despite the widespread opinion that Littlewood's rehearsal work on a script evolved into a play quite unlike what the author had written—the changes were relatively minor. Delaney did not see the production until the end of rehearsals and was unable to detect any differences from her original until they were described for her. Comparing the first and last versions, Taylor reveals that, regardless of considerable tightening of the dialogue, "most of the celebrated lines are already there" and the chief role, that of Jo, is substantially as she is in Littlewood's rendition. The other changes, including that of the ending, merely serve to improve the play. Taylor concludes. "Essentially the process of communal revision has served (and here the true genius of Joan Littlewood as a director emerges) to bring out the best in the author's work while staying completely true to its spirit."[13]

THE HOSTAGE

Even greater acclaim for Littlewood and her group resulted from the first offering of the 1958–59 season, Behan's *The Hostage,* a play written at Littlewood's suggestion, and given a rambunctious treatment at Stratford East. The play was Stratford's entry at the Paris Festival that year; in 1960 it became Littlewood's first New York production. Behan's one-act Gaelic play, *An Giall,* had been done in Ireland, and Littlewood had asked for an English translation. When Behan fell behind the date by which he had promised to have the script ready, Littlewood, desperate for a play, accepted a rough draft, hoping to work the piece out in rehearsal. The play she ultimately staged was almost a new work, with additional characters, dialogue, and songs.

The Hostage is set in a brothel and tells of an eighteen-year-old British soldier (Murray Melvin) kept there as a hostage by the IRA following the arrest of an Irish youth implicated in the killing of an Ulster policeman. Littlewood's production fleshed out a play one-third as long as its final version, unlike her work on *The Quare Fellow,* in which her alterations, though changing the tone and viewpoint of certain parts of the play, made no major additions. Music-hall devices such as talking to the audience, song-and-dance routines, self-parodistic dialogue, and nightly adlibbing were used and so opened the play's borders that the incidental details and laughs practically obscured the point of the original. Some cracks were aimed directly at audience members, especially latecomers and those choosing to leave early. Audiences took away the impression of an improvisational free-for-all, very much in the spirit of the *commedia dell'arte,* with new material taken from the daily papers inserted into each performance to keep it as topical as possible. Ulrick O'Connor reports that the nightly adlibs mentioned anachronistic subjects, such as "Khruschev, Tony Armstrong-Jones, the Lord Chamberlain, the Duchess of Argyll, Franco, parking meters, deb's delights, football teams, the weather and even myself,"[14] timely jokes completely out of place in the period of the late forties in which the play is set.

Highly critical of the Littlewood version, O'Connor describes how bawdy music-hall lines like "Up the Republic" were answered by shouts of "Up the Arsenal." He acknowledges, however, that Littlewood's unconventional approach was a major reason for the play's success in censorship-bound London, though as an Irishman he is especially sensitive to the mocking anti-IRA tone taken by the Theatre Workshop interpretation. (The terrorist activities of the IRA were still a thing of the future.) Behan himself stood firmly behind Littlewood, saying, "She has the same views on theatre that I have, which is that Music Hall is the thing to aim for to amuse people and any time they get bored divert them with a song or a dance."[15]

LATER PRODUCTIONS

In February 1959, shortly after *A Taste of Honey* had moved to Wyndham's Theatre, Littlewood's production of Frank Norman's *Fings Ain't Wot They Used t'Be* opened, her only other staging of the season, apart from a revival of *The Dutch Courtesan. Fings* was another hit and was transferred to the West End. It was the outstanding example of Theatre Workshop's collective improvisational creativity, being worked up from a forty-eight-page script (different sources give different size scripts, although Norman insists the correct figure is forty-eight) about the sleazier side of Cockney life in London's Soho district. Lionel Bart provided the songs which helped transform Norman's intended drama into musical comedy. Though he originally agreed to the Littlewood approach, Norman later said that, though grateful for his royalties, he would never want a script of his treated similarly again. He seems to be the first writer to have expressed such dissatisfaction with Littlewood's methods. Nevertheless, it was not very long before she was staging another Norman work. Norman also contributed to her 1972 production, *Costa Packet*.

If Norman was unhappy, Wolf Mankowitz was utterly depressed by Littlewood's disregard for his writing. *Make Me an Offer,* which opened in October 1959, was a musical based on his novel of the same name about business practices. It had a fine young cast including Daniel Massey, Sheila Hancock, and Diana Copeland. These actors had to be jobbed in because the company had been scattered by the West End moves; this destructive pattern did not get any better. Non-Stratford actors often had serious difficulty adjusting to Littlewood's unique methods.

Mankowitz says he "had to fight her for the survival of the script. It was only fifty-fifty in the end." He went on to castigate Littlewood for the excesses she took with Behan's work and argued that Behan, a notorious alcoholic, let her take liberties because "he was pissed out of his mind anyway when most of the changes were made."[16] At any rate, *Make Me an Offer* became the fourth Stratford show to transfer to the West End.

One final Littlewood production for 1959–60 arrived in May with James Clancy's *Ned Kelly,* about a famed nineteenth-century Australian outlaw. At that year's Paris Festival Littlewood presented her slapstick version of Ben Jonson's *Every Man in His Humour* and brought it to Stratford in July; it was followed in August by Stephen Lewis' *Sparrers Can't Sing,* concerned with the trivialities of life on an East End street. It was a success, was transferred to the West End (where it flopped), and was made by Littlewood into a film in 1962, the only one she ever directed. Murray Melvin later revealed that when, as an observer, he attended the first reading of the play and seemed delighted with it, Littlewood asked him if he wanted a part in it, although there was none for him at the time. His role—as was Littlewood's custom—was created during the rehearsal period and ultimately became the most important in the play.[17]

One other Littlewood credit of 1960 is of note, her staging in Berlin of a

German production of *Operation Olive Branch*. January 1961 witnessed Littlewood's direction of American writer Marvin Kane's *We're Just Not Practical*, about a couple mismanaging a boardinghouse. It was succeeded by James Goldman's *They Might Be Giants*. Kane had joined the ranks of disillusioned writers when he saw how casually his script was being handled (he was eventually barred from rehearsals), but Goldman (another American), whose new play about a former judge with a Sherlock Holmes fixation was a far more finished work than others with which Littlewood had worked, remained faithful and adoring in spite of what some saw as serious bungling of a promising work. *They Might Be Giants* was sent to Littlewood by American producer-director Harold Prince, who had been delighted by her treatment of *A Taste of Honey* and *Fings*. Littlewood's working methods soon alarmed Prince, however, when he attended a rehearsal three days before the scheduled opening and saw her still doing improvisational exercises with the actors. In contrast, Goldman was so impressed by her talent that he remained unperturbed and allowed her to continue making drastic changes in the script, even though the work had been in rehearsal for two months. As it was, she wanted to delay the opening so she could rehearse an extra week. Prince, understanding that her shows usually made their greatest improvements after they had been running, forced her to open on time. A critical drubbing ensued.

Littlewood's essential regard for the script as a springboard for company elaboration suited both loosely developed materials and scripts that were in nearly finished form. Prince and others feel that her approach was most appropriate for the undeveloped script, but her success with plays like *The Quare Fellow* and *A Taste of Honey,* for all their revisions and reorientations, may put such opinions in doubt. Similarly, her successful revivals of the classics have shown a powerful directorial technique, for here the scripts, though cut, were not rewritten. She achieved excellent results with both structured and unstructured texts, and also failed with both. Her apparently greater proclivity for unstructured material stems primarily from her spectacular success with only two productions, *The Hostage* and *Oh, What a Lovely War!* (1963), though considerable acclaim was also given several other works, notably *Sparrers Can't Sing, Fings Ain't Wot They Used t'Be,* and *Mrs. Wilson's Diary.*

RESIGNATION FROM THEATRE WORKSHOP

Upset by critical reaction to *They Might Be Giants,* by a depressing situation in which her hit productions continued to deprive her of good actors (so that others reaped the profits of her hard work), and by her inability to develop a working-class audience, Littlewood found herself in 1961 at a crossroads. Financial worries still plagued her theatre. She also felt dissatisfied with the conditions of an eight-week rehearsal and longed for the leisure to open a play only when she felt it was ready. Burdened by these problems, she shocked London in July by announcing her resignation from Theatre Workshop for a two-year period. She told the press:

There is no formula for success—you have to change your skin everytime or you're finished—dead. . . . You either have to achieve freedom from having no money and no attention paid to you, as we did in the old days, or by having so much money and attention, that like Brecht, you can go on and on working on a production until it's just as you want it.[18]

THE FUN PALACE

Littlewood was in Africa during 1961–63, directing Wole Soyinka's *The Lion and the Jewel* in Nigeria. Among her other activities during this period was the formulation of plans for an ideal amusement and cultural complex that she termed a Fun Palace. As always, she was concerned with finding measures for dissolving the barriers between art and life; the Fun Palace represented a chance to transform her dreams into concrete reality. The project still remains a dream. This "mobile theatre" which could be erected almost anywhere was to be a multimedia fun park equipped with psychological games, free musical instruction, instruments to play, records of all types of music, poetry and dance recitals, lectures and demonstrations, closed-circuit TV, news presentations, places for lengthy discussions, acting, psychodrama, arts and crafts in all media, closed and open areas, and multilevels, and was to be used for active participation or just browsing. For this work of planned obsolescence, all was to be built of disposable materials lasting no longer than ten to fifteen years.

The public was to walk by itself or be carried on conveyor belts from place to place. No formal entrances or exits were to be included, so all could come and go as they pleased, with everything for free. Despite years of planning, writing, and discussion, nothing ever came of the idea because of financial difficulties compounded by the lack of an appropriate site.

By 1969 her ideas for a Fun Palace led to the conception of a Bubble City. This would be a medieval feast of theatre, where the audience could go from attraction to attraction and experience a totality of artistic, scientific, and philosophical experiences. Despite the availability of every possible resource, said Littlewood, the theatre today does not offer the audience a jot. The plays of John Osborne, Edward Albee, and others of their nature, offer "characters locked up in a womb of theatre."[19] Theatre today can offer a renaissance environment only if it takes advantage of its resources, especially the technological ones, she concluded.

OH, WHAT A LOVELY WAR!

As she promised, Littlewood returned to Theatre Workshop in March 1963 and immediately set to work on a show that was to be the most successful of her career—a success she would never again match. Preparatory rehearsals for *Oh, What a Lovely War!* began with the director suggesting books on World War I for her cast to read; she then used this research as a background for a series of improvisations on the cause and nature of war. A sense of shared purpose led to a communally created production so powerful in its impact that reviewer Kenneth Tynan "stumbled home . . . blinded by tears."[20]

It was Gerry Raffles who, thinking that a show based on World War I songs would be entertaining, first broached the idea. Charles Chilton, who had put together a radio show of World War I songs that had inspired the new work, was in charge of writing the continuity for the play, although many involved with the show say his actual contributions were nil. Littlewood managed the difficult feat of producing a charming, thoroughly entertaining musical while telegraphing a searing antiwar message. Some critics, however, found the commercial values of the show a travesty of her professed ideals. The show was also sharply rapped by those who still believed in the sentimental, allegedly glorious aspects of World War I; the family of General Haig, who was scathingly satirized in the show, did what they could to hinder its continuing success.

Oh, What a Lovely War! played to packed houses and, after a showing at the Paris Festival, moved to the West End; there, to the distaste of some, the scathingly cynical ending seen at Stratford was softened and sentimentalized. Although the theatre's management was scored for the change, the actual producers were Littlewood and Raffles, whose motives in making the revision were never clarified. A Littlewood-directed production of the play opened at New York's Broadhurst Theatre in September 1964, and both East and West Berlin saw it in 1965. It was an energetic but brutal look at the sentiment and foolishness of wartime attitudes, undercut by constant reminders of war's bloody actuality. A cast of nineteen, wearing costumes clearly derived from *commedia dell'arte,* the men in white Pierrot-like outfits, the women in see-through pantaloons and ballet skirts, cavorted to the tunes of songs like "Pack Up Your Troubles in Your Old Kit Bag," "Keep the Home Fires Burning," and "We Don't Want to Lose You But We Think You Ought to Go," while the offstage sounds of shells exploding provided counterpoint to the onstage caperings. Behind the actors was a movie screen on which wartime newsreel footage was projected while a running electric light sign flashed news headlines and casualty counts. "300,000 CASUALTIES DURING AUGUST—GAIN NIL," flashed one sign. "BRUSSELS FALLS," flashed another. A minimum of props and dialogue was used, mime communicating everything essential. In one scene:

On a darkened stage, with half a dozen Tommies huddled over the footlights and two German ships glimpsed against a bare background, [Littlewood] creates a wary, innocent Christmas Eve fraternization in the trenches. From a line of recruits armed only with walking sticks and a sergeant major spitting out angry gibberish, she can expound a mime which shows us the comic horror of decent men infected with blood lust.[21]

Following the success of *Lovely War* Stratford East was used with increasing irregularity by Theatre Workshop. Littlewood's single play there in 1964 was Norman's *A Kayf Up West,* a rambling failure about the corruption of a young man in the late 1940s, with a *dramatis personae* of forty characters played by a cast of thirteen. After it closed it was three years before Theatre Workshop resumed work at Stratford East.

HENRY IV

At the 1964 Edinburgh Festival Littlewood presented a controversial mixed modern-dress production of *Henry IV* with Parts I and II combined as a single play. It was played on a 48' × 15' platform at the Assembly Hall that ran straight down the hall from north to south. Most critics were seriously disturbed by Littlewood's directorial innovations. Apparently undismayed, she responded that Shakespeare "wasn't a scholar, he was a nut like us. We did him the way he'd have wanted."[22] It was argued that her textual arrangement made the play incoherent, that the actors spoke the verse with neither good projection nor clarity (a frequent jibe at her classical work), that the music was too loud, and that the anarchic costume choices were bizarre. All the lines were spoken as if they were contemporary prose, Falstaff wore neither beard nor padding, and was quite shorn of sentimental qualities. John Russell Brown found that "his bulk, high-living, and capacity for friendship were as much a part of his fantasy as his valour," but that there was too great an abyss between the characterization and the text. Brown, who thought the production "witty and intelligent," appreciated the well-rounded presentation of the minor roles, and considered the "highway, tavern and rustic scenes" to be highlights; nevertheless, he had strong reservations about the rest.

She saw the king and nobles as cold politicians, uniform in dress and clipped and unemotional in speech. . . . A single, huge cannon, awkwardly pushed into position behind Henry IV for the battle of Shrewsbury, showed that the king was *meant* to lack stature on his own account. So half the play dwindled at the director's command; through manner of speech and action, costume, stage-movement, this half became a demonstration of inadequacy.[23]

Henry IV was to be Littlewood's last Shakespeare production. She struck back at the critics who panned the production by asserting that the work represented a valid attempt to put her Theatre Workshop theories into practice within the framework of a classical play. She defended the use of regional accents, as opposed to the traditional formality of well-bred Shakespearean speech, on the grounds that working-class accents were as worthy of respect as those of the upper-class. To her, "the dreary respect" which is accorded Elizabethan verse is foolish, for this poetry was formed by a wild and rowdy bunch of artist-commoners, "leery misfits, anarchists, out-of-work soldiers, [and] wits," who belched forth their verbiage in the atmosphere of pubs and brothels. The Elizabethan drama was a people's theatre, raw and vigorous, unconcerned with questions of "art" and "direction," dealing with man and not with puppets.[24]

SUBSEQUENT PRODUCTIONS

In subsequent years Littlewood's directing career slackened off considerably. She had a disastrous experience in 1965 with *Twang!!,* a Lionel Bart musical. She walked out of the show during its tryout period, and it is not listed in her *Who's Who* credits. The show was produced as a commercial venture apart from Theatre Workshop and revealed the difficulty she had in employing her favorite rehearsal techniques outside the Stratford East environment. She had undertaken the project in hopes of raising cash for her special projects.

Littlewood left Stratford-atte-Bowe for two years, touring the globe, working on *Twang!!,* and evolving a project in Tunisia, where she staged a play called *Who Is Repito?* at the Hamamet Arts Festival in 1966. In this African nation, she said she

worked for what amounted to a year altogether with a mixture of nationalities to play out their fear of each other. Syrian for Algerian, Algerian for Tunisian, Arab for Jew, Jew for Arab, French for Algerian. This they played out, and they became a very exciting piece of theatre, almost a therapy.[25]

Back again at Theatre Workshop in 1967, Littlewood opened the season with a painful failure, Barbara Garson's American political burlesque, *MacBird.* Theatre Workshop had to be turned into a private club for the production because the Lord Chamberlain's office had forbidden public performances of the controversial play. A major criticism was that the political sting had been removed in favor of a series of music-hall turns. Martin Esslin observed: "Barely a line of Barbara Garson's Shakespearean verse has survived. Instead there is prose that bears the marks of having been hurriedly improvised during rehearsal."[26]

Following a heavily cut, broadly acted *Intrigues and Amours,* based on Sir John Vanbrugh's Restoration comedy *The Provok'd Wife,* a hit came once more in September 1967 with *Mrs. Wilson's Diary,* a musical political satire largely improvised by the actors and shaped by the writers Richard Ingrams and John Wells, with music by Jeremy Taylor. It was based on a satirical series then running in the comic journal *Private Eye* and fictitiously attributed to the wife of then Prime Minister Harold Wilson; the piece laughed at the daily goings on at No. 10 Downing Street. Critic Charles Marowitz wrote that "it is the first time since Walpole invented the Lord Chamberlain, with his power of stage censorship, that public figures have been openly lampooned on a public stage."[27] *Mrs. Wilson's Diary* was the last Littlewood show to go to the West End, as, soon afterwards, she decided she could no longer stand to lose her talented people to the lures of the commercial theatre. Littlewood followed *Mrs. Wilson's*

Diary in November with a play about a great music-hall star, *The Marie Lloyd Story*, by Daniel Farson and Harry Moore, with a score by Norman Kay. Avis Bunnage gave a commanding performance in the title role, and the play was very well received.

It was another several years until Joan Littlewood staged a Theatre Workshop production, although she had been actively engaged there since 1967 in a therapeutic and recreational program for neighborhood youths. Another preoccupation from 1968 on was the gradual demolition of Angel Lane, the street on which the theatre stood, as the street was being redeveloped with new office and residential buildings. Raffles and Littlewood fought unavailingly to have the theatre made the center of a cultural and entertainment complex. Rubble surrounded the theatre for years. The theatre itself came under the threat of the wrecking crew, but strenuous efforts by Raffles and others succeeded in having it preserved under a historical landmark designation in 1972. The same year, a reasonable, if still insufficient, subsidy was granted to the company which, in 1970, had returned to put on plays.

Of the two plays Littlewood staged in late 1970, the more intriguing was one called *The Projector*. Her intent was to put on a play to underline a 1968 municipal scandal involving a Ronan Point disaster in which a high-rise development collapsed and several people were killed. She observed the trials of those involved and wanted to develop a play from the notes she took, but learned that such an endeavor would not be legally permissible. Instead of a new play, she chose a play purportedly written in the eighteenth century by William Rufus Chetwood which dealt with an unscrupulous 1733 building contractor who erected a housing project that collapsed, killing and injuring inhabitants. "Adapted" by John Wells, it was an entertaining romp which Alan Brien described as a work of "lusty, high-spirited vulgarity, [and] burlesque fun, [with] camp and transvestite intentions."[28] The press, however, soon started questioning the authenticity of the supposed source. No copy of the original could be found, nor could any reference to it be unearthed. It was suspected that the claim was a hoax, but Wells admitted nothing. Eventually George Dorris investigated the matter and revealed that Wells and Littlewood had created a clever pastiche of a Chetwood work called *The Mock Mason* (1733), which itself was the comic subplot of Chetwood's *The Generous Free Mason*.[29] *The Projector* was one of several plays dealing with local problems staged by Littlewood at this period. The others were Ken Hill's *Forward, Up Your End* (1970), a political satire, and *The Londoners* (1972), a well-liked musical adaptation of *Sparrers Can't Sing*, its score by Lionel Bart.

In 1971 Littlewood took a leave from Theatre Workshop and directed Connor Cruse O'Brien's political drama about Patrice Lumumba and Dag Hammarskjöld, *Murderous Angels*, in Paris at the Théâtre National Populaire.

She did three plays for Theatre Workshop in 1972, one of which was a revival of *The Hostage*. Her interpretation, however, was nothing like that of the first production. Instead of the hilarious farcelike tone of the 1958 mounting, the play was now seen in a realistic, straightforward light. Eight members of the original company were in it. "The tones have darkened," wrote Peter Ansorge, "the songs interrupted, and each of the characters has been given a coherent purpose and place in the context of a real, as opposed to fantasy, Dublin brothel."[30] Littlewood's rewritten production was done with specific reference to the Irish political troubles, which had intensified tragically since the more relaxed days of the original production. Bomb scares plagued the theatre, which twice had to be evacuated.

Her final projects for Theatre Workshop were 1972's *Costa Packet*, a successful musical satire on package tours, with two songs by Lionel Bart and a score by Alan Klein, who also developed Frank Norman's original script, and 1973's *So You Want to Be in Pictures?* The latter, the last play she directed, was by Peter Rankin, took place on a Rome film set, and poked fun at the world of moviemaking.

Littlewood's last year at Stratford saw her pursue an increasingly careless managerial policy, which disturbed many of her coworkers. She moved to France following the close of *So You Want to Be in Pictures?* and, although she may have planned on returning, never did. Ken Hill took over the management of Theatre Workshop; in 1975 Littlewood's close associate and lover Gerry Raffles died (she had been divorced from MacColl), aged only fifty-one, and the distraught Littlewood declared that her theatre activity was over.

POPULAR THEATRE

Littlewood's career reveals her consuming passion for a relevant theatre that would appeal to the average man. Her productions, modern and classic, always sought to deal with current issues and universal themes in a way which anyone, no matter how lacking in formal education, could understand and enjoy.

Littlewood's importance lies more in the method and manner of her presentations than in her directorial breadth. She did not consciously choose to be an actress or a director, she says, but—being a lover of life in all its variations, someone who loves watching and working with people—she ended up in the theatre because it gave her "a place where it would be fun for people to work. I wanted a place where you could just take off, take the high jump; that's why I direct."[31] Talking about theatre in terms of "art" annoys Littlewood, for she prefers to think of it as an element of life, not something apart. "I don't do theatre, love," she told a journalist. "What I do is explore delight and pain, sometimes on the stage. What *am* I then? Well you could say I'm a concierge— I open doors."[32]

A rebel against the political and artistic establishment, yet one whose overwhelming success allowed her to watch her rebellious ideas become conventional, Littlewood always sided with the underdog and downtrodden and sought to make her theatre one where they would feel at home. In her opinion, England's leading establishment theatres are the "walking dead" because they lack a sense of the here and now. Theatre should be capable of capturing the passing moment and must not live on its past reputation like a mummy in a museum. The famous theatres have no connection with the pain and joy of life, she said, and exist as in a womb. As she told Kenneth Tynan, "We must have places where we can eat, drink, make love, be lonely, be together, and share in the theatre of living. That is my theatre."[33]

To make her theatre serve life, not art, she instilled it with whatever she found vital in the ideas and techniques of modern and ancient theatre, taking her methods from the commedia, Stanislavsky, Brecht, Piscator, Laban, Vakhtangov, Meyerhold, the Elizabethans, and the circus clown. She saw the great modern companies of Europe as having emerged to answer local needs for popular theatres providing their audience with entertainment and moral instruction. She cited the theatres of Copeau, Brecht, Stanislavsky, and the Habimah of Israel as creative ensembles working harmoniously to establish methods by which they could reflect the world around them. In England only the work of Irish director Terence Gray in the 1920s bore the impulse of a popular theatre, she believed, but Gray's productions did not lead to any popular tradition.

By "popular theatre" Littlewood meant not plays which enjoy capacity audiences but those which fulfill a specific function based on their significant exploration of current ideas and needs. Theatre occurs in the here and now, she insisted. Give her a writer of the masses like Brendan Behan, who can take the words of the common man and make great theatre of them. She took pride in having brought to the stage the accents of the workingman, in contrast to the Oxfordian and Etonian tones so long familiar there. Actors whose speech prevented their employment elsewhere were happily supplied with jobs by Littlewood.

Essential to her vision is a place for Rabelaisian laughter. Audiences must be "delighted," she asserted. "They need to remember that it is a planet we live on, that laughter's the only thing that can stop war and chauvinism. We ought to just laugh those things off the face of the planet. Laughter's the job, love."[34]

Littlewood's comic style was marked by rapid pacing, as in the old Mack Sennett silent film comedies. "Custard pie" comedy remained one of the strongest ingredients of her work. She would tell her actors to "play as if the camera's running too fast," or "Keep it all like comic cuts and camera." James Schevill, watching her rehearse, declared that

more than any other director I've seen working in theatre, she saw that the physical presence of the actors . . . could be used for transitions in the same bold way that films are cut. The actor could not disappear as easily, of course, but even if he remained on stage a gesture or a change in style could be used to emphasize a change in mood or scene and maintain the kind of rapid time sequence that fits modern, urban life.[35]

Because theatre must be "in the present tense," Littlewood stressed topicality in most of her work. Plays were often revised nightly to bring in current references, thereby keeping the actors fresh and the audiences alert. As we have seen, trouble with the Lord Chamberlain was likely to occur as a result of changing an officially approved script. Her work also suffered censure for its frequent vulgarity. Though she rarely exploited lewdness, its presence did give her productions a ribald earthiness much loved by Theatre Workshop audiences.

BRECHTIAN NATURALISM

Like Brecht, who has often been considered her greatest influence, Littlewood normally employed strikingly naturalistic characterizations. Closely observed in all their social relationships, the characters immediately conveyed these upon entering. According to John Elsom, when an actress in *Sparrers Can't Sing* "came on stage . . . the audience was able to guess that she was the sister of so-and-so, the daughter, the grand-daughter, girlfriend and rival of others."[36]

Naturalism was especially helpful in the plays she staged dealing with local conditions, Elsom said, documentary dramas that, in their "short, naturalistic scenes, company teamwork, avoidance of central 'heroes,' ballads, songs and music [created a genre] which became particularly popular in the late 1960's, [and] remains Littlewood's great contribution to British theatre."[37]

Again, like Brecht, Littlewood often employed naturalism in a nonillusionistic way to help bring home the thematic point. She also shared Brecht's Marxist politics, but differed markedly from him in her far less overtly didactic purposes. Instead, as John Harrop explains, she wanted to return to her working-class public "the cultural heritage which she believed they had been deprived of by their upper-class masters."[38]

Harrop sums up the similarities between Brecht and Littlewood by comparing *Mother Courage* and *Oh, What a Lovely War!*, which are somewhat related in subject matter. Both employ open staging techniques, with rather bare stages, few props, and rapid and flexible scene shifts—executed with a minimum of technical fuss in the Elizabethan manner. Projections and slogans are another common device. Musical scene bridges in Brecht use biting original tunes, but in Littlewood are authentic period songs which comment sardonically on themselves by their ironic juxtaposition with the show's critical view of war.

Regardless of the apparent similarities to Brecht in her work of the fifties and early sixties, Littlewood's nonintellectual style, her affinity for Stanislavsky acting methods, and her preference for unfinished scripts are among the diverse ways in which she and Brecht are in different camps. Further, Harrop points out that,

like Brecht, Littlewood assumes that the theatre is not an "illusion" in the old sense of the word, but the nature of her "non-illusionistic" theatre is, again, something very different from Brecht's. In Littlewood's theatre there is an emphatic and sensual coop-eration between the actor and audience which Brecht avoided. For her, the actors, while playing their parts, are still people who are talking to other people; therefore an actor can ad-lib on stage, or can talk directly to the audience without any conspicuous purpose of breaking the audience's illusion—the truth of the theatre includes the spectator's emotional agreement to participate in the sensual and intellectual experience.[39]

MUSIC

Music enhanced most of Littlewood's productions, including the straight plays like *A Taste of Honey*. Elsom declares that she inspired a new British musical style "far removed from the Ruritanian splendours of Ivor Novello and the university charms of Sandy Wilson and Julian Slade."[40] Familiar musical styles such as her audience were fond of—including rock, jazz, and pop—filled the air at Littlewood's shows, though nostalgic music from the past often made a strong impression as in *Oh, What a Lovely War!* In *Make Me an Offer* and *Fings Ain't Wot They Used t'Be* the astringent music sharply reminded Martin Esslin of Brecht. He wrote that

She was also responsible for what must be regarded as the only notable work which owed a debt to the Brechtian use of music in Britain in [the late fifties]: Brendan Behan's *The Hostage* (1959) with its many parallels to the *Threepenny Opera*.[41]

SCENIC DESIGN

Littlewood's chief designer for the period of her greatest glory, from 1954 to 1963, was a man who began his theatre career as an actor in her company. John Bury later became one of the world's leading scene designers and was appointed head of design at England's National Theatre. Because of the company's limited funds, Bury had to stretch his great imagination to devise exciting sets with a minimum of means. In his earlier designs black drapes played a significant role, but he had to develop a more concrete scenic style for those plays that required, at the least, selective elements of realism. Tom Milne observed that Bury's style was in perfect harmony with Littlewood's intentions,

and his settings, in their starkness, are platforms from which her productions are launched at the audience. Their bareness is not a merit rising out of material necessity, but a merit in itself, using the whole range of the stage, vertically and horizontally, to frame the play without detracting from it by unnecessary trappings.[42]

A designer of extremely selective means, Bury used the simplest arrangements with great dramatic force, stemming from a metaphorical rather than representational view of the stage space, though, as in Brechtian design, naturalistic details were occasionally of significance. Bury also provided effective lighting designs, producing unusual effects through his metaphoric methods.[43] (In the sixties and seventies most of Stratford East's scenery and lighting was designed by Guy Hodgkinson and Mark Pritchard. Costumes normally were by Willie Burt.)

APPROACH TO ACTING

Most critics agree that Littlewood brought to the British stage a completely new style of acting, at extreme variance with the suave perfectionism of the traditional theatre. The lifelikeness of her actors, their coarse earthiness, the detailed realism of their manner, the music-hall familiarity with which they addressed the spectators, their mimic expressiveness, their contemporary casualness in the classics, and the unity of their ensemble work were previously unknown qualities in English theatres. Working together as permanent company members, Littlewood's men and women developed a clear-cut stylistic identity, an identity emerging from constant training and playing together in quest of a shared ideal. Many of England's finest players were trained at Theatre Workshop, including Harry Corbett, Maxwell Shaw, Richard Harris, Howard Goorney, Frances Cuka, and Murray Melvin. Many others played there, providing new blood and replacing those moving on, beginning in the late fifties. For such actors, it was often difficult to work in the approved Littlewood manner. She demanded that actors have imagination, truth, a sense of humor, human warmth, great freedom from inhibitions, and a devotion to the company concept.

Littlewood was against the star system and found her actors largely among untrained aspirants, whom she preferred to train from scratch. Overtrained actors with all their stock tricks appalled her. She wanted actors who were willing to work in whatever way she thought appropriate for a production, flexible players to suit her whim for experimentation. Her continuing goal was to create a true ensemble, all of its members thoroughly trained in the same company acting method. Before the company concept began to weaken as a result of her commercial successes, she succeeded in creating an outstanding corps of exciting, fresh, and honest young players lacking the artificial speech and attitudes of conventional actors.

WORKING WITH ACTORS

Littlewood always inclined toward the concept of a group of collaborative artists working together toward a common goal, and therefore decried those directors who make their actors into robots. Hers, she claimed, was an actor's theatre where she and her company worked together to find the best solutions to the problems at hand. Molière and the artists of *commedia* provided inspiration for her vision. She was convinced that a play is composed of so many physical and intellectual ingredients that it is impossible for a director single-handedly to conceive an end result for it. Only through the arduous process of group rehearsal in movement and speech can the play evolve into a vital and artistic production.

''Professional directors'' are, to her, people who take a script, plan out all its rhythms, visualizations, and vocalizations, and overintellectualize their material in the process.

But there is something else that happens [she explained]. I don't care who we are. If five of us are gathered at random in this room and we have a subject and it's exciting, we'd get together on it; you read one bit, I'll read another, someone can dance, someone knows about music. The objective is in the team looking for protein; they might not find it but they might find something quite different.[44]

The idea of an "Olympian" director who hands down instructions from above to the actors is one with which Joan Littlewood found little sympathy, although some actors remember times when her cooperative ideals crumbled and the autocrat in her took over. She even resorted to a megaphone to bark out her orders when necessary. Still, her unique method was largely a collaborative one, and it is in this method that her greatest achievements lie.

A process-oriented director who wished she could go on rehearsing without the deadline of an opening night, she rehearsed mainly by a method of imaginative improvisations. She would continue such techniques until the very day of the opening, and even after, when she could. Her aim was to keep the actors fresh through the vivid exploration of new problems in playing their roles.

Even Littlewood's auditions were likely to be improvisatory. According to Kenneth Tynan, she once told an auditioning actor: "Let's drop all that and improvise. You want X pounds a week. Argue with me and prove that you need it. Lie as much as you like. If you can convince me, you get the job."[45] And he did.

Sometimes, she would audition an actor by asking him to perform all the parts in a script. After reading a wide range of characters, young and old, male and female, and feeling silly as a result, an actor was informed, "Well, at least you don't mind making a fool of yourself—and any man who has courage on the stage and is willing to make a fool of himself can, in fact, become a good actor."[46]

Littlewood was pragmatic and would use whatever technique she felt was best suited to a play. Analytical discussions with the cast, for example, were distasteful to her, but she employed them on occasion. Her methods were closer to those of Stanislavsky in his later period—when he stressed the "method of physical actions"—than they were to his earlier work, in which emotion memory was a central feature. Even this latter technique was used by Littlewood, however, when she felt it was useful for solving a problem.

Research and careful preparation were always extremely important before Littlewood began rehearsals. This was especially true regarding period plays. Yet her attitude at rehearsals was never closed to new impulses and ideas from her collaborators. Often she would guide the company in their own process of research on an old play, studying the historical and social background, and then develop improvisations in movement, style, and character to explore what they had found. Howard Goorney remembers the improvisations during the early period of the Jacobean play *The Dutch Courtesan*. "We enacted elaborate mimes to the accompaniment of encouraging shouts from Littlewood: 'You don't care if your teeth are falling out so long as you can still get your fucking!' "[47]

Often, Littlewood would not give her actors the text of the play until they had gone through an extensive period of work on the subtext. This was her approach, for instance, to *Richard II*. The company did careful work on discovering through physicalization and movement what the play's pulse beat was. They found how each character's watchful, suspicious air could be conveyed through his manner of walking and gesturing. Exercises in the Laban system of movement were practiced for many hours. Only after weeks of emotional and physical exercises was the script brought in. The words, when spoken, were seen as part of a total matrix in which they were merely the verbal expression. This speaking was scored by many critics. As we have observed, Littlewood did not care for the artificial manner in which classical verse is spoken on the English stage; she preferred to colloquialize the verse and make it honest rather than stagey.

She did not, in her classical work, avoid the problems of verse speaking, but went at them from her own unique perspective. To make it sound real, not phony, she stressed the communication of meaning through attention to the internal rhythms. Sometimes she would require an actor to beat out the rhythms of a speech with his fists, like a boxer. This technique allowed the actor to discover the meaning of the verse through his physical involvement with it.

Richard II was an example of a play rehearsed early on a semblance of the actual set. This gave the actors a feeling of great familiarity with their scenic environment and allowed them to develop movement patterns in accord with the physical and atmospheric attributes of the scene. Other scenic elements like props and costumes were usually evolved in the course of rehearsals, and grew from the choices made in the group improvisations.

Littlewood's rehearsals were geared toward stripping the actor of all his actorish defenses, all the hollow tricks he employed to hide his basic humanity and warmth. She wanted her people to give themselves to the work unreservedly, with all their attention and will. Freshness, truth and spontaneity were basic concepts. All set ways and notions were irrelevant to the process of opening up and finding new things the person scarcely knew were there. New actors working with Littlewood were told:

1. Jettison any preconceived ideas about your part or the play.
2. Forget how you rehearsed with other directors.
3. Be prepared for anything.
4. Wear old clothes.[48]

Following Stanislavsky's principles, each character's action onstage was seen by Littlewood as the expression of an attempt to satisfy an objective. The objectives were the core features of the blocks of action, called units (or beats), into which the play was broken down. Each unit is a complete segment, no matter whether it is only a line or two, or an extended scene. The play consists of all the units, with their integral objectives, linked together to form an organic whole. Work on the units was usually executed through improvisational exercises in which related subject matter was enacted with the actor's own words and business. A classical situation might be played by using modern equivalents, such as changing a courtier and a king to an employee and his boss. A scene imagined to have taken place prior to that in the play might be improvised, such as a pub scene showing Macbeth's act of hiring the murderers of Duncan. When Brendan Behan attended rehearsals of *The Hostage*, he often told the cast Irish stories to provide background for the play. These stories were then used as the basis for improvisations related to what was in the play.

Every play presents a different set of improvisational problems for rehearsal; Littlewood's solutions to these were often brilliant. To get the actors into the appropriate frame of mind for *Macbeth* she had them do cowboy-and-Indian improvisations; the culminating battle led directly into playing the drama's opening scene. To develop the proper physical responses for the mother and daughter in the beginning of *A Taste of Honey*, Littlewood had the actresses drag big, heavy suitcases about the stage for an hour, improvising their search for lodgings on a rainy day. The result was a truthful sense of how they would have felt upon finally reaching their chosen flat.

In preparatory sessions for *The Quare Fellow*, which takes place in a prison, the company was brought to the gray, slate roof of the theatre. They had not seen the text and knew only the basic subject matter. In the prison-yard-like roof environment the actors were marched about endlessly as during a prison exercise period—until they felt the strain as actual prisoners would have felt it. Even their short breaks were improvised in convict style. Other improvisations of prison life were performed until the sense of prison reality grew personal and intense. Pieces of the play were fed to the actors as they continued rehearsing, but no one was definitely cast in any role until a fairly late stage in rehearsals. The actors were delighted to discover that much of what they had improvised turned out to be part of the play's action. They simply had to learn Behan's dialogue and apply it to the situations.

Twang!!, a musical about Robin Hood, used a great many improvisations in rehearsal, though the production was being produced commercially and not in the relatively relaxed atmosphere of Stratford East. She preferred to call the improvisations "games" or "parallels," and was especially fond of those she called "Keystone Cops" or "Custard-pie comedy," in which very rapid music was accompanied by rapid action.

Improvisations were also part of some plays when performed, most notably *The Hostage*. Littlewood knew that actors, given the freedom to improvise before an audience, could get carried away and weaken the fabric of the play. She told the New York *Hostage* company, for instance, that all adlibbing had to be rooted in the specific unit and its objectives. Only when the actors fully understood their objectives and those of the other characters could they know what to adlib. If this self-scrutiny was used, the humor of the unit would be communicated and would be truthful.

No one onstage was ever to perform without a full understanding of his character and its relationship to the given circumstances. She informed her actors in rehearsing the 1971 version of *The Hostage*:

Each character must know why they are standing in a certain position, each movement must be based on their strained or harmonious relations with the other characters. The women in the house have a subtle understanding of each other—they must almost move and change positions together.[49]

The impression a visitor to a Littlewood rehearsal normally received was one of chaos. Hal Prince was astounded at the casual attitude of the rehearsal he saw three days before the scheduled opening of *They Might Be Giants*. Not only was Littlewood still improvising—with the author's willing consent—she was also doing such experimental exercises as having the actors play parts other than their own (one of her favorite devices).[50] Sometimes this meant having a male character played by a female, and vice versa. Yet, regardless of the apparent confusion of these rehearsals, as Ansorge points out, "Joan Littlewood's final commitment is to perfection of detail and movement in the slow construction of immaculate stage pictures."[51]

Littlewood's blocking and consequent picturization emerged naturally from the truthful interior basis of the improvisational activity. Obviously, preplanned blocking played no part in her system. Only by a careful investigation of units and objectives could the most meaningful organic blocking be found. Rather than simply telling an actor where to go she would suggest something like: "In this scene you're coming out of a cellar, and fighting your way down a long, dark passage. You can't see, but you just know you have got to get out and through the door at the end."[52] The proper stimulus led the actor to find the most expressive moves; these always came from an inner justification. Movement deriving from this method was usually visually striking and sharply communicative of interior content, though never a result of conscious planning. "If the characters are right, the feelings are right, and if the motivations are right, the grouping must be right."[53]

Anyone present at a Littlewood rehearsal was likely to find him or herself drawn into the session. Frequently, the playwright took an active part as we have seen was true with Brendan Behan. Frank Norman was engaged in the rehearsals of *Fings Ain't Wot They Used t'Be* to help develop the dialogue. His knowledge of criminal behavior was often the clue for an improvisation by the company. When rehearsing Wolf Mankowitz's *Make Me an Offer* and an actor had trouble with a line, Littlewood had Mankowitz try to say the line himself. Whenever he had difficulty saying the line, he had to change it, realizing the fault was his and not the actor's. Nevertheless, Littlewood never changed a line without first getting the author's consent.

Kenneth Tynan points out that Littlewood was not so free in her attitude toward fully written scripts. She had the ability to make the lines meaningful without hiding behind funny or clever stage business. An actor in *The Dutch Courtesan,* recounts Tynan, had to get a laugh from a very tough speech about a long-forgotten Elizabethan book by John Lyly. Littlewood told him to approach it from a technical point of view. "If you gather the first half of the speech, and scatter the second, the sense will come over" [said the director]. "Well [stated the actor], I knew what she meant. So I gathered like mad and scattered like hell, and got a big laugh."[54]

This example stresses Littlewood's ability to use the most effective means for stimulating actors. If an improvisation was inappropriate, she would rely on verbal suggestions, couching her ideas in vivid images to make the point clearly. A Canadian actor in *Richard II* who needed help to feel like an English nobleman was told, "Pretend that stretching out before you is your future, your sons and their sons in a great long line. Behind you is a man with a dagger, about to plunge it into your back."[55] When she had a specific aim in mind, she would often have the actors respond to telling action verbs, giving them instructions like: "Sweep her out of the room. Take over. That's your underlying objective." Urging them to carry out the action with determination and directness, she would say, "Don't worry about details. Let's see about the sequence."[56] She once got the reaction she wanted from an actor who had to appear embarrassed by whispering something in his ear which at once turned his face bright red. Whatever the response, she insisted on reality. James Schevill heard her frequently say to the cast, "That'll have to be extended and made *true.*"[57]

If required, Littlewood would even demonstrate what she wanted, because she was a talented actress and capable of making her ideas visible through physical means. Obviously, she preferred less direct ways of working. Some actors, those with long experience and settled methods, found working with Littlewood unpleasant, and there are many stories of less experienced actors who felt that she could be painfully destructive, but the great majority loved being directed by her. She had an instinctive knowledge of how to reach into actors and expose their deepest qualities. She never held back when dissatisfied with an actor and would tell him frankly what she perceived as his problems. It was indeed part of her technique (and personality) not to allow actors ever to become complacent and self-satisfied, and she would often make a stinging comment aimed at deflating an actor who she felt was too comfortable with his work. Her theory was that an actor should be on the edge and insecure in his work; when Howard Goorney went to the bathroom during rehearsals of *Twang!!* missing his scene, he returned to find that his lines in the scene were cut. " 'Blimey,' said Howard, 'I only went for a pee; it's a good job I didn't go for a shit, I'd a lost my part.' "[58] Moreover, she was not content with too cozy a company atmosphere and would deliberately create tensions in the hope that they would transfer to the work onstage, although never in a way that would harm the play.

Each actor received total attention, no matter how many were in the same scene; her considerate care for the players, whom she called her "children," "darlings," "kinder," "nuts," "tosspots," and other terms of endearment, fostered genuine love and respect for her and a willingness to do anything she asked, no matter how foolish they might appear. She was rarely rigid, and would listen to all worthwhile ideas and try alternatives, preferring compromise to dictatorship. Never satisfied with the work she'd accomplished, she was always going back and "fixing" scenes that actors had grown used to and that audiences accepted without question. Her search was always to recapture the scene's original spontaneity, and material that was already effective was sometimes damaged in the pursuit. When she did this once to a scene involving writer Henry Livings during his brief acting stint with the company, she asked him,

"Better, wasn't it?" I rejoined that it was the worst fucking seven minutes I'd ever spent on stage. Her eyes softened to clear entrancing blue pools of love, and she murmured, "There has to be a destructive as well as a creative art, you know, they go together."[59]

Like a mother hen, she continued to worry over her brood even into the run of a show and would post nightly messages to them on performance problems she had observed. Midway in the run of one show, for instance, the following note was posted for the cast's consideration:

Can we stop regarding the audience as morons, cut out the rubbish, get back a bit of tension, pace and atmosphere in Act II. Can we stop wriggling our anatomies all over the script, over-acting, *bullying* laughs out of the audience and playing alone, for approbation. . . . *You cannot* play alone, stop wanting the audience to adore you and you only, they do anyway . . . so relax and let them have a look at the play for a dig.[60]

Her notes to actors were often couched in biting invective, but were usually right on target and of considerable assistance. Actors would find them in their dressing rooms, on the company board, or—sometimes to their great embarrassment—be forced to listen to them over the public address system.

CONCLUSION

Disdain for conscious artistry did not prevent Joan Littlewood herself from becoming one of the most galvanic of contemporary artistic forces in the theatre. She sought an audience of people "who sweat and swear, eat fish and chips with their fingers, drink beer noisily, and bawl out bawdy music-hall songs,"[61] but she could survive only by catering to the bourgeois public she had wished to avoid. Depending on one's politics, this was either her tragedy or the great good fortune of the theatregoing middle class. No matter what people thought of her as an artist, she wished to be considered a "vulgarian."

I could have been a great director [she once said]. . . . I didn't want to be trapped into something I didn't want, and I didn't want greatness. Art, art, I don't care about art. To hell with all art. There are too many dead gods around. I'm interested in our madness.[62]

Joan Littlewood stands alone in the English theatre in the attempt to use collaborative means to achieve popular theatricalism. Her techniques and style have given rise to a host of successors, but not one has yet reached the pinnacle represented by her great work of the fifties and early sixties. Littlewood's work still remains the most important directorial contribution to the development of a noncommercial people's theatre modern Britain has known. It is unparalleled in its wholehearted devotion to creating a deintellectualized, truthful, energetic, musical, and comedic workingman's theatre form, one with direct pertinence to the sensual and political interests of its customers. Away with gentility and poeticism, cries Joan Littlewood. Give us a theatre of grandeur, vulgarity, simplicity, artlessness, pathos—one which will make us weep, perhaps, but, better still, one which will make us shout with laughter and dance with joy.

NOTES

1. Quoted in Ewan MacColl, "Grass Roots of Theatre Workshop," *Theatre Quarterly* 3 (January/March 1973): 67.

2. Ibid.

3. Ibid., p. 65.

4. Ibid., p. 68.

5. Quoted in Michael Coren, *Theatre Royal, 100 Years of Stratford East* (London: Quartet Books, 1984), pp. 23–24. Coren gives a helpful, if attenuated, overview of Littlewood's work at Theatre Royal. The fullest account of her career and company will be found in Howard Goorney, *The Theatre Workshop Story* (London: Eyre Methuen, 1981).

6. Anthony Bailey, "Would Little Joan Littlewood Were Here!" *Esquire* 64 (January 1964): 113.

7. Goorney, *Theatre Workshop Story*, pp. 101–2.

8. Ibid., p. 101.

9. Norman Marshall, *The Producer and the Play*, rev. ed. (London: Davis-Poynter, 1975), p. 299.

10. John Russell Taylor, *Anger and After: A Guide to the New British Drama* (London: Methuen, 1962), p. 110.

11. Lindsay Anderson, "A Taste of Honey," in *The Encore Reader: A Chronicle of the New Drama*, ed. Charles Marowitz, Tom Milne, et al. (London: Methuen, 1965), p. 79.

12. Quoted in Coren, *Theatre Royal*, p. 35.

13. Taylor, *Anger and After*, pp. 113, 114.

14. Ulrick O'Connor, *Brendan Behan* (London: Hamish Hamilton, 1970), p. 197.

15. Ibid., p. 207.

16. Wolf Mankowitz, quoted in ibid., p. 196.

17. Coren, *Theatre Royal*, p. 41.

18. Joan Littlewood, quoted in Amanda Sue Rudisill, "The Contributions of Eva Le Gallienne, Margaret Webster, Margo Jones, and Joan Littlewood to the Establishment of Repertory Theatre in the United States and Great Britain" (Ph.D. diss., Northwestern University, 1972), p. 213.

19. Ibid., pp. 5–6.

20. Kenneth Tynan, "Joan of Cockaigne," *Holiday* 26 (November 1964): 121.

21. Alan Brien, "Openings: London," *Theatre Arts* 48 (June 1966): 70.

22. Quoted by Jane Howard, "Merry, Angry Mother Hen," *Life,* 27 November 1964, p. 62.

23. John Russell Brown, "Three Kinds of Shakespeare," *Shakespeare Survey,* vol. 18 (Cambridge, Eng.: Cambridge University Press, 1965), pp. 153, 154.

24. "Joan Littlewood Hits Back at Crix," *Variety,* 2 September 1964.

25. Quoted by Margaret Croyden, "Joan Littlewood," in *Behind the Scenes: Theater and Film Interviews from the "Transatlantic Review,"* ed. Joseph F. McCrindle (New York: Holt, Rinehart and Winston, 1971), p. 10.

26. Martin Esslin, "London Broils *MacBird,*" *New York Times,* 16 April 1967.

27. Charles Marowitz, "Oh What a Lovely Diary," *New York Times,* 8 October 1967.

28. Alan Brien, "London: On Contemporary Relevance," *New York Times,* 7 December 1970.

29. George Dorris, "*The Projector, The Mock Mason,* and Miss Littlewood," *Modern Drama* 16 (December 1973): 265–68.

30. Peter Ansorge, "Lots of Lovely Human Contact! An Inside Look at Joan Littlewood," *Plays and Players* 19 (1972): 19.

31. Croyden, "Joan Littlewood," p. 1.

32. Howard, "Merry, Angry Mother Hen," p. 62.

33. Tynan, "Joan of Cockaigne," p. 114.

34. Howard, "Merry, Angry Mother Hen," p. 64.

35. James Schevill, *Break Out! In Search of New Theatrical Environments* (Chicago: Swallow Press, 1973), pp. 324–25.

36. John Elsom, *Post-War British Theatre* (London: Routledge and Kegan Paul, 1976), p. 101.

37. Ibid., p. 103.

38. John Harrop, "Brecht's Baby, A Misconception about Joan Littlewood," *Drama at Calgary* 3 (March 1969): 74.

39. Ibid., p. 78.

40. Elsom, *Post-War British Theatre,* p. 83.

41. Martin Esslin, "Brecht and the English Theatre," *The Drama Review* 11 (Winter 1966): 65.

42. Tom Milne, "Art in Angel Lane," in *Encore Reader,* ed. Marowitz, Milne, et al., p. 85.

43. Ibid.

44. Croyden, "Joan Littlewood," p. 9.

45. Tynan, "Joan of Cockaigne," p. 121.

46. Clive Goodwin and Tom Milne, "Working with Joan," in *Directors on Directing: A Source Book of the Modern Theatre,* ed. Toby Cole and Helen Krich Chinoy, rev. ed. (Indianapolis: Bobbs-Merrill, 1963), p. 399.

47. Howard Goorney, "Littlewood in Rehearsal," *The Drama Review* 11 (Winter 1966): 102.

48. Goodwin and Milne, "Working with Joan," p. 395.

49. Ansorge, "Lots of Lovely Human Contact!," p. 21.

50. Harold Prince, *Contradictions. Notes on Twenty-Six Years in the Theatre* (New York: Dodd, Mead, 1974), p. 75.

51. Ansorge, "Lots of Lovely Human Contact!," p. 21.
52. Goodwin and Milne, "Working with Joan," p. 396.
53. Ibid.
54. Quoted in Tynan, "Joan of Cockaigne," p. 394.
55. Goorney, *Theatre Workshop Story*, p. 171.
56. Schevill, *Break Out!*, pp. 324–25.
57. Ibid.
58. Henry Livings, quoted in Goorney, *Theatre Workshop Story*, p. 193.
59. Ibid.
60. Goodwin and Milne, "Working with Joan," p. 398.
61. Harrop, "Brecht's Baby," p. 74.
62. Quoted by Paul Gardner, "Joan Littlewood: Call Me a Vulgarian," *New York Times*, 27 September 1964.

CHRONOLOGY

All productions London, unless noted. Littlewood's *Who's Who in Theatre* listing is incomplete. The best listing of Theatre Workshop's productions is in Howard Goorney's *The Theatre Workshop Story* (London: Eyre Methuen, 1981), although he omits one or two plays. For help in compiling the present list I am grateful to Profs. J. P. Wearing and Clive Barker (a former Littlewood actor); the latter received assistance from Goorney. An asterisk denotes plays that remained in the repertory—if only briefly—beyond their initial presentation. Only important revivals of plays already staged are noted, the focus being on new productions.

1915	born in Stockwell, South London
1931	scholarship to Royal Academy of Dramatic Art
1934	acts with Manchester Rusholme Repertory Company; cofounds left-wing Theatre of Action in Manchester with Ewan MacColl (Jimmy Miller)
1934–36	produces a series of left-oriented plays and sketches in makeshift surroundings; includes *Newsboy, Waiting for Lefty,* and *John Bullion—A Ballet with Words*
1935	marries Ewan MacColl
1936	cofounds Theatre Union in Manchester; Lesser Free Trade Hall, Manchester: *Miracle at Verdun; The Sheepwell*
1938	Lesser Free Trade Hall: *The Good Soldier Schweik*
1939	Manchester: *The Masters of Time*
1940	Round House, Manchester: *Last Edition*; show closed by authorities because of antigovernment viewpoint
1941	Milton Hall, Manchester: *Lysistrata; The Flying Doctor; Classic Soil*
1942	World War II forces breakup of company
1945–53	founding of Theatre Workshop in Kendal; over next eight years located in Kendal; Ormesby Hall, Manchester; and Glasgow; survives mainly by touring the provinces in one-night stands
1945	provincial tour: *The Flying Doctor;* * Johnny Noble;* * The Love of Don Perlimplín for Belissa in His Garden* *

1946 provincial tour and Scotland: *Uranium 235*; also briefly visits London

1947 Library Theatre, Manchester, and provincial tour: *The Proposal*;* *The Gentle People*;* *The Other Animals*;* *Operation Olive Branch*;* *Professor Mamlock*; formal London debut, Rudolf Steiner Theatre; tour to West Germany

1948 Library Theatre and tours to Czechoslovakia, Sweden

1949 schools tour, Manchester: *Twelfth Night*; Library Theatre: *Rogues' Gallery*; Epworth Hall, Edinburgh Theatre Festival: five-play repertory; schools tour, Manchester: *As You Like It* (for schools)

1950 provincial tour and Theatre Royal, Stratford-atte-Bowe, London: *Alice in Wonderland*; provincial tour; Adelphi Theatre, London: *The Gentle People*; South Wales tour: *A Midsummer Night's Dream* (for schools)

1951 South Wales tour: *Landscape with Chimneys*;* Scandinavian tour; tour of northeast provinces; Oddfellows Hall, Edinburgh: *Uranium 235; Johnny Noble; The Flying Doctor*; South Wales: *Hymn to the Rising Sun; The Long Shift;* schools tour: *Henry IV, Part I*

1952 northeast tour and Scotland; Embassy Theatre, London, and Comedy Theatre, London: *Uranium 235*; Oddfellows Hall: *The Travellers*; schools tour, Glasgow: *Twelfth Night*

1953 company established at Theatre Royal (TR) (Stratford East, London): *Twelfth Night; The Imaginary Invalid; Paradise Street; Juno and the Paycock; Colour Guard; Hindle Wakes; Arms and the Man; Lysistrata; Three Men on a Horse; Anna Christie;* Oddfellows Hall, Edinburgh Festival: *The Imaginary Invalid; Uncle Vanya;* TR: *The Troublemakers; The Alchemist; The Government Inspector; A Christmas Carol*;* *Treasure Island**

1954 TR: *Richard II; Van Call; The Dutch Courtesan; The Devil's Disciple; The Fire Eaters; Amphitryon 30; Red Roses for Me; An Enemy of the People; The Long Voyage Home; Arden of Faversham; Cruel Daughters; The Good Soldier Schweik; The Chimes; The Prince and the Pauper; The Legend of Pepito*

1955 TR: *Richard II; Volpone; The Midwife; Arden of Faversham*; Théâtre Hébertot, Paris International Theatre Festival: *Volpone; Arden of Faversham*; Devon Festival, Barnstaple: *Mother Courage; Richard II*; TR: *The Sheepwell; An Italian Straw Hat; Big Rock Candy Mountain*

1956 Scandinavian tour: *Arden of Faversham*; TR, Duke of York's Theatre, London, and Théâtre Sarah Bernhardt, Paris International Theatre Festival: *The Good Soldier Schweik*; TR: *Edward II; The Quare Fellow*; the latter then plays Brighton, Comedy Theatre, London, and engagements at Streatham Hill, Liverpool, Cambridge

1957 Schauspielhaus, Zurich, Moscow Art Theatre, Moscow, TR, and Playhouse, Oxford: *Macbeth*; TR: *You Won't Always Be on Top; And the Wind Blew*

1958 TR: *Celestina; Unto Such Glory* and *The Respectable Prostitute* (double bill); *A Taste of Honey; The Hostage*

1959 TR, Wyndham's Theatre, London, and Criterion Theatre, London: *A Taste of Honey*; TR and Wyndham's: *Fings Ain't Wot They Used t'Be*; TR and Wyndham's: *The Hostage*; TR and New Theatre, London: *Make Me an Offer*

1960   TR: *Ned Kelly*; Sarah Bernhardt, Paris International Theatre Festival, and TR: *Every Man in His Humour*; TR: *Sparrers Can't Sing*; Cort Theatre, New York: *The Hostage*; Maxim Gorky Theater, East Berlin: *Operation Olive Branch*

1961   TR: *We're Just Not Practical*; *Sparrers Can't Sing* transfers to Wyndham's; TR: *They Might Be Giants*

1961–63   leaves company for two years; Nigeria: *The Lion and the Jewel*; Theatre Royal leased to outside producers

1963   TR and Wyndham's: *Oh, What a Lovely War!*

1964   TR: *A Kayf Up West*; Assembly Hall, Edinburgh Theatre Festival: *Henry IV*; Broadhurst Theatre, New York: *Oh, What a Lovely War!*

1964–67   Theatre Royal leased to independent producers; Littlewood develops Fun Palace concept

1965   walks out on *Twang!!*; East and West Berlin: *Oh, What a Lovely War!*

1965–66   Centre Culturel Internationale, Hamamet, Tunisia: *Who Is Repito?*

1967   TR: *MacBird; Intrigues and Amours*: TR and Criterion Theatre, London: *Mrs. Wilson's Diary*; TR: *The Marie Lloyd Story*

1968   TR's surrounding neighborhood undergoes extensive redevelopment

1970   TR: *Forward, Up Your End; The Projector*

1971   Théâtre National Populaire, Paris: *Murderous Angels*

1972   TR: *The Londoners; The Hostage; Costa Packet*

1973   TR: *So You Want to Be in Pictures?*

1975   declares her theatre work over; moves to France

Peter Brook

(1925–)

There is a passage in Peter Brook's book *The Empty Space* where he says that for the American theatre to move ahead, it is necessary "for a Meyerhold to appear, since naturalistic representations of life no longer seem to Americans adequate to express the forces that drive them."[1] Few will doubt that when Brook himself appeared, the English theatre at last found its own Meyerhold, for Brook's genius revealed a world of theatrical possibilities in which the Russian master would have felt quite at home. Indeed, Brook and Meyerhold are perhaps the century's two most outstanding examples of the director-experimentalist, the artist-scientist who uses the theatre as a laboratory to see what chemical effect the combination of selected theatrical ingredients will have on the end result. Such men are forever searching, asking questions, trying to discover that which is essentially undiscoverable—what is the theatre, what are its natural properties, and why does it exist?

EARLY YEARS

Peter Stephen Paul Brook is of Russian parentage, having been born to Simon and Ida Brook in London in 1925. His investigative bent comes naturally, as both his parents were trained scientists. Schooled in England and Switzerland, Brook attended Oxford University, where he soon began to show evidence of being a youthful prodigy. In 1943, a year before he received his degree (at nineteen), Brook set up his own theatre, the Torch, and staged his first play, *Dr. Faustus,* with an amateur company. His aim at the time was to become a film director (he made his first film in 1944, an adaptation of Laurence Sterne's novel *A Sentimental Journey*), but his subsequent career shows his film work, though important, to have been relatively minor when compared with the extensiveness of his theatre activity. By 1945 he was working in London at the out-of-the-way Chanticleer Theatre, gaining attention through his staging of Jean Cocteau's *The Infernal Machine*.

Following a production of Rudolf Besier's *The Barretts of Wimpole Street* at London's "Q" Theatre and one of George Bernard Shaw's *Pygmalion* for an ENSA (Entertainments National Service Association) tour, he was engaged by Sir Barry Jackson to direct at the latter's famed Birmingham Repertory Company where, with *Man and Superman,* he first worked with Paul Scofield, who eventually starred in more Brook productions than any other major actor. Of English stars, only John Gielgud has acted with Brook nearly as much. Before 1945 was over, Scofield had appeared in Brook's mountings of Shakespeare's *King John* and Henrik Ibsen's *The Lady from the Sea*.

Scofield later recalled that his twenty-year-old director "would have a conception of the play at the first reading which, to us at the Birmingham Repertory Theatre, seemed almost impertinent. That anyone so young should presume such grasp." But Brook's brilliance soon became apparent, for it was clear "his grasp was fully backed up."[2] At the time, Brook's interests were more in visual and atmospheric effects than in acting. Still, Scofield remembers Brook's effect on him as being "traumatic" enough to jar him and the other actors from their complacency.

In 1946 Brook began directing at the Shakespeare Memorial Theatre, Stratford-on-Avon, where he began with *Love's Labour's Lost* (Scofield acted Berowne), adding *Romeo and Juliet* in 1947. Both were considered highly unconventional productions. The former is remembered for its lovely Watteau-influenced decor, which Brook decided on as a means of making the play as appealing and intelligible for a modern-day audience as the theatre's resources would allow. He explained that he had chosen Watteau "because the style of his dresses, with its broad, undecorated expanses of billowy satin, seemed the ideal visual correlative of the essential sweet-sad mood of this play." Similarly, he added a silent character, not in the original, to the scenes in the Princess' court, "a chalk-faced, white-clothed zany . . . who remained to the end as a forlorn, drooping symbol, in period as much Schumann as Shakespeare, of the atmosphere of these scenes."[3] A profound image was created when, in a scene of a summer evening displayed in pale pastels, the unsettling image of the black-garbed Mercade was injected. His melancholic disposition evoked a feeling of reality's intrusion in the presence of death. With *Romeo and Juliet* Brook took textual liberties, such as removing the scene between Juliet and Friar Laurence and excluding the reconciliation scene between the Montagues and Capulets. To capture the virility of the Elizabethan spirit, Brook eliminated all traces of sentimentality in acting, decor, and music, stressing instead the heated passions of the participants. Moreover, much ado was made of his choice of very young actors to play the leads, including the eighteen-year-old Daphne Slater as Juliet.

Meanwhile, Brook was gaining attention with his 1946 London stagings of Alec Guinness' adaptation of *The Brothers Karamazov* and Jean-Paul Sartre's *Vicious Circle* (better known in English as *No Exit*); Guinness starred in both.

The following year saw more Sartre in *Men without Shadows* and *The Respectable Prostitute*. Two opera productions at the Royal Opera House, Covent Garden, occupied Brook in 1948 (he would do a number of important opera mountings in the following years), but he was back with legitimate drama in 1949, gaining West End fame with a commercially successful version of Howard Richardson and William Berney's fanciful American folk play, *Dark of the Moon,* which, with its cast of rather inexperienced young actors, exuded great bursts of energy and enthusiasm. Critic Kenneth Tynan, remembering Brook's "incredibly inventive way of handling entrances," says that a witch girl in this play "made her entrance leaning backwards from the proscenium, so she appeared to be suspended in mid-air upside down while talking to you."[4]

Dark of the Moon was succeeded by more opera work, but in 1950 Brook concentrated on plays, offering Jean Anouilh's *Ring Round the Moon* (Scofield starring), *Measure for Measure* at Stratford, and André Roussin's *The Little Hut*.

MEASURE FOR MEASURE

Brook's *Measure for Measure* with Gielgud as Angelo was an outstanding achievement, and is still regarded as one of this play's finest modern incarnations. *Measure for Measure* was surprisingly straightforward in conception. Tynan felt Brook included only one novel device:

The grisly parade of cripples and deformities which Pompey introduces in that leprous Viennese gaol. Last of all appears "Wild Half-Can who stabbed pots": a very aged man, naked except for a rag coat, twitching his head from side to side, and walking poker-stiff, bolt upright on his bare heels, with his toes turned up. All the ghastly comedy of the prison scene was summed up in this horribly funny piece of invention.[5]

Brook's masterly use of daring pauses made the production even more exciting. Tynan points out that Act II of *Measure for Measure* is a "scene of such coincidences and lengthy impossibilities" that it is usually played at a rapid pace to get it over with before its exaggerations become too obvious. Brook chose to play it with great deliberation, and had Isabella take a full thirty-five-second pause before deciding to plead for Angelo's life. This created such suspense that he "had every heart in the theatre thudding."[6] Brook's talent as a designer was in evidence here; he styled both sets and costumes, using ideas derived from Bosch and Breughel, having seen "the *zeitgeist* of Vienna as the dark underside of the Elizabethan world—and, indeed, of our world."[7]

Even more impressive than the stylistic mood with which he infused the design was the technical mastery of Brook's overall scenic conception. He designed a unit setting which was capable of clearly suggesting all changes in locale by the addition or subtraction of scenic plugs and other details. The set consisted of two rows of soaring arches progressing regularly from center stage upstage to the wings on either side. When the sky drop upstage could be seen through the arches the scene was out of doors; different plugs placed in the arches would then reveal where the interior scenes were taking place. A further permanent feature was a heavy postern gate placed downstage at either side for use in those intimate scenes which would have been overwhelmed by use of the full stage space. Area lighting enhanced the smaller scenes by cutting them off from the rest of the stage.

THE 1950s

Brook was very active in the 1950s, directing in Brussels, Paris, London, and New York. His first international directing job was at Brussels in 1951, a French-language production of *Death of a Salesman*; back in London he staged John Whiting's *A Penny for a Song, The Winter's Tale* (with Gielgud), and Anouilh's *Colombe* the same year. A year off to make a film was followed with 1953 productions of Thomas Otway's rarely done Restoration tragedy, *Venice Preserv'd* (starring both Gielgud and Scofield), and the New York mounting of *The Little Hut,* as well as projects in other media. Christopher Fry's *The Dark Is Light Enough* was Brook's first project of 1954; the year was rounded out with Arthur Macrae's *Both Ends Meet* and, on Broadway, *House of Flowers,* the whimsical musical by Truman Capote and Harold Arlen and starring Pearl Bailey. More Anouilh and Shakespeare was on deck for Brook in 1955, when he presented the former's *The Lark* and the latter's *Titus Andronicus* at Stratford (and, later, London) and *Hamlet* (Scofield played the prince) in the West End; *Hamlet* also toured to Russia.

An adaptation of Graham Greene's *The Power and the Glory* (with Scofield as the priest) started Brook off in 1956, and T. S. Eliot's *The Family Reunion* (again with Scofield), Arthur Miller's *A View from the Bridge,* and a French translation of Tennessee Williams' *Cat on a Hot Tin Roof* in Paris (Jeanne Moreau played Maggie) kept Brook busy for the rest of the year. A 1957 Stratford staging of *The Tempest,* starring Gielgud, was Brook's first attempt of three at this classic; it also came to London. Among his various projects this year was the European tour of *Titus Andronicus,* including its appearance at Paris' Théâtre des Nations. The year following witnessed Brook's French-language production of *A View from the Bridge* in Paris, the Broadway staging of Swiss playwright Friedrich Dürrenmatt's *The Visit* starring Alfred Lunt and Lynn Fontanne, and a return to musical comedy with an English version of the popular French show *Irma la Douce* back in London. The decade's work was rounded out with Brook's 1959 Broadway production of yet another Anouilh play, *The Fighting Cock,* with Rex Harrison and Natasha Parry, whom Brook had wed in 1951, and who would one day become a mainstay of his theatre work.

This array of outstanding plays and productions established Brook as one of the world's foremost serious directors, both in the importance of his repertory and the international scope of his endeavors. Many of these works profited from his talents as a designer and composer as well.

In *Venice Preserv'd* Gielgud and Scofield were a matchless pair of leads in a production which saw Brook restrain his fanciful inventiveness to achieve a tragic intensity of enormous power. Brook performed major text surgery, cutting, transposing, tightening, and finally persuading his cast to relay the vivid emotionality of the characters and situations. For his now-famous version of *Titus Andronicus,* starring Laurence Olivier and Vivien Leigh, Brook not only designed the sets and costumes but composed startling music in the mode of *musique concréte*. To stage this chilling play he exposed its ritualistic core, took liberties with the text to eliminate the possibility of the audience's tittering at the more ghastly moments, and managed to create a devastatingly effective production. He avoided embarrassing his audience through the Grand Guignol theatrics to which many feared he would resort. Ivor Brown observed that his

method was to drain off the rivers of gore, never to parade the knife-work, and instead to symbolize a wound with a scarlet ribbon. Lavinia hacked and gashed could still be an endurable sight and, since Vivien Leigh played the part, a very pretty one despite all her surgical and spiritual tribulations.[8]

Titus was one of his chief achievements of Shakespeare staging in the 1950s, and gained international acclaim during its London season and European tour.

In *The Visit* Brook chose to avoid the extreme theatricalization of earlier European versions, and opted for a subtler, more suggestive and imaginative approach with simplified sets and acting rather than the more overtly stylized requirements called for by the original text. Brooks Atkinson of the *New York Times* was overwhelmed by Brook's staging, especially the climactic scene of the town meeting when the villagers accede to the killing of Anton Schill. He was impressed by

the silent weight of public determination visible in the impassive look on the faces of the people, the feeble collapse of the opposition, the orderly assembly of the villagers to witness the strangling, the hideous shuffling of feet and the panic-stricken drawing back from the spectacle of a passionless crime. In these heartless details Mr. Brook conveys everything that the script implies without exploiting it. His taste is as impeccable as his skill.[9]

Brook has declared that his 1960 Paris production of Jean Genet's *The Balcony* marked a turning point in his career. He considered it his final "illusionist" work before moving into pure presentational theatre in the 1960s. It was during this latter decade that Brook became renowned as the *sine qua non* of British avant-garde theatre and reached the pinnacle of his profession. Improvisational and collaborative techniques now became a principal practice in his work.

ROYAL SHAKESPEARE COMPANY

In 1960 a triumvirate consisting of Brook, Michel Saint-Denis, and Peter Hall was named to take over the running of the old Shakespeare Memorial Theatre at Stratford, now renamed the Royal Shakespeare Company (RSC). Their aim was to modernize Shakespearean productions in keeping with the needs of contemporary audiences. A London company was formed in addition to that in Stratford, the former to do experimental work which would feed into the latter notions on the staging of the Bard. Brook was to make notable use of the experimental opportunities afforded under this arrangement.

The 1960s were a remarkable decade for Brook; the total number of his productions declined but the relative proportion of unforgettable masterpieces was unusually high. Paul Scofield made his final starring appearance under Brook in the landmark *King Lear* at the RSC in 1962. It was, however, the first time Irene Worth, who played Goneril, acted under Brook; she would become a faithful standby in some of his most demanding work. Dürrenmatt's *The Physicists* (also with Worth) was Brook's first work of 1963, a year which also saw his second *Tempest* at Stratford, a musical called *The Perils of Scobie Prilt* at Oxford, a French-language production of John Arden's *Sergeant Musgrave's Dance* in Paris, the Paris staging of Rolf Hochhuth's controversial docudrama *The Representative* (also known as *The Deputy*), and the visit of *King Lear* to the Théâtre des Nations. In 1964, apart from a tour of *Lear* to Eastern Europe and America, Brook was immersed in work on his widely discussed Theatre of Cruelty season, his unusual production of Genet's *The Screens,* and his landmark version of Peter Weiss' *Marat/Sade*. The following year, at the start of which he was awarded the title Commander of the British Empire, Brook (with David Jones) presided over a public reading of Weiss' holocaust drama, *The Investigation,* but he did not handle a full production again until 1966 when he prepared *Marat/Sade* for its New York opening. That same year he directed the collaboratively written *US,* about the U.S. involvement in Vietnam, but theatre audiences had to wait until 1968 for his next stage surprise, Seneca's *Oedipus,* for the National Theatre, with Gielgud and Worth. Also that year, he worked with an international group in Paris, the seed of the company he would form two years later. Stemming partly from this early group came Brook's third version of *The Tempest,* at London's Round House. The end of the decade (or the beginning of the next one, depending on one's viewpoint) arrived with Brook's revolutionary interpretation of *A Midsummer Night's Dream* for the RSC, in the wake of which he founded the International Center for Theatre Research in Paris. Within this corpus of work, new concepts of the theatre's possibilities were put to the test, new configurations of the nature of the audience-actor love-hate affair were explored, and new strata of the actor's art were uncovered. Not all were critically well received; but all represented new and unusual topography on the Brookian landscape. The highlights are limned below.

KING LEAR

Brook's feelings about Lear coincided with ideas that Polish critic Jan Kott was then promulgating through his recently published *Shakespeare Our Contemporary*; as Charles Marowitz expressed it, Kott saw a resemblance between Shakespeare's tragedy and the plays of Samuel Beckett (especially *Endgame*), "a metaphysical farce which ridicules life, death, sanity and illusion."[10] Kott views Shakespeare through the cynical eyes of a World War II survivor, claiming, in Margaret Croyden's words, "that Shakespeare was dark, savage, and cruel, that power, politics, and murder were crucial to the morality of Elizabethan times, that treachery, greed, and violence are elemental."[11]

As director-designer, Brook realized his vision of this world in a harsh visual metaphor of scenic elements seemingly rusted and corroded through ages of rugged use. A great deal of attention was paid to the problem of discovering costumes that would appear to be of no specific period yet suggest a cross between a pre-Christian barbarism and the highly developed era of the Renaissance. All costumes were notably simplified, distressed to seem worn, and adorned with few decorative features. Scofield's Lear existed within a starkly lit, forbidding, ominous environment which was matched by the slow-moving, dry, alienated acidity of the acting style adopted. The cool and astringent commentary on the action and characters conveyed by the acting and staging was clearly influenced by Brook's familiarity with the Brecht style at the Berliner Ensemble. A concrete example of a Brechtian alienation device, designed to aid the spectator in comprehending what he viewed in order to judge events dispassionately, was seen at Gloucester's blinding. Brook had the house lights turned on full at this moment to impress the scene on the audience before it proceeded to break into applause as the act ended. Few who witnessed the production seem to have felt the stirrings of sympathy or grief usually associated with the play.

In keeping with his bleakly unsentimental approach, Brook increased the possibility of sympathy for Lear by allowing Regan and Goneril to seem as if their attitude toward their father is justified; Lear's arrogance was such that he practically begged to be bitten by his children's serpent's teeth. Brook's existentialist interpretation had carefully pruned the drama of anything that might have led to such emotions. James H. Clay and Daniel Krempel describe how

the battle scene is probably the single most characteristic and unforgettable directorial invention in this production. . . . Kneeling, tiny and alone in the center of this great, gaping, vacuous mortar of a set, the blinded Gloucester sits immobile, staring, waiting to be ground and crushed. Seemingly from all around us, the sound of the unseen battle swells to cover us and our mirror image, Gloucester. It is a terrifying, welling ocean of beating, rumbling: a vortex of dissonance, the mindless, monstrous tide of evil in nature overwhelming the speck of humanity on stage—the hundreds of us—alone—watching him.[12]

THEATRE OF CRUELTY WORKSHOP

In 1964, Brook and the American expatriate critic-director Charles Marowitz were instrumental in establishing an experimental London workshop under RSC auspices. The ideas of the French theorist Antonin Artaud were the inspiration for a Theatre of Cruelty Workshop, titled after Artaud's famous essay. In this workshop Brook established the basis for the collaborative approach to working with actors which has come to be so distinctive a part of his technique. His explorations of the limits of conventional language and the possibilities of a nonverbal form of theatrical expression also are to be traced to this workshop, which engaged in three months of grueling work, averaging forty-five hours a week of intensive improvisational training in preparation for public presentations of the work-in-progress.

Brook had come to believe that to avoid the clichéd shallowness of what he calls the Deadly Theatre it was necessary to discover the elements of a Holy Theatre based on rituals which would be recognized as true for our time and culture. He wondered whether the loss of impact, which he believed to have occurred within contemporary stage language, could not be repaired through newfound imagistic means. Was the theatre capable of employing images discoverable within the production process to replace those normally found in words, using

another language just as exactly as for the author, as a language of words? Is there a language of actions, a language of sounds—a language of word-as-part-of-movement, of word-as-lie, of word-as-parody, of word-as-rubbish, of word-as-contradiction, of word-shock or word-cry?[13]

Such questions lay behind the creation of the Theatre of Cruelty investigations.

Much of Brook's future development was prefigured during the workshop's season as, in the words of Marowitz,

Little by little we insinuated the idea that the voice could produce sounds other than grammatical combinations of the alphabet, and that the body, set free, could begin to enunciate a language which went beyond sub-text, beyond psychological implication and beyond monkey-see-monkey-do facsimiles of social behaviorism. And most important of all, that these sounds and movements could communicate feelings and ideas.[14]

The results were presented for a five-week season in the eighty-seat Donmar Rehearsal Rooms at the LAMDA (London Academy of Dramatic Art) Theatre. The basic program—which occasionally varied—was made up of two parts, the first including a pair of nonsense sketches by Paul Ableman; a presentation of Artaud's surrealist playlet *Spurt of Blood*, acted first only with sounds and then with the original words; a mimed version of a story by Alain Robbe-Grillet; a pair of theatrical collages created by Brook, *The Public Bath* and *The Guillotine*, the former based on the Christine Keeler call-girl scandal (with a brilliant performance of Keeler by young Glenda Jackson); several scenes from Genet's *The Screens*; a mime piece, *The Analysis*; and John Arden's short piece, *Ars Longa, Vita Brevis*; the second part was Marowitz's unusual twenty-minute collage version of *Hamlet,* in which the script was shredded, fragmented, rearranged, and dislocated. There were also two so-called free portions of the evening, one of them devoted to improvisations run by Marowitz, the other to "specials," that is, whatever someone wanted to try in that section, from rehearsals of a scene to an open discussion of the evening's purpose. In addition to the lessons he learned concerning the nature of the theatre experience, Brook also found that the intensive improvisational work with young actors helped to bind the company into a very cohesive unit. He discovered too the value of a long-range creative project which did not culminate in a completely finished production.

It was a natural step from this experimental season to Brook's next project, a collaboration with Marowitz on a full production of *The Screens* (at the Donmar Rehearsal Rooms), which depicts the Algerian war within a context of highly charged ritualism and theatricality; Genet's aesthetic links to Artaud were a definite inspiration for Brook as well. Brook managed to mount this supposedly unstageable, multiscened play of epic proportions through imaginatively pared-down means; Sally Jacobs' set was made up essentially of tall white screens fitted with rollers, and moved about by stagehands dressed in white Arab-like robes with cowls. These allowed for the incorporation of scenes derived from exercises used during the Theatre of Cruelty season. David Williams describes one of these, an exercise in which the actors expressed their feelings by depicting them in paint and chalk in improvised "action" paintings.

To represent the burning of the orchard (tableau x), the "arabs" frantically splashed flames on to the screens while others created the sounds of crackling flames, at the same time twisting and crushing pieces of bright orange paper in their hands. In another scene (tableau xii), images of violent disembowelment, rape, murder and expressions of fear were drawn rapidly, until the whole surface of the screens was covered with the scribblings of evil: a catalogue of horrors in a frenzied dance of death.[15]

Like the Theatre of Cruelty workshop, *The Screens* was important more for its process-oriented explorations than for the so-called success of any final result, but it did contain scenes of great originality and power.

MARAT/SADE

In 1964 Brook firmly cemented his reputation as one of the world's leading directors, for this was the year which saw his London Royal Shakespeare Company production of Peter Weiss' *The Persecution and Assassination of Jean-Paul Marat as Performed by the Inmates of the Asylum of Charenton under the Direction of the Marquis de Sade (Marat/Sade)*. Here Brook brought to fruition the lessons he had garnered from his last two major endeavors, *King Lear* and the Theatre of Cruelty workshop, in a production which fused the two apparently disparate styles of Brecht and Artaud. His genius in finding a bridge between the distancing effects of Brecht's objective theatre and the emotional whirlwind of Artaud's subjective approach brought to life a production which many consider a highlight of modern theatre history, on a par with Gordon Craig's Moscow *Hamlet,* Max Reinhardt's *The Miracle,* Vsevolod Meyerhold's *The Inspector-General,* Yevgeny Vakhtangov's *Turandot,* and Harley Granville-Barker's *A Midsummer Night's Dream* (Brook's own version of this last play could easily join these immortals). Brook chose *Marat/Sade* because he found in it a density of excitement, experience, and poetry akin to that existing in Elizabethan drama. He perceived the play's style to be a combination of Brechtian and Artaudian qualities but rejected the claim that these were in conflict.

I believe [he wrote] that theatre, like life, is made up of the unbroken conflict between impressions and judgements—illusion and disillusion cohabit painfully and are insepa-rable. . . . [Marat/Sade] is designed to crack the spectator on the jaw, then douse him with ice-cold water, then force him to assess intelligently what has happened to him, then give him a kick in the balls, then bring him back to his senses again.[16]

As the play's full title suggests, *Marat/Sade* concerns the performance of a play (in 1808) at an insane asylum by its inmates under the direction of fellow inmate, the Marquis de Sade (whose performance by Patrick Magee was modeled on Brook himself). This establishes a basis for an abstract philosophical dis-cussion concerning the need for totalitarian control, no matter how much blood is spilled, as expressed by a madman playing the revolutionary Marat (Clive Revill in London; Ian Richardson in America), confined to his tub for a terrible skin disease, and complete individual freedom, the viewpoint of the libertine Sade. Considerable debate was stirred concerning who was deemed the winner of the debate (the Marxist playwright ceded the palm to Marat), but the play and production appeared so politically ambivalent and its theatrical opportunism so insistent that various critics thought the work evasive and sophistic.

Employing a play-within-a-play framework, Brook's actors explored the many levels of madness in a terrifyingly realistic manner (Brook had the advice of his psychiatrist brother), yet the structure of the script allowed for an enormous range of imaginative theatrical coups, worked out improvisationally during the rehearsal process. With Weiss' text, according to Margaret Croyden, "Anything could be justified and believable, and everything could be interchanged. Hair could be a whip; a knife, a penis; a bathtub, a hearse."[17] Exercising his genius for the creation of symbolic actions, Brook devised such scenes as that in which the effect of the guillotine was suggested by having asylum inmates slam down wooden shutters at the rear while a pit full of inmates at the front of the stage showed only a mass of bobbing heads. To heighten the thematic implications of the mass "executions," buckets of blood in various colors were poured into a funnel, red for the people, blue for the nobility, and white for the intellectuals.

Among the most controversial moments was that in which Marat stepped out of a tub and displayed his naked buttocks to the audience. In 1964 this was a shocking gesture. At the play's conclusion the madmen in the asylum broke out in a horrifyingly realistic riot of noise and action, threatening to do violence to the audience; at a crucial moment someone came onstage and blew a whistle, bringing everything to a halt. Then, as the actors began to relax and to remove their wigs and the audience, sighing in relief, began to clap, the actors started slowly to clap back—forcing the audience to shift perspectives and contemplate the event anew. Brook was carrying out the Artaud-Brecht dialectic to the bitter end.

US

In 1966 Brook turned to a project with overtly political themes. His growing reliance on improvisational, collaborative techniques, based on his Theatre of Cruelty experiences, led him to use a company of RSC actors in the evolving of a text based on their own personal reactions to the Vietnam War. Its title was *US*, an obvious play on words which was changed to *Tell Me Lies* for its movie version. It was hoped that a truly collaborative ensemble could work together creatively over a fifteen-week rehearsal period both to develop and express its own artistic and political ideas and to stimulate the thinking of the audience. Brook sought to make the theatrical experience a confrontation by English actors and their audience in a shared space on a subject of concern to all. He wanted to determine how they could relate to the Vietnam War, a war over which they had no apparent control and which had provoked no such unified English stance as, for instance, Nazism had given rise to in World War II. Brook felt compelled to create this work because no one else was producing anything dealing with the war. He was outspoken in his disdain for the lack of any worthwhile theatre piece dealing with Vietnam.

The company read extensively about the conflict, developed improvisations based on their research and discussions, looked into various artifacts of American myth and culture, explored the contemporary movement of "happenings," and created a Living Newspaper–like collage that was refined by writers Denis Cannan and Charles Wood (who left the project in mid-rehearsals), and continually revised during the run at London's Aldwych. Assistance in the preparation of the work was accepted from such visitors as Susan Sontag, Joseph Chaikin, and Jerzy Grotowski. Much of the final material was deliberately humorous in effect, a sort of laughing in the face of ineffable catastrophe.

In rehearsing *US* Brook had his actors deal improvisationally with their own responses to Vietnam. Over a period of months their growing sense of helplessness and shame overcame them as they dropped their initial prejudices and came together in shared anguish with their fellows. Brook viewed this development of communal angst as a social breakthrough in that it strengthened the group's ties to one another and also led to a heightened sense of self in each actor. To Brook, an actor could accomplish no worthier goal. Song, dance, mime, masks, a huge Artaudian effigy, and all sorts of other ritualistic and theatricalist props and effects were employed. However, costumes were not among the more overtly theatrical elements present as Brook and designer Sally Jacobs, impressed by the actors' appearance in rehearsal clothes two days before the opening, decided to cut the regular costumes. The most controversial moment came near the end when a butterfly (actually made of paper) was ceremoniously burnt alive, mirroring the self-immolation of Buddist martyrs.

Criticism was quite mixed, the negative opinions lacerating the work for, among other things, its oversimplification of complex problems, failure to provide answers, confused conclusions, preaching to the converted, and—from outraged politically conservative quarters—lack of balance in failing to show the Viet Cong side of the question. It was also scored for sloppy acting and aesthetics. Positive views credited the work with effectively demanding a meaningful public response to what was then the world's most burning issue.

OEDIPUS

In his next production, two years later, Brook shifted directions sharply and came up with a revival of the rarely done *Oedipus* of Seneca, in a new version by British poet Ted Hughes based on a literal translation by David Anthony Turner. Brook claimed, however, that *Oedipus* was related to *US* in its pondering the increasingly persistent problem of man's willful avoidance of the truth. Moreover, the script—packed with images of brutality and primitivism—held vague resonances of recent events in Vietnam. John Gielgud, Irene Worth, and Colin Blakely appeared in a spiritually and aesthetically ascetic production emphasizing unusual vocal techniques with physical movement cut to the barest minimum. This "concert performance" employed severely simple modern costumes of brown and black velvet and had the chorus dispersed throughout the auditorium where it moaned and wailed in a shamanistic manner suggestive of primitive rites; this reminded some of the effects Artaud might have demanded. Brook designed a set consisting of a giant metal revolving cube positioned at center stage, reflecting light in sparkling rays as if directed by supernatural forces. The cube was made so the chorus could open it to reveal new acting areas.

Its front sides could be lowered separately or simultaneously to provide enclosed space, an open platform with ramps—or it could swallow characters for entire scenes. Hung over it was a huge golden lid. . . . Smaller golden cubes upon which the actors sometimes sat were also drums for them to beat.[18]

The play opened with the chorus chanting to a musical arrangement composed by Brook and Richard Peaslee. The actors onstage then began to beat their golden drum-seats while those in the auditorium beat the pillars. A growing intensity of beating suddenly stopped, the cube opened out to form a stage, and the play commenced.

Throughout *Oedipus*, the audience was kept emotionally removed from the action by the impersonal hieratic style. No attempt at realism in the character depiction was allowed, Gielgud's Oedipus being neither made up to look aged nor permitted to limp. His self-imposed blindness was suggested by the donning of dark glasses, taken off the face of Tiresias. Worth as Jocasta died onstage (by impaling herself on a sword in a memorably symbolic image of sexual sacrifice) and then calmly walked off accompanied by two chorus members. Entrances through the audience were used to special effect, especially one moment when, Oedipus having called for all local shepherds to appear, "the audience is suddenly frozen by the faint sound of an actor's feet shuffling down the aisle towards the stage."[19]

Marowitz says Brook chose this work because it challenged him to stage a work using "orchestral sound, tonal values and the rendition of the literary narrative"[20] as primary features. Brook's most notorious conceit was the wheeling on at the end of a seven-foot golden phallus as the music for "Yes, We Have No Bananas" was performed by a jazz band and the company danced around the "maypole." "Joyously they dance and shout," wrote Boyce Richardson, "leap from the stage to aisle and back again, follow the jazzmen around the auditorium and break into a wild session of jiving and dancing, flinging their golden robes into the air."[21] It was conceived as a moment of bacchanalian revelry to provide relief from the intensity of the preceding tragic events, but seems to have succeeded only in pointing attention to itself—to the dismay not only of the audience members but to actors in the cast as well.

THE TEMPEST

Brook's 1968 version of *The Tempest*, unlike the *Oedipus*, did not shortchange movement enthusiasts. Always now exploring the relation of the actors to the audience, he sought to discern what principles were involved in varying these factors by a radical adjustment of the playing space. Brook's previous work had been essentially in proscenium theatres but now, after opening his production in Paris, he moved it to a deserted London railroad station called the Round House where he and designer Jean Monod could freely improvise with the spatial environment.

Spectators were invited to sit on scaffolding where they would literally be swept up by the action going on around them (these were the "dangerous" areas) or on "safe" seats where they could observe the action dispassionately. Richard Schechner, environmental theatre spokesman, soon employed similar principles in his New York production of *Dionysus in '69* and other plays.

Brook used an international company set up at the invitation of Jean-Louis Barrault as part of the Théâtre des Nations Festival events in Paris. This international company concept eventuated in the 1970 International Center for Theatre

Research, to be discussed below. In *The Tempest,* Brook attempted to find with his foreign actors a universal, synthetic theatre style. They treated Shakespeare's text as so many words and images which they felt free to alter, mutilate, rearrange, and cut at will; the method was reminiscent of Marowitz's collage *Hamlet.* A scrambled plot, newly devised character relationships, startling time shifts, choral chanting, words as sound effects rather than as symbols of meaning, incantations, overt sexual imagery, acrobatics, disparate costumes, Grotowski face-masks, mingling with the audience—all were features of this much criticized experiment. Even before the production began the actors were visible to the audience, doing warmups during which they played games and performed vocal and physical exercises. Despite the adverse critical reviews Brook was undaunted. He did not think of the piece as a finished production but rather as a work-in-progress for which an audience was needed so that the actors might gauge the reactions of living spectators to the event. Here was Brook the scientist faithfully pursuing his course, seeking answers to his questions no matter what the world might think. He believes, in fact, that for such experimental work an audience of children would be better than one of severe and critical adults with their preconceived ideas. In his *Tempest* the actors were seeking a freedom from conventional restraints, a freedom in which they could attempt emotional and physical flights rarely allowed them in the establishment theatre. The freedom afforded the actors was incorporated, with new exercises and methods, in Brook's next milestone production, *A Midsummer Night's Dream.*

A MIDSUMMER NIGHT'S DREAM

Shakespeare's *Dream* was the crowning achievement of Brook's ultratheatricalist decade. His goal was to free the play from its conventional accoutrements of saccharine scenery and acting, accumulated during a long history of production, and find instead a means of making a play about magic meaningful to a twentieth-century audience. He rid the play of every traditional artifice and introduced a world of simplicity and light. A white squash court–like cube of a set with several vertical black ladders leading to an overhead gallery; chunky adult male fairies in loose grey silk pajama-like costumes inspired by those of Chinese acrobats; circus elements including trapezes, spinning plates, and stilts; a forest of shining steel coils manipulated by actors with fishing poles in the overhead gallery; an imaginative Richard Peaslee score using offbeat instruments; and a Bottom whose ass-costume was little more than cloglike shoes, a black clown's nose, and donkey ears were some of the revolutionary visual concepts devised by Brook and designer Sally Jacobs. This was to be a theatrical celebration, and there was no more appropriate image for such a fest than that of the circus.

Brook told Jerry Tallmer of the *New York Post* why he chose a white scenic environment:

The first thing this play has running through it is darkness. . . . And from that everything else descends. All we wanted was to make nothingness around the work. So we went to brilliant white, which would be completely neutral and said nothing except what the actors were saying at the moment.[22]

The worlds of fantasy and reality within the play were bound and intermingled through the use of double casting—Theseus as Oberon, Philostrate as Puck, Egeus as Quince, Hippolyta as Titania. Nonverbal techniques of recent research were abandoned, and the words came forth clearly and without affectation. Unlike the 1968 *Tempest,* Shakespeare was quite himself here, with all his words intact. Stanley Kauffmann remarked that the cast album of this show would probably sound like that of a company from 1890: "Barring a few instances, the verse is read with classical intent, and the comic lines are treated in a style that would have pleased Beerbohm Tree."[23] An interesting criticism of Kauffmann's, though, was that the abstract scenic embodiment clashed sharply with the conventional verbal style, the scenic conception seeming to lack justification as a result. Another criticism held that the actors were allowed to illustrate the text with what was occasionally excessive (and misleading) indicative behavior, ignoring the audience's ability to imagine the meanings of the lines for themselves. And, of course, there were those who felt that for all Brook's claims to be allowing Shakespeare's text to stand forth clearer than ever, this was after all the "Peter Brook Show," and was more an excuse for directorial inventiveness than Shakespearean illumination.

Following its run at Stratford, the *Dream* traveled to the United States (including New York) and Canada in 1971; in addition to playing on Broadway, it played for two weeks at the Brooklyn Academy of Music (BAM), where Brook was to engage in a number of important ventures during the coming years. It was produced at London's Aldwych in 1971, toured Europe in 1972, and a world tour ensued in 1973.

INTERNATIONAL CENTER FOR THEATRE RESEARCH

Brook had reached a new high-water level above which it would be difficult to rise. As might be expected, he now did the unexpected. Because his focus since *The Tempest* had become increasingly concentrated on the development of the actor and of the problems of the actor-audience relationship, he decided to leave the world of commercial and institutional theatre. In 1970, with French agent and producer Micheline Rozan as his partner, he established in Paris the International Center for Theatre Research (*Le Centre Internationale de Recherches Théâtrales*); to it was added in 1974 the International Center for Theatre Creation (ICTC). The idea for this ambitious venture had been born in 1968 when, as mentioned earlier, Brook ran a Théâtre des Nations workshop composed of theatre artists from many cultural backgrounds. Now, with a group of professionals from a dozen countries, selected from over 150 applicants whom Brook personally interviewed, the center set up workshops in a huge room of an old tapestry factory (the Mobilier National); financial backing was provided by the French Ministry of Culture and foundation grants. Here Brook was free to work in his own way with no commercial pressures impeding his investigations. Only by stepping out of the commercial system in toto could he ignore the typical problems of theatre (i.e., arena, proscenium, thrust, environmental, etc.), audience expectations, economic factors, and so on. Working with an internationally mixed company of Roumanian, French, German, English, African, Japanese, Mali, and American actors, he was able "to explore whether something new could be learned through the clash of different cultures working toward a shared expression." He found that actors of different cultures working together can "sometimes crack open the clichés that their cultures have become. . . . The complete truth is global: the theatre is the place where this great jigsaw can be played."[24]

ORGHAST

Brook and his company—including Irene Worth—worked long hours each day, beginning at 10:00 A.M., doing many exercises in the use of language, sound, and movement. Experts from different nations visited and led the company through a wide assortment of vocal and physical techniques. The company's first public presentation came in 1971 at the Fifth Shiraz International Festival of the Arts in Persepolis, Iran, where they presented *Orghast,* a play developed in collaboration with Ted Hughes. Iranian performers had worked on the piece with Brook's actors in Paris and took part in the finished work; also, the ritualistic Iranian theatre form of *ta'zieh* had an influence on the performance. *Orghast* was the culmination of months of experiments with a new language—Orghast, which was created especially for the event out of ancient Greek, Latin, and Avesta, the intent being to see what emotional vibrations this language could set up when used in the Artaudian sense of language as sound and incantation rather than strictly as the bearer of literal meaning. Orghast "harnessed the consonants, vowel sounds and syllables of the constituent vocabulary to a complex-seeming tonal scale and onomatopoeic sound-structure." Brook's program notes contained the following passage:

What is the relation between verbal and non-verbal theatre? What happens when gesture and sound turn into word? What is the exact place of the word in theatrical expression? As vibration? Concept? Music? Is any evidence buried in the sound structure of certain ancient languages?[25]

Orghast was staged out of doors amid spectacular surroundings the topography of which dictated the physical form of the presentation. Part I was played on a platform before the Royal Tombs of the Persian Kings Darius and Artaxerxes I, dating back twenty-five hundred years. It was played at sundown and at nightfall lit by torches and flares. The subject matter was a ritualistic reenactment of ancient myths, including that of Prometheus, though the audience was not always sure of what was happening. The work was "conceived as a strange and exotic ritual, as impenetrable as a religious ceremony in a foreign country and in an unfamiliar language,"[26] according to one observer.

Part II was done six miles from Persepolis at the supposed tombs of Darius II and Artaxerxes I and III, at Nagsh-i-Rustam. In this part the audience was not immobile as in Part I but was allowed to move from place to place as demanded by the movement of "the actors, who performed either in the cliff-face, or on the plain, or came tearing from the slightly raised ground, behind [the audience], like soldiers in a military tattoo, to re-enact the destruction of the Persian army by the Greeks."[27]

THE CONFERENCE OF THE BIRDS

Having concentrated on the nonverbal performance style of *Orghast* in its first year, Brook's company emphasized exercises in sound and movement during its second year. Part of the work involved research done in conjunction with the National Theatre for the Deaf, which was in residence. This culminated in a performance of a variety of "free versions" of Peter Handke's *Kaspar* in French. In late 1972 Brook and his company headed for rural Africa where they toured extensively, experimenting improvisationally with a twelfth-century Persian poem called *The Conference of the Birds,* Ted Hughes again being responsible for the creation of the verbal aspect. *The Conference of the Birds* is an allegorical poem by the Sufi poet Farid Uddin Attar. It is about the search for God (the Simorgh) which reveals to the searchers that God resides within them and that before immortality can be achieved worldly vanity must first be discarded. The characters are a conference of birds of various sorts, led by the Hoopoe.

With this work Brook hoped to find a meeting place between the world of the imagination and everyday reality, not the separate imaginary world of the conventional theatre shut off by a curtain from the audience's everyday existence. Believing that these worlds coexist in the mind of a child, Brook traveled to Africa, where he felt a similar capacity would be found among rural people who were unsophisticated about what was expected of them at a theatrical performance and yet would be able to see reality on both the imaginary and concrete levels. He trusted the spontaneous reactions of such audiences, which leave as soon as they lose interest in the proceedings. This, he thought, would reveal fundamental human nature. He was longing to find answers to a new set of questions now.

What in theatre has to be prepared in advance and what must be left free? What is a character, what is a human situation, and can an imitation of reality ever be true? Does the theatre eventually stand or fall by what it says—or is theatre something quite different, a form of intoxication produced by a certain release of energy?[28]

John Heilpern followed Brook's company on their three-month African od-
yssey, watching them travel from town to town in Land Rovers to set up their
carpet in a myriad of locales as they attracted crowds ranging from several dozen
to one thousand or more. He reports that though they performed on many occasions (thirty-four times, in fact) they infrequently did *Conference of the Birds,*
this piece merely being the central focus of their rehearsals and workshop activity.
It was never seen in Africa in its finished form, remaining mostly in the realm
of rough improvisation. Most of these "carpet shows" were improvisatory, with
the actors usually having no idea of what they would present even minutes before
the actual show. Brook loved the sense of "danger" this created and wished to
see what the actors would come up with under the stress of various performing
conditions. The improvisations, normally done as broad farce, typically began
with situations centering on boldly drawn emotional conflicts within universal
human relationships or as scenes deriving from imaginative—and unconventional—responses to specific objects, such as a shoe, a stick, or a loaf of bread.
American composer Elizabeth Swados also guided many experiments in musical
voice and sound improvisations, especially those which explored the relationship
of an improvising solo performer to a choral rhythm. Often the work failed
miserably, though those rare times when it succeeded were treasured by the
company as intimations of what theatre as Brook dreamed of could be.[29]

After their African experience, in mid-1973 the group took the continually
developing *Conference of the Birds* to Paris, and then to California where they
worked with Louis Valdez's El Teatro Campesino for eight weeks, became
involved with labor issues among the migrant farmers, and performed at strike
meetings. Participation of Valdez's troupe in *Conference* altered its form considerably. Soon after, the company worked with the Native American Theatre
Ensemble on the Chippewa Indian reservation. They ended their stay in the
United States at BAM, where five weeks of public experiments were conducted
with the material—different groups (including Grotowski's) constantly being
engaged in the work. Brook also took his actors into local ethnic neighborhoods
where improvisations were staged in streets and schools. On their last night at
BAM, after a period of nightly cast rotations aimed at bringing forth new impressions from the material, they offered three performances, an improvised, com-
ically robust one at 8:00 P.M., a reverently sober, ceremonially whispered version
lit by candles at midnight, and one done as a ritualistic improvised chorale an
hour before dawn. They hoped that someday the essence of all three versions
could somehow be combined.

Ideas garnered from the improvisational versions of *Conference* done at BAM
and elsewhere were resuscitated in 1979 when Brook decided to revive the work
with a script written by Jean-Claude Carrière (Ted Hughes had worked on the
earlier versions) and in a scenic embodiment created by Sally Jacobs. (Accompanying the work was a new piece, *L'Os* [*The Bone*], adapted by Carrière and
company actor Malick Bowens from an African story by Birao Diop.) *Conference*
now became a formal, polished theatre piece, quite unlike its earlier manifes-

tations. The scripted version premiered at the Avignon Festival, briefly toured Europe, played in Paris, and figured as the highlight of the company's work when it toured to New York in 1980 and played at La Mama E.T.C. in the East Village. In this latest embodiment, Brook's actors performed in a simple setting consisting of a large Persian rug on the floor and an equally large rug attached to a wall at the rear. Wearing a lovely tunic and robe, each actor assumed the personality of a bird, mainly by dexterously manipulating beautifully crafted hand puppets. Mime, storytelling, masks (mostly Balinese), and music (from the Japanese musician Toshi Tsuchitori) combined to make the work an elegant demonstration of effective mingling of Asian and Occidental styles; yet—despite Brook's strenuous efforts to make the material as universally appealing as he believed it was—for some viewers a hovering cloud of mysticism refused to disperse.

TIMON OF ATHENS

A surprising return to Shakespeare followed in 1974 with *Timon of Athens* at Paris's Théâtre Bouffes du Nord, a once-elegant 1876 playhouse whose interior was a charred shambles following a 1952 fire. The rundown theatre, located in the depressed working-class district of St. Denis, was renovated in a way that allowed the place to remain a self-consciously shabby-looking ruin, with the signs of its former opulence peeping through the peeling paint and plaster. The Bouffes du Nord, which usually charges the same low price for each of its approximately 500 seats, remained the center of Brook's work into the eighties. *Timon*'s staging was not very surprising, though, as Brook was returning to the basic free-form style he used in the 1968 *Tempest,* employing a good deal of audience involvement, an idiosyncratic interpretation of the text, and the international cast speaking Carrière's French translation of Shakespeare's barely cut verse in a welter of almost incomprehensible pronunciations. The action took place in the orchestra area, where the seats had been removed, and the audience was seated on wooden benches: it involved much physical activity and acrobatic movement. The production brought to the staging of Shakespeare the easy audience-actor informality that Brook and his company had developed during their so-called carpet shows in Africa. As in most of Brook's work in the previous decade, harsh white lighting was used throughout, with no special lighting effects for mood or atmosphere. Audience and actors were clearly in a shared space, barely differentiated from one another. These arrangements, which also allow for seating in three balcony areas, prevailed for all of Brook's subsequent productions here.

Contemporary thematic ideas were stressed, Brook seeing the play as dealing with inflation. ''Timon's Athens is the colonels' Athens and Timon himself a living emblem of the industrial West brutally awakened from its paradisial consumer's dreams by the oil crisis.'' The actors wore an eclectic blend of modern costumes, with a strong suggestion of Arab cultural elements apparent in the overall look. Some even wore djellabahs. An Arab-style feast and Arab dancing were also included. Apemantus was cast with a black actor, costumed as an Algerian laborer. His presence commented on Timon's extravagance. Alcibiades was played as "the symbol of the military coup which is the only solution to the decadence and corruption of Athens."[30]

THE IK

A year afterward (1975), Brook's group presented *The Ik,* an austere production based on anthropologist Colin Turnbull's *The Mountain People,* showing how a poor mountain tribe in northern Uganda becomes dehumanized in the wake of government legislation that deprives them of their traditional hunting privileges. It was adapted by Colin Higgins and Denis Cannan, the French version being prepared by Jean-Claude Carrière. A small company of six actors and two children performed the simple drama on a dirt-strewn floor. Aside from one actor who played an anthropologist, the others enacted a variety of village characters. In 1976 *The Ik* was produced for a six-week season at London's Round House, toured South America, various American universities, and Eastern Europe, was seen in Australia in 1980 with other Center-produced works, and arrived at the La Mama Annex in New York shortly afterwards.

As performed in New York, the piece presented the harrowing account of the depravity and loss of humanity to which lack of food drove the Ik, by resorting to a greatly simplified "poor theatre" type of staging in which shabby clothes substituted for the naked black skins of the characters; moreover, the international cast made little attempt to create the feeling that they really were the hungry Africans. Theatrical coups were minimal though one potent image was provided by two actors stuffing their faces with grain and then instantly regurgitating it as they dragged relief supplies to the other villagers. Also interesting was the erection by the actors of the complete framework of a village hut.

The production was the result of an intensive rehearsal period involving many exercises and improvisations aimed at re-creating the physical conditions of life among the Ik. Photos and films by Turnbull were the source of physical activity that attempted to duplicate precisely what they revealed of postures and facial expressions. Their most illuminating discoveries were incorporated in the script, which evolved during the course of rehearsals.

Of the three programs brought to La Mama (the other two were *Ubu* and *L'Os*), *The Ik* was the least successful with most New York critics. Its deep pessimism and emotional coolness, which was related to its use of various Brechtian distancing methods, combined with its slow pace and dry understated manner, led many to dismiss it, despite a general recognition of its thematic pertinence. Brook himself insisted that its theme was actually the decline of the cities of the Western world, which becomes even clearer when reading Turnbull's own summation of his experiences. As David Williams explains, much of Brook's work since *Lear* has borne a nihilistic substructure informed "by the

belief that in certain extreme situations, civilizing social restraints reveal themselves to be false and shallow, crumbling to unleash the human beast within''[31]
(cf., for example, Brook's 1964 film, *The Lord of the Flies*). Some claimed that
the piece was merely another piece of self-serving liberalism, but equally devastating were the critical reminders that *The Ik* and its fellow productions were
drawing on theatrical devices that jaded avant-gardists were beginning to find
outdated and boring.

ENDING THE DECADE

In 1977 the Théâtre Bouffes du Nord witnessed Brook's highly farcical, spare,
and simplified production of *King Ubu at the Bouffes* (shortened to *Ubu* when
it toured), a conflation by Carrière of all four of Alfred Jarry's turn-of-the-
century antibourgeois, proto-absurdist ''Ubu'' comedies, with *King Ubu* occupying the bulk of the text. It toured Europe and Latin America in 1977 and
1978, including a stop in London and one at the Théâtre des Nations, Caracas.
It was also in the Brook repertory that visited Australia and New York in 1980.
Unlike *The Ik*, *Ubu* (played in French with frequent English interpolations)
abounded in clever theatrical ideas, despite (more likely because of) its minimalist
sets and costumes. Reliance on improvisations led to a great deal being made
of ''found'' properties, such as sticks and bricks, especially two large electric
cable spools; at one point the larger one was used to bowl over a three-man
army. As it passed over them they flattened out on the floor as if they were the
victims of a steamroller. All the props were put to imaginative, sometimes highly
symbolic, multiple uses. Instead of the abstract, puppet-like costuming and
makeup called for by the original, Brook allowed his characters to be played as
recognizable human beings, with Ubu himself an ordinary worker. A good deal
of byplay with the audience was employed, though this tended to become self-
conscious at times. The ultimate achievement of the piece, as in the simple fable-
play *L'Os*, staged as its curtain-raiser, was the energy and sense of fun in
performing exuded by the company. A true feeling of the ''rough'' theatre of
which Brook writes came across, as if these actors were a band of cabotins who
could create theatre anywhere by simply willing it into being.

L'Os, a morality play, is a very simple account of a man who refuses to part
with a marrow bone, even if he has to die in the process. *L'Os* uses story-theatre
techniques to communicate its cautionary point of view. It had its final revival
to date in 1982, when it was taken on a short European tour, including a London
engagement.

The productions of *L'Os* and *Ubu*, *The Ik*, and *The Conference of the Birds*
were intended to be viewed as a sort of trilogy on the theme of hunger. In John
Heilpern's words:

Alfred Jarry's *Ubu*: an absurdist hunger for power; *L'Os*, an African folk tale: hunger
for possessions; Colin Turnbull's adaptation of *The Ik*: hunger for survival; *The Conference
of the Birds*: hunger for an alternative way of life.[32]

An important adjunct to Brook's work in the late seventies was the trips taken by the company to various places where they could perform for "unsophisticated" audiences and test their responses to the material. Eric Shorter watched them play to a group of immigrant Algerians in a new town near Versailles in 1978. Playing as usual in makeshift quarters, they improvised according to the reactions of their viewers.

The idea [says Shorter] is to divert casual audiences and make them realize . . . that spontaneous acting has a theatrical value beyond its importance for the players—that is to say, that artistically it can give as much pleasure to the spectator as a rehearsal text[33]

and concurrently establish a close relationship between audience and players.

The Bouffes du Nord was home to a new and well-received Brook interpretation of *Measure for Measure* in 1978. Carrière's translation was done by the Center troupe in stripped-down workshop style using no music and in a setting made up of little more than several benches and some straw; the costumes suggested the current era, and the approach to the play's political and sexual themes—including Isabella's being acted as a Joan of Arc–like feminist and the Duke's having a homosexual attraction to Lucio—was seen to mirror present realities.[34]

Less than a month before *Measure for Measure* opened, Brook's English-language staging of *Antony and Cleopatra* starring Glenda Jackson and Alan Howard was produced by the Royal Shakespeare Company at Stratford; a somewhat revised version was soon seen in London. The austere production—which used an almost complete text, classically spoken—was designed by Sally Jacobs, who, according to Michael Kustow, provided

a set of woodframed screens made of translucent material, which enclose a central playing area defined by a thick, natural raffia rug, unpainted benches, and a couple of shiny stools. Through the screens you can see ghost-images of characters as they enter. The translucent surfaces collect the glow from costumes and floor. It's a distillation of the luminosity of sun, sea, and sand, a reminder that the play is set at the Egyptian and Italian ends of the Mediterranean basin, and a realization of the play's many images of dissolution and metamorphosis.[35]

Brook used the concept of scenic shifts sparingly, making visible changes only when crucial to the action and emotion.

A semi-visible area behind the screens, animated with bursts of light and, at times, running figures, is used to suggest the great battles, and during the final clash, in which Antony is defeated, awful red wounds splash against the back of the screens. For Cleopatra's death scene, a red carpet is lowered, picking up the colors of the blood splotches, for a majestic final tableau.[36]

Costumes were similarly simple and suggestive; the entire company was dressed in robes like those worn in Arabia or North Africa. As the play progressed, this similarity of costume gradually was replaced as specific elements, designed to clarify the distinctiveness of the characters, were added. As in his productions of *King Lear* and *A Midsummer Night's Dream,* Brook found inspiration or confirmation of his views in Jan Kott, but some specialists were dismayed by his thus having reduced the work from one that takes cognizance of both the private and public worlds to one almost exclusively private; the outside world, seen vaguely through the translucent panels, seemed remote and unreal. The work's epic scale was so reduced that the effect was of a chamber version.

Some of Brook's staging ideas were noteworthily original. Among them was his onstage display of the slaying of Pacorus, son of the Parthian king, to contrast it with the scene of partying in Pompey's galley. Another was his suggestion of Cleopatra's monument by the red carpet mentioned above; instead of having Antony hoisted to Cleopatra, the dying hero merely had to be moved horizontally to her where he could be enmeshed by her in scarves.

THE 1980s

During the eighties Brook continued to stir controversy and draw atention to his always startling new conceptions. The most conventional of his offerings was the 1983 hit revival of François Billetdoux's poignant 1959 drama, *Tchin-Tchin*, staged (in collaboration with Maurice Benichou) in minimalist scenic style—a few screens, the stage's unadorned rear wall exposed, stagehands moving the furniture in view of the audience—at Paris's Théâtre Montparnasse with Italian star Marcello Mastroianni making his first appearance on the stage in fifteen years; Natasha Parry was cast opposite Mastroianni.

Brook's other theatre work of the decade was in the classic vein, beginning with *The Cherry Orchard* and a radical treatment of the opera *Carmen* (retitled *The Tragedy of Carmen*) in 1981, and an epochal staging of *The Mahabharata* in 1985. All were originally done in French and subsequently revived, toured internationally, and produced in English.

THE CHERRY ORCHARD

Chekhov's *The Cherry Orchard* was produced at the Bouffes du Nord in a new version prepared by Brook (who reads Russian and knows at least six foreign languages) and Carrière; it sought to be as faithful to Chekhov as possible, even respecting his punctuation. A specially selected company—including Natasha Parry as Mme. Ranevskaya—rehearsed for ten weeks, employing improvisations and immersing themselves in Chekhov's stories. The staging was done mostly in the three-quarters round, but sometimes employed the entire theatre as an acting space, as when the occupants of the Ranevsky house, preparing busily to take leave of it, were seen in balconies, corridors, and stairways, with Lopakhin alone at center stage drinking champagne. True to Brook's goal of peeling away all superfluities, Chloé Obolensky's decor was skeletal, with only the barest minimum of scene-setting furniture and props; a couple of chairs, several large screens, a bookcase. Several lovely Persian carpets were a primal focus; the actors generally sat on them or on the several cushions that were strewn about. A striking image was created when the carpets were removed to denote the departure of the family at the end, the bare stage floor emphasizing the desolation of the moment. Obolensky's exquisite costumes, however, were historically accurate and revelatory of character. Brook's staging was considered decidedly unsentimental and intensely true to Chekhov's text, which he saw as a combination of actuality and myth. One critic found the production decidedly in the Beckettian mold of Brook's *King Lear*. There was an unexpected fullness in each role (most surprisingly, that of Lopakhin), and the performance offered an exhilarating blend of humor and sadness (with the emphasis on the former); the naturalistic ensemble acting style unearthed many nuances, yet the exuberant pace allowed the uncut text to be performed in only two hours and a quarter (there were no intermissions).

In 1983 *The Cherry Orchard* was revived at the Bouffes, and in 1988, an English-language version by Elisaveta Lavrova was prepared for production at BAM; soon after, it was seen in Moscow (where it was acclaimed as more Chekhovian even than Russian versions) and elsewhere in the USSR before heading for Japan. The American version continued to enjoy Parry's Ranevskaya, but otherwise employed a new company, with famed Swedish actor Erland Josephson considered a standout in the role of Gaev. The multinational cast, however, disturbed some because of the melange of accents.

THE TRAGEDY OF CARMEN

The Tragedy of Carmen—which opened in Paris in 1981, came to New York's Vivian Beaumont Theatre late in 1983, and toured to Japan in 1986—was a major theatre event, despite its operatic origins. A ten-week rehearsal period involved the usual emphasis on improvisation plus extensive work on movement, because of Brook's commitment to freeing the singers of conventional operatic clichés, and unifying their physical means of expression with their vocal ones. Bizet's famous score was considerably reduced and rearranged by Marius Constant to suit a fourteen-piece chamber ensemble, often placed in two sections directly upstage of the action; the music was secondary to the dramatic effects that could be derived from Prosper Merimée's tragic story, which—at the hands of Brook and Carrière—underwent considerable revision from the Meilhac-Halévy libretto. Critic Frank Rich described the result:

Heated up and stripped of its social context, *Carmen* is no longer a conflict between Carmen's liberated gypsy passions and José's imprisoning bourgeois values. Carmen and José are now equal partners in a raw, brutal tale of mutual self-destruction that's fuelled by both lust and existential bloodlust—and is as deadly for others as it is for themselves.[37]

The entire performance lasted only about an hour and twenty minutes. Many music lovers were outraged at what they considered a sacrilegious manhandling of the work, but others appreciated the way the new presentation made the dramatic element emerge more than in standard productions.

Several roles were shared at alternating performances, most notably that of Carmen who was played by a multinational succession of three sopranos; for the American production, five Carmens were on hand and the multinational element was expanded to a multiracial one. Brook's casting favored singers who could act and look their parts, instead of those gifted only with vocal talent. Brook openly defied the opera convention of having romantic leads played by excessively heavy star singers, especially since many physically attractive and vocally talented singers were available. Numerous means were exploited for conveying Carmen's overwhelming sensuality. Brook staged the arias as vivid dramatic scenes, and not as purely musical interludes.

The Vivian Beaumont stage was used in its thrust arrangement; the essentially sceneryless platform was covered with sand and earth as in a bullring, and around the perimeter coarsely covered cushions were placed for spectators charged a reduced admission of $10. The ring was backed by a curved wall of wooden planks. Costumes were grittily realistic. Much use was made of ritualistic elements, such as the opening, focused on fortune-telling cards, and a later incantatory lighting of fires in the mountain scene. For commercial reasons, during the New York run, the French-language performance (with occasional interpolations in English) was put into alternation with a new one in English.

THE MAHABHARATA

Brook's most recent production was *The Mahabharata,* a distillation by him and Carrière—they had developed the work over a ten-year period—of India's great Sanskrit epic poem, which exists in eighteen volumes and is fifteen times longer than the Bible. The stories and ideas expressed in it and the other great Sanskrit epic, *The Ramayana,* are at the heart of most South East Asian religion and culture, where they are represented in numerous artistic and literary forms, both classical and contemporary. Its preparation involved a number of trips by Brook and Carrière to India, where they investigated various popular forms of Indian performance, and a two-week visit there with the entire company right in the midst of the rehearsal period. The script was consistently revised during the rehearsals and even after the show was in performance.

Brook and Carrière conceived their play as a trilogy to be played in three three-hour-plus presentations on successive nights (the separate pieces being titled *The Game of Dice*, *Exile in the Forest,* and *The War*), although it was also given a number of performances in which audiences could experience the entire play in a one-day marathon viewing; with intermissions and a dinner break these performances lasted over eleven hours. As usual, Brook's despairing view of mankind was a prime motivating factor in the creation of the work, which, loosely translated, means "The Great Poem of the World"; among its many complex metaphysical and moral threads, the episodic story of the mythical battle between the five Pandava brothers and their evil cousins, the Kauravas, could be viewed as the quintessential struggle of opposing human forces; the culmination of their animosity in the use of an ultimate weapon killing eighteen million people, an apocalypse expressed in the production as a huge explosion, needed no footnotes to explain its significance. An epilogue set in paradise allowed the work to conclude on a vaguely reconciliatory note. Brook pointed out that the play asked many pertinent questions, such as "What does it mean to commit yourself to conflict? Is this a terrible thing or a good thing? Is it part of the inevitable pattern of human existence? Is it better to try to renounce violence or accept it?" He added, "All the questions we are living through today are dramatized by this work."[38]

The Mahabharata premiered at the Bouffes du Nord in the spring of 1985 and then played at Avignon's summer festival and on tour to Athens, Madrid, and Frankfurt before returning to Paris. At the Avignon Festival, it was seen on Saturday nights from dusk to dawn in an impressive out-of-doors environment at a temporary theatre built in a limestone quarry at Boulbon, on the Rhône River south of Avignon; to get to it audiences had to travel by boat and then make their way over hilly terrain.[39]

A strenuous ten-month rehearsal period was devoted to improvisational work and training in various disciplines, including such martial arts as kung fu. Musical and movement exercises (the former guided by Toshi Tsuchitori) helped in the freeing of the actor's rhythmic and gestural vocabulary.

Eschewing the methods of classical Indian theatre, which would at any rate have been impossible to master without a lifetime of training, the company became imbued with the spirit of the popular theatre, including the use of a storyteller recounting the tale to a young boy—representing the audience—as a way of tying the many strands of the narrative together. Indian theatre styles were only hinted at in the production, never copied, and a host of techniques from other traditions were employed whenever appropriate; the effect was universal in scope, not limited to any national theatrical method. The same was true of Chloé Obolensky's predominantly red and gold costumes, which were Indian in effect, but also mingled elements from other traditions. Minimalist means prevailed, such as the repeated use of sticks and bamboo screens to serve a multitude of purposes. Horses were mimed, and to represent the chariots in the central battle of Arjuna and Karna, their respective charioteers each rolled along a single large wheel. A slain warrior's guts were represented by red ribbons chewed on by his bloodthirsty conquerer. A babe in arms was signified by an actress' swift manipulation of her veil into swaddling clothes. A group of actors used their bodies to suggest an elephant on which rode a goddess. The suicide of a warrior in the wake of his son's death was shown by having the actor very slowly empty a water-jug filled with blood over his head. Slow motion was used in a number of other sequences as well, most notably when Arjuna takes aim with his bow and arrow at the great warrior Bhishma, and as time comes to a stop, the supposedly invisible demigod Krishna grabs the arrow and carries it in slow motion across the stage to Bhishma's heart. Music was provided by a small onstage ensemble led by Tsuchitori, many of their effects being improvised. The playing area was arranged as a three-quarters round arena, and the scenery— designed by Obolensky—was merely a red earthen floor, a stream of water in front of the rear wall, and a pool of water further downstage. Locations were changed constantly by the simple means of rearranging swathes of material on the ground. To complement the elements of earth, water, and air, each of which was endued with shifting metaphysical purposes, considerable use was made of fire in the performance, as when a magical flame burned on the earth around the pool, trapping a band of warriors within its borders, or when the final conflagration was suggested by an awesome magnesium flare.

The Mahabharata was a work of comedy, tragedy, storytelling, and mysticism in a moving conception of sweeping grandeur, bearing echoes of Homer, Greek tragedy, Shakespeare, and the Bible; it used (in its American version) a company of twenty-four actors (and two children) representing eighteen nationalities, many of them playing multiple roles. Its critical reception abroad was overwhelmingly favorable, but in New York, despite several ecstatic notices, a number of serious caveats were expressed; while its visual splendors were hailed, it was accused of being too emotionally distanced, talky and verbally unimpressive (Brook did the English version), possessed of an excessively complex narrative, and spiritually slippery and facile. Still, most would have agreed with *Time* critic William A. Henry III that "whatever the longueurs and idiosyncrasies, all cavils are minor. The work itself is major, a spellbinding journey through myth and fable, blessed with an unfailing sense of wonder."[40]

This exceptional work toured Europe briefly in September 1985, and began a world tour of an English-language version in 1987, including a stay at BAM's Majestic Theatre, two blocks from BAM itself. The once-elegant 1904 playhouse, fallen into disuse, was subjected to an extraordinary makeover as part of BAM's long-term commitment to showcase Brook productions. Five million dollars was spent, not to make the theatre resemble a pristine version of its former self, but to re-create the kind of pitted and brutalized atmosphere of the Bouffes du Nord; the effect was dazzlingly original, as the walls were scraped and painted to suggest layers of peeling paint but in a precisely designed way that was aesthetically striking. In addition, a forestage area resembling that created at the Bouffes was constructed, and major renovations were made to the auditorium structure itself.

THE EXPERIMENTALIST

The diversity of Peter Brook's career reminds one of those twisting scenic roads along the California coast, where turning a sudden corner means never knowing what will be coming from the other direction. He hates to be pigeon-

holed or labeled as a director of this or that school or inclination, for—as he
restlessly seeks new answers to the questions he keeps posing—he sees his work
as ever changing, ever growing. Ultimately, he admits that even the solutions
are not a final goal, for, as he says, he believes more in the search than in the
solution. His many published comments on theatre practice display his experimental compulsion as he has moved from idea to idea through the years. In *The
Empty Space* he revealed that his words were merely ''a picture of the author
at the moment of writing: searching within a decaying and evolving theatre. As
I continue to work, each experience will make these conclusions inconclusive
again.''[41]

A study of Brook's career thus reveals a prodigious range of styles which
have been grist to his mill. He has touched all theatrical bases, from the *nō*
theatre to *commedia dell'arte,* from music hall to circus, from documentary
drama to spectacle, from text-worshipping classical revivals to free-form improvisations based on the same material. Influences on him have ranged from
Artaud to Brecht, from Barry Jackson to Meyerhold, from Craig to Terence
Gray and Grotowski, from the criticism of Jan Kott to the philosophy of G. I.
Gurdjieff to the paintings of Bosch, Breughel, Watteau, and Goya. Yet through
the welter of styles and ideas, Brook has never faltered in his adherence to one
basic tenet: that the theatre must fulfill a worthwhile purpose, must be of pertinence to its audiences, must fill a hunger for them. His research always has
been geared to the demands of this audience, to determine just what those hungers
are that cry out to be satisfied.

A play to Brook is like a specimen to a laboratory scientist; he scrutinizes it
under the microscope of his artistic vision, searching out its hidden heartbeat,
looking for what it has to say to a modern spectator. Once he has glimpsed this
secret life, he seeks the most expressive means by which he can translate it into
production terms within an environment where actors and audience come together
to share a united experience. Brook considers his work experimental, a search
for answers, but he never intends to offer the results of an experiment as a
definitive solution backed up by fully expounded theory. As he says, ''The fact
of the wish to experiment only states one thing—an awareness that the existing
form is not right. The experiment is an attempt, publicly, to define the new
direction.''[42]

No one breakthrough or idea should constitute an answer. Each subsequent
work poses its own problems, but the solutions are not necessarily applicable to
succeeding productions. ''No experiment can succeed or fail, because every
experiment is a potential success,'' he states. ''Potential, because success depends on the observer. Does he wish to know?'' Responding to criticism of his
experimentation at the Round House in 1968, he pointed out that he was seriously
concerned with such questions as ''What is a theatre? What is a play? What is
a spectator? What is the best relationship between them all? What conditions
serve this relationship best?''[43]

To confuse the issue by looking at the results as good or bad, success or failure is an error. The artist can search for answers only in the crucible of actual theatrical work, not at his desk, and he must be granted critical freedom to do so.

THE EMPTY SPACE

Brook's early directing work was notable for the stunning effectiveness with which he could unite superb acting, brilliant visual coups, and a dynamic background of music and sound effects within a unique and individualistic, if not idiosyncratic, view of the plays he handled. When Brook was only twenty-five, Tynan was convinced that he was "probably the most mature and certainly even the most exacting producer in England,"[44] and compared him favorably to the reigning theatricalist director, Tyrone Guthrie.

Most of Brook's work was done in proscenium theatres, the limitations of which he has come to despise, especially those in England such as the Royal Shakespeare Theatre at Stratford, whose acoustics are dreadful. Shakespeare, above all, requires "an acoustic miracle"[45] to make his language live, he claims. The proscenium theatre is an anachronism, in Brook's latest thinking. Its separation of actor from audience prevents true theatre events from happening. Ironically, his erstwhile admirer, Tynan, considered Brook "the last real master-director of the proscenium stage."[46]

Much of Brook's recent directing has been outside the framework of the proscenium. A variety of locales have been used—often in natural surroundings—in which he has been free to alter the spatial relationship between actors and audience. Some of this work has involved mobilizing the audience, forcing it to follow the action from place to place, rather than watching from a fixed vantage point. Other experiments have included producing a play one way for one theatre and another way elsewhere. When *A Midsummer Night's Dream* played at the 300-seat Midlands Art Centre in Birmingham, a house quite dissimilar to the Stratford theatre for which it had been conceived, the company performed it in a freewheeling, improvisatory manner, aiming not to reproduce the Stratford production but to adjust the spirit of the work in accordance with the new environment. Though the play had new life and vitality as a result, it was clear the same methods would fail dismally at Stratford. Brook continued to experiment in this way with the pieces developed at the ICTC in Paris. This company played where and when it wanted to and with no fixed set of rules to follow except the duty to do its best.

DIRECTING SHAKESPEARE

Shakespeare's name appears more frequently in the Brook oeuvre than any other playwright's. Because he wants to evoke the living Shakespeare, Brook occasionally has taken liberties with the texts in an attempt to point up those pertinent themes and ideas which he discerns. Brook has not been opposed to adding words to the dialogue to clarify archaic usages, and cutting chunks out to punctuate contemporary insights. He candidly affirms that rewriting Shakespeare's plays is a completely acceptable practice. No matter what anyone does with them, they endure. Brook has no set approach to Shakespeare. Each play has its own needs to which the director must be extremely sensitive. *A Midsummer Night's Dream,* he thought, was perfect, so nothing was cut, while other plays may suggest a strong need for omissions and rearrangements.

Brook's purposes and methods in directing Shakespeare have changed considerably over the years. When he began directing the Bard with *Love's Labour's Lost,* he had to have and express a personal vision of the play. He approached it with a filmmaker's mentality, through a variety of visual images he wished to set in motion. This resulted in a long, pictorial production reminiscent of the old-fashioned romantic stage. He continued to work that way through his 1950 *Measure for Measure,* on the principle that the director's task was to discover images within the play to which he could fully respond. He would then translate these images into visual concepts through his design for the play. Images being so evident in this age, Brook often combined the director's function with that of the designer with the understanding that the two functions actually are one.

He gradually evolved from the view that the director must create new imagery for a play to "an awareness that the total overall image was so much less than the play itself." From his later work outside conventional theatre structures he realized that a Shakespearean production could exceed the single imagistic concept and begin from the director's premise "that this is the play for now."[47] Thus, the play's contemporary relevance, its thematic values, became the predominant production factor. The play had to be meaningful both to him and to people in general. This new orientation became the chief factor for him in the process of play selection.

He states that he has never done a Shakespeare play he did not want to do. He prefers to direct a play because it presents the possibility of making discoveries, not simply because it appeals to him through its opportunities for exciting illustrative ideas. Instead of "I like it, and I'll show you why I like it," he will say, "I like it because it parallels all that I need to know about in the world."[48]

In answer to those critics who have accused him of putting the director before Shakespeare, he argues that a director may freely interpret a play in terms of its immediate relevance, no matter what these terms may be, but no one should impose such a one-sided view as to neglect all its other values. To do so would be to deprive both the director and his audience of the chance to make new discoveries in the play. The play must not be *used,* for this distorts it and misses out on its "re-exploration of the truth."

Discussing Shakespearean costuming, Brook says that the director should avoid selecting any specific historical period, for to do so is to introduce irrelevancies which impede communication of the play's reality. Historical costuming detracts from the inner life of the drama. Each production must solve the problem anew, there being no fixed answers. Mixing the styles is superior to a consistent look, since too unified a design would be tantamount to putting Shakespeare into a straitjacket. The danger is one of being too eclectic, for that too could prove distracting. The appearance of unity is an impression, an optical illusion.

Brook's approach to Shakespeare's language has varied in each of his recent productions. *A Midsummer Night's Dream* and *Antony and Cleopatra* were quite traditional in their verse-speaking, while the 1968 *The Tempest* and *Timon of Athens* were unconventionally spoken. Brook explains that Shakespeare's words cannot be limited to single meanings, for each word gives off rays that connect it to several meanings—all of which the actors must be open to. He would rather think of Shakespeare not as someone who *means,* but as an artist who *creates* works of drama like works of pottery. The play should be detached from its author and seen on its own terms, as with a piece of primitive art.

Brook's unusual use of language in several of his recent Shakespeare productions stems from his current notions that Shakespeare's language no longer bears the impact it once did and that a new theatrical equivalent, expressed in kinesthetic and auditory imagery, must be discovered to replace it. A large part of Brook's work at the ICTC has been concerned with just such ideas.

SCENIC STYLES

Peter Brook is a director in the Craigian sense of one who is in charge of the total mise-en-scène, often designing his own sets, lights, and costumes, and composing the music. As noted earlier, he once believed it an advantage for the director to do his own designs, for he can thus develop his ideas of the play at the same time as he is working them out in concrete form. As he has written:

A scene may escape the director for several weeks—then as he works on the set he may suddenly find the place of the scene that eludes him; as he works on the structure of the difficult scene he may suddenly glimpse its meaning in terms of stage action or a succession of colours.[49]

In recent years he has turned the design duties over to specialists, notably Sally Jacobs and Chloé Obolensky and has concentrated mainly on his work with the actors. However, when the director has someone else do his designs, this collaboration can only work when they operate at the same pace. The designer should be able to alter his conceptions as the director alters his, until a unity of form occurs. The design process should then be simultaneous with the development of the production and not complete when the design sketches are submitted early in the production process. His work with Sally Jacobs on the *Dream* reveals his carrying out of theory into practice, as the final designs for the play did not evolve until late in the rehearsal process; throughout, Jacobs was free to experiment, scrapping some ideas and redeveloping others as needed.

A good example of Brook's early work with a designer was his experience with Teo Otto on *The Visit*. At first, Brook had rejected the playwright's request that Otto be used, as the designer already had done several European versions of the play and Brook wanted a fresh conception. When he saw Otto's designs hung on the walls of Dürrenmatt's house, however, he changed his mind and agreed to use him. Otto agreed without reservation to alter his designs to suit Brook. Although Otto had wanted the actors to represent trees in a forest, Brook chose to suggest the forest by a simple bench on a bare stage. In Otto's production in Switzerland the play ended by Schill being killed only after a baroque proscenium and ornate curtain had been flown in to "distance" and theatricalize the act's brutality; the killing was done behind the curtain where the audience could not see it. Since this convention was unfamiliar to American and English audiences, Brook had Otto design "a Gothic hall with hanging lamps in a dark and somber mood"[50] as a replacement. This collaborative process produced a notable success.

Brook's impetus for staging a play during his pre-1970s period often grew out of a scenic impulse. His scenic conceptions were often rather elaborate in the more decorative tradition of modern scenography. However, his scenic tastes altered markedly in his later period. Brook went from the visually striking and innovative to the simple and essentially unadorned; carpets and cushions replaced furniture, and scenic units were often found objects that could serve a variety of functions. Probably the major impetus in this direction was his production of *King Lear,* for which he originally had designed an imposing and complex setting; as rehearsals were about to commence, Brook decided that the set—on which he had worked for a year—was "absolutely useless," and scrapped almost all of it, stripping it to its barebone essentials. In several recent works he has employed natural materials, such as earth, water, and fire as scenic elements. Brook's earlier belief in scenery as fundamental to the conception of a play was revised to one favoring a unity between the text, the actors, and the audience; scenery should serve as a bridge to effect this unity but should not be granted a separate life of its own. Thus, the scenic environment for a Brook production is basically that of an empty space, with a few well-chosen elements, such as carpets, to establish a visual focus, but with the brunt of the decor residing in the person of the costumed actor and his personal props. Lighting—unlike his earlier, more atmospheric, practice—is conceived in a Brechtian mode using little more than white lights, Brook's principal injunction to the lighting designer being "Very bright!" "I want everything to be seen, everything to stand out clearly, without the slightest shadow,"[51] Brook states.

SOUND AND MUSIC

Music and sound in a Peter Brook production are normally as exceptional as the visual components. Brook constantly searches for new musical backgrounds, from his own *musique concrète* to the imaginative sounds of Richard Peaslee, to the "nonsense music, pop music, English country songs, and workmen's dirges"[52] heard in his various works. His fertile inventiveness in the creation of his own compositions was especially noteworthy in *Venice Preserv'd*. It "was scored for harpsichord, guitar and bells [notes J. C. Trewin, Brook's biographer], being plucked on a fantastic instrument as high as the proscenium." In *Titus Andronicus* he tried to create a truly primitive sound through similar means, working with composer William Blezard. The pair pursued many sounds and musical experiments, aiming to find a sound in which "only textures, rhythm and timbre were important. They worked with such things as ashtrays and pots and pans, pencils on Venetian glass phials, and wire baskets used as harps."[53] Similarly, Brook takes great pains with the nonmusical sound effects for his plays, as with his careful symphony of dockyard noises for *A View from the Bridge*.

Much of the effectiveness of his work since *Ubu* has been owing to the work of Toshi Tsuchitori, a multi-instrumental musician who designs his brilliant musical effects collaboratively with the actors during the rehearsal process. He and the musical ensemble are normally in view of the audience when they perform. Tsuchitori's work was of vast importance in the evolution of the music for *The Mahabharata,* which went to great lengths to create the proper musical background and employed an unusual combination of African and Oriental instruments; the composer spent two years in India absorbing its music in preparation for the project. One of his musicians, an experienced wind musician, spent three months just learning how to play an exotic Indian wind instrument, the *nagaswaram*. At the same time, when Brook felt that a play required no music, he assiduously avoided it. The exemplar of this approach was *King Lear,* which made effective use of thunder sheets for the storm, but otherwise made no use of music at all.

GOOD THEATRE/BAD THEATRE

All contemporary references to categories like "actor's theatre," "director's theatre," and "writer's theatre" are false and misleading to Brook. There is either good theatre or bad theatre, no matter whose contribution is the primary one. Good theatre is good because all of it is good—the directing, the designs, the acting, the writing. He has been criticized for overdirecting, but he insists that the opposite is true, that his manner is to underdo, not overdo—to strip away, to get to the bone. This often results in his discarding the timeworn conventionalities people have come to expect. By removing the excess and getting to the essentials, he seeks to deal with a play's fundamental problems. His opera productions have been rebuked because he removed the false encrustations of scenery and acting, excisions which critics claim distract them from the music. But Brook thinks audiences want these familiar aids because they are benumbed by and do not have to pay attention to them. When he did *King Lear* his sole purpose was to bore to the drama's core by eliminating everything extraneous. This meant getting rid of all the familiar physical trappings and moral positions that have accrued to the play. A similar argument could be made for other major works, like *Oedipus* and *A Midsummer Night's Dream*. The problem is that critics come with preconceptions about theatrical conditions. When the new directorial approaches become more familiar they will cease to shock the unprepared.

PREPARATION FOR PRODUCTION

Because he is a perfectionist Brook cannot abide the limited rehearsal period to which most commercial theatre is restricted. He longed for a totally subsidized company, such as the Berliner Ensemble or Moscow Art Theatre, where work on a production could take as much time as necessary before being shown to the public. Fortunately for him, his RSC involvement in the sixties provided him with longer periods for rehearsal than he would have had on the West End; a typical Brook production of those years used anywhere from eight to ten weeks of rehearsal time. Of course, Brook often did preparatory work on a production far in advance of rehearsals, taking a year, for example, to conceptualize *Titus Andronicus.* At the ICTC Brook took far longer to work on a piece, as he felt no compulsion here to present a work until the piece itself dictated that it was ready for an audience. *The Mahabharata,* for example, rehearsed for ten months before opening.

Despite his lengthy prerehearsal cogitations, Brook has not, for many years, engaged in preblocking his shows. In his first productions the opposite was true; he would come to rehearsal with every move, every lighting and sound cue, thought out in advance in a thick promptbook. Because he was preoccupied with the visual side of production, he used scenic models and cardboard figures to work out his blocking, although he was ready even then to make adjustments when required by the needs of the actors. "It seemed to me then," he recalls, "that I should try to produce a striking set of fluid pictures to serve as a bridge, between the play and the audience."[54] It was not until his seventh production, *Love's Labour's Lost,* that he changed his methods after realizing that, no matter how carefully prearranged his effects, these were far less interesting than what the living actors themselves devised spontaneously.

I stopped and walked away from my book [he writes], in amongst the actors, and I have never looked at a written plan since. I recognized once and for all the presumption and the folly of thinking that an inanimate model can stand for a man.[55]

Having given up his promptbook, he worked ad hoc, by trial and error:

If you plan too precisely in advance . . . you get parental, possessive, and proprietary; if you don't plan, you don't mind scrapping what you've done. The danger in the latter technique, however, is that in continually revising you sometimes scrap something that is excellent and ought to be retained.[56]

A Peter Brook production, then, is an attempt at true collaboration between actors and director. The company's ideas are, in the end, almost as important as are those of Brook himself. He has tried to explain the process:

It's as though one starts from something that one feels very strongly. One can even talk about it and define it to a degree, but it hasn't quite got a form, and you go towards that with the people concerned—amending, changing, adapting, finding—and at the end, as the form emerges, you realize that this is where you've been going from the start.[57]

Elsewhere he declares,

I start with a profound formless hunch which is like a smell, like a colour, like a shadow. That's the basis of my job, my role—that's my preparation for rehearsals with any play I do. There's a formless hunch that is my relationship with the play. It's my conviction that this play must be done today, and without that conviction I can't do it. I've no technique.[58]

Brook refuses to impose his own interpretation on an actor, since he believes the actor, if he or she is a good one, is closer to the part than he is. During his rehearsals for *Antony and Cleopatra,* he told an interviewer,

at every minute we stop and discuss a passage and I say that I think this means such and such a thing and Glenda Jackson says, "No, I think that actually she means this," and we discuss it, and the other actors join in. We all discuss it. But eventually she has to know better because she has to play it. I mean, she is living with it.[59]

As Brook recently told Margaret Croyden,

Directing is pointing, not imposing. Someone asks you the way, you direct them. If they set off misunderstanding you, you stop them and say no, and point them in the right direction, which is very different from a director who has it all figured out beforehand.[60]

Consequently, he hates to impose any definitions from the outside, feeling that no play would be worth attempting if its aims were too specifically pinpointed in advance. He seeks the definition with his actors during the rehearsals, often learning that the play in performance is considerably different from his preconceptions.

As Brook works with the actors, he encourages them to try anything they want to do; a tremendous number of choices thus are not made until—by a painstaking process of elimination, during which he continues to probe and provoke the actors—the form of the production gradually begins to emerge. He insists that his aim is never to evolve a production from a preconceived idea; instead, the process of chipping away during rehearsals is intended to reveal the play's "organic form" lurking within. "Because the form is not a form imposed on a play, it is the play illuminated, and the play illuminated is the form."[61]

As a result of Brook's actor-centered way of working, those new to his methods have sometimes questioned whether he presages the disappearance of the director. His assistant on *Carmen,* Michel Rostain, observed, "Placing the actor in a position where he is responsible for bringing, inventing, feeding life at every moment. Are we witnesses to the abolition of the director?'' But he answers himself, ''First of all there is this fantastic creative demand made on the actors and singers. But behind this demand, there is someone called the 'director': with all that he brings in his own right: a working direction, a research style, theatrical techniques.''[62] Italian actor Vittorio Mezzogiorno, who first worked with Brook on *The Mahabharata,* was totally at sea when he began rehearsals, as Brook offered him no apparent help. ''Then after a certain point my survival instinct forced me to understand that what was being asked of me was to free things from within myself, to give, to be myself. So what started as discomfort became freedom.''[63]

CASTING

Brook must obviously be careful about the actors he casts if he is going to get them to work in his uniquely collaborative way. He therefore opts for actors who appear to have temperaments similar to his own, who are ''open'' and ready to discard achieved effects and search for new and better ones. Actors who seek immediate results clearly do not fit into his approach. Older stage veterans find it hard to adjust to Brook's techniques, while young ones are far more susceptible to it. An older actor who is an exception is John Gielgud, a man with whom Brook has an excellent rapport and who has starred in five Brook productions. Gielgud has a reputation for being a highly flexible performer who keeps changing his attack on a role during rehearsals until he finds the best of all possible solutions. Brook takes to the improvisational, instinctual methods of Gielgud, for both operate within the parameters of the trial-and-error style of creation.

Brook recognizes the need for typecasting in the limited conditions of conventional production; he prefers not to cast by type, though, for he knows that, given a long rehearsal period, actors will often reveal facets of their talent which are totally unexpected. His own casting is often a mixed assortment of actors with different backgrounds and training whom he blends together into an ensemble despite all odds. His dream is of a company such as he has worked with at ICTC, one that can

play to 20, 200, or 2,000 people of all strata and ages, that can play free theatre, ritual theatre, Shakespeare, or modern drama; a company that will be a fusion of temperaments, styles, techniques, and background. . . . There are no set rules except one—that the actor must be ready to go beyond himself.[64]

WORKING WITH ACTORS

Brook is a pragmatist who uses whatever means are available to reach his goals. His rehearsal techniques are wide-ranging and varied, depending more on inspiration and selectivity than on any clearly formalized methodology. Though improvisations are his most frequent tool, he often uses other techniques when circumstances demand them. With one actor a verbal explanation may be the answer; with another a mere gesture may suffice. When beginning a production he feels a director should avail himself of many stimuli for the cast, including "improvisation, exchange of associations and memories, reading of written material, reading of period documents, looking at films and photographs."[65] Rehearsals may vary depending on the problem being worked on. He notes:

There is a place for discussion, for research, for the study of history and documents, as there is a place for roaring and howling on the floor. Also there is a place for relaxation, informality, chumminess, but also there is time for silence and discipline and intense concentration.[66]

The good director is one who is aware of when the right time for the right method has arrived. He must never push his actors in early rehearsals but must be patient with them, for when the right time comes the merest hint will stimulate the initially anxious and confused performer. Many actors will corroborate Brook's patience. As Bruce Myers has said, "He can wait until you find for yourself what you need."[67]

In the 1940s and 1950s Brook was likely to begin his rehearsals by having the cast read through the entire play. Usually he prefaced this by giving a lengthy talk on the play and its production style. He disliked the director's reading the script because it bored him to do so. The cast reading itself served only one purpose, to break the ice for those who are going to work together in the company. During the reading Brook would interrupt to comment on the theme, locale, and characters. On the second day he began to block the play, as he hated lengthy analytical talk fests. When roughly blocked, the play would be broken down into small pieces and these worked on separately. He described this method as similar to creating an oil painting. "First I make a large free sketch, then I put in more and more details, but I keep changing and adding throughout the rehearsal period. I give the actors rough positions but each day I make changes until exactly the right places are found."[68] Rather than answer the actor's questions directly he would work with the actor to discover the answers in rehearsals, perhaps taking three weeks to find them.

Brook always has been adept at the psychological manipulation of actors to get good work from them. Kenneth Tynan recounts how Brook

would talk an elderly actress into climbing a rickety staircase . . . simply by letting it be known to other members of the company that he thought she was physically unable to do it, and that he would never dream of asking her . . . and she virtually insisted on doing it.[69]

Most observers agree that Brook could wring fine performances out of the unlikeliest prospects. Marowitz saw him handle a crowd of knights in *Lear* after they failed to act convincingly. By dealing with them privately and convincing them of the importance of their work within the context of the production, as well as by individualizing each as a separate character, he was able to get them to launch ''into the same scene, with a conviction and clarity of purpose which, apart from transforming the scene, managed to bring the rehearsal chandelier crashing down onto the stage.''[70]

A good part of the Brook mystique emerges from the man's personality. He has been described as an intellectual, a nonintellectual, a warm and even-tempered person, a Napoleon who rarely gives vent to his emotions, and in various other contradictory ways, depending on who is describing him. The impression Brook produces is that of a chameleon who can change his spots according to the situation.

He has gathered a string of nicknames, including the Guru, the Ogre, the Monster, the Buddha, and King of the Trolls. A short, cherubic man, balding with tufts of gray hair, he is gentle-voiced and highly expressive with his gestures. He is famous for never losing his temper, but he is equally well known for the rarity with which he compliments his actors; his preference for constantly revising their work instead of accepting it as fixed does not sit equally well with everyone. Equally disturbing to some is Brook's seemingly indefatigable workaholic constitution, his ability to rehearse for twelve hours, attend to additional postrehearsal business, and be completely fresh at the next day's rehearsal.

IMPROVISATION

A Peter Brook rehearsal typically begins with the cast seated in a circle on the floor on cushions. All discussions and exercises to be carried out begin from the premise of the group gathered in this circle. As already noted, the method he is most likely to employ as the work progresses is improvisation. Although he began to use this technique at the beginning of the 1960s in productions like *The Balcony,* he did not really become addicted to it until his Theatre of Cruelty Workshop. Prior to this his method had been based primarily on stars and directorial ingenuity. His *Lear,* done shortly before the workshop, used Paul Scofield in the lead but made some preliminary attempts to give all the players a good deal of freedom in the development of movements and characterization. He rehearsed the play by continually eliminating earlier choices, asking new questions, and reversing old solutions. A number of improvisational techniques were employed, including Brecht's third-person narrative exercises and mask exercises for exploring character and situation. Scofield, however, found such exercises wasteful and divisive of his energy. Interestingly, it was his last Brook production to date.

Brook is convinced that improvisations are a crucial factor in avoiding the trap of what he calls Deadly Theatre. Improvisations make the actors find truths instead of lies; they lead to real, not phony or imitative, performances. The actor is forced to dig down inside until he experiences his falsity, allowing him to open up to truer impulses.

An insight into Brook's improvisational method can be gleaned from his rehearsals of *Oedipus*, where he placed full stress on vocal techniques of pacing, rhythm, and tone. He allowed his cast much liberty, telling them what to avoid but not what to do. No clear concept was imposed on the actors. Following a period of several weeks of discussion necessitated by the script's not being ready, the company engaged in exercises in T'ai Chi, a favorite Brook device. During the rehearsal period everyone in the cast got to play everyone else's part as a means of developing the ensemble. To evoke the play's sense of horror they were asked to tell stories of horrible experiences they had encountered, then to tell these without using words, vocally with no body movement, bodily without vocal sounds, and with neither movement nor vocalization. This latter refers to special breathing exercises used for the communication of ideas. A snake exercise aimed at developing corporeal expressiveness. Using his whole body, the actor had to portray a snake in an imaginary situation, using body rhythms to communicate ideas of movement and emotional state. Then parts of the body would be used as the snake, so that for example, two snakes might be shown by one finger of each hand.

Oedipus also contained the unique problem of handling a chorus. As Brook had no past experience in this convention and had no models to draw upon, he had to develop his own approach. The choral work was broken down into seven "discovery problems" which I have paraphrased here:

1. To discover the meaninglessness of preconceived notions of choral chanting.
2. To discover nonrealistic vocal possibilities.
3. To discover the chorus' realistic function.
4. To discover the differences between personalized and depersonalized emotion in speaking techniques.
5. To discover how the body can be used to evoke vocal effects.
6. To discover the ways in which formal movement and speech may be used as valid means of expression.
7. To discover how the group may work cohesively through a wide range of exercises in intergroup communication.[71]

In his article on the *Oedipus* chorus, Brook cautions that any exercise can only be understood within the context of the need to which it is being applied, and cannot be used out of that context. When the need is evident, the means to satisfy that need are applied. An example was the exercise he gave Irene Worth to help her capture the proper vocal "weight" at the conclusion of *Oedipus*. He tried to have her realize vocally the

image of a charred, ashen ruin. . . . I suggested that she speak only in inbreaths—an impossible challenge which she mastered amazingly. But this could not, physically, be sustained. So out of it she evolved a new sound and rhythm of her own. And so it went. In each case the good inventions grew out of *need*, they were not shaped by tricks or formulas.[72]

For the *Dream* Brook created a rehearsal atmosphere where anything was possible. Early rehearsals revolved around a number of readings of the play as the company delved into its themes. Soon they were all practicing circus tricks for the first half hour of each rehearsal, developing discipline of mind and body with balls, plates, and sticks. The company worked at eliminating over-rationalizing in order that their inner subjective impulses could be put to work in shaping the production. Exercises included wordless conversations and circus acrobatics as a means of communication. Considerable time was spent on such exercises even before rehearsals commenced.

Much of Brook's recent technique has been oriented toward the actor's vocal effects. Rehearsals for *The Conference of the Birds* saw the company creating "a system of signs, syllables and silence—and in addition, bird sounds." The cast practiced Greek daily to familiarize themselves with sounds which they could adapt and around which they could improvise. Other sound sources were Japanese and African songs demanding special vocal usages. In this work, "Brook is striving for the meaning of *sound* [wrote Margaret Croyden] rather than the meaning of words and for a theatrical language that is more physically expressive than English and more universal."[73] He and his company wanted to see what possibilities the use of language in his terms has; formal language no longer satisfied him for it could no longer act as man's greatest evolutionary feat.

As much of the above reveals, Brook's work with his actors is far more than simply a way of creating better theatre; he seeks with them to find a better way of living, an ethic that will correspond to the spiritual precept of *dharma* (the way of righteous behavior) that provides the foundation of *The Mahabharata*. Many of his actors emerge from working with him transformed as human beings, especially in their experience of moving to a higher consciousness. One of them, Bruce Myers, has declared, "It's not only that Peter is a great director, but being around him increases one's sense of the richness and intensity of life."[74] And Andrzej Seweryn has observed,

What you learn here is not only a job, a craft; you also come to recognize what is human, and what it is to be human. I hope to become—I almost said "better"—more demanding of ourselves, more disciplined, more open, more respectful of others. The theatre becomes a way of life.[75]

VISITORS

Though Brook has been known to invite specialists to work with his company—such as Jerzy Grotowski and Joseph Chaikin, who participated on *US*—he dislikes outsiders watching his rehearsals, except toward the end when the actors need an audience to play to. An audience's presence disorients the actors early in the rehearsal process and prevents total relaxation. Nevertheless, his ICTC work was frequently viewed in a workshop state by well-known visitors from the world theatre. This new openness reflects simply another shift in Brook's kaleidoscopic attitudes toward the meaning of his work.

CONCLUSION

Brook has written that a director should be a strong unifying force, providing clear leadership even at the risk of despotism. He admits that he was a definitely autocratic director from the 1940s through the early 1960s, becoming a truly collaborative artist with his Theatre of Cruelty season. This new approach cut him off from his most successful old tools, the showman's technical and artistic skills in judging the strength or weakness of a work as an audience will perceive it. In his current work, he, "like his actors, is trying to confront his own barriers and deceptions, enrich himself through unknown territory: open himself to it."[76] He now views a director as one "who is there to attack and yield, provoke and withdraw until the undefinable stuff begins to flow."[77] And, in another passage, "the director is always an imposter, a guide at night who does not know the territory, and yet he has no choice—he must guide, learning the route as he goes."[78] Peter Brook is a magnificent imposter; for no matter how little he knows the path his experiments will take him, the world of theatre will follow after, implicitly believing that somehow he will find the way.

NOTES

1. Peter Brook, *The Empty Space* (New York: Avon, 1968), p. 25.

2. Quoted in Ronald Hayman, *Playback* (New York: Horizon Press, 1974), pp. 61–62.

3. Peter Brook, "Style in Shakespearean Production," in *The Modern Theatre: Readings and Documents,* ed. Daniel J. Seltzer (Boston: Little, Brown, 1967), p. 254.

4. Kenneth Tynan, "Director as Misanthropist: On the Moral Neutrality of Peter Brook," *Theatre Quarterly* 7 (Spring 1977): 20.

5. Kenneth Tynan, *A View of the English Stage 1944–1963* (London: Davis-Poynter, 1975), p. 85.

6. Ibid., p. 86.

7. Tynan, "Director as Misanthropist," p. 21.

8. Ivor Brown, *Shakespeare Memorial Theatre 1954–1956* (London: Max Reinhardt, 1956), p. 10.

9. Brooks Atkinson, followup review of *The Visit, New York Times,* 18 May 1958.

10. Charles Marowitz, "Lear Log: Rehearsal Notes on Peter Brook's Production of *King Lear,*" in *Theatre at Work,* ed. Charles Marowitz and Simon Trussler (New York: Hill and Wang, 1967), p. 133. Brook denies that he was "influenced" by Kott, as many have asserted. He told an interviewer, "I really read nothing about Shakespeare that's

of any help. You have to work directly with the author, you can't read any commentaries. But, by chance, Kott's piece was really close, almost parallel, to the way we were evolving and so I felt that what we were doing and what he was theorizing completely married." Daniel Labeille, " 'The Formless Hunch': An Interview with Peter Brook," *Modern Drama* 23 (Spring 1980): 221.

11. Margaret Croyden, *Lunatics, Lovers and Poets: The Contemporary Experimental Theatre* (New York: McGraw-Hill, 1974), p. 232.

12. James H. Clay and Daniel Krempel, *The Theatrical Image* (New York: McGraw-Hill, 1967), pp. 210–11.

13. Brook, *The Empty Space*, p. 44.

14. Charles Marowitz, "Notes on the Theatre of Cruelty," *The Drama Review* 11 (Winter 1966): 155.

15. David Williams, *"The Screens,"* in *Peter Brook, A Theatrical Casebook*, ed. and comp. David Williams (London: Methuen, 1988), p. 53.

16. Peter Brook, introduction to Peter Weiss, *The Persecution and Assassination of Jean-Paul Marat as Performed by the Inmates of the Asylum of Charenton under the Direction of the Marquis de Sade* (New York: Pocket Books, 1966), p. 6. A thorough analysis of this production is in David Richard Jones, *Great Directors at Work: Stanislavsky, Brecht, Kazan, Brook* (Berkeley: University of California Press, 1986).

17. Croyden, *Lunatics, Lovers and Poets,* p. 241.

18. Joyce Doolittle, "Oedipus-Sophocles-Seneca-Brook," *Drama at Calgary* 3 (November 1968): 39.

19. Boyce Richardson, "Holy Experience," *Enact*, nos. 24–25 (January-February 1969); n.p.

20. Charles Marowitz, "From Prodigy to Professional, as Written, Directed and Acted by Peter Brook," *New York Times,* 24 November 1968, sec. 2.

21. Richardson, "Holy Experience," n.p.

22. Jerry Tallmer, "Daily Closeup," *New York Post,* 27 January 1971.

23. Stanley Kauffmann, *Persons of the Drama* (New York: Harper and Row, 1976), p. 55.

24. Peter Brook, "The Complete Truth Is 'Global,' " *New York Times*, 20 January 1974.

25. Ossia Trilling, "Playing with Words at Persepolis," *Theatre Quarterly* 5 (January/March 1972): 33. Andrei Serban and Arby Ovanessian worked with Brook as codirectors. For the fullest account of the work see A. C. H. Smith, *Orghast at Persepolis* (New York: Viking, 1972).

26. Quoted in Trilling, "Playing with Words," p. 33.

27. Ibid., p. 40.

28. Brook, "The Complete Truth Is 'Global.' "

29. See John Heilpern, *"Conference of the Birds": The Story of Peter Brook in Africa* (London: Faber and Faber, 1977),

30. Pierre Schneider, "Paris: The Privacy of the Impressionist's Engravings," *New York Times,* 23 December 1974. An excellent description of the Bouffes du Nord and of the production there of *Timon of Athens, The Ik, Ubu,* and a re-created version of *The Conference of the Birds* is in David Williams, " 'A Place Marked by Life': Brook at the Bouffes du Nord," *New Theatre Quarterly* 1 (February 1985): 39–74; most of it is reprinted in Williams' *Peter Brook: A Theatrical Casebook.*

31. David Williams, " 'A Place Marked by Life,' " p. 53.

32. John Heilpern, "Magic of the Birds," *Observer*, 11 May 1980.

33. Eric Shorter, "Off the Cuff—with Peter Brook and Company," *Drama*, no. 129 (Summer 1978), p. 28.

34. Wolfgang Sohlich argues that Brook's interpretation failed to resolve the various ambiguities it suggested; see his "Prolegomenon for a Theory of Drama Reception: Peter Brook's *Measure for Measure* and the Emergent Bourgeoisie," *Comparative Drama* 18 (Spring 1984): 54–78.

35. Michael Kustow, "Letter from London, II: Theatre of the Soul," *Village Voice*, 6 August 1979.

36. Eileen Blumenthal, "Toils of Grace," *Village Voice*, 27 November 1978.

37. Frank Rich, review of *The Tragedy of Carmen*, *New York Times*, 18 November 1983.

38. Quoted in "Peter Brook Directs a Sanskrit Epic," *New York Times*, 31 July 1985.

39. This production is discussed in considerable detail in a series of articles and interviews in *The Drama Review* 34 (Spring 1986).

40. William A. Henry III, "An Epic Journey through Myth," *Time*, 19 October 1987, p. 85.

41. Brook, *The Empty Space*, p. 91.

42. Peter Brook, "We're All Menaced," *Flourish* (August 1968): n.p.

43. Ibid.

44. Tynan, *A View of the English Stage*, p. 84.

45. Quoted by Hayman, *Playback*, pp. 46, 47.

46. Tynan, "Director as Misanthropist," p. 25.

47. Quoted in Ralph Berry, *On Directing Shakespeare* (London: Croom Helm, 1977), p. 133.

48. Ibid.

49. Brook, *The Empty Space*, pp. 91–92.

50. Quoted by Randolph Goodman, ed., *Drama on Stage*, 2nd ed. (New York: Holt, Rinehart, and Winston, 1978), p. 571.

51. Peter Brook, *The Shifting Point: Theatre, Film, Opera, 1946–1987* (New York: Harper and Row, 1987), p. 14.

52. Croyden, *Lunatics, Lovers and Poets*, p. 258.

53. J. C. Trewin, *Peter Brook: A Biography* (London: Macdonald, 1971), p. 112.

54. Brook, *The Shifting Point*, p. 11.

55. Brook, *The Empty Space*, p. 97.

56. Quoted by Goodman, *Drama on Stage*, p. 571.

57. Quoted in Hayman, *Playback*, p. 33.

58. Quoted in Labeille, "The Formless Hunch," p. 223.

59. Quoted in ibid., pp. 222–23.

60. Quoted in Margaret Croyden, "Peter Brook Creates a Nine-Hour Epic," *New York Times Magazine*, 4 October 1987, p. 40.

61. Quoted in Labeille, "The Formless Hunch," p. 226.

62. Michel Rostain, "*The Tragedy of Carmen*: A Rehearsal Log," in *Peter Brook: A Theatrical Casebook*, ed. David Williams, p. 347.

63. Quoted in "An Interview with Vittorio Mezzogiorno (Arjuna) by Martine Millon," in ibid., p. 376.

64. Croyden, *Lunatics, Lovers, and Poets*, p. 259.

65. Brook, *The Empty Space*, p. 113.

66. Ibid., pp. 113–14.

67. Quoted in Croyden, ''Peter Brook Prepares a Nine-Hour Epic,'' p. 44.

68. Quoted in Goodman, *Drama on Stage,* p. 571.

69. Tynan, ''The Director as Misanthropist,'' p. 21.

70. Marowitz, ''From Prodigy to Professional.''

71. Peter Brook, ''The Chorus for the Senecan *Oedipus,*'' *Drama at Calgary* 3 (November 1968): 41.

72. Ibid.

73. Croyden, *Lunatics, Lovers and Poets,* p. 280.

74. Quoted in Croyden, ''Peter Brook Prepares a Nine-Hour Epic,'' p. 44.

75. Quoted in ''An Interview with Andrzej Seweryn (Duryodhana) by Martine Millon'' in *Peter Brook: A Theatrical Casebook,* ed. David Williams, p. 380.

76. John Heilpern, ''Peter Brook, the Grand Inquisitor,'' *Observer,* 18 January 1966.

77. Margaret Croyden, ''Peter Brook's 'Birds' Fly to Africa,'' *New York Times,* 21 January 1973, sec. 2.

78. Brook, *The Empty Space,* p. 35.

CHRONOLOGY

All productions London, except where noted.

1925	born in London
1942–44	attends Oxford University
1942	Torch Theatre: *Dr. Faustus*
1945	Chanticleer Theatre Club: *The Infernal Machine*; ''Q'' Theatre: *The Barretts of Wimpole Street*; ENSA tour: *Pygmalion*; Birmingham Repertory Company, Birmingham: *Man and Superman; King John; The Lady from the Sea*
1946	Shakespeare Memorial Theatre, Stratford-on-Avon: *Love's Labour's Lost*; Lyric, Hammersmith: *The Brothers Karamazov*; Arts Theatre: *Vicious Circle*
1947	Shakespeare Memorial and His Majesty's Theatre, London: *Romeo and Juliet*; Lyric, Hammersmith: *Men without Shadows* and *The Respectable Prostitute* (double bill)
1949	Lyric, Hammersmith, and Ambassador's Theatre: *Dark of the Moon*
1950	Globe Theatre: *Ring Round the Moon*; Shakespeare Memorial and West Germany: *Measure for Measure*; Lyric, Hammersmith: *The Little Hut*
1951	Belgian National Theatre, Brussels: *Death of a Salesman* (in French); Haymarket Theatre: *A Penny for a Song*; Shakespeare Memorial Theatre: *The Winter's Tale*; New Theatre: *Colombe*; marries actress Natasha Parry
1953	Lyric, Hammersmith: *Venice Preserv'd*; Coronet Theatre, New York: *The Little Hut*
1954	Aldwych Theatre: *The Dark Is Light Enough*; Apollo Theatre: *Both Ends Meet*; Alvin Theatre, New York: *The House of Flowers*
1955	Lyric, Hammersmith: *The Lark*; Shakespeare Memorial: *Titus Andronicus*; Moscow Art Theatre, Moscow, and Phoenix Theatre: *Hamlet*

1956   Phoenix: *The Power and the Glory; The Family Reunion*; Comedy Theatre: *A View from the Bridge*; Théâtre Antoine, Paris: *Cat on a Hot Tin Roof* (in French); Stoll Theatre, London: *Titus Andronicus*

1957   Shakespeare Memorial and Theatre Royal, Drury Lane: *The Tempest*; tour to Paris (Théâtre des Nations), Venice, Belgrade, Warsaw, Vienna, and Zagreb: *Titus Andronicus*

1958   Théâtre Antoine: *A View from the Bridge* (in French); Lunt-Fontanne Theatre, New York: *The Visit*; Lyric Theatre: *Irma la Douce*

1959   ANTA Theatre, New York: *The Fighting Cock*

1960   Théâtre de Gymnase, Paris: *The Balcony*

1962   named codirector, Royal Shakespeare Company (RSC), Stratford-on-Avon; RSC and Aldwych: *King Lear*

1963   Aldwych: *The Physicists*; RSC: *The Tempest*; New Theatre, Oxford: *The Perils of Scobie Prilt*; Théâtre de l'Athenée, Paris: *Sergeant Musgrave's Dance* (in French); *The Representative* (in French; codirected with François Darbon); Théâtre des Nations, Paris: *King Lear*

1964   LAMDA Theatre: Theatre of Cruelty season (codirected with Charles Marowitz); East European and U.S. tour, including State Theatre, New York; *King Lear*; Donmar Rehearsal Rooms, Covent Garden: *The Screens*; Aldwych (RSC): *The Persecution and Assassination of Jean-Paul Marat as Performed by the Inmates of the Asylum of Charenton under the Direction of the Marquis de Sade (Marat/Sade)*

1965   RSC public reading, Aldwych: *The Investigation* (codirected with David Jones)

1966   Martin Beck Theatre, New York: *Marat/Sade*; Aldwych (RSC): *US* (codirected with Geoffrey Reeves)

1968   National Theatre: *Oedipus*; workshop at Mobilier National, Paris, with international Théâtre des Nations company; Round House: *The Tempest*; publishes *The Empty Space*

1970   RSC: *A Midsummer Night's Dream*; founds International Center for Theatre Research, Mobilier National, Paris, with Micheline Rozan

1971   Billy Rose Theatre, New York, tour of United States and Canada, Brooklyn Academy of Music (BAM), and Aldwych: *A Midsummer Night's Dream*; Fifth Shiraz International Festival of the Arts, Persepolis, Iran: *Orghast* (codirected with Andrei Serban, Arby Ovanessian, Geoffrey Reeves)

1972   International Center for Theatre Research, Paris: *Kaspar*; this and all subsequent work premiering in France originally given in French; English versions later on tour; *A Midsummer Night's Dream*, European tour; African tour, including work on *The Conference of the Birds*

1973   tour of United States, including California (with El Teatro Campesino), Minnesota, New York, Brooklyn (BAM): *Conference of the Birds*; world tour including United States and Japan: *A Midsummer Night's Dream*

1974   adds International Center for Theatre Creation (ICTC) to Paris project; Théâtre Bouffes du Nord (ICTC), Paris: *Timon of Athens* (codirected with Jean-Paul Vincent)

1975   Bouffes du Nord (ICTC): *The Ik*; improvisational versions of *Conference of the Birds; Timon of Athens* in alternating repertory with *The Ik*

1976   Round House, South American tour, U.S. university tour, and European tour: *The Ik*

1977   Bouffes du Nord (ICTC): *Ubu at the Bouffes, L'Os*; European and Latin American tour: *Ubu*

1978   Young Vic and Théâtre des Nations, Caracas: *Ubu*; RSC: *Antony and Cleopatra*; Bouffes du Nord (ICTC): *Measure for Measure*

1979   European tour: *Measure for Measure*; Avignon Festival, European tour, and Bouffes du Nord (ICTC): *Conference of the Birds; L'Os*

1980   tour to New York, La Mama E.T.C.

1981   Bouffes du Nord (ICTC): *The Cherry Orchard; The Tragedy of Carmen*; European tour including Almeida Theatre, Islington, London: *L'Os*

1983   Bouffes du Nord: *The Cherry Orchard*; Théâtre Montparnesse, Paris: *Tchin-Tchin*; United States, including Vivian Beaumont Theatre, New York: *The Tragedy of Carmen*

1985   Boulbon, France (Avignon Festival; ICTC), European tour, and Bouffes du Nord: *The Mahabharata*

1986   tour to Japan: *The Tragedy of Carmen*

1987   world tour, including Majestic Theatre (BAM), Brooklyn: *The Mahabharata*; publishes *The Shifting Point*

1988   Majestic: *The Cherry Orchard*

Select Bibliography

GENERAL

Many of the works listed here treat several of the directors discussed in the text. Works dealing primarily with individual directors are listed under the director's name.

Atkinson, Brooks. *Broadway*. New York: Macmillan, 1970.
————. *Broadway Scrapbook*. New York: Theatre Arts, 1947.
Bentley, Eric. *In Search of Theatre*. New York: Vintage, 1957.
Bradby, David, and David Williams. *Directors' Theatre*. New York: St. Martin's Press, 1988.
Braun, Edward. *The Director and the Stage: From Naturalism to Grotowski*. London: Methuen, 1982.
Brockett, Oscar, and Robert R. Findlay. *Century of Innovation: A History of European and American Theatre and Drama Since 1870*. Englewood Cliffs, N.J.: Prentice-Hall, 1973.
Burton, Hal, ed. *Great Acting*. New York: Hill and Wang, 1967.
Carra, Lawrence. "The Influence of the Director—for Good or Bad, Covering the Years 1920–1969." In *The American Theatre: A Sum of Its Parts*. New York: Samuel French. 1971.
Cheney, Sheldon. *The New Movement in the Theatre*. New York: Benjamin Blom, 1971.
Chinoy, Helen Krich. "The Profession and the Art: Directing in America, 1860–1930." In *The American Theatre: A Sum of Its Parts*. New York: Samuel French, 1971.
Clark, Barrett H., and George Freedley, eds. *A History of the Modern Drama*. New York and London: Appleton-Century, 1947.
Clay, James H., and Daniel Krempel. *The Theatrical Image*. New York: McGraw-Hill, 1967.
Cole, Toby, and Helen Krich Chinoy. *Directors on Directing: A Source Book of the Modern Theatre*. rev. ed. Indianapolis, Ind.: Bobbs-Merrill, 1963.
Crawford, Cheryl. *One Naked Individual*. New York: Bobbs-Merrill, 1977.
Croyden, Margaret. *Lunatics, Lovers and Poets: The Contemporary Experimental Theatre*. New York: McGraw-Hill, 1974.

Fuerst, Walter René, and Samuel J. Hume. *Twentieth Century Stage Decoration*. New York: Dover, 1967.

Funke, Lewis, and John A. Booth, eds. *Actors Talk About Acting*. New York: Random House, 1961.

Gassner, John. *The Theatre in Our Times*. New York: Crown, 1954.

———. *Directions in Modern Drama and Theatre*. New York: Holt, Rinehart and Winston, 1967.

Goldman, William. *The Season: A Candid Look at Broadway*. New York: Bantam Books, 1970.

Goodman, Randolph, ed. *Drama on Stage*. 2nd ed. New York: Holt, Rinehart and Winston, 1978.

Gorelik, Mordecai. *New Theatres for Old*. New York: Samuel French, 1940.

Hayman, Ronald. *Playback*. New York: Horizon Press, 1974.

———. *The Set-Up: An Anatomy of the English Theatre Today*. London: Eyre Methuen, 1973.

Hinchcliffe, Arnold P. *British Theatre 1950–1970*. Totowa, N.J.: Rowman and Littlefield, 1974.

Innes, Christopher. *Holy Theatre: Ritual and the Avant Garde*. Cambridge, Eng.: Cambridge University Press, 1981.

Johnson, Albert, and Bertha Johnson. *Directing Methods*. South Brunswick, N.J.: A. S. Barnes, 1970.

Jones, David R. *Great Directors at Work: Stanislavsky, Brecht, Kazan, Brook*. Berkeley: University of California Press, 1986.

Kirby, E. T., ed. *Total Theatre: A Critical Anthology*. New York: E. P. Dutton, 1969.

Leiter, Samuel, ed. *Shakespeare Around the Globe: A Guide to Notable Postwar Revivals*. Westport, Conn.: Greenwood Press, 1985.

Lillywhite, Harold. "The Evolution of the Director in the American Theatre." *Quarterly Journal of Speech* 27 (February 1971).

Macgowan, Kenneth. *The Theatre of Tomorrow*. New York: Boni and Liveright, 1921.

Marowitz, Charles. *Prospero's Staff: Acting and Directing in the Contemporary Theatre*. Bloomington and Indianapolis: University of Indiana Press, 1986.

Marowitz, Charles, and Simon Trussler, eds. *Theatre at Work: Playwrights and Productions in the Modern British Theatre*. New York: Hill and Wang, 1967.

Marowitz, Charles, Tom Milne, et al., eds. *The Encore Reader: A Chronicle of the New Drama*. London: Methuen, 1965.

Marshall, Norman. *The Producer and the Play*. rev. ed. London: Davis-Poynter, 1975.

Motherwell, Hiram. "The Unseen Director." *The Stage* 10 (November 1932).

———. *The Theatre of Today*. New York: John Lane, 1914.

Nathan, George Jean. *The Magic Mirror*. Ed. Thomas Quinn Curtis. New York: Alfred A. Knopf, 1960.

Prince, Harold. *Contradictions: Notes on Twenty-Six Years in the Theatre*. New York: Dodd, Mead, 1974.

Roose-Evans, James. *Experimental Theatre: From Stanislavsky to Today*. New York: Avon, 1971.

Ross, Lillian, and Helen Ross. *The Player: A Profile of an Art*. New York: Simon and Schuster, 1962.

Rowe, Kenneth Thorpe. *A Theatre in Your Head: Analyzing the Play and Visualizing Its Production*. New York: Funk and Wagnalls, 1960.

Samachson, Dorothy, and Joseph Samachson, eds. *Let's Meet the Theatre*. New York: Abelard-Shuman, 1954.

Schevill, James. *Break Out! In Search of New Theatrical Environments*. Chicago: Swallow Press, 1973.

Seltzer, Daniel, ed. *The Modern Theatre: Readings and Documents*. Boston: Little, Brown, 1967.

Speaight, Robert. *Shakespeare on the Stage*. Boston and Toronto: Little, Brown, 1973.

Styan, J. L. *The Shakespeare Revolution*. Cambridge, Eng.: Cambridge University Press, 1977.

Tynan, Kenneth. *Curtains*. New York: Atheneum, 1961.

Wiles, Timothy J. *The Theatre Event: Modern Theories of Performance*. Chicago: University of Chicago Press, 1980.

Wills, J. Robert, ed. *The Director in a Changing Theatre*. Palo Alto, Calif.: Mayfield, 1976.

Young, Stark. *Immortal Shadows*. New York: Hill and Wang, 1948.

Unpublished Materials

Cochran, James Preston. "The Development of the Professional Stage Director: A Critical-Historical Examination of Representative Professional Directors on the New York Stage, 1896–1916." Ph.D. diss., State University of Iowa, 1958.

Cox, Charles W. "The Evolution of the Stage Director in America." Ph.D. diss., Northwestern University, 1957.

Hazzard, Robert Tombaugh. "The Development of Selected American Stage Directors from 1926 to 1960." Ph.D. diss., University of Minnesota, 1962.

Rudisill, Amanda Sue. "The Contributions of Eva Le Gallienne, Margaret Webster, Margo Jones, and Joan Littlewood to the Establishment of Repertory Theatre in the United States and Great Britain." Ph.D. diss., Northwestern University, 1972.

DAVID BELASCO

Albert, Dora. "A Power in the Theatre at Seventy-Five." *Forecast* 36 (November 1929).

Belasco, David. "How I Stage My Plays." *Theatre Magazine* 2 (December 1902).

———. "David Belasco Reviews His Life's Work." *Theatre Magazine* 6 (September 1906).

———. "My Life's Story." *Hearst's Magazine* 25–26 (March 1914–December 1915).

———. *The Theatre Through Its Stage Door*. Edited by Louis V. Defoe. New York and London: Harper Brothers, 1919.

———. "About Acting." *Saturday Evening Post*, 24 November 1921.

———. "Why I Produce Unprofitable Plays." *Theatre Magazine* 49 (March 1929).

Bell, Archie. "David Belasco Attacks Stage Tradition." *Theatre Magazine* 13 (May 1911).

Brown, John Mason. *Upstage: The American Theatre in Performance*. Port Washington, N.Y.: Kennikat Press, 1960.

Coward, Edward Fales. "The Men Who Direct the Destinies of the Stage." *Theatre Magazine* 15 (October 1912).

Dodge, Wendell Phillips. "Staging a Popular Restaurant." *Theatre Magazine* 16 (October 1912).

Dransfield, Jane. "Behind the Scenes with Belasco." *Theatre Magazine* 35 (April 1922).

Eaton, Walter Prichard. "Madame Butterfly's Cocoon: A Sketch of David Belasco." *American Scholar* 5 (Spring 1936).

Huneker, James Gibbons. "American Producers III: David Belasco." *Theatre Arts Monthly* 5 (October 1921).

Kane, Whitford. *Are We All Met?* London: Elkin, Mathews and Marrot, 1931.

Lanston, Aubrey. "A Rehearsal under Belasco." *Theatre Magazine* 5 (February 1905).

Marker, Lise-Lone. *David Belasco: Naturalism in the American Theatre*. Princeton, N.J.: Princeton University Press, 1975.

Middleton, George. "Adventures Among the French Playwrights," *New York Times*, 23 October 1938, sec. 9.

———. *These Things Are Mine: The Autobiography of a Journeyman Playwright*. New York: Macmillan, 1947.

Moses, Montrose J. "The Psychology of the Switchboard." *Theatre Magazine* 10 (August 1909).

———. "Belasco: Stage Realist." *Theatre Magazine* 23 (March 1916).

———. "David Belasco: The Astonishing Versatility of a Veteran Producer." *Theatre Guild Magazine* 7 (November 1929).

Murphy, Brendan. *American Realism and American Drama, 1880–1940*. Cambridge, Eng.: Cambridge University Press, 1987.

Timberlake, Craig. *The Bishop of Broadway: The Life and Work of David Belasco*. New York: Library Publishers, 1954.

Vardac, Nicholas. *Stage to Screen: Theatrical Method from Garrick to Griffith*. New York: Benjamin Blom, 1968.

Winter, William. *The Life of David Belasco*. 2 vols. New York: Moffat, Yard, 1918.

Yurka, Blanche. *Bohemian Girl: Blanche Yurka's Theatrical Life*. Athens: University of Ohio Press, 1970.

HARLEY GRANVILLE-BARKER

Archer, William, and Granville Barker. *A National Theatre: Scheme and Estimates*. London: Duckworth, 1907.

Barbour, Charles M. "Up Against a Symbolic Painted Cloth: *A Midsummer Night's Dream* at the Savoy, 1914." *Educational Theatre Journal* 28 (December 1975).

Barker, [Harley] Granville. "Rehearsing a Play." (part 1) *Theatre Magazine* 30 (September 1919).

———. "Rehearsing a Play." (part 2) *Theatre Magazine* 30 (October 1919).

(See also Granville-Barker, Harley, below.)

Bartholomeusz, Dennis. *"The Winter's Tale" in Performance in England and America. 1611–1976*. Cambridge, Eng.: Cambridge University Press, 1982.

Bridges-Adams, W. "Granville Barker and the Savoy." *Drama*, no. 59 (Spring 1952).

Byrne, M. St. Clare. "Fifty Years of Shakespearean Production." *Shakespeare Survey*, vol. 2. Cambridge, Eng.: Cambridge University Press, 1949.

Carter, Huntley. *The Theatre of Max Reinhardt*. New York: Benjamin Blom, 1964.

Casson, Lewis. "Granville Barker, Shaw and the Court Theatre." In *A Theatrical Companion to Shaw*. Edited by Raymond Mander and Joe Mitchenson. London: Folcroft, 1954.

Coward, Edward Fales. "Barker's New Shakespearean Spectacles." *Theatre Magazine* 21 (April 1915).

Dymkowski, Christine. *Harley Granville Barker: A Preface to Modern Shakespeare.* Cranbury, N.J.: Folger, 1986.

Eaton, Walter Prichard. *Plays and Players: Leaves from a Critic's Notebook.* Cincinnati: Stewart and Kidd, 1916.

Fernald, John. *A Sense of Direction: The Director and His Actors.* London: Secker and Warburg, 1968.

Gielgud, John. "Granville Barker's Shakespeare." *Theatre Arts Monthly* 31 (1947).

————. *Stage Directions.* London: Heinemann, 1963.

"Granville Barker, The New Art of the Theater and the New Drama." *American Review of Reviews* 51 (April 1915).

Granville-Barker, Harley. *The Exemplary Theatre.* Boston: Little, Brown, 1922.

————. "The Heritage of the Actor." *Quarterly Review* 140 (July 1923).

————. "A Letter to Jacques Copeau." *Theatre Arts Monthly* 13 (October 1929).

————. *The Study of Drama.* Cambridge, Eng.: Cambridge University Press, 1934.

————. *On Dramatic Method.* New York: Hill and Wang, 1956.

————. *Prefaces to Shakespeare.* Edited by M. St. Clare Byrne. Princeton, N.J.: Princeton University Press, 1963.

————. *The Use of the Drama.* New York: Russell and Russell, 1971.

————. *More Prefaces to Shakespeare.* Edited by Edward G. Moore. Princeton, N.J.: Princeton University Press, 1974.

(See also Barker, [Harley] Granville, above.)

Hunt, Hugh. "Granville-Barker's Shakespearean Productions." *Theatre Research* 10 (1969).

Jackson, Anthony. "Harley Granville-Barker as Director at the Royal Court Theatre, 1904–1907." *Theatre Research* 12 (1972).

Kauffmann, Stanley. "A Life in the Theatre." *Horizon* 17 (Autumn 1975).

Kennedy, Dennis. *Granville Barker and the Dream of Theatre.* Cambridge, Eng.: Cambridge University Press, 1985.

Kitchin, Laurence. *Drama in the Sixties: Form and Interpretation.* London: Faber and Faber, 1966.

Knight, G. Wilson. *Shakespearean Production.* London: Routledge and Keagan Paul, 1964.

MacCarthy, Desmond. *The Court Theatre, 1904–1907: A Commentary and Criticism.* Edited by Stanley Weintraub. Coral Gables, Fla.: University of Miami Press, 1966.

MacOwan, Michael. "Working with a Genius." *Plays and Players* (July 1955).

Mander, Raymond, and Joe Mitchenson. *A Theatrical Companion to Shaw.* London: Rockliff, 1954.

Mazer, Cary M. *Shakespeare Refashioned: Elizabethan Plays on Edwardian Stages.* Ann Arbor, Mich.: UMI Research Press, 1981.

————. "Actors or Gramophones: The Paradoxes of Granville Barker." *Theatre Journal* 36 (March 1984).

Mehra, Manmohan. *Harley Granville-Barker: A Critical Study of the Major Plays.* Calcutta: Naya Prokash, 1981.

Meriden, Orson. "Greek Tragedies in C.C.N.Y. Stadium." *Theatre Magazine* 21 (June 1915).

Moses, Montrose J. "Greek Drama in Beautiful Settings." *Theatre Magazine* 22 (July 1915).

Nesbitt, Cathleen. "Cathleen Nesbitt Talks to Michael Elliot about Harley Granville-Barker." *Listener,* 13 January 1972.

———. *A Little Love and Good Company*. Owings Mills, Md.: Stemmer House, 1977.

Odell, George C. *Shakespeare from Betterton to Irving*. New York: Dover, 1966.

Patterson, Ada. "Behind the Scenes with Mrs. Granville Barker." *Theatre Magazine* 21 (May 1915).

Pearson, Hesketh. *Modern Men and Mummers*. New York: Harcourt, Brace, 1922.

———. *The Last Actor-Managers*. New York: Harper and Brothers, 1950.

———. "A Great Theatrical Management." *Theatre Arts Monthly* 31 (September 1955).

Purdom, C. B. *Harley Granville-Barker: Man of the Theatre, Dramatist, and Scholar*. London: Barrie and Rockliff, 1955.

Robinson, Lennox. *Curtain Up*. London: Michael Joseph, 1942.

Rosenfeld, Sybil. *A Short History of Scene Design in Great Britain*. Oxford: Basil Blackwell, 1973.

Salenius, Elmer W. *Harley Granville Barker*. Boston: Twayne, 1982.

Salmon, Eric. *Granville Barker: A Secret Life*. London: Heinemann Educational Books, 1983.

———, ed. and annot. *Granville Barker and His Correspondents*. Detroit: Wayne State University Press, 1986.

Savage, Richard. "Who Will Be Director of the 'New Theatre'?" *Theatre Magazine* 7 (September 1907).

Schmidt, Karl. "How Barker Puts Plays On." *Harper's Weekly,* 30 January 1915.

Shaw, George Bernard. "Barker's Wild Oats." *Harper's Weekly,* 19 January 1947.

———. *Bernard Shaw's Letters to Granville Barker*. Edited by C. B. Purdom. New York: Theatre Arts Books, 1957.

———. *Shaw on Theatre*. Edited by E. J. West. New York: Hill and Wang, 1958.

Smith, Harrison. "The Revival of Greek Tragedy in America." *Bookman* 41 (June 1915).

Steell, Willis. "Granville Barker May Head the New Theatre Here." *Theatre Magazine* 21 (February 1915).

Thomas, Noel K. "Harley Granville-Barker and the Greek Drama." *Educational Theatre Journal* 7 (December 1955).

Trewin, J. C. *Shakespeare on the English Stage, 1900–1964*. London: Barrie and Rockliff, 1964.

Whitworth, Geoffrey. *Harley Granville-Barker, 1877–1946*. London: Sidgwick and Jackson, 1948.

Williams, Gary J. "*A Midsummer Night's Dream*: The English and American Popular Traditions and Harley Granville-Barker's 'World Arbitrarily Made.' " *Theatre Studies,* no. 23 (1976–77).

Wilson, J. Dover. "Memories of Barker and Two of His Friends." In *Elizabethan and Jacobean Studies Presented to Frank Percy Wilson*. Edited by Herbert Davis and Helen Gardner. Oxford: Oxford University Press, 1959.

Unpublished Materials

Elberson, Stanley Denton. "The Nature of Harley Granville Barker's Productions in America in 1915." Ph.D. diss., University of Oregon, 1968.

Kelly, Helen. "The Granville-Barker Shakespeare Productions: A Study Based on the Promptbooks." Ph.D. diss., University of Michigan, 1965.

GEORGE ABBOTT

Abbott, George. "A Director's Lot. . . . " *New York Times Magazine,* 5 April 1951.
———. "My Ten Favorite Plays." *New York Sun* (n.d.), clipping, Lincoln Center Library for the Performing Arts, New York City.
———. *"Mr. Abbott."* New York: Random House, 1963.
"All the Four Horsemen." *New York Herald Tribune,* 24 November 1934.
Atkinson, Brooks. "Morales for Kings." *New York Times,* 27 September 1931.
———. Review of *Ladies' Money. New York Times,* 2 November 1934.
———. "Slapstick Comedy." *New York Times,* 9 October 1952.
Beebe, Lucius. "Stage Asides." *New York Herald Tribune,* 30 May 1937.
Berger, Marilyn. "Theatre's George Abbott: On the Road to 100." *New York Times,* 22 June 1986.
Bolwell, Edwin. "George Abbott Again Caring for a Broadway Bound Patient." *New York Times,* 10 November 1967.
Eustis, Morton. "The Director Takes Command." *Theatre Arts Monthly* 20 (February 1936).
Gilbert, Douglas. "Making Plays into Shows." *New York World Telegram,* 21 January 1936.
Hammond, Percy. "The Theatre." *New York Sun,* 8 January 1932.
Hickey, Neil. "Mr. Abbott, Sir!" *American Weekly,* 15 May 1960.
Hummler, Richard. "Still Rolling Up Those Sleeves after 100 Years, Abbott Keeps Perpetuating 'Mr. Broadway' Tag." *Variety,* 24 June 1987.
———. *"Broadway." Variety,* 1 July 1987.
Kanin, Garson. "A Born Dancer's 'Abbott Touch.' " *Variety,* 24 June 1987.
Kipps, Charles. "Remembrances of 'George.' " *Variety,* 24 June 1987.
Kissel, Howard. "Going Through the Paces with George Abbott." *Women's Wear Daily,* 12 April 1976.
Klein, Alvin. " 'Yankees,' Hit of Old Is Revived in Milburn." *New York Times,* 28 September 1986, sec. 11.
Little, Stuart. "It's an Old Story for Abbott—The Rehearsal of a New Play." *New York Herald Tribune,* 3 October 1962.
Mandelbaum, Ken. "Welcome Back, Mr. Abbott!" *Theater Week* 3 (October 16, 1989).
Millstein, Gilbert. "Mr. Abbott: One Man Theatre." *New York Times Magazine,* 3 October 1954.
"Prince Recalls: 'Abbott Was First to Tell Me, You Are a Director.' " *Variety,* 24 June 1987.
"The Talk of the Town: Rehearsal." *New Yorker,* 30 October 1978.
Wallach, Alan. "He's Still Got the Abbott Touch." *Newsday,* 11 May 1986, part 2.
Wasserstein, Wendy. "Directing 101: George Abbott on What Works." *New York Times,* 8 October 1989, sec. 2.
"Working for Abbott no Leadpipe Cinch, Art Carney Recalls." *Variety,* 24 June 1987.
Zadan, Craig. *Sondheim and Co.* New York: Macmillan, 1974.
Zolotow, Maurice. "Broadway's Most Successful Penny-Pincher." *Saturday Evening Post,* 29 January 1955.

Unpublished Materials

Hess, Dean. "A Critical Analysis of the Musical Theatre Productions of George Abbott." Ph.D. diss., University of California Press, 1976.

MacClennan, Robert. "The Comedy of George Abbott." Ph.D. diss., Bowling Green State University, 1975.

TYRONE GUTHRIE

Beck, Ervin. "*Tamburlaine* for the Modern Stage." *Educational Theatre Journal* 28 (March 1971).

Casson, John. *Lewis and Sybil*. London: Collins, 1972.

Chayefsky, Paddy. "Tyrone Guthrie: A Playwright's View." *Drama Survey* 3 (Winter 1963).

Clurman, Harold. "Guthrie!" *Playbill* (January 1967).

Davies, Robertson. "The Genius of Dr. Guthrie." *Theatre Arts* 40 (March 1956).

Davies, Robertson, Tyrone Guthrie, and Grant Macdonald. *Renown at Stratford*. Toronto: Clarke, Irwin, 1953.

Davies, Robertson, Tyrone Guthrie, Tanya Moiseiwitsch and Boyd Neel. *Thrice the Brinded Cat Hath Mew'd*. Toronto: Clarke, Irwin, 1955.

Duncan, Angus. "An Interview with Tyrone Guthrie." *Equity Magazine* (September 1957).

Forsyth, James. *Tyrone Guthrie. A Biography*. London: Hamish Hamilton, 1976.

Friel, Brian. "The Giant of Monaghan." *Holiday* 35 (May 1964).

Guinness, Alec. *Blessings in Disguise*. New York: Alfred A. Knopf, 1986.

Guthrie, Tyrone. "Producing a Play." *Scottish Stage*, February 1932.

———. *Theatre Prospect*. The Adelphi Quartos, no. 3. London: Wishart, 1932.

———. "Hamlet and Elsinore." *London Mercury,* 31 July 1937.

———. "Some Notes on Direction." *Theatre Arts* 28 (November 1944).

———. "Shakespearean Production." In *The Year's Work in the Theatre, 1949–50*. London: Longmans, Green, 1950.

———. "Shakespeare Finds a New Stratford." *Theatre Arts* 47 (September 1953).

———. "The World of Thornton Wilder." *New York Times Magazine,* 27 November 1955.

———. "Shakespeare Comes to Stratford, Ontario." *Shakespeare Survey*. vol. 8. Edited by Allardyce Nicoll. Cambridge, Eng.: Cambridge University Press, 1955.

———. "*Tamburlaine* and What It Takes." *Theatre Arts* 40 (February 1956).

———. "Broadway vs. London." *New York Times,* 22 April 1956, sec. 2.

———. "Shakespeare Comes to Stratford (Ont.)." *New York Times Magazine*, 10 June 1956.

———. "Case for an 'Arts Council' Here." *New York Times Magazine*, 25 November 1956.

———. "Ode to Oedipus." *New York Times,* 7 January 1957, sec. 2.

———. "Tribute to Age." *New York Times*, 14 July 1957, sec. 2.

———. "Is There Madness in the Method?" *New York Times Magazine*, 15 November 1957.

———. "Greek Tragedy and the Producers of Today." *World Theatre* 6 (Winter 1957).

———. "Some Other Notes on Shakespeare Production." *Playbill*, week of 29 September 1958.

———. "10 Best for a Repertory Theater." *New York Times Magazine*, 9 November 1958.

———. *A Life in the Theatre*. New York: McGraw-Hill, 1959.

———. "Repertory Theater—Ideal or Deception?" *New York Times Magazine*, 26 April 1959.

———. "On the Critical List." *Theatre Arts* 42 (November 1959).

———. "Why and How They Play *Hamlet*." *New York Times Magazine*, 14 August 1960.

———. "Dominant Director." *New York Times*, 21 August 1960, sec. 2.

———. "The Star's the Thing." *New York Times Magazine*, 23 October 1960.

———. "A Modern Producer and the Plays." In *The Living Shakespeare*. Edited by Robert Gittings. Greenwich, Conn.: Fawcett, 1961.

———. "Greatness in the Theatre." *Horizon* 4 (January 1961).

———. "The Case for a National Theatre." *London Sunday Observer*, 12 March 1961.

———. "The Theatre and God." *Drama Survey* 1 (Spring 1961).

———. "Directing a Play." Transcript of Folkways Records Album #FL 9840. September 1961.

———. "On Producing *Coriolanus*." Introduction to *Coriolanus* by William Shakespeare. New York: Dell, 1962.

———. "Threat of Newness to Olde Stratford." *New York Times Magazine*, 22 April 1962.

———. "So Long as the Theatre Can do Miracles." *New York Times Magazine*, 28 April 1963.

———. "If a Theater Is to Prosper." *New York Times Magazine*, 28 July 1963.

———. "*Hamlet* in Modern Dress." *Drama Survey* 3 (Spring/Summer 1963).

———. "A New and Hopeful Role for Repertory." *New York Times Magazine*, 10 November 1963.

———. "Drama." *Esquire* (December 1963).

———. "The Director Comments. . . . " *The Tyrone Guthrie Theatre Souvenir Program*. Minneapolis, Minn.: Select Publications, 1964.

———. "Ten Favorites from Shakespeare." *New York Times Magazine*, 15 March 1964.

———. *A New Theatre*. New York: McGraw-Hill, 1964.

———. "Why I Refuse Invitations to Direct on Broadway." *New York Times*, 20 December 1964, sec. 2.

———. "A Director's View of *The Cherry Orchard*." In *The Cherry Orchard* by Anton Chekhov. Translated by Tyrone Guthrie and Leonid Kipness. Minneapolis: University of Minnesota Press, 1965.

———. "Filling the Blank." *Theatre: The Annual of the Repertory Theatre of Lincoln Center*. vol. 2. New York: Hill and Wang, 1965.

———. *In Various Directions: A View of the Theatre*. New York: Macmillan, 1965.

———. "Poetry Is Where You Find It." *New York Times*, 18 April 1965, sec. 2.

———. *Tyrone Guthrie on Acting*. New York: Viking, 1971.

Guthrie, Tyrone, et al., *Twice Have the Trumpets Sounded*. Toronto: Clarke, Irwin, 1955.

Hatch, Robert. "Tyrone Guthrie: The Artist as Man of the Theatre." *Horizon* 5 (November 1963).

Houghton, Norris. "Sir Tony at the Phoenix: A Personal Memoir." *Drama Survey* 3 (Winter 1963).

Hunt, Hugh. "Sir Tyrone Guthrie and the Rediscovery of the Shakespearean Playhouse." In *Innovations in Stage and Theatre Design*. Edited by Francis Hodge. New York: American Society for Theatre Research, Theatre Library Association, 1972.

Kitchin, Laurence. *Mid-Century Drama*. London: Faber and Faber, 1960.

Marshall, Norman. "Guthrie Here, There and Everywhere: A Portrait of a Man Who Won't Sit Still." *Drama Survey* 3 (Winter 1963).

Peck, Seymour. "Tyrone Guthrie's Three Ring Circus." *New York Times Magazine,* 23 December 1956.

Roberts, Peter. "Guthrie at the Vic." *Plays and Players* (January 1963).

Rogoff, Gordon. "Guthrie's Shakespeare." *New Republic*, 11 March 1957.

Rossi, Alfred. "Minneapolis Rehearsals." *Drama Critique* 7 (Winter 1964).

———. *Minneapolis Rehearsals: Tyrone Guthrie Directs "Hamlet."* Berkeley: University of California Press, 1970.

———. *Astonish Us in the Morning: Tyrone Guthrie Remembered*. Detroit: Wayne State University Press, 1980.

Stokes, Sewell. "Tyrone Guthrie." *Theatre Arts Monthly* 28 (April 1943).

Whittaker, Herbert. *The Stratford Festival, 1953–1957: A Record in Pictures and Text of the Shakespeare Festival in Canada*. Toronto: Clarke, Irwin, 1958.

Wood, Roger, and Mary Clarke. *Shakespeare at the Old Vic, 1955–56*. London: Hamish and Hamish, 1956.

Worsley, T. C. *The Fugitive Art*. London: John Lehman, 1952.

Unpublished Materials

Capbern, August. "Tyrone Guthrie: A Study of His Artistic Accomplishments in the U.S.A." Ph.D. diss., University of California at Los Angeles, 1969.

Rossi, Alfred A. "A Critical Study of the Philosophy of Theatre and the Technique of Stage Direction of Tyrone Guthrie." Ph.D. diss., University of Minnesota, 1965.

Turgeon, Thomas S. "The Super Artist of the Classical Revival: A Study of the Productions of Orson Welles and Tyrone Guthrie, 1936–1939." Ph.D. diss., Yale University, 1968.

MARGARET WEBSTER

Brock, H. I. "The Taming of the Bard." *New York Times Magazine,* 30 January 1944.

Brown, John Mason. *Dramatis Personae: A Retrospective Show*. New York: Viking, 1965.

Campbell, Oscar J. "Miss Webster and *The Tempest*." *American Scholar* 14 (July 1945).

Choate, Edward. "The Road Show." *Theatre Arts* 33 (December 1949).

Crawford, Cheryl. "Repertory Returns." *New York Times,* 3 November 1946, sec. 2.

Downer, Alan S. "The Dark Lady of Shubert Alley." *Sewanee Review* 54 (January 1946).

Duberman, Martin. *Paul Robeson: A Biography*. New York: Alfred A. Knopf, 1988.

Engel, Lehman. *This Bright Day: An Autobiography*. New York: Macmillan, 1974.

Esterow, Milton. "Shakespeare Takes the Bus." *New York Times,* 26 September 1948, sec. 2.

Evans, Maurice. *All This . . . and Evans Too!: A Memoir*. Columbia: University of South
    Carolina Press, 1987.

Heggie, Barbara. "Profiles: We." *New Yorker,* 20 May 1944.

Hermann, Helen Markel. "Saint Joan from Wisconsin." *New York Times Magazine,* 30
    September 1951.

Houghton, Norris. "It's a Woman's World." *Theatre Arts* 31 (January 1947).

Isaacs, Hermine Rich. "*Tempest* in the Making." *Theatre Arts* 29 (February 1945).

Le Gallienne, Eva. *With a Quiet Heart*. New York: Viking, 1953.

Ormsbee, Helen. "An Accessory to Murder, She Likes It." *New York Herald Tribune,*
    23 November 1941.

"The Tempest." *Life,* 12 February 1945.

Webster, Margaret. "Costume and the Actor." *Amateur Theatre* 8 (8 June 1934).

————. "Credo of a Director." *Theatre Arts* 22 (May 1938).

————. "On Sir John Falstaff." *New York Times,* 9 October 1938, sec. 9.

————. "Will S. in Flushing." *New York Times,* 23 April 1939, sec. 10.

————. "The Golden Eggs: The Broadway, 1940, Grade." *New York Times,* 17 March
    1940, sec. 10.

————. "The Theatre Takes Stock: A Symposium." *Theatre Arts Monthly* 24 (May
    1940).

————. "To W. S., an Open Letter." *New York Times,*17 November 1940, sec. 9.

————. "Pipe Dream on a Train." *Stage* 1 (February 1941).

————. "Late Extra! Murder in Scotland." *New York Times,* 9 November 1941, sec.
    9.

————. "Producing Mr. Shakespeare." *Theatre Arts* 26 (January 1942).

————. "A Better Way to Meet Shakespeare." *Good Housekeeping,* January 1943.

————. "Pertinent Words on His Moorship's Ancient." *New York Times,* 17 October
    1943, sec.2.

————. "A Letter to Chekhov." *New York Times,* 23 January 1944, sec. 2.

————. "Such Stuff as Dreams Are Made On." *New York Times,* 28 January 1945,
    sec. 2.

————. "A Note on *Battle of Angels*." *Pharos Magazine* 1 (Spring 1945).

————. "Dame May Whitty Acts for Her Daughter." *New York Times,* 7 October 1945,
    sec. 2.

————. "Plea for a Rebirth of the Theatre." *New York Times Magazine,* 25 November
    1945.

————. "We Believe: American Repertory Theatre." *Theatre Arts* 30 (March 1946).

————. "On Cutting Shakespeare—And Other Matters." *Theatre Annual* 5 (1946).

————. "Repertory Problems: Time and Cooperation Are Urgent Needs." *New York
    Times,* 2 February 1947, sec. 2.

————. "Vistas Along That Other 'Road.' " *New York Times,* 8 January 1950, sec. 2.

————. "To Travel Hopefully." *Theatre Arts* 34 (February 1950).

————. "Why Shakespeare Goes Right On." *New York Times Magazine,* 12 August
    1951.

————. "Ways of Interpreting 'Joan.' " *New York Times,* 4 November 1951, sec. 2.

————. "On Directing Shakespeare." In *Producing the Play*. Edited by John Gassner.
    rev. ed. San Francisco: Rinehart, 1953.

————. "Director Offers Views on the Staging of Shakespeare's Plays." *New York
    Times,* 6 September 1953, sec. 2.

———. *Shakespeare Without Tears*. rev. ed. New York: World, 1955.

———. *Shakespeare Today*. London: J. M. Dent, 1957.

———. "*Macbeth*—Two Ways." *New York Times,* 20 October 1957, sec. 2.

———. "Soliloquy on Methusalah Shaw." *Theatre Arts* 42 (April 1958).

———. "Going, Going, Gone." *Theatre Arts* 43 (April 1959).

———. "Shakespeare in His Time." In *The Living Shakespeare*. Edited by Robert Gittings. London: William Heinemann, 1960.

———. "Whither Bound." *Theatre Arts* 44 (November 1960).

———. "Dateline—South Africa: Six Thousand Feet Up and Bitter Cold." *Show* 2 (March 1962).

———. "Shakespeare Can Take It." *Show* 4 (February 1964).

———. *The Same Only Different*. New York: Alfred A. Knopf, 1969.

———. *Don't Put Your Daughter on the Stage*. New York: Alfred A. Knopf, 1972.

Zorina, Vera. *Zorina*. New York: Farrar, Straus, Giroux, 1986.

Unpublished Materials

Silverman, Ely. "Margaret Webster's Theory and Practice of Shakespearean Production in the United States, 1937–1953." Ph.D. diss., New York University, 1969.

Worsley, Ronald Craig. "Margaret Webster: A Study of Her Contributions to the American Theatre." Ph.D. diss., Wayne State University, 1972.

ELIA KAZAN

Anderson, Robert. "Walk a Ways with Me." *Theatre Arts* 38 (January 1954).

Basinger, Jeanine, et al. *Working with Kazan*. Middletown, Conn.: Eastern Press, 1973.

Bentley, Eric. *What Is Theatre? A Query in Chronicle Form*. Boston: Beacon Press, 1956.

———. *The Dramatic Event*. Boston: Beacon Press, 1956.

Ciment, Michael. *Kazan on Kazan*. New York: Viking Press, 1974.

Clurman, Harold. *Lies Like Truth*. New York: Grove Press, 1958.

"Elia Kazan: Candid Conversation." *Show Business Illustrated*, February 1962.

Gelb, Arthur. "Williams and Kazan and the Big Walk-Out." *New York Times,* 1 May 1960.

Gilman, Richard. *Common and Uncommon Masks: Writings on the Theatre, 1961–1970*. New York: Vintage Books, 1972.

Hewes, Henry. "A Minority Report on *J.B.*" *Saturday Review,* 3 January 1959.

Hyams, Barry, ed. *Theatre: The Annual of the Repertory Theatre of Lincoln Center, 1965*. New York: Hill and Wang, 1965.

Isaacs, Hermine Rich. "First Rehearsals: Elia Kazan Directs a Modern Legend." *Theatre Arts* 28 (March 1944).

Israel, Lee. *Miss Tallulah Bankhead*. New York: Putnam, 1972.

Kazan, Elia. "Ten Best for a Repertory Theater." *New York Times Magazine,* 9 November 1958.

———. "Theater: New Stages, New Plays, New Actors." *New York Times Magazine,* 23 September 1962.

———. *On What Makes a Director*. Los Angeles and New York: Directors Guild of America, 1973. (pamphlet)

———. *Elia Kazan, a Life*. New York: Alfred A. Knopf, 1988.

Kazan, Elia, and Archibald MacLeish. "The Staging of a Play." *Esquire* 59 (May 1959).

Martin, Ralph G. *Lincoln Center for the Performing Arts*. Englewood Cliffs, N.J.: Prentice-Hall, 1971.

Mielziner, Jo. *Designing for the Theatre: A Memoir and a Portfolio*. New York: Bramhall, 1965.

Morehouse, Ward. "Keeping Up with Kazan." *Theatre Arts* 41 (June 1957).

Morgan, Thomas B. "Elia Kazan's Great Expectations." *Harper's Magazine* 225 (September 1962).

Morton, F. "Gadg!" *Esquire* 57 (February 1957).

Novick, Julius. "The Old Regime at Lincoln Center." *Educational Theatre Journal* 18 (May 1964).

Oppenheimer, George. "On Stage: Kazan Answers the Critics." *Newsday*, 14 November 1964.

Peck, Seymour. "The Temple of the Method." *New York Times Magazine*, 6 May 1956.

Poling, J. "Handy Gadget." *Collier's*, 31 March 1952.

"A Quiz for Kazan." *Theatre Arts* 40 (November 1956).

Rogoff, Gordon. "A Streetcar Named Kazan." *Reporter*, 17 December 1964.

Schechner, Richard. "Sentimental Kazan." *Tulane Drama Review* 9 (Spring 1965).

———. "The Bottomless Cup: An Interview with Geraldine Page," in *Stanislavski in America*. Ed. Erika Munk. Greenwich, Conn.: Fawcett, 1967.

Schechner, Richard, and Theodore Hoffman. (Interview with Kazan) "Look, There's the American Theatre." *Tulane Drama Review* 8 (Winter 1964).

Schumach, Murray. "A Director Named 'Gadge.' " *New York Times Magazine*, 9 November 1947.

Stevens, Virginia. "Elia Kazan, Actor and Director of Stage and Screen." *Theatre Arts* 31 (December 1947).

Taubman, Howard. "Arthur Miller's Play Opens Repertory." *New York Times*, 24 January 1964.

Williams, Tennessee. "A Note of Explanation." *Theatre Arts* 41 (June 1957).

———. *Memoirs*. New York: Bantam Books, 1976.

Zolotow, Maurice. "Viewing the Kinetic Mr. Kazan." *New York Times*, 9 March 1952.

Unpublished Materials

Clark, Leroy W., Jr. "The Directing Principles and Practices of Elia Kazan." Ph.D. diss., Kent State University, 1976.

Schueneman, Warren Walter. "Elia Kazan, Director." Ph.D. diss., University of Minnesota, 1974.

JOAN LITTLEWOOD

Ansorge, Peter. "Lots of Lovely Human Contact! An Inside Look at Joan Littlewood." *Plays and Players* 19 (1972).

Bailey, Anthony. "Would Little Joan Littlewood Were Here!" *Esquire* 64 (January 1964).

Bradshaw, Jon. "Truth about *Twang!!*" *Plays and Players* 13 (April-May 1966).

Brien, Alan. "Critic's Choice: The London Season." *Theatre Arts* 43 (May 1959).

———. "Openings: London." *Theatre Arts* 48 (June 1966).

———. "London: On Contemporary Relevance." *New York Times,* 7 December 1970.

Brown, John Russell. "Three Kinds of Shakespeare." *Shakespeare Survey.* vol. 18. Cambridge, Eng.: Cambridge University Press, 1965.

Coren, Michael. *Theatre Royal, 100 Years of Stratford East.* London: Quartet Books, 1984.

Dorris, George. *"The Projector, The Mock Mason,* and Miss Littlewood." *Modern Drama* 16 (December 1973).

Elsom, John. *Post-War British Theatre.* London: Routledge and Keagan Paul, 1976.

Esslin, Martin. "Brecht and the English Theatre." *The Drama Review* 11 (Winter 1966).

———. "London Broils *MacBird." New York Times,* 16 April 1967.

Gardner, Paul. "Joan Littlewood: Call Me a Vulgarian." *New York Times,* 27 September 1964.

Goorney, Howard. "Group Theatre: Acting in It." *Encore* 6 (May-June 1959).

———. "Littlewood in Rehearsal." *Drama Review* 11 (Winter 1966).

———. *The Theatre Workshop Story.* London: Eyre Methuen, 1981.

Grant, Steve. "Fings Ain't What They Used to Be." *Plays and Players* 23 (April 1976).

Harrop, John. "Brecht's Baby: A Misconception about Joan Littlewood." *Drama at Calgary* 3 (March 1969).

Howard, Jane. "Merry, Angry Mother Hen." *Life,* 27 November 1964.

"Joan Littlewood Hits Back at Crix." *Variety,* 2 September 1964.

Littlewood, Joan. "Plays for the People." *World Theatre* 8 (Winter 1959–60).

———. "Non-Program: A Laboratory of Fun." *Drama Review* 12 (Spring 1968).

MacColl, Ewan. "Grass Roots of Theatre Workshop." *Theatre Quarterly* 3 (January-March 1973).

McCrindle, Joseph F., ed. *Behind the Scenes: Theatre and Film Interviews from the "Transatlantic Review."* New York: Holt, Rinehart and Winston, 1971.

Marowitz, Charles. "Oh, What a Lovely Diary." *New York Times,* 8 October 1967.

O'Connor, Ulrick. *Brendan Behan.* London: Hamish Hamilton, 1970.

Rogoff, Gordon. "Joan and the Good Guys." *Reporter,* 19 November 1964.

Taylor, Charles. "Workshop with a Lust for Life." *Theatre Arts Monthly* 43 (May 1959).

Taylor, John Russell. *Anger and After: A Guide to the New British Drama.* London: Methuen, 1962.

Tynan, Kenneth. "Joan of Cockaigne." *Holiday* 26 (November 1964).

Unpublished Materials

Goodman, Judith Lea. "Joan Littlewood and Her Theatre Workshop." Ph.D. diss., New York University, 1975.

PETER BROOK

Ansorge, Peter. Interview with Peter Brook. *Plays and Players* 18 (October 1970).

Auslander, Philip. " 'Holy Theatre' and Catharsis." *Theatre Research International* 9 (Spring 1984).

Banu, Georges. "Talking with the Playwright, the Musician, and the Designer." *Drama Review* 30 (Spring 1986).

Bernard, Kenneth. "Some Observations on the Theatre of Peter Brook." *Yale/Theatre* 12 (Fall-Winter 1980).

Berry, Ralph. *On Directing Shakespeare*. London: Croom Helm, 1977.

Billington, Michael. "RSC in *US*." *Plays and Players* 14 (December 1966).

———. "Written on the Wind: The Dramatic Art of Peter Brook." *Listener* 21 and 28 December 1978.

Blumenthal, Eileen. "Toils of Grace." *Village Voice,* 27 November 1978.

Brook, Peter. "Oh for Empty Seats." *Encore,* January 1959.

———. "From Zero to the Infinite." *Encore,* November 1960.

———. "The Road to *Marat/Sade*." *New York Herald-Tribune,* 26 December 1964.

———. "We're All Menaced." *Flourish* (August 1968).

———. "The Chorus for the Senecan *Oedipus*." *Drama at Calgary* 3 (November 1968).

———. *The Empty Space*. New York: Avon, 1968.

———. "Looking for a New Language." *Performance* 1 (December 1971).

———. "The Complete Truth Is 'Global.' " *New York Times,* 20 January 1974.

———. *The Shifting Point: Theatre, Film, Opera, 1946–1987*. New York: Harper and Row, 1987.

Brown, Ivor. *Shakespeare Memorial Theatre 1954–1956*. London: Max Reinhardt, 1956.

Burns, John F. "Chekhov Goes to Moscow by Way of Brooklyn." *New York Times,* 6 March 1988.

Cox, Frank. Interview with Peter Brook. *Plays and Players* 15 (April 1968).

Croyden, Margaret, "Exploration of the Ugly: Brook's Work on *Oedipus*." *The Drama Review* 13 (Spring 1969).

———. "Peter Brook's *Tempest*." *The Drama Review* 13 (Spring 1969).

———. "Peter Brook Learns to Speak Orghast." *New York Times,* 3 October 1971, sec. 2.

———. "Peter Brook's 'Birds' Fly to Africa." *New York Times,* 21 January 1973, sec. 2.

———. "Peter Brook's Search for Essentials." *New York Times,* 4 May 1980, sec. 2.

———. "Comedy, Tragedy and Mystical Fantasy: Peter Brook's New Trilogy." *New York Times,* 25 May 1980, sec. 2.

———. *The Centre: A Narrative*. Paris: C.I.C.T., 1980.

———. "Peter Brook Transforms an Indian Epic." *New York Times,* 25 August 1985.

———. "Peter Brook Creates a Nine-Hour Epic." *New York Times Magazine,* 4 October 1987.

David, Richard. "Shakespeare's Comedies and the Modern Stage." *Shakespeare Survey*. vol. 4. Cambridge, Eng.: Cambridge University Press, 1951.

Doolittle, Joyce. "Oedipus-Sophocles-Seneca-Brook." *Drama at Calgary* 3 (November 1968).

Eder, Richard. "The World According to Brook." *American Theatre* 1 (May 1984).

Esslin, Martin. "The Theatre of Cruelty." *New York Times,* 6 March 1966, sec. 2.

———. "Oedipus Complex." *Plays and Players* 15 (May 1968).

Gibson, Michael. "Brook's Africa." *The Drama Review* 17 (September 1973).

Gussow, Mel. *"Conference of the Birds": The Story of Peter Brook in Africa*. London: Faber and Faber, 1977.

———. "Peter Brook Returns to Chekhov's Vision." *New York Times,* 9 August 1981.

Heilpern, John. "Peter Brook's 'Birds' Fly to Africa." *Observer,* 18 January 1966.

Henry, William A., III. "An Epic Journey Through Myth." *Time,* 19 October 1987.

Hentoff, Nat. "Brook: Yes, Let's Be Emotional About Vietnam." *New York Times,* 25 February 1968, sec. 2.

Hughes, Ted. "*Orghast*: Talking without Words." *Vogue,* December 1971.

Kauffmann, Stanley. *Persons of the Drama.* New York: Harper and Row, 1976.

Kauffmann, Stanley, and Irving Drutman. "The Provocative *Marat/Sade*: Was Peter Brook Its Brain?" *New York Times,* 9 January 1966, sec. 2.

Kott, Jan. *Shakespeare Our Contemporary.* London: Methuen, 1978.

Kustow, Michael. "Letter from London, II: Theatre of the Soul." *Village Voice,* 6 August 1979.

Labeille, Daniel. " 'The Formless Hunch': An Interview with Peter Brook." *Modern Drama* 23 (Spring 1980).

Lahr, John. "Knowing What to Celebrate." *Plays and Players* 23 (March 1976).

Lawson, Stephen R. Interview with Peter Brook. *Yale/Theater* 7 (Fall 1975).

Lewis, Anthony. "Peter Brook's Theatre Is a Living Event." *New York Times,* 15 January 1971.

Marowitz, Charles. "Lear Log." *The Drama Review* 8 (Winter 1963).

———. "Notes on the Theatre of Cruelty." *The Drama Review* 11 (Winter 1966).

———. "From Prodigy to Professional, as Written, Directed and Acted by Peter Brook." *New York Times,* 24 October 1968, sec. 2.

———. "Brook: From *Marat/Sade* to *Midsummer Night's Dream*." *New York Times,* 13 September 1970, sec. 2.

———. *Confessions of a Counterfeit Critic.* London: Eyre, Methuen, 1973.

Millon, Martine. "Talking with Three Actors." *The Drama Review* 30 (Spring 1986).

Milne, Tom. "Cruelty, Cruelty." *Encore* 11 (March-April 1964).

———. "Reflections on *The Screens*." *Encore* 11 (July-August 1964).

Munk, Erika. "Looking for a New Language." *Performance* 1 (December 1971).

"Peter Brook Directs a Sanskrit Epic." *New York Times,* 31 July 1985.

Pitt-Rivers, Julien. "Peter Brook and the Ik." *Times Literary Supplement,* 31 January 1975.

Rea, Kenneth. "The Physical Life of the Actor: Kenneth Rea Talks to Peter Brook and Adrian Noble." *Drama* 153 (Autumn 1984).

Read, Bill. "Peter Brook: From Stratford-on-Avon to the Gare du Nord." *Boston University Journal* 24 (1975).

Reeves, Geoffrey, "The Persepolis Follies of 1971." *Performance* 1 (December 1971).

Rich, Frank. Review of *The Tragedy of Carmen. New York Times,* 18 November 1983.

Richardson, Boyce. "Holy Experience." *Enact,* nos. 24–25 (January-February 1969).

Robertson, Nan. "Making Way for *Mahabharata*." *New York Times*, 30 September 1987.

Schechner, Richard. "*Marat/Sade* Forum." *The Drama Review* 10 (Summer 1966).

———. "*The Mahabharata*." *The Drama Review* 30 (October 1985).

———, et al. "Talking with Peter Brook." *The Drama Review* 30 (Spring 1986).

Selbourne, David. *The Making of "A Midsummer Night's Dream."* London: Methuen, 1982.

Serban, Andrei. "The Life in a Sound." *The Drama Review* 20 (December 1976).

Shevtsova, Maria. "Peter Brook Adapts *Carmen*." *Theatre International* 2 (1983).

Shorter, Eric. "*Timon of Paris*." *Drama,* no. 115 (Winter 1974).

———. "Off the Cuff—With Peter Brook and Company." *Drama,* no. 129 (Summer 1978).

Smith, A.C.H. *Orghast at Persepolis.* New York: Viking, 1972.

Sohlich, Wolfgang. "Prolegomenon for a Theory of Drama Reception: Peter Brook's *Measure for Measure* and the Emergent Bourgeoisie." *Comparative Drama* 18 (Spring 1984).

Tallmer, Jerry. "Daily Closeup." *New York Post,* 27 January 1971.

Taylor, John Russell. "Peter Brook, or the Limitations of Intelligence." *Sight and Sound* 36 (Spring 1967).

Trewin, J. C. *Peter Brook: A Biography.* London: Macdonald, 1971.

Trilling, Ossia. "Playing with Words at Persepolis." *Theatre Quarterly* 5 (January-March 1972).

Trussler, Simon. "Private Experiment—in Public." *Plays and Players* 11 (February 1964).

Tynan, Kenneth. *A View of the English Stage 1944–1963.* London: Davis-Poynter, 1975.

———. "Director as Misanthropist: On the Moral Neutrality of Peter Brook." *Theatre Quarterly* 7 (Spring 1977).

Weiss, Peter. *The Persecution and Assassination of Jean-Paul Marat as Performed by the Inmates of the Asylum of Charenton under the Direction of the Marquis de Sade.* Introduction by Peter Brook. New York: Pocket Books, 1966.

Williams, David. " 'A Place Marked by Life': Brook at the Bouffes du Nord." *New Theatre Quarterly* 1 (February 1985).

———, ed. and comp. *Peter Brook: A Theatrical Casebook.* London: Methuen, 1988.

Wright, David. "The Actor and Vietnam." *Plays and Players* 14 (January 1967).

Zarrilli, Phillip. "The Aftermath: When Peter Brook Came to India." *The Drama Review* 30 (Spring 1986).

Unpublished Materials

Dawes, Carrol Cecily. "Peter Brook and the Living Event." Ph.D. diss., Yale University, 1971.

Index

About the Author

SAMUEL L. LEITER is Professor of Theatre at Brooklyn College, City University of New York, and the Graduate Center, CUNY. His previously published books include *The Art of Kabuki: Famous Plays in Performance; Ten Seasons: New York Theatre in the Seventies; The Encyclopedia of the New York Stage, 1920–1930*; and *The Encyclopedia of the New York Stage 1930–1940* (Greenwood Press, 1979, 1986, 1985, and 1989). He also edited *Shakespeare Around the Globe: A Guide to Notable Postwar Revivals* (Greenwood Press, 1986). Professor Leiter is editor of the *Asian Theatre Journal*.

3 1543 50122 0703

792.0233
L533f

DATE DUE

Cressman Library
Cedar Crest College
Allentown, Pa. 18104

DEMCO